NIKOLAI TOLSTOY is an English-Russian author and was Patrick O'Brian's stepson, their relationship spanning forty-five years during O'Brian's marriage to Mary Tritten a number of books, includ of the Novelist, The Coming of is a Fellow of the Royal Societ

'This biography draws extensively on the diaries, letters and accounts . . . Shows us another, more attractive side of O'Brian . . . Tolstoy well describes the hardscrabble existence of the first few years – the sheer bloody grind of making a living as a professional author . . . Many moments of light relief . . . [We see] O'Brian at his best as a novelist: his extraordinary knowledge of the period blended perfectly with his innate command of narrative and his elegant, often witty prose. Not for nothing was Jane Austen his favourite author'
The Times

'Millions of O'Brian devotees around the world, and this reviewer is one, thrill to the wonderful roman-fleuve of his Aubrey–Maturin series, the 20½ seafaring novels (the last was unfinished) set during the Napoleonic Wars. They know rather less about the author who was, as Nikolai Tolstoy's title suggests, an immensely private man, deeply wounded by a sometimes brutal, generally loveless and impoverished childhood'
Sunday Times

'O'Brian was a fine biographer himself . . . So, what was sauce for the goose must be sauce for the gander . . . Tolstoy contributes important background knowledge, and makes the case that O'Brian's unhappy childhood, his disastrous first marriage, his extreme poverty for many years, his love for Mary and his deep attachment to Collioure in French Catalonia, where he lived, all provided raw material for his books . . . For those who love Patrick's great creation Stephen Maturin, it is indeed fascinating to see how much of himself the author put into the character: the cyclical depression, the blind rages, the sometimes cruel wit, the intelligence, the capacity for love, the courage'
Spectator

'Full and fond biography ... Essential to understanding O'Brian's later actions and much of his writing ...Tolstoy quotes from voluminous family papers, particularly O'Brian's diary...Tolstoy's access to such material gives this biography a comprehensiveness that no other biographer of O'Brian will be able to match. It contains much detail of family misunderstandings and misinterpretations. Tolstoy throughout seeks to counter the judgements and assumptions made by an earlier unauthorised biographer ... O'Brian's was a writer's life. In this discursive biography, which includes much on his own relations with his stepfather, Tolstoy convincingly demonstrates how the life fed the fiction and, for O'Brian, how writing fiction was the only way to make sense of life'   *Literary Review*

'Tolstoy writes well about O'Brian's debilitating attacks of profound depression, his frequent misgivings about his literary talent and his financial troubles for any years ... Devotees of the Aubrey and Maturin sequence of novels, from *Master and Commander* onwards, will want to read this book. It finally reaches the point in O'Brian's life when he embarked on writing the series, and sheds some light on the creation of the two gloriously vivid and idiosyncratic characters at its heart'   *The Oldie*

Also by Nikolai Tolstoy

The Founding of Evil Hold School (1968)
Night of the Long Knives (1972)
Victims of Yalta (1978)
The Half-Mad Lord (1978)
Stalin's Secret War (1981)
The Tolstoys: Twenty-Four Generations of Russian History (1983)
The Quest for Merlin (1985)
The Minister and the Massacres (1986)
The Coming of the King: The First Book of Merlin (1988)
Patrick O'Brian: The Making of the Novelist (2004)
The Oldest British Prose Literature: The Compilation
of the Four Branches of the Mabinogi (2009)
The Mysteries of Stonehenge: Myth and Ritual
at the Sacred Centre (2016)

PATRICK O'BRIAN
A Very Private Life

NIKOLAI TOLSTOY

WILLIAM
COLLINS

William Collins
An imprint of HarperCollins*Publishers*
1 London Bridge Street
London SE1 9GF

WilliamCollinsBooks.com

First published in Great Britain in 2019 by William Collins
This William Collins paperback edition published in 2020

1

Copyright © Nikolai Tolstoy 2019

Nikolai Tolstoy asserts the moral right to be identified as the author
of this work in accordance with the Copyright, Designs and Patents Act 1988

A catalogue record for this book is available from the British Library

ISBN 978-0-00-835062-8

All photographs courtesy of the author

Typeset in Sabon by
Palimpsest Book Production Limited, Falkirk, Stirlingshire
Printed and bound by CPI Group (UK) Ltd, Croydon CR0 4YY

MIX
Paper from
responsible sources
FSC   FSC C007454
www.fsc.org

This book is produced from independently certified FSC™ paper
to ensure responsible forest management.

For more information visit: www.harpercollins.co.uk/green

I dedicate this book to my late cousin Adrian Slack and his sister Julia, the dearest of friends as well as closest of relatives since those distant days of childhood at Appledore beside the Severn Sea.

At home in the cloister of Correch d'en Baus

Indeed I cannot conceive a more perfect mode of writing any man's life, than not only relating all the most important events of it in their order, but interweaving what he privately wrote, and said, and thought; by which mankind are enabled as it were to see him live, and to 'live o'er each scene' with him, as he actually advanced through the several stages of his life.

James Boswell, *The Life of Samuel Johnson, LL.D.*
(London, 1793), i, p. 6

CONTENTS

Preface

A fortnight after Patrick O'Brian's death, the playwright David Mamet wrote of his literary achievement:

Recently I put down O'Brian's sea novel 'The Ionian Mission' and said to my wife, 'This fellow has created characters and stories that are part of my life.'

She said: 'Write him a letter. He's in his 80s. Write him and thank him. And when you are in England, look him up, go tell him.

'How wonderful,' she said, 'to be alive, when he is still alive. Imagine living in the 1890s and being able to converse with Conan Doyle.'

Mamet promptly rehearsed the eulogium with which he would address his literary hero, and began preparing a letter of introduction at his breakfast table. Then, glancing at the newspaper beside him, he saw to his dismay an announcement of the melancholy news of Patrick's death.[1]

I have no doubt that Patrick would have been delighted by such praise from his acclaimed fellow writer, and that had my mother still been alive she would have inserted the letter in her box-file 'Valuable Fans and very good reviews'. My hope is that, while nothing can quite replace a face-to-face conversation, this book may compensate by enabling Mamet and others of Patrick's world-wide legion of admirers to learn much more of his life and personality than might have been obtained from any interview with the famously reclusive writer.

This book covers the latter part of Patrick O'Brian's life, from the moment of his and my mother's arrival at Collioure in the south of France in the autumn of 1949. It is the period during which he wrote all his major works. Since my mother's death twenty years ago, I remain the sole intimate observer of Patrick's astonishing career from impoverished and little-known writer in 1955, when I first met him, until his death at the height of his international fame at the turn of the millennium forty-five years later. Nevertheless, it never occurred to me at any point during his lifetime to compile his biography – not least because I was well aware of his detestation of inquisitive enquiries into his private life.

My unanticipated decision to undertake the task began in the aftermath of Patrick's death at the beginning of the year 2000. I was witness to the acute distress caused him by the imminent appearance of an unauthorized biography.* My dismay was briefly allayed by its publication soon afterwards, when I was asked to review it. My initial impression was that the book appeared largely harmless. Knowing little at the time about Patrick's early life, and his relationship with his first wife Elizabeth and son Richard, I felt I had no reason not to accept the author's account of Patrick's life before I knew him as broadly accurate, and besides dismissed it as of little relevance to his reputation as a writer.

What I was not prepared for, however, was the startling extent to which a small but vociferous coterie of journalists and reviewers eagerly swallowed everything related in the book that could be interpreted as detrimental to Patrick's reputation, regardless of its truth – or in many instances even likelihood.† Regrettably, it was

---

* This should not be taken to imply that I particularly approve *authorized* biographies, which all too often end up as hagiographies.

† A striking counterbalance is provided by the American Patrick O'Brian scholar Anthony Gary Brown. Lacking any biographical material beyond that contained in the published biography, he nevertheless politely but damningly shows that, on their internal evidence alone, barely any of the writer's speculations stands up

in some of the more meretricious cases that his detractors arranged for their pieces to be posted on the internet for futurity.

Before long it occurred to me that I was uniquely placed to provide a more balanced and credible picture. Not only had I known Patrick intimately throughout the greater part of his life,* but in addition I possess almost all his personal papers, extending from his appearance in a pram at the age of one to his final melancholy sojourn in Dublin. This includes such invaluable sources as my mother's and his own diaries covering every day of the greater part of the period 1945 to 1999, my mother's financial accounts from 1945 to 1997, Patrick's correspondence with his literary agents, publishers and admirers, manuscripts of many of his unpublished works, recorded interviews with his friends and family, extensive personal notes, preliminary drafts of his novels, his precious library, and much else. In addition, I knew intimately many of his and my mother's friends inhabiting Collioure or visiting them there, almost all of whom are now sadly dead. However, I soon realized that, much more significantly than a desire to refute the damaging effect of media vilification, a biography based on authentic evidence would constitute a remarkable chronicle of love, endeavour, and in some ways unique triumph over daunting odds. In addition it would reveal much of the genesis and inspiration of his admired works of fiction and biography, which continue to enthral millions of readers around the world.

For the rest, it is my hope that this biography will enable readers to arrive at judgements based on evidence, rather than efflorescent

---

to critical scrutiny. See his 'Still Waters: A Review of Dean King's "Patrick O'Brian: A Life Revealed', at Anthony Gary Brown's internet 2009 Homepage – Saignon.

* Johnson declared that 'nobody can write the life of a man, but those who have eat and drunk and lived in social intercourse with him' (Boswell, *The Life of Samuel Johnson*, ii, p. 22). He was of course exaggerating for emphasis, as he himself compiled biographies of people he had never met. Nevertheless, there is clearly an advantage in being able to picture with vivid immediacy the character whose history the biographer is recounting.

imagination. In my experience, truth tends to be vastly more interesting than the most lurid of conjectures. I conclude with an assurance that I have suppressed nothing material from memories extending over five decades and the extensive archive in my possession, save one matter of trifling consequence which for the present I feel it proper to withhold.

Nikolai Tolstoy, 2019

Acknowledgements

I would like to thank the following for their generous help during the protracted genesis of this book. Many of them knew Patrick and my mother personally, and I have greatly benefited from their differing perspectives.

Les Amis de Patrick O'Brian à Collioure; Mme Youg Azzopard-Vinour; Mlle Danielle Banyuls; Professor John Bayley; Mr Stuart Bennett; Mrs John Elliott (our daughter Anastasia); Mr Ben Fenton; Mr Robert Broeder; Lady Buckhurst (our daughter Xenia); Mrs Patrick Bucknell (my sister Natasha); Miss Mary Burkett; Mme Hélène Camps; Mr John Cole; Mr Arthur Cunningham of the British Library; The Rt. Hon. Lord Justice Deeny; Mr Christopher Dowling of the Imperial War Museum; M. Gildas Girodeau; Mme Odette Girodeau; Mr Robert Hardy; Mrs Sherryl Healey of Bovey Tracey Library; Mr Geoff Hunt; Mr Mark Horowitz; Mme Claude Jonquères d'Oriola; Mr Brian Lavery; Admiral Sir Michael Layard; Professor Raymond Levy; the Lilly Library; the London Library; Dr Richard Luckett, Pepys Librarian; Dr David Lyon; Mrs Anne Louise Moore; Mr Edwin Moore; Dame Iris Murdoch; Mr and Mrs Richard Ollard; Miss Sarah Plimpton; Mr James Puckridge; Mrs Brigid Roffe-Silvester; Mr Charles Russ; Mrs Saidie Russ; Mr Stephen Russ; Mr Harry Russell; Mrs Gwen Russell-Jones; Mr Chris Smith of HarperCollins; Countess Alexandra Tolstoy-Miloslavsky; Count Dmitri Tolstoy-Miloslavsky; Count Ivan Tolstoy-Miloslavsky; Mr John Saumarez Smith; Mrs Elizabeth Russ Wood; Mrs Annemarie Victory.

Terry Zobeck lent me exceptional aid. He is preparing what will undoubtedly be the authoritative bibliography of my stepfather's works. In addition to sharing his specialized knowledge with me, providing in some cases copies of published material which I lacked, he generously gave of his time to read the text more than once during its gestation, providing me with invaluable advice on issues great and small.

My especial thanks go to my old friend and ally Sir Roger Scruton for introducing me to my capital literary agent Caroline Michel of Peters, Fraser & Dunlop, who in turn introduced the book to Patrick's long-term publisher HarperCollins. Iain Hunt undertook the editorial work with a meticulous care not always encountered in these difficult days for publishers.

I must also emphasize the exceptional benefit I gained from Oliver Johnson's painstaking editing of the first volume of this biography, from which I have continued to profit in the present work.

Finally, and most important of all, I must thank my dear wife Georgina. Not only has she provided invaluable support of every kind over long years of preparation, but from her first stay at Collioure in 1971 she came to know my parents intimately. As a consequence I was not only able to consult her shared memories, but to discuss with her at every stage Patrick's enigmatic character. Further to this, she read attentively the entire typescript, detecting many tiresome little errors of chronology and the like which I had overlooked.

I

Collioure and *Three Bear Witness*

I went in the loft & there found not only old account books so
beautifully kept but our old formally-kept diaries of nearly 30 years
ago. How vividly alive we were in those days, or seem to be in this
reflection, & how v v little we lived & loved on.

Patrick's diary, 9 December 1981

In the summer of 1945 Patrick and my mother Mary were
compelled to leave London, following the abrupt termination
of their wartime employment at Political Warfare Executive.
Although they had been very happy during the three years' tenancy
of their elegant Queen Anne house in Chelsea, it was with buoyant
excitement that they began their new life in a tiny cottage in a
remote valley of North Wales. Patrick welcomed the prospect of
entering on a romantic wilderness existence with my mother. His
deprivation of many of the normal pleasures of childhood, above
all the fellowship of contemporaries, made him by nature unusually self-sufficient. Furthermore, he and my mother were still young
(Patrick being then thirty, and my mother twenty-nine), adventurous, and very much in love.

His ambitions were clear. Ever averse to dependence on others,
he intended to live so far as possible by the work of his hands,
while resuming his precocious career as a writer, which five years
of war had compelled him to abandon. Prospects appeared as

promising as might be. My mother possessed a modest private income on which they were able to scrape by in their two-roomed house at Cwm Croesor in Snowdonia, whose rent amounted to a mere £4 a year. They were fit, resourceful, and unmaterialistic: a perfect team. Neither ever baulked at hard work, and they rarely repined at the constraints of poverty. Over the bitter winter of 1945–46 they laboured undauntedly to make their home habitable, and toiled at their little garden in order to make themselves as self-sufficient as possible in the coming year. Patrick's shooting and fishing among the mountains and lakes completed their supply of food.

Nevertheless, the spring of 1946 found him increasingly assailed by frustration and pessimism. Try as he would, his pen failed to flow with its former facility. While my mother's faith in his talent as a writer never wavered, Patrick increasingly experienced prolonged bouts of writer's block, a condition which by the end of their four years in Wales had all but overwhelmed him. Moving to a larger house nearby in the valley generated only the briefest spasm of revived creativity, and during the winter of 1948–49 he began to despair of ever fulfilling his consuming ambition. He grew more and more tense, irritable, self-doubting, and agitated by agonizing thoughts of death and dissolution.[1] In addition the long dark wet winters of North Wales imposed debilitating physical gloom over their lives. Eventually he and my mother decided that their only recourse was to effect a total severance with their current unhappy existence.

After living together for six years, in the summer of 1945 Patrick had married my mother, when he further adopted the decisive course of changing his surname from Russ to O'Brien. Contrary to widespread speculation when this was belatedly made public at the end of his life, I have shown elsewhere that he did not select his new name in order to pass himself off as an Irishman. Indeed, the name itself was chosen effectively at random. His overriding motive was to achieve a total break with his past: above all, to banish all association with his selfish and frequently tyrannical father. However, as failure dogged his every effort to extract himself from the grim predicament he found himself facing, he became increasingly troubled by an obsessive fear that his father's destructive shadow hung over him, frustrating his every effort to break free. Even the rugged recesses of Snowdonia proved too little protection from the hated oppressor, whose presence he sensed looming above him in forbidding screes or tearing down the valley in raging storms, and eventually it seemed that a second flight afforded the only avenue for escape and renewal.

The bleak Welsh winters no longer proffered an invigorating challenge, but exerted a dampening gloom permeating the little household. By the early summer of 1949, the young couple fastened on the south of France, as refuge from the more and more desperate impasse into which Patrick found himself driven. He returned from an exploratory expedition with the exciting news that he had discovered the ideal spot where they could rebuild their lives.

The little town of Collioure lies on the Mediterranean coast, a few miles from the Spanish frontier. Years later, in his broadly autobiographical novel *Richard Temple*, Patrick provided a vivid sketch of the impression it first made on him:

> The village stood on a rocky bay, with a huge castle jutting out into the middle, and a path led round underneath this castle to a farther beach and farther rocks . . . A jetty ran out at the end of the second beach . . . and as he walked along the jetty . . . he took in a host of vivid impressions – the brilliance of the open sea, white horses, the violet shadows of the clouds. From the end of the jetty the whole village could be seen, arranged in two curves; the sun had softened the colour of the tiled roofs to a more or less uniform pale strawberry, but all the flat-fronted houses were washed or painted different colours, and they might all have been chosen by an angel of the Lord . . . the high-prowed open fishing-boats were

also painted with astonishing and successful colours: they lay in two rows that repeated the curves of the bay, and their long, arched, archaic lateen yards crossed their short leaning masts like a complexity of wings.[2]

The couple arrived at the town in the beginning of September, which is generally one of the best months of the year on the Côte Vermeille. Tourists had departed, and the little town reverted to its workaday existence. The brilliant sunshine was tempered by a pleasant freshness in the air, with the Pyrenees looming behind the town standing out sharp and clear against a pure azure sky.

During his prefatory visit Patrick had already made a few friends. Among these was a beautiful *Colliourencque** (as the town's female inhabitants are termed), Odette Boutet. Odette was married to a sculptor and painter named François Bernardi.[†] They met again the day after Patrick's return with my mother, when the two couples immediately became fast friends. During his initial visit Odette had helped Patrick find a small *apartement* on the second floor of 39, rue Arago,[‡] situated opposite a great gateway opening through the town wall onto the seafront. There was a living room, bedroom, a windowless nook known as 'the black hole', a bathroom with shower, and a tiny lavatory.

Always hospitable to a fault, when guests came to stay my parents customarily abandoned the bedroom, ensconcing them-selves on lilos, inflatable mattresses, in the black hole. Electricity only arrived in the *apartement* nine months after their arrival. Inadequate heating was initially provided by a small bottled-gas

---

* *Cotlliurenca* in Catalan.
† Soon after my parents had settled into the rue Arago, Bernardi painted the fresco depicting the grape harvest and fishers of Collioure, still to be seen in the restaurant on the ground floor of the house where Patrick and my mother lived. The yet more splendid fresco in the railway station is also by him.
‡ The numbers of the street have been changed since.

cooker, and it was not until towards the end of 1953 that they managed to afford 'a beautiful blue enamelled stove, a flexible desk-light for P. & various other things . . . Very pleased with stove. It was too heavy for P & me but P & Rimbaud managed.' This was the Mirus, a handsome and extremely effective heater, capable of burning coal or wood. Cooking was conducted on a small 'Wonder Oven', operating on bottled gas.

Apart from the inevitable proliferation of tourist shops and restaurants and the regrettable removal of cobblestones from the streets, the appearance of Collioure within its town walls is not greatly changed since my parents first lived there. Most streets are so narrow that the inhabitants might almost touch hands from opposite windows. Behind the rue Arago, clustered houses along winding passages ascend the hillside to the base of Fort Miradou, while a couple of streets away the Place de la Mairie provided a pleasant refuge under the shade of its plane trees, where townspeople strolled and gossiped in the evenings.

In one major respect, however, Collioure has changed beyond recognition. Some time ago, when I was discussing the town with an old family friend, widow of a retired *Colliourench* fisherman, she described the new Musée de Collioure in the Faubourg. It contains many pleasing relics of former local life: fishing gear, old photographs, household implements, and so forth. 'But one aspect it can never show,' Hélène Camps observed emphatically, 'is the incessant and extraordinary noise we all knew in those days' – whether inside or outside the town. For many years all coastal road traffic to Spain passed through the heart of Collioure. Eventually this came to be diverted inland through a massive road tunnel constructed beyond the railway line.

In 1954 Patrick wrote this lively description for the American magazine *Homes and Gardens*:*

---

* For some reason the piece was not published.

Where the foothills of the Pyrenees plunge directly to the sea, the smooth-rounded Mediterranean sea that has bitten away the land in black cliffs there, the road winds and winds interminably: hair-pin bends writhe down to the gaunt bridges that stand over naked, dried up river-beds, and from each ravine the road twists upwards through cuttings in the red-black rock to the narrow back of the hill – up, and down again. It is a nightmare for a nervous driver in a hurry, for the lorries from Port Vendres, the buses and the cars tear furiously round the corners – blind corners – screaming brutally with their tyres, klaxons, horns. They all disregard the most elementary precautions (no Latin soul should ever drive a car) and a stranger might well demand whoever had established the theory that the French drive on the right side of the road.

But in the autumn, when the tide of summer cars has slackened, and before the schooners from the south have begun to bring up the oranges that load the lorries in the port, then one can walk safely on the road, follow its turning through the hills and look with tranquillity on the sea below or up to the mountains on the right hand.

This is the time of the vendanges. The hills, terraced with inconceivable labour to the height of the fertile land, are covered everywhere with vines, and the vines are ready.

Although families native to Collioure still live in and around the town, many houses and flats now sadly belong to absentee owners, a proportion of whom I understand do not even appear for some eleven months of the year. In contrast, Collioure in the Forties and Fifties was overwhelmingly home to *Colliourench* fishermen and their families. Most were closely interrelated through marriage, with links in many cases extending back for centuries. An unfortunate consequence of this was a never-ending spate of raucous conversations conducted throughout the day and much of the night, not only within the houses, whose windows for much of the year were opened wide to the mild air, but also between relatives or neighbours living on opposite sides of the narrow streets. My mother, who might have felt herself back in the Devonshire fishing village of her childhood, was able to tolerate this with fair equanimity. For the edgy and introspective Patrick, however, the hurly-burly proved a constant trial of his temper. His ears were jarred by hoarsely jocose cries of fishermen, high-pitched exchanges between wives and daughters, and maddening screams from their children. 'Everyone evidently assumed everyone else was deaf,' he once remarked to me.

Rare objections to the cacophony achieved little more than to exacerbate it:

Last night the Puits [the restaurant on the ground floor] made such a din: Mme R[imbaud]. told me Franco it was who threw the bottle last year: Pilar told her today. P[ilar] & F[ranco] keep cailloux [pebbles] on their window-sill.

This entry in my mother's diary alludes to an outraged assault on late-night revellers in the restaurant on the ground floor. A year later, to her evident satisfaction, there was a repeat attack: 'Last night someone threw a bottle outside the Puits: it made a fine noise.' These incidents provoked inconclusive police and private investigations, all conducted at stentorian level on the spot, the fallout from which their friend Odette once told me had not entirely subsided half a century later.

As though this were not trial enough, Patrick understood barely a word of these vociferous exchanges, since almost everyone's first or even sole language was Catalan. The occasional bilingual exchange was as often as not equally hard to understand. As my mother recorded:

The woman opposite went bankrupt, & left to live at Elne. There she took up with a man & they came back to live at her house here. His wife found out where they were, & on Sunday came &

7

tried to get at them. They barred their door & she sat on a chair in the Street for six hours. A filthy scene (woman screeching French – man Catalan) by the arch 3 days ago must have been them, I think. The woman was dragging a 4–6 year old child with her.*

If the human cacophony momentarily waned in the early hours, it was only to be replaced by horrid war cries uttered by the martial cats of Collioure, who waged internecine conflict around gutters, doorways, and up and down stairs – there being generally no doors at street level to communal entrances. Even my parents' tough little Welsh hunt terrier Buddug could barely hold her own against these feline hosts of Midian. She was enabled to sally forth at will through an entrance cut in the door to the flat. One fine spring day my mother reported: 'Cats (toms) infest stairs, & Budd rages. She came in with v. bloody nose this morning.' Their morals were as depraved as their conduct was aggressive. On 9 September 1951 my mother adopted a kitten from the *rue*, whom she named Pussit Tassit, entering her arrival at the appropriate date in her childhood *Christopher Robin Birthday Book*. The following May, Patrick 'saw our cat being covered in the street by a large black tom while half a dozen others sat quietly watching'.

My mother's diary entries regularly attest to the strain imposed by the unrelenting cacophony:

'Our rue gets more & more noisy'; 'Oh God I am so sick with hearing vicious slaps & more vicious screaming at Martine. Patrick tried to read a T.S.E[liot]. poem [*Burnt Norton*] aloud yesterday but was drowned by the noise in the rue. Both boiled this morning

---

* Incidents like this show that Patrick did not exaggerate when referring to 'those screaming, tearing scenes that broke out three or four times a day somewhere along the street' (*The Catalans*, p. 30). 'How Mme Rimbaud ill-treated [her daughter] Martine: vicious slaps & howls,' my mother recorded in her diary in October 1953.

as cats howling kept us from sleeping'; 'V. bad night: noises'; 'Street noises formidable'; 'Neither of us can sleep: too much noise.'

When their neighbour Madame Rimbaud fell ill and was visited by the doctor, his ministrations were accompanied by well-intentioned 'Shoutings of choruses of women down there all day'.

Despite the disadvantages of their cramped quarters and noisy surroundings, my parents remained at first broadly satisfied with their new home, and swiftly became profound lovers of Collioure and its inhabitants. Their isolated and unproductive life in Snowdonia had long strained Patrick's nerves to desperation, and there could be no doubting the truth of his parting aphorism: 'it is better to be poor in a warm country.'*

In fact the weather at Collioure was far from being balmy throughout the entirety of the year. Winters could prove bitterly cold, and one snowstorm was so heavy that roofs collapsed beneath the weight. In January 1954 my mother recorded: 'Snow thick from Al Ras to Massane; cold & it rained all night', and shortly afterwards: 'Rain in the night, & today the Dugommier hillside specked with snow. They say 15° [Fahrenheit] below zero at Font Romeu.' I remember seeing in the town at that time photographs of what I recall as enormous waves frozen in mid-air as the sea hurled itself against the town walls. Life in the tiny flat above the rue Arago could be harsh indeed: 'Ice on comportes in the rue; glacial wind. Mirus [stove] full blast hardly keeps us warm'; 'Still 23° without, washing frozen into boards . . . Frightful cold: P. works au coin du feu.'

In spring the 'maddening, howling tramontane' battered the region for frustrating weeks, while in the autumn 'Wind (from Spain) & clouds prevented plage. C'est le vent d'Espagne – il fait humide – c'est pas sain.'

---

* It is a curious fact that the local inhabitants of my parents' homes in both Wales and France were for the most part monoglot speakers of indigenous tongues.

Port d'Avall and Château St Elme under snow in 1954*

Of course much of the year was generally hot, but even then freak weather could strike Collioure's microclimate, arising from its situation between the mountains and the sea. July 1953 saw a 'fantastic hail storm . . . River vast red flow.' Much of this belongs to the past, owing to climate change, but is important to recall when reliving my parents' early days in Collioure.

A hostile critic has conjectured that Patrick's move to Collioure was undertaken 'perhaps, in order to be a long way from the family he had abandoned'.[3] In reality, seven years had passed since he finally left his first wife Elizabeth for my mother. Moreover, he continued in close touch with his young son Richard, the only other member of his immediate family, whom he had no intention of abandoning, while he maintained intermittent correspondence with his brothers, sisters and stepmother throughout the long years that lay ahead.

---

* Note the absence of houses in Correch d'en Baus (on the slope of the hill below the castle), where my parents were soon to build their home.

It is true that relations with his son had been troubled, although nothing approaching the extent alleged by subsequent critics. Richard O'Brian was, by his own admission, somewhat indolent as a child, and made unsatisfactory progress at the Devonshire preparatory school to which his father and my mother had sent him for two and a half years at great financial sacrifice to themselves. At the end of the summer term of 1947 Patrick was obliged to withdraw him, and set about teaching him at the house where he and my mother were living in North Wales. Although the boy's education improved considerably in consequence, in some respects the experience was an unhappy one. Patrick's own wretched childhood had left him constitutionally ill-equipped (for much of his adult life, at any rate) to deal with small children, a failing on occasion so pronounced as to be all but comical. Walking above Collioure in November 1951, he fled down a sidetrack on 'seeing some beastly little boys' – one of several similarly alarming encounters. He imposed what might now appear excessively rigorous discipline on his son during lessons. Although Richard regularly stayed with his mother in London during the 'school holidays', during his time in Wales he had missed her and his beloved boxer Sian acutely. Patrick and my mother were fond of dogs, but it was impossible to introduce Sian into the sheep-farming community of Cwm Croesor.

This regime continued for two years, during which time excruciating attacks of writer's block made Patrick more and more testy and uncompromising in his efforts to educate the boy. It is likely that Patrick's frustration with Richard's lack of satisfactory progress was exacerbated by his own inability to achieve anything constructive in his writing. On the other hand, outside lessons he became in marked contrast a strikingly adventurous and imaginative parent. My mother's unwavering affection, too, went far to ameliorate Richard's life. Eventually, the ill-conceived scheme came to an end, with the departure of Patrick and my mother for Collioure in September 1949. That July Richard's mother Elizabeth married her longstanding lover John Le Mee-Power, which enabled her to make a successful application to the courts to recover custody of her son.

Patrick was deeply concerned to secure the best education possible for Richard. In 1945 he had registered him for entry to Wellington College, a public school with a strong military tradition, with a view to his eventually obtaining a career in the Army. Unfortunately this was my father's old school, which I in turn entered in January 1949. When my father was informed by Elizabeth that the O'Brians planned to send Richard there, he managed to persuade the Master of the undesirability of his attending the same school as me. The fact that my mother was at the time denied all contact with me presumably influenced the College's concurrence with my father's objection, which would now seem harsh and arbitrary. It is possible that some future unhappiness might have been avoided, had Richard and I been permitted to become friends from an early age.

The sincerity of Patrick's concern to advance Richard's education and future career cannot be doubted. The annual fees for Wellington were £160–£175 a year, which together with travel and additional expenses required a total expenditure of about £200 per annum. Yet his and my mother's combined income for 1950–51 amounted to £341 6s 9d.* Nor was the proposed sacrifice any fanciful project, since they had earlier paid about £170 a year for Richard's preparatory school fees and expenses.[4]

Eventually Richard came to believe that his father had contributed nothing material towards his education. In a press interview conducted over half a century later, he declared: 'My father never offered to help . . . [I] had been sent to a boarding school in Devon by [my] mother . . . [My] mother found the fees increasingly difficult to pay.'[5]

Although Richard is unlikely to have been concerned at the time

---

* This income was to become severely depleted in ensuing years.

by the question of who paid his school fees, in retrospect his mother's poverty-stricken circumstances (by her own account, she earned 'between £3. 10. 0. and £4. 0.0. a week', from invisible mending conducted in their home) might have made it plain that it could not have been she. Nor, given her upright character, does it appear likely that she would have made any attempt to deceive her son over the issue. Again, the fact that it was to Patrick and my mother that Richard looked for provision of all extras, ranging from school uniform and games kit to pocket money and railway travel, must have made it plain at the time who was meeting the bills.

Richard's memory could well have deceived him after half a century. Unfortunately, it is necessary to demonstrate that it did do so, in order to counter accusations levelled at Patrick by others.

Denied entry to Wellington, in the autumn of 1949 Richard was enrolled at Cardinal Vaughan School in Holland Park. A place was found for him by Father de Zulueta, aristocratic priest of the Roman Catholic church in Chelsea, where Richard and his mother lived. My mother's accounts show that she and Patrick spent substantial sums on Richard each year, although this did not include school fees, the institution being funded by the London County Council. Occasional financial assistance was probably also contributed by my grandfather, who was then living in Upper Cheyne Row around the corner from Richard and his mother. My mother's brother Howard, known to the family as 'Binkie', recalled: 'My Father told me that Patrick's son had been brought to him in a hungry state by that kind Father Zulu. I have no doubt but that Pa would have given him a hand out despite his aversion to Patrick.'

Some years ago I heard from an old schoolfriend of Richard's. Bob Broeder remembered him well:

Richard stood out from the rest of us as he spoke in a refined accent while most of us spoke in what can only be described as a London accent. As boys do, we asked each other which schools we had come from. When it came to Richard, he told us that he had been educated [i.e. tutored] by his father. This made him stand out even more.

Miserable though it had in part been at the time, it seems that Richard had already come to value his father's didactic course of instruction – as he undoubtedly did not long after this. He might, after all, have confined himself to naming the Devonshire preparatory school he had attended previously.

A letter sent by Richard to Collioure at this time recounts his progress. (Here as elsewhere I retain his delightfully idiosyncratic spelling, which adds to the charm of the correspondence.)

Dear Daddy and Mary, I am very sorry I did not reply to your letter. The only subject I find easy is Greek, but altogether I get on nicely, in Latin we are doing the Relative pronoun, in French we are learning the presents of some irregular and regular verbs, in history we are doing Tudor times, in arithemetic we are about to begin fractions, in algebra we have not started similtanious equations, in geometry we are learning Euclid 1 .13. I find home-work very boring, but I do it, so far I have had only three penances. Here is a bit of news for Mary, I have growen out of my good old boots, I can't get them on though last two months I could, my mother says please can I have several pairs of socks and some ~~pugams~~ pyjamers. My Mother says I will be taking my Exam in the spring or else I might stay where I am. I like the idea of the feast and wished I was there, but we can't buy wishing-carpets. I will try very hard for a silent dog whistle [for Buddug] when I have time but most propally I'll end up some where else. Please could I have a little money? I am very glad you are in your new home, have you had a shower-bath, I think when I come over I will invent a sort of bellows which you start off and stop when you want. I have never heard of a Praying Montis. I do not like getting up early but I do. I hope you and Daddy and Buddug are well? With love from Richard.

The 'Exam' in question was the Common Entrance for admission to public schools. The attempt to enter Richard for Wellington having been blocked, Patrick now sought to have him admitted to St Paul's, a prestigious London public school. This would have enabled him to attend as a day boy, thus avoiding the heavy expense of boarding. Richard prepared for the examination in the summer of 1950, which in the event poor academic progress appears to have prevented his sitting. There is incidentally a suggestion that my mother attempted to persuade her father to break the modest financial trust he had settled on her, in order that she might devote the capital to Richard's education. A passage in Patrick's autobiographical novel *Richard Temple* may well allude to such a plea: 'On the same reasoning he [Mrs Temple's father, Canon Harler] had refused to let her touch the capital of her little trust-fund to send Richard to a better school: besides, he had never approved of her marriage and would lend its results no countenance.'[6]

Grim personal experience of the terrible financial crash of 1929 had left my grandfather with a visceral aversion to dispersion of capital.

Richard's initial experience at Cardinal Vaughan had been less than happy. As his friend Bob Broeder further recalls:

As time went on he was the subject of verbal bullying and was given a nickname – 'Sheep's Brains' . . . Things came to a head one day, when a large lad (who later went on to play rugby for the Wasps) confronted Richard & threatened him with violence. By this time I had had enough and although smaller than this lad I told him in no uncertain terms to pack it in. Psychology worked and he never troubled Richard again, the other boys saw what had happened and they in their turn left Richard alone.

Before long he had settled down well, at least with his fellow pupils. Writing to Collioure, he cheerfully declared: 'Dear Daddy

. . . I hope I pass the common entrance to St Pauls, though I am quite happy where I am.' He and Bob Broeder had become fast friends. The latter retains a vivid memory of Richard's cramped little home:

> As time went by I was invited to his home to meet his mother. They lived in a flat on the first floor at 237, Kings Road Chelsea. Adjacent to the first floor landing was the kitchen/dining area then up some more stairs to the living room – quite large and very cold in Winter, despite a small fire.
>
> I found his mother Elizabeth a small, charming and very well spoken lady with whom I had a good rapport. Little mention was ever made about his father, except that he lived in the south of France. At that age you accept things readily and don't question.

Subsequently, Bob found conditions at Richard's home materially improved:

> One day I arrived at Richard's home and went into the living-room with him, discovered it was no longer cold but nicely warm. He pointed to a brand new stove that had been installed in the fireplace and which gave out a marvellous warmth . . .
>
> One Christmas I was invited to Christmas dinner. Elizabeth had prepared a wonderful feast. There was a complete roasted goose with all the trimmings – it was an unforgettable occasion. Elizabeth was a kind and generous lady who worked hard as a seamstress. I often saw her patiently repairing nylon stockings for customers. Such luxury items were hard to come by and then very expensive. She also worked at the Chelsea Arts Club in the evening.

Richard was now thirteen, when a combination of factors served to place his relationship with his father on an altogether happier basis. No longer confined in isolated contiguity with his at times testy parent, he was also outgrowing tiresome childish failings which all too easily provoked Patrick's simmering wrath. The permanent rift which was one day to develop between them lay far in the future, and as will be seen did not in any case originate with Patrick. It looks as though Richard's eventual decision to abandon relations with his father led him (as may too often occur in such unhappy cases) to reinterpret or confuse his memories of the past. Looking back from 2000, he recalled of this period:

> Later, my father moved to France and I was delighted to return to my mother. Over the years I continued to visit my father and Mary but our relationship didn't develop much further. He was not an easy person to get near. He was not affectionate; there were no quick hugs or pats on the shoulder. Nor was there much fun about him. Everything was a little bit heavy. He could also be very, very sarcastic. There was one incident that I remember clearly. He was extremely good at sharpening knives. 'That looks interesting,' I thought, so I had a go. His comment was: 'I've seen angle-irons sharper than that.' He could have thought of something pleasant to say.

I can confirm that Patrick was instinctively averse to 'quick hugs or pats on the shoulder', which he had rarely experienced in his own childhood. But so in my experience were many fathers at that time, and this, like much else in Richard's subsequent assessment, suggests judgements formed in a radically different era. While the clumsy attempt at humour (which I suspect the knife-sharpening exchange to have been) may or may not have upset the boy at the time, there exists abundant evidence that Richard's memory in later life could deceive him in material respects.

In the 1950s Patrick appears to have been unaware of any suggestion of coldness in their relationship. Pondering the matter, he jotted in a notebook:

The dialogue between a man and his son an inner dialogue. The well-known lack of communication is no more than a lack of contact on the surface – words, formal communication – and in fact the generations are linked to a sometimes intolerably intimate degree – secret glances instantly and wholly understood, disapproval felt, affectations detected hopelessly because hereditary . . .

This passage is further interesting, suggesting as it does Patrick's sincere, if at times excessive, concern to eradicate failings in his son which he ascribed to his own boyhood experience.

Richard, like many of us on occasion, was undoubtedly capable of unconsciously 'editing' his early childhood memories long years after the event. An illuminating example is provided by an episode he recounted in a press interview, in which he attacked his father's memory. 'When I was five he sent me a present – a bottle of malt and cod liver oil, something no five-year-old would want. That was the year that [Richard's sister] Jane died.'[7]

This reads as though it were a direct memory of a long-distant event. In reality, he first learned of it from a letter discovered by his mother Elizabeth in 'an old box', which she sent to Richard's daughter Joanna. Elizabeth's letter is undated, but since Joanna was born in 1969 it is unlikely to have been written before the 1980s. The trove of material discovered in the old box included the letter in question (also undated), which conveyed birthday wishes and what Patrick described as 'a rather revolting sort of birthday present – to wit, some malt and cod-liver oil. But reflect that it is good for you, and see if you can enjoy it.' To this Patrick appended some amusing verses and accompanying sketches, after the style of Hilaire Belloc.

Elizabeth, whose memory must in this case be preferred to that of her then infant son, wrote that he was at the time not five as he later asserted, but 'about 3 years old' – i.e. two years before his sister Jane died. In view of Richard's age, the letter plainly represented a *jeu d'esprit*, intended for the mother's amusement rather than that of the small unlettered infant. Furthermore, given that we know nothing of the context, it seems not unlikely that Richard really was ill (his birthday was at the beginning of February), and the announcement that the medicine was a birthday present reflected nothing more than a private joke to be shared with his mother. Indeed, the letter concludes with a mock-sinister verse about a scorpion, on which Patrick commented: 'I'm afraid that last one won't appeal to you very much, but your mother might like it.'*

Letters from Richard's Chelsea home delighted my parents after their arrival in Collioure in 1949, including as they did many artless touches of boyhood enthusiasm. 'I have been four day's in bed with tonsilitis,' he reported: 'that means I will have my tonsils out, maybe I will grow wiser on account of my tonsils being cut out.' He was beginning to evince encouraging interest in literature, and used the pocket money they sent him to buy such sterling boys' fare as the works of Rider Haggard, Alexandre Dumas and R.M. Ballantyne. There were regular reports on Sian the boxer's welfare and her occasional 'weddings', which resulted in numerous offspring. He attended his first communion at Chelsea's Catholic church: 'Father de Zulueta is giving me a Bible as my own [Authorized Version] is anti-catholic, however I shall keep it.'

Excitement mounted as across the river preparations began for the 1951 Festival of Britain in Battersea Park, which Richard roundly condemned as an expensive white elephant. He received letters from his father and my mother almost every week, money being punctiliously despatched whenever required, and at whatever sacrifice to the impoverished O'Brians. As a growing boy, he regularly required new clothing. On one occasion they provided

---

* Patrick O'Brian Collection, the Lilly Library. Could the fact that Elizabeth carefully preserved Patrick's letters, written at this most acrimonious of times, suggest that she may not always have nurtured the degree of lifelong detestation which has been posthumously ascribed to her?

him with a complete cricket outfit, which he was aware 'was very expensive'. Gratifyingly, 'when I put all the clothes on I looked like a proffessional cricketer'. Patrick took a keen interest in Richard's sporting activity, and the latter responded with detailed accounts of matches: 'Thank you for the lovely parcle of buscuits and advise on cricket.' He was looking forward to coming out to France, but 'was rather horrified at the thought of the journey.' Furthermore, 'I am afraid I have forgotten all my French as we say almost the same thing every lesson, "come and stand here", "do you come here?" I think the master askes most silly questions.' When my mother told him she was teaching Odette Bernardi to speak English, Richard rejoiced at the prospect of being able to speak to her.

In July 1949 the judge presiding over the custody hearing had ruled that Patrick 'be at liberty to take the said child out of the jurisdiction of this Court to France for half of the Summer Holidays, the Respondent [Patrick] undertaking to return the said child within the jurisdiction at the end of the said period'.[8] Richard accordingly spent part of his 1950 summer holiday at Collioure, which he hugely enjoyed. The next term he submitted an eight-page essay 'on the most exicting part of the holidays', with an account of a bullfight in the little arena beside the Collioure railway station. A healthy and active boy, he revelled in swimming from the plage St Vincent, exploring the neighbouring countryside, and walking with his father and stepmother in the Pyrenees. Nor was life lonely, as it had been to such an exacting extent in North Wales. Patrick and my mother had made close friends in the town since their arrival. Among their friends, Richard saw much of Odette and François Bernardi, as also the voluble and amusing painter Willy Mucha, and his attractive and equally garrulous (when permitted) wife Rolande.

That autumn Richard fastened on the career he wanted, writing eagerly to his father:

I am very happy at school. Please could you arrange for me to go into the Royal Navy, please? Please could you arrange for me to go into the Submarine Service? Could you write to the Admilaltary now, and find out what exams I must pass so I can be in at the age of 16. I am very keen for this to happen.

Patrick, whose own lack of formal education had prevented his gaining entrance to the Royal Naval College at Dartmouth, responded with enthusiasm. No career for his son could please him more, and Richard threw himself into the project with mingled energy and apprehension:

At school we are going to have the exams, which are horrors, on Thursday. The masters make it sound so easy and pleasant but I am dreading the results and the terrible report. Thank you so much about the Navy but I am afraid of the exams. I know that it is right for me to go into the R.N., and I will work very hard for it.

Patrick himself had never passed (quite likely never sat) a single examination during his drastically curtailed schooldays, and remained throughout his life markedly sympathetic toward children encountering problems with their school work. As it happened, on this occasion Richard's results were good, and he evinced particular aptitude for geometry. A plea to have virtually all his clothes replaced ('All the boys at school are well dressed and I am about the shabbiest one there') immediately elicited a cheque for the substantial sum of £10/5/-, with a pair of goggles for swimming thoughtfully thrown in for good measure. His enthusiasm for mechanical toys also pleased Patrick, who loved dismantling and reassembling clocks and other intricate machinery.

Father and son further shared a common delight in the natural world. In March 1951 Patrick sent Richard a copy of Henry

Williamson's *Tarka the Otter*, and the boy was already looking forward to his next holiday in Collioure:

> When I come over I shall bring the Union Jack tent, air-pistol, flute and one or two books, and (if I can get one) a little pet snake, the pet shop in lower Sloane Street may have a few young vipers.
>
> Thank you so very for Tarka and the electrical book . . . Can one tame young hoopoos? I would like one. Do we often have sharks in the bay as Daddy told me he saw one?

In March 1951, Richard's mother, with whom my mother regularly exchanged correspondence concerning Richard's needs, wrote to report that her son was unhappy at home, and enquired whether he might be allowed to live permanently with them at Collioure.* Poor Elizabeth had been ill for much of the winter, and was finding it an increasing strain combining her arduous work with looking after the lively boy in her little upstairs flat. My mother replied that they would be delighted to have him. However, Patrick, as always concerned for his son's best interest, asked their old wartime friend Walter Greenway to take Richard out to tea, and discover how matters really stood. In due course my mother noted: 'Walter wrote that Richard seems very happy & settled at Cardinal Vaughan's school & he himself says he would not like to leave it & come here altogether.'

It turned out that Richard, who frequently struggled to keep up with school work, tended to grow restless and unhappy as the term drew to its close. At the same time, he looked forward to coming over 'for the summer hols'.

My mother undoubtedly loved Richard as though he were her

---

* Early in the next month, Richard himself wrote: 'I think my mother is finding it a strain in doing her job and looking after me. She has been very unwell this winter.'

own son, and her affection can only have been accentuated by an unhappy exchange of correspondence in the early summer of 1951. In view of her desertion, and continued 'living in sin' with Patrick until their marriage in 1945, a court had granted my father custody of my sister Natasha and myself. He himself had remarried in 1943, and as a promising barrister with a substantial private income was in a position to provide a suitable home for us.

My mother in the early 1950s

I was to be sixteen in June 1951, and in April my mother wrote to the London solicitor who had handled her divorce proceedings, 'to ask if in fact Nikolai can choose to know me if he likes after his 16th birthday'. After some delay the solicitor confirmed that there was no reason why she should not at least enquire. Accordingly, she wrote both to her parents, who remained in close contact with my sister and me, and also directly to me. I received the letter at Wellington College, accompanied by a birthday present of a handsome book: William Sanderson, *A Compleat History of the Lives and Reigns of Mary Queen of Scotland, And of Her Son and Successor, James The Sixth, King of Scotland* (London, 1656).

My mother must somehow have learned of my devotion to the House of Stuart, following my enraptured introduction to Scott's Waverley novels by the enlightened headmaster of my preparatory school.

Needless to say, I was delighted with the present, but bemused to know how to respond. Before I could do so, however, my father arrived at the College in a state of grim agitation. He was at pains to impress on me how appallingly my mother had behaved, not the least of her crimes being an insidious attempt to make contact with me by entering Richard for Wellington. He accordingly urged me not to reply. When I enquired what I should do with her present, he smiled and suggested I keep it. Although I felt instinctively that there was something not quite right about this, I complied, and still have the book.

Children tend to be remarkably adaptable to circumstances. I myself was generally unhappy at home. Probably as a consequence of the loss of his own mother at the age of three, followed by terrifying childhood experiences during and after the Russian Revolution, and finally my mother's desertion, my poor father had become a solitary, parsimonious, and generally morose figure, while my Russian stepmother was a relentless scold, who made no secret of the fact that she resented my presence in the house. Although set in a delightful situation beside the Thames at Wraysbury near Windsor, our home appeared to me a gloomy prison visited by few: so much so, that each holiday I compiled a calendar, whose function was to record and strike out on a half-daily basis the approach of the longed-for return to my friends at school. Yet, despite this dismal condition, I accepted all that my father urged on me, and remained persuaded throughout my schooldays that my mother was a very wicked woman. Shortly after the episode described above, she received letters from my father and her mother, impressing on her the undesirability of approaching me when I was already experiencing emotional problems at home and school. It is not hard to picture her anguish. Fortunately, she had Patrick to sustain her. 'Dear P.', as she wrote appreciatively that night in her diary.

Small wonder, then, that my mother poured so much affection onto her young stepson. While he continued devoted to his own mother, he had long become correspondingly fond of his step-mother, and swiftly grew enraptured with life at Collioure. His nostalgia for the town was such, that on the occasion of one return to London he requested a phial of sand from the beach, which on its arrival he much prized: 'The sand has turned moist as the air is damp. If you send me any more curios I can start a penny-peep-show-museum.'

At this time Patrick and my mother were living on a more and more heavily taxed income amounting to £48 a quarter from the trust established on my mother by her father, supplemented by modest literary and other irregular earnings. My mother in addition occasionally taught English to *Colliourenchs* and their children, translated and typed letters, and engaged in other modestly remunerative activities. From this meagre income they had to meet continual requests from the growing Richard and his mother for new clothes, school extras and private entertain-ment. This they invariably did to the best of their ability, and the fact that his requests feature with such blithe regularity in his correspondence confirms that they neither reproached nor stinted him.

Any unforeseen expenditure was in danger of sinking their precar-ious little boat. On 1 September 1951, my mother was 'Rudely awakened this morning by cheque of £32 instead of expected seventy. We have £13 a month until March . . . Richard never wrote: P. wrote again to him today. Dreadful letter from Mrs. Power suddenly demanding "maintenance".' This was Richard's mother, who had finally married her lover John Le Mee-Power in May 1949. On what grounds she believed she could now make a claim on Patrick was unclear, but nonetheless alarming. Some weeks later, however, my mother heard again from the unhappy Elizabeth:

'Letter from . . . Mrs. Power: poor thing, husband gone two years ago, not enough money.'* Power had proved to be a drunken, irresponsible bully. Elizabeth's demand proved to be a momentary cry of despair, since by this time she appears to have accepted that my parents lacked any means of providing more financial help than that which they already lavished on Richard.

Now that Richard was fast becoming a young man, Patrick could share pleasures with him, imbuing them with that infectious enthusiasm which was one of his most endearing characteristics. Overall, the relationship had reached a happy modus vivendi. Patrick, my mother and Richard had grown into a compact little family, corresponding regularly and affectionately, and meeting from time to time for extended holidays and London treats. My mother's parents, Howard and Frieda Wicksteed, as ever concerned for Richard's welfare, regularly intervened to plug her recurrent financial holes. Fortunately, they lived in Upper Cheyne Row, a short walk around the corner from his mother in King's Road. There Elizabeth eked out an existence marred by poverty and illness, while he continued devoted to her and she to him. Even the once bitter feud between Elizabeth and Patrick appears to have subsided into a mutually acceptable truce, with letters passing between the two households concerning Richard's welfare, and my mother during visits to her parents calling to collect him from Elizabeth's little upstairs flat round the corner. Other exchanges included Patrick's arranging for her to be given their Hoover. How happy might it have been had these amicable relations continued! The only lasting sadness was that which constantly assailed my mother: deprivation of opportunity even to correspond with her own son and daughter Natasha. And whatever distressed my mother deeply troubled her devoted Patrick.

As this account has established, it is a regrettable but undeniable

---

* It appears from this that Power deserted Elizabeth almost immediately after their marriage, though I possess no confirmation of the fact.

fact that Patrick was by nature and upbringing ill-suited to engage with young children, whose waywardness, unreflecting lack of tact and blithe innocence of the ways of the world tended all too readily to affront and alarm his fragile composure. However, once they attained an age which he regarded as providing a measure of rationality and intelligence, his attitude shifted remarkably. In one of his novels he describes how: 'When Madeleine was a little girl she was a plain creature, and timid. Her form was the undistinguished, pudgy, shapeless form of most children.' As an adolescent, however, she swiftly blossoms into a beautiful, intelligent, self-possessed young lady.[9] It is clear that he recognized this evolutionary transformation from caterpillar to butterfly in the case of his son. Furthermore, as I have shown in the first volume of this biography, it is worthwhile to stress that it was only when teaching Richard that his patience was tried: outside the 'classroom' Patrick became charm and enthusiasm personified.

Following the move to France, Patrick's equanimity was restored by the generally promising path of his literary work. Shortly before their departure from Cwm Croesor, he had assembled a collection of short stories. Although in 1947 he had published *A Book of Voyages*, an anthology of seafaring episodes, this slim collection was to comprise the sum total of his original published literary projects since 1939, when the first of its tales was written. Although reflecting his sparse creative output over the preceding decade, the stories are beautifully written and highly imaginative, and were received enthusiastically by his literary agent, Spencer Curtis Brown. He passed them in turn to Fred Warburg, of the publishers Secker & Warburg, who on the eve of Patrick's departure for France expressed similar appreciation:

We have now read and admired the remarkable stories of Patrick O'Brien [*sic*], at present entitled COUNTRY CONTENTMENTS, and should certainly like to publish the book . . . We do not like the title proposed by O'Brien and tentatively suggest THE LAST POOL as a possibility.

Patrick had adopted the title *Country Contentments* from his copy of a delightful work of that name, a guide to rural activities by the seventeenth-century writer Gervase Markham, which Patrick had sought to put into practice in Wales.[10] There seems little doubt, however, that Warburg's choice was preferable (several stories in the collection are markedly *dis*contented, being positively gloomy and even macabre), and *The Last Pool* (the title of the first story in the book) is what the title became. Curtis Brown stood firm in Patrick's interest, insisting *inter alia* that he retain US rights for the book. Warburg gave way graciously on the issue, and the contract was signed on 27 September 1949. In it Patrick further committed himself 'to write a book on Southern France and to proceed to France within the next two months in order to collect material for such a book'. For this 'the publisher undertakes to pay to the Author forthwith the sum of £75 (seventy-five pounds) towards the expenses of the Author's visit to France'. In fact, Patrick had by this time already crossed the Channel.

In addition the publisher obtained an option on Patrick's next book, and when the two of them had lunched together on 24 August of that year Warburg learned that it was to be 'a full length novel with a Welsh background'. Next day Warburg wrote to Spencer Curtis Brown, thanking him 'for putting this most unusual book [*The Last Pool*] our way and very much hope it will have the success it deserves'. At the same time he (surely wisely) rejected Patrick's tentative suggestion for the alternative title *Dark Speech upon the Harp*.

Patrick appears to have persuaded Secker that the prime motive of their journey was to gather material for the 'book on Southern France'. Either way, the money came in extremely handy towards meeting the expense of their move. In the event, they arrived at Collioure shortly before the contract was completed. The removal cost £9.10/-, and since the rent of the flat in the rue Arago amounted to some £10 a year (which their genial landlord, M. Germa, seems to have collected erratically), for a while at least they should have been quite comfortably off. However, by next February they were alarmed by a statement from their bank in London, explaining that no more money could be forwarded, as they had attained the limit of £250 which it was at that time permitted to take abroad. Towards the end of May Patrick was still struggling to liberate Warburg's £75 advance from an impassive bureaucracy. He noted grimly: 'Wrote to C.J. Foreign Div. & Parry – The last two letters Mrs O'Brian wrote to you are still unanswered. This sort of treatment is really intolerable, and I must insist upon an immediate final.'

Unfortunately, it turned out that they did not qualify for remission of the advance.

At Warburg's invitation, Patrick forwarded from my grandparents' house in Chelsea (whose lease they had taken over from him at his departure in 1945) 'some biographical scraps' for inclusion on the dustjacket. Although Warburg thanked him for 'the biographical material, which is excellent', nearly eight months later he oddly repeated the request for 'your biographical details, i.e. date and place of birth, education, appointments held and any other relevant information . . . speed is of the essence'. Since it was Patrick's persistent habit to preserve copies of such material, it is hard to conceive of any reason why he should have failed to comply with the second request after being so prompt in fulfilling the first. It seems likely therefore that in the event Warburg decided against inclusion of a potted biography. As the sizeable dustjacket blurb implies that the tales arose out of the author's own communing with the countryside which provides their setting, this may have appeared to suffice for a personal description.

The Last Pool was published on 17 August 1950. Its best stories contain some of Patrick's finest writing, while all are entertaining. A Latin dedication 'To Mary, my wife and Dearest Friend' acknowledged her indispensable support and help. The book's atmospheric green dustjacket design by Edward Bradbury, depicting three fine trout in the foreground, and shadowy images reflecting country sports circling dimly through refracted water, make it a handsome volume, now much sought by bibliophiles.

Reviews in the press were largely favourable: in some cases, enthusiastic. The novelist L.A.G. Strong perceptively described him as 'A real new writer, with a voice of his own. He shows a real power to describe physical sensations.' Patrick's response to all this was guarded. In a letter to his editor Roger Senhouse written in the following February, he provided an assessment of critics which came from the heart: 'I do grow passionate about criticism from fools, from people who have not really read what they criticise and from those whose aim is to show off; but I am really grateful for genuine criticism.'*

He welcomed Senhouse's comments on his next book, but clearly had coverage of *The Last Pool* in mind, for he continued with some sharp reflections on 'the damned silly review Dunsany produced in the Observer. Did you see any worthwhile reviews of The Last Pool? I only saw a long and offensively fulsome one in the Irish Times, and a short and stupid one in the Spectator, apart from the Observer.'

At first glance, Patrick's testy dismissal of the *Observer* review appears perverse. Lord Dunsany, a well-connected Irish peer, literary figure and keen rider to hounds, was surely ideally placed to review such a book. What seems particularly to have riled Patrick was a well-intentioned laudatory comment, much canvassed since: 'This charming book by an Irish sportsman is a genuine collection of tales of the Irish countryside.' For a start, it might suggest that Dunsany had done little more than glance through the text. Although five of the thirteen tales have Irish settings, a careful reader would have noted that the three located in Wales evince a much more fundamental grounding in local toponymy, landscape and speech.

Still more upsetting appears to have been Dunsany's gratuitous allusion to the author as 'an Irish sportsman'. This was presumably

---

* Patrick's own book reviewing in later years was almost invariably sympathetically constructive in its criticism – sometimes, I felt, to the point of being overly charitable.

inferred by Dunsany from Patrick's surname,* together with the Irish setting of several of the stories. That an influential Irish writer publicly hailed him as a compatriot placed Patrick in an embarrassing quandary. As was explained in the first volume of this biography, his change of name was selected in order to banish an unbearable past – not to invent a new one. An obsessively private individual, the last thing he wanted was to find his personal life paraded before an inquisitive public. After all, Dunsany's erroneous assumption could lead to his being derided as an imposter. What could he do? A correction (in the unlikely event of the newspaper's publishing it) must inevitably invite enquiry into his actual background.

While this might be criticized as an absurdly paranoid reaction, it was to become unexpectedly justified when belated revelation of his change of name half a century later aroused bitter diatribes in the media beyond anything Patrick at his most vulnerable might have anticipated. He instinctively believed a substantial body of the literati to be an innately envious and consequently malevolent crew. Sadly, he lived to find this jaundiced view not altogether mistaken. It may surely be enquired, were he as concerned to lay claim to Irish ancestry as ill-natured critics have proclaimed, why he did not seize the opportunity to do so in *The Last Pool*, nor seek to profit from Lord Dunsany's flattering allusion.†

When Patrick came under pressure by publishers on other occasions to provide autobiographical notices, he either evaded doing so altogether, or submitted some patently humorous fantasy. The dustjacket of his early novel *Hussein* (1938), for example, informed its readers:

---

* Dunsany might have noted the idiosyncratic spelling 'O'Brian', which is rare almost to non-existence in Irish usage. I have shown in the first volume of this biography how Patrick adopted it entirely at random from a copy of a nineteenth-century marine insurance certificate (now in my possession).

† Dean King asserts that Patrick 'put this to good use: to confirm his nationality, all he had to do now was circulate Dunsany's review'. There exists no evidence whatever known to me that endorses this jaundiced assertion.

Patrick Russ has seen much of life in his 26 years. When he was stoking a Portuguese tramp steamer, he came to Rabat and made the acquaintance of two professional story-tellers with whom he wandered up and down French Morocco for a couple of months. It was from them, conversing in mixtures of French and Berber Arabic that he got much of the material widely current throughout the Mohammedan world, which goes to form the story of Hussein.

It is presumably the rarity of this dustjacket which has thus far protected Patrick from being accused by humourless critics of intending these imaginative exploits to be taken *au pied de la lettre*.[11]

Although beautifully written, the stories in *The Last Pool* proved to be no more than a swansong to the otherwise alarmingly arid period from which he was at last emerging. I have described in the first volume of this biography how they were spasmodically compiled over the decade of 1939–49, during which time the interruption caused by wartime employment, followed by nearly four years of mounting writer's block, eventually brought to fruition no more than this sparse collection. After their luncheon meeting in August 1949, Fredric Warburg noted: 'I gathered that in this field he had, for the moment, written himself out.' In fact, all he had had in mind for further writing was 'a book on the French Catalans'.

It appears, however, that not long after their arrival at Collioure, Patrick began to find memories of life at Cwm Croesor flooding back. Now distanced from the life of hardship and frustration they had endured there, he began to picture it all anew in his mind's eye. In a notebook he jotted down a plan for a novel set in the dark valley:

Do not forget the idea of having the man (or one of his friends) a sociologist nor overlook the possibility of presenting slabs of Welsh life in the manner either of direct reporting or now I come to think of it, what about having the farm situations seen from many angles – all the others 3rd person – no one being wholly true. From each slab one could regard the farm.

The 'sociologist', professional observer of the workings of humanity, is clearly derived from Patrick himself, and indeed in the finished work he appears under palpably thin disguise as its protagonist Pugh, who arrives as a visitor in the valley. The name itself was possibly drawn from 'old Pugh', a servant who worked at the house at Kempsey where Patrick had lived as a boy in 1923–24. He had retained in his mind a vivid picture of life in Cwm Croesor, as also its inhabitants, with whom he and my mother maintained warm if intermittent contact for several years after their departure. In January 1952 Bessie Roberts, the neighbouring farmer's wife, sent them a charming photograph of their two young sons Gwynfor and Alun ('Taken at school in September / With there love and many thanks to "Antie Vron"'),* which my mother lovingly preserved.

Gwynfor and Alun Roberts

---

* 'Auntie Vron': my mother lived at Fron Wen.

In September 1951 'Pierce sent £5 for the old bikes' they had left behind to be sold, and four years after their settlement in France my mother was still singing Welsh songs. In addition to his memories, Patrick drew on the journal he had kept during the first nine months of their Welsh existence, on which he relied extensively for descriptive passages in his novel.

Long afterwards he provided this summary analysis of his work:

About forty years ago I did write a mildly experimental book called Testimonies in which all the main characters, having left this world, sat peacefully in the next, each independently delivering an account of his or her recent life to a simple, objective being whom readers of the fifties at once understood to be a kind of non-sectarian recording angel. The novel has just been reissued and to my astonishment many of those who read it today, or at least many reviewers, though very kind about the tale itself, are sadly puzzled by my angel. 'Who is this investigator?' they cry. 'Who him? What is this guy doing around the joint?'

On another occasion he explained further:

I was writing hard, working on a novel called *Testimonies*, which I placed in Wales, though the situation it dealt with might just as well have arisen on the seacoast of Bohemia: I finished it very late one night and, in a state of near-prostration – how I wish I could, in a line or so, convey the strength of generalised emotion and delight at times like this, when one feels one is writing well. (I speak only for myself, of course.) The book was politely received in England, much more enthusiastically in the States where the intellectual journals praised it very highly indeed. It did not sell well, but New York magazines asked me for stories.[12]

The claim that 'the situation it dealt with might just as well have arisen on the seacoast of Bohemia' must be taken with a large grain of salt. The valley setting is described with wonderful vividness, reflecting the fact that it is indeed the Cwm Croesor, unchanged (save for some readily identifiable toponyms), of their four years' exile. In addition, so far as I have been able to identify them, virtually every character reflects a real individual. Broadly speaking, it is the melodramatic plot alone that derives from Patrick's imagination.

It is not my purpose to analyse the story. With my mother excluded from the story, Pugh is a combination of Patrick as he really was, and in some respects what he wished to be. Pugh is a university Fellow at Oxford, who is preparing a learned tome on *The Bestiary before Isidore of Seville*. This was the topic selected by Patrick for a book he hoped would establish his scholarly credentials, on which he had worked in the British Museum before the War. He had also nurtured an early ambition to go up to Oxford, and enjoy the prestige of gaining academic qualification.

Pugh's antecedents confirm the self-portrait. A forebear had established himself as a draper in Liverpool, while 'my father, a sociable man, living in a time of acute social distinctions, felt the Liverpool-Welsh side of his ancestry keenly.* He dropped all Welsh contacts and added his mother's name, Aubrey, to ours. He had never cared for me to ask him about it.'[13] Patrick's grandfather had been a successful furrier in London, while his father embarked on a medical career. It is needless to emphasize the change of name, nor (in another context) the selection of 'Aubrey' as a gentlemanly alternative. (Pugh further has a close friend named Maturin!) For 'Liverpool-Welsh' may be read 'German', the original nationality of the Russ family.

The tall red-haired farmer Emyr Vaughan is Patrick's neighbour Harri Roberts, while his comely wife Bessie provided the model

---

* In Patrick's most intensely autobiographical novel, the hero's father is likewise dismissively ascribed a Liverpool-Welsh background in trade (*Richard Temple*, p. 28).

for Bronwen, tragic heroine of the novel.* Readers may wonder, but for myself I doubt that Patrick himself indulged in serious fantasies about Bessie Roberts. He admired and appreciated attractive women, but was too innately monogamous and devoted to my mother to harbour dangerously improper thoughts. Bessie was simply the model for the fictional Bronwen. Moreover it was a dramatic requirement that the heroine be living immediately below the brooding Pugh in his tiny cottage, while the Roberts farm was the only house adjacent to Fron Wen.

The taxi driver who brings Pugh to his cottage at the beginning was in real life Griffi Roberts, owner of the garage at Gareg, while the *gwas* (farm boy) John, Pugh's informant on Welsh lore, was Edgar Williams, our good friend who still lives in Croesor. The originals of other characters are less readily identified today, but there can be little doubt that they reflect to various degrees others with whom Patrick came in contact.

The unmistakable extent to which Patrick drew on real people for his novel dismayed his friend Walter Greenway, who had stayed with him in Cwm Croesor. As Walter later told me, he feared it could cause offence in the valley. However, cordial Christmas greetings and other occasional communications continued to be exchanged annually between Collioure and Cwm Croesor,† and doubtless Patrick assumed with good reason that few if any people there were likely, or even able, to read a book published in English.

Three Bear Witness (his American publisher retained Patrick's preferred title *Testimonies*) was written in 1950, and as my mother only began keeping a diary from January 1951 I do not know as much as I could wish about its composition. With the physical hardship and mental turmoil of life in Cwm Croesor distanced in

---

* *Bronwen* ('White Breast') is both a classic Welsh name and that of my parents' cottage Fron (pronounced 'Vron') Wen.

† In November 1952 my mother 'went to Port Bou & bought & sent off Christmas presents . . . 3 to Croesor Fawr' (the Robertses' farmhouse).

time and space, Patrick could contemplate his former existence dispassionately, even with nostalgia. Observing the mountains above Collioure, he noted one day: 'I love the absolute hardness and contrast of the mountain and just that pure sky: the Cnicht ridge had it often.' At about the same time he jotted down this verse:

> The raven of the Pyrenees
> Cries harsh and folds his wings to fall.
> On Moelwyn Mawr the watcher sees
> The folded tumble, hears the call.*

The contract for *The Last Pool* provided for the publisher's retention of an option on his next book, together with an opportunity to consider the proposed book about Southern France. Four months later, on 1 February 1951, Patrick signed the contract for *Three Bear Witness*. It was in many ways an experimental work, with the imaginative contrivance of the protagonists interrogated in turn for their versions of the same events by an unidentified 'Recording Angel'. In later life he recalled that 'I do remember that writing parts of it quite destroyed me'. He also felt it was the best book he had written, and remembered the night he finished it:

'I was writing very hard that evening, and at three in the morning I went like so on my desk,' he says, folding himself over his elbows in an exhausted swoon. 'When I knew it was done I had the feeling of achievement and loss simultaneously'.[14]

Although Patrick, always ill at ease when conducting interviews, was on occasion prone to modify or embroider his memories, it does indeed seem likely that the book was written under considerable stress. Poverty at the little *apartement* at 39, rue Arago was extreme at the time, and there was no knowing whether anyone

---

* In May 1950 Patrick observed ravens nesting near Collioure.

beyond my mother would appreciate a book that meant so much to him. In fact her initial reaction was one of disapproval: 'P. finished T.B. which I did not like.' However, I suspect this was due to alarm at the extent to which their kindly Welsh neighbours featured in largely recognizable guise throughout the tale. Or was she disturbed by its hero Pugh's silent adoration of the attractive farmer's wife next door?

At Secker & Warburg, on the other hand, his editor Roger Senhouse expressed approval. He added some reservations – what he conceived to be excessive use of Welsh words and placenames, a need to locate the 'Recording Angel' in time or space, 'the whole conception of the physical side of Pugh's infatuation needs careful revision', and so forth. Since it does not appear that the manuscript or proof of the book has survived, we have only glimpses of its original state, and the alterations Patrick was persuaded to accept. As the contract was signed on 1 February 1951, and Senhouse's fairly drastic 'improvements' were forwarded via Curtis Brown a fortnight later, the book must have made its mark as it stood. By March, however, Patrick was expressing extreme annoyance with Senhouse. When in August they learned that he had been in their neighbourhood, my mother wrote: 'We are relieved to have been away from Collioure & to have missed him. You can tell by his letters he is a pansey.'*

Although no one at his publisher's could guess the extent to which Pugh represented a self-portrait, Patrick resented Senhouse's verdict:

Character of Pugh. Naturally I don't want to make him a romantic hero, but there is surely no reason why even a middle-aged scholar should be so unsympathetic. He gives himself away: his hypochon-

---

* What provoked this dismissive judgement I do not know, but Senhouse was in reality a dedicated sado-masochist, who engaged in a bizarre affair with Lytton Strachey.

dria, his lack of affection, his timidity . . . and ineptitude (as opposed to mere helplessness and vagueness). All this is really sordid, and as a result I have found something repellent about the idea of his being madly in love.

The criticism is not altogether unfair, and naturally could not take into account Patrick's unconscious motive, which was I believe in part to purge himself of characteristics of which he continued deeply ashamed. Pugh is endowed with much of the 'difficult' side of Patrick's character, while being denied almost any of his compensating virtues: his mischievous humour, exemplary patience, pertinacity, resilience, courage, unselfishness and generosity. The underlying confessional function of the book meant that a more balanced portrayal of the real-life Pugh might not have acted as confession at all. The same process may be detected in Patrick's other largely autobiographical novels, *The Catalans* and *Richard Temple*. In the latter case, the protagonist provides an extensive confession of his earlier degraded ('silly') existence. Significantly, this confession is vouchsafed during a protracted spell of imprisonment and torture, inflicted in order to extract 'the truth', and concludes with Temple's liberation (by the French Resistance). Although it does not appear that Patrick was ever formally admitted to the Catholic Church, he occasionally implied that he was a communicant, and it is not difficult to imagine how the confessional would have appealed to his deep-rooted feelings of shame and guilt.

On one point to which he attached importance, Patrick felt compelled to give way. His title *Testimonies* was objected to by his English publisher on grounds that 'it sounds far more like a treatise on codicils, or last words and testaments'. Next: 'Senhouse wrote: they (or he alone) want to change the title from Testimonies to Bronwen Vaughan. I am against it, but I don't want to offend them just at this point, so I left it up to him if they feel very strongly about it.'

Finally, the publishers settled on *Three Bear Witness*.

In her diary my mother reports that Patrick continued to find Senhouse patronizing, petty-minded and obstructive. In March 1951, 'P. sent C[urtis].B[rown]. a card this morning, worried for Manuscript, & this afternoon had a letter from C.B. with loathesome comments from Senhouse & "a femal[e] reader" on Testimonies.'

Another irritating obstruction, likewise apparently ascribable to Senhouse, was a perverse disregarding of Patrick's request for inclusion of the dedication: *À mes amis de Collioure*. This was no empty gesture, and in due course he presented complimentary copies to friends and neighbours. He even managed to sell one to a more prosperous acquaintance.

By the end of the year Patrick declared he could no longer work with Senhouse, and Spencer Curtis Brown wrote to Fred Warburg:

> The confidential part of this letter is that apparently Patrick O'Brien really does not get on at all well with Roger Senhouse, so that if you want to keep him on your list, as I hope you will do, it might be a good plan if you could take over most of the correspondence with him. I have never found him in any way a difficult author, and I don't believe that you would do so.

Warburg had been away in New York during the early part of the year, and now promptly complied with Spencer's suggestion. In due course Patrick was to wreak characteristic punishment on his troublesome editor. Nearly forty years later, in *The Letter of Marque* (London, 1988, p. 27), Stephen Maturin learns of the fate of 'poor Senhouse', who ascended into the sky in a hot-air balloon whose excessive supply of gas ensured that he 'was never seen again'.

On 3 January 1952 Warburg sent Patrick strong praise for the book, which he had at last found time to read:

I think you have written an extremely promising first novel and indeed even better than that, for in many ways the novel shows a maturity of outlook and a power of construction which augurs well for the future. I cannot somehow take too much interest in your male hero, although he is clearly and distinctly drawn . . .

On this issue Warburg was broadly at one with Senhouse. After explaining his reasons, he continued:

But these minor criticisms pale before the accomplishment in other directions, above all the splendid rendering of the Welsh Hills and vales, villages and villagers, and the eternal life of the farms and the treatment of animals, and the surely magnificent description you give of the sheep shearing which stands out in my mind with a clarity and vividness which prove how well you have done it.

One issue on which Patrick expressed a forceful view was the design of the dustjacket. At Collioure his good friend Willy Mucha had agreed to provide an abstract illustration, an offer which Patrick was anxious to see implemented. As he pointed out to Senhouse, Mucha was an artist of considerable reputation: 'Matisse, Dufy, Braque and Léger think highly of him. (They have given him pictures that I envy enormously).' The suggestion was however declined by Secker, as also by Harcourt Brace in America, and the collaboration of novelist and painter had to await publication of the more appropriate vehicle of *The Catalans*.

Finally, there remained the delicate issue of the author's customary biographical notice. Both the promptness with which he had despatched one for *The Last Pool* (subsequently mislaid by the publisher), and the accuracy of its information, suggest that it was he who provided that which appears on the back sleeve of *Three Bear Witness*:

Patrick O'Brian was born in 1914, and started writing early. He produced four books before the war, and also worked for many years, in Oxford, Paris and Italy, on a book on Bestiaries. Most of this valuable material was, however, lost in the war.

During the war he drove an ambulance in London during the blitz, and later joined the Political Intelligence Department of the Foreign Office.

He and his wife lived at one time in a remote Welsh valley, where Mr. O'Brian fished, shot and hunted whenever possible. He is at present living on the Mediterranean coast of France.

It will be noted that this broadly accurate autobiographical notice contains no allusion to Ireland, still less any claim to Irish nationality or origin. A close paraphrase of this potted biography features on the dustjacket of the American edition of Patrick's later work *Lying in the Sun*, which was entitled *The Walker and other stories* in the USA. However, there it begins with the additional words 'Patrick O'Brian was born in the West of Ireland and educated in England.' It looks as though this item was added by a copywriter at Harcourt Brace – especially as Patrick omitted the notice altogether in the English edition.

The extent to which well-intentioned publishers occasionally made up for Patrick's dislike of supplying personal data is illustrated by a comment made by my mother in 1952: 'Irish Writing came with N.L.T.P.T.R.A.;* very surprised to find biographical notes after I'd refused them because P. doesn't like it.' Fortunately, this issue remained for the present a minor irritation. Two overriding concerns exercised Patrick and my mother throughout this critical period in their lives. How was he to relaunch his literary career? And, still more pressingly, how might the impoverished couple survive financially?

---

* The short story 'Not Liking to Pass the Road Again'.

II

The Catalans

When a man wakes in the night and finds his head filled with
remorse and bitter, old regret, if he chose he could reflect that no
other man in the world would be suffering precisely that remorse
nor exactly that regret . . . Of course, he would not choose to do
so, for he would be too busy dodging about in his mind, trying to
escape – unless, that is, he were occupied with feeling the wound
to see how much it still hurt and trying to persuade himself that
there was virtue in mere remorse.

Patrick O'Brian, 'The Voluntary Patient'

With Secker & Warburg's acceptance of *Three Bear Witness*
in February 1951, Patrick had reason to feel confidence in
his regenerated career as a writer. Not only was it his first adult
novel, but the first novel he had published since *Hussein* in 1938.
At last he had emerged from the creative chasm inflicted by the War
with his accompanying personal crises of divorce and remarriage,
followed by the dire impact of his troubled exile in North Wales.

At the same time, he had come to feel he had finally shed the
oppressive effect of his father's dark shadow. In the summer of
1949, shortly before his and my mother's departure from Cwm
Croesor, a solitary walk brought him to a precipitous, sunless
valley amidst the mountains. 'When I was going up to Llyn yr
Adar there seemed to be a thing at the top of the high black barren

cliff that forms the backside of Cnicht.' What it was he found hard to identify:

> I watched it for some time, but it did not move; and all the way along the valley I kept looking up, but it seemed immobile . . . When I came back it was still there. Gargoyle-ish, brooding, jutting out, small in the distance, but menacing and in control. The next time I went up to the lake it was not there.

This uncanny experience occurred when Patrick had attained the nadir of his increasingly frustrating Welsh exile, shortly before he made the dramatic decision to escape to sunny France. Returned from his walk, he wrote the powerful story 'Naming Calls', which was later published in *The Last Pool*. It recounts the terrifying experience of a writer who withdraws to a small house set in the sinister valley explored by Patrick. The tale concludes with the destruction of the frantic outcast, when a raging storm drives up the valley and dislodges 'a vast mass of rock' from the mountain-side above: 'Abel shrieked high and the door burst open, swinging wide and shuddering on its hinges.' The elemental force of the tempest is unmistakably intended as an evocation of the man's father, 'a formidable, roaring tyrant', whose spirit he had inadvert-ently conjured forth.

It is clear that Patrick had come to associate his oppressive malaise with his frequently bullying giant of a parent, who had repeatedly afflicted him with demoralizing terror during his infancy. Now, however, when in *Three Bear Witness* he adverted to the same uncanny episode, it was to dismiss it comfortingly as an unpleasant memory banished to the past. After a spasm of appre-hension, 'I felt positively merry – a glance upwards showed it there, of course, an insignificant rock, though curious. When I had finished my sandwiches it was gone.'[1]

Unfortunately, the couple's financial predicament remained as alarming as ever. Secker's acceptance of *Three Bear Witness* brought only the briefest respite. An advance of £100 was contracted on 1 February 1951, half on acceptance and half at publication. Sympathetic to his client's worrying predicament, Spencer Curtis Brown charitably forwarded him the second £50, which was not otherwise due to be paid for at least another year. 'Even agents can have kind hearts on occasion,' he wrote to the publisher, who failed however to reimburse Curtis Brown in turn. Sadly, Curtis Brown's generosity was all but negated by the rapacious grasp of government. As my mother learned: 'C.B. now has to deduct income tax at 9/- in the £: with that & his 10% Testimonies £100 has shrunk to £49.'

While the prospect of his novel's publication went far to restore Patrick's self-esteem, until it *was* published openings for further literary employment remained constricted.* Shortly before their move to France, Patrick confessed to Warburg that he had 'written himself out', so far as short stories were concerned. Gradually, however, the colourful turbulence of Collioure brought him a fresh harvest of imaginative themes. During the year following November 1950, he composed no less than thirty-three short stories. Many were set in and around Collioure, drawing on his observations of the town, its inhabitants, customs and traditions.

Why then did he not launch at once into the work on Southern France, which he had discussed with Fred Warburg, and for which an option was stipulated in the contract for *Three Bear Witness*? It looks as though one of his recurrent failures of confidence inhibited his undertaking a full-scale book during the anticlimactic year which stretched between his completion of *Three Bear Witness* and its publication in the spring of 1952. Ever his own sternest critic, it was about this time that he penned this frank assessment of his approach to writing:

---

* In May 1951 Patrick received a puzzling, though welcome, cheque for £28 13s 9d from Oxford University Press. It was not until nearly two years later that he discovered it to be payment for a new German edition (1950) of *Hussein*, which was first published on the eve of the outbreak of war in 1939.

I often, or at least sometimes, like my writing when I am doing it, but so much more often I feel uneasy and ashamed afterwards. All the affectations, poses and 'special' attitudes stare out – hideously pimpled youth smirking in the looking-glass yet finds his confidence decay and enters a public room fingering himself – and often the 'clever pieces' appear shallow and dull as well as quite unauthoritative, the 'poetic touches' arty, long-winded and false, and dreadfully often the whole thing comes to pieces at the end – shuffles off in the lamest manner possible. This is because I think of a good beginning, grow excited and embark upon the story, taking it for granted that it will finish itself.

In November 1951 Patrick sent off his collection, provisionally entitled *Samphire and Other Stories*:

I have just posted the MS to Curtis Brown: yesterday I sent six stories to the New Yorker and one, with two poems, to Irish Writing.* That they may prosper. The postage was very expensive: I did not think about Spain [for cheap postage] until this morning. But even so I do not think I would have posted them from there; they are too precious, and I want to hear <u>soon</u>. After re-reading and re-typing both, I am fairly sure that Samphire is much better than The Lemon: not so clever, much more concentrated (the Lemon tries to say too much and grows diffuse) and because of the hatred in it, more lovingly handled. So I have called the book Samphire and put that story first. It was a slimmer parcel than usual, but it is between 60 and 65 thousand . . . I feel rather low now, with the typewriter folded up and the MS gone: I regret my hurry; I could have polished more.

---

* Terry Zobek informs me that the *New Yorker* never published a story by Patrick, while *Poetry Ireland* published the single poem 'Song' in their April 1952 issue.

Sadly, disappointment swiftly followed. A month later Fred Warburg wrote to Curtis Brown:

> I have now had a report on the new stories of Patrick O'Brian, SAMPHIRE, and some of them are good, though others seem to us basically to fail. However I think it is absolutely essential that we publish the novel now called THREE BEAR WITNESS instead of TESTIMONIES and see if we can do well with it before committing ourselves to further work from O'Brian particularly in the short story field.

Eventually most of the stories were published in book form, although not for some years. It was an eclectic selection that Patrick had despatched. 'Samphire', on which he particularly prided himself, is simply summarized. A young couple is walking beside a seacliff: he complacent, insensitive, and possessed of a tiresomely adolescent sense of humour; she a quiet, nervous, sensitive girl, whose nerves are stretched to breaking point by her husband's relentlessly patronizing jocularity. When he stretches down to pick a sprig of samphire, she suddenly loses self-control and vainly attempts to push him over the edge. Even the insensitive soul to whom she is married recognizes with shock the impassable gulf suddenly opened between them, and realizes that nothing will ever be the same again.

In 1985, Patrick explained to the publisher Bell and Hyman how he came to write the story:

> I was reflecting . . . as I walked along the cliffs that overhang the sea near our house [at Collioure], and a striking example occurred to me – that of a particularly elegant, intelligent woman who in her extreme and utterly inexperienced youth had married a bore or, at least a man who had developed into a bore, a didactic eternally prating bore. At some point in my walk I noticed some plants growing quite far down on the rock face: the lines about the

samphire-gatherer in King Lear drifted into my mind, & as I walked on in a vague, uneasy state of the two notions combined and this took form without any conscious effort on my part.

This account is not entirely candid. The story makes uneasy reading for me, since the husband is unmistakably a recognizable, if uncharitable, portrait of my father, and the delicate young wife my mother, who was eighteen when they married. It was lingering guilt, I suspect, that impelled Patrick to write a story stressing that the marriage was doomed from the outset, regardless of intervention by any third party.

The extent to which Patrick at this experimental stage of his literary career utilized his fiction as an instrument of attack or defence in relation to aspects of his own life is exemplified by two other stories in the collection. In the first, 'The Flower Pot', a couple of Germans, living in what is manifestly Collioure, lovingly tend six flower pots on their windowsill. A fierce tramontane blows up, an increasing gale tearing through the streets: one of the pots is dislodged, and kills a fisherman below. The man responsible is filled with horror:

A man struck dead, or maimed for ever: struck down and by his fault. The great wave of hatred rising from the street. The foreigners at René's have killed père Matthieu. The pointing and the great just wave of hate; and his head only, peering from the window, peering down to meet the hatred and the pointing.

One might imagine this gloomy little tale arose from a flight of fancy, but for this notice in my mother's diary for St Patrick's Day 1951:

P. finished the Flower Pot yesterday . . . after we had been on the jetty. There was a fantastic dry warm wind three days ago which knocked the pinks off bedroom window-sill. It landed just beside

M. Ribeille, who only laughed. We felt terribly guilty & P. has fastened all the pots with wire.

Their dismay was understandable, but Patrick's emphasis on the great wave of collective hatred arising against the hapless outsider plainly reflects his continuing sense of isolated insecurity, originating in the damaging circumstances of his solitary childhood.

Another tale illustrates Patrick's propensity, at least in the early days of his literary career, to deploy his fiction as a weapon of psychic attack. 'The Lemon' concerns a man whose isolated existence has transformed him into a psychopath. The first part of the story comprises an arresting analysis of his bewildering condition, and its symptoms. Despite this, he is on good terms with his neighbours, who are:

> working people, kind, sensible, very tolerant. Good people, my neighbours: all except the man and woman who kept the restaurant on the ground floor. They were a bad couple; the man a flashy, smarmy-haired little pompous rat; the woman a short-legged, hard-faced shrew of about forty . . . They drank heavily, quarrelled and screamed until dawn sometimes. Their place was frequented by their friends and by foreigners on the spree, and they bawled and sang and shrieked above the blaring wireless until four or five in the morning.

A sluttish waitress, ceaselessly singing loudly and tunelessly during the day, by night slept indiscriminately with the clientèle.

The restaurant in question is unmistakably Le Puits, which occupied the ground floor of the house in the rue Arago, two storeys below the flat in which Patrick and my mother lived. On 19 February my mother wearily recorded: 'The Puits kept it up until 6 a.m.: an infernal racket.' On 27 May Patrick stayed up most of the night writing 'The Lemon'. In the story he (for I fear the nameless protagonist is he) creeps downstairs, removes the fuse controlling the lighting for the restaurant, and hurls a hand grenade ('the lemon') into the darkness. As he carefully restores the fuse and tiptoes back up to his *apartement*, a blinding flash and shattering roar proclaim the destruction of the entire crew of revellers in Le Puits. Ah, if only . . .*

Of the thirty-three stories Patrick wrote during the year 1950–51, nine were never published. Of these, three ('Federico', 'Moses Henry' and 'Fort Carré') appear to be lost. The manuscripts of the remaining six are in my possession, and make interesting reading. 'Mrs Disher' concerns an old man's confused reflections on his dying housekeeper, while 'The Clerk' explores a disturbing memory of medieval antisemitism encountered in a remote English town by a visiting enthusiast for church architecture.

'George' (which he retitled 'The Tubercular Wonder') is the most revealing of these unpublished tales in respect of Patrick's own life. In the first volume of this biography, I suggested that it provides an illuminating exposé of his troubled state of mind at the time he began his secret affair with my mother, betraying an overriding sense of guilt in respect of his betrayed wife Elizabeth.[2] The theme of another story, 'Beef Tea', recalls that of 'Samphire', with its dull and relentlessly facetious husband, who drives his long-suffering wife to insanity. It looks like a further attempt to dismiss the reproachful figure of my father, representing him as utterly impossible to live with.

The personal application of the story 'A Minor Operation', which is one of those published in the collection, speaks for itself. A young English couple come to live in an old French town by the sea. We learn that 'they were virgins; virgins from principle, mystic and practical'. They are very poor, but so well liked by the inhabitants that they are continually sustained by regular gifts of food. Much

---

* There exists some sort of cosmic justice, however. In real life the dissolute maid of Le Puits departed in search of a customer who had made her pregnant, while the owner died of alcoholism a year later.

of this popularity they put down to the 'affectionate, well-mannered dog they had brought with them'. After a while Laurence is troubled by a severe affliction to his hand. Eventually an operation becomes necessary, which unexpectedly proves so sanguinary that the surgeons depart, leaving their patient for dead. However, he is not. Arising from the operating table, the victim races frantically back to his *apartement*, brutally kicks their beloved dog downstairs, and apparently (it is not entirely clear) kills his wife.

Patrick wrote the story on 12 and 13 June 1951, originally entitling it 'A Nice Allegory', and later 'Hernia, Stranguary and Cysts'. That the couple is Patrick and my mother, and the dog their Buddug, is evident from the opening description. Three weeks earlier, my mother had written in her diary: 'P. showed Dr Delcos swelling on his hand. It has to be removed.' Five days later 'P. had his hand done, fainted, poor P., is splinted & bound & in a sling.' For over a fortnight he continued in great pain, suffering continual discharges of pus from the infected wound, and enjoying little sleep.

It looks as though this protracted suffering led Patrick, as in 'The Lemon', to reflect on how far an inordinate degree of psychological distress or physical pain might wholly distort a man's nature, exposing the perilous fragility of the mind's control over destructive elements of the subconscious. The threat is emphasized by the frenzied patient's violent assault on the very beings to whom he is closest.

There exists what may be a tentative draft of the tale in one of Patrick's notebooks. There he contemplates writing the story of 'A very sensible childless pair [who] decide that the husband had best beget one on a healthy girl'. This he does, with predictably stressful effect on the wife. This perhaps appearing too trite or unrealistic a theme, it seems Patrick converted it into a savage melodrama, whose principal content derived from his own experience.

Another story written at this time is 'William Temple', which remains unpublished. Ultimately a precursor to Patrick's novel *Richard Temple* (1962), it begins on an unmistakably autobiographical note. Like Patrick during his wartime service with Political

Warfare Executive, Temple is employed by a branch of Intelligence whose members do not normally operate in occupied Europe. Again, I suspect like Patrick himself, 'he had often pictured to himself William Temple as one of that great secret army that was being built up in France'. Unexpectedly, he is selected to be dropped on a special mission to the French Resistance 'in the mountains between Spain and France'. After a realistic account of his reception by the maquis, he is diverted into a hunt for a magnificent boar, which he finally tracks down and shoots.

The story is very much longer than others written at this time, being reckoned by Patrick at 23,500 words. The indications are that it was at first intended as a novel, which for some reason came to an unanticipated halt. Possibly, with the (symbolic?) death of the boar, he simply found further inspiration lacking. At any rate, he decided to include it among the collection submitted to Fred Warburg. In view of its exceptional length, it was divided into two parts, oddly entitled 'A Pair I' and 'A Pair II'. The adventure is fluently narrated, but from its length ill-suited to a collection of short stories.

Disheartened by Warburg's rejection, Patrick brought his short-story writing to an abrupt close. Not until well over a year had passed did he attempt another. As his publisher pointed out, the twenty tales are widely varied in quality. Without straying into excessive analysis, it has to be said that in several cases the plots appear somewhat contrived, and I am inclined to suspect the baneful influence of Somerset Maugham in what appears to be Patrick's apparent need to round off with a quirky or violent conclusion. Again, several stories are driven by a desire to sublimate personal fantasies, wish-fulfilments or resentments which do not always fully accord to dramatic requirement. More, too, might perhaps have been made of those descriptive passages at which Patrick excelled, evoking the Catalan people and their harsh but beguiling landscape.

Another possibility for generating desperately needed additional income occurred to Patrick at this time. In November 1951 Curtis Brown passed an enquiry to Fred Warburg: 'Patrick asks if I know of any books which a publisher would like him to translate from the French. It occurs to me that he might be a very good translator. Have you by any chance any such book in mind?'

Warburg could offer nothing, and the proposal fell by the wayside. Eventually Curtis Brown was to be proved right, and Patrick became an admired translator of contemporary French writing. But another ten years were to pass before he was afforded opportunity to undertake that lucratively dependable employment.

Over the winter of 1950–51 the couple's hopes were largely founded on the success of *Three Bear Witness*, for which Warburg had expressed such high regard. It was a desperately worrying time. In January 1952 my mother lamented that: 'The year continues to go badly: Seckers don't want W[illy Mucha]'s maquettes. Very much gloom.' They were eager to have the dust-jacket illustrated by their friend. At the beginning of the next month 'Secker sent list with T.B.W. in it.' A month later the strain had become almost unendurable: 'I could not sleep for thinking of TBW, copies being liable to arrive any time now.' Eventually, on 22 April, 'TBW came; parcel on the stairs. P. infinitely kind, sat by me.'

Unhappily, the excitement proved ephemeral. Press reception in Britain was muted, and although one or two reviewers voiced approval of the book's finer qualities, it slipped rapidly from public consciousness. For all their exceptional resilience and recurrent surges of optimism against hostile odds, for much of the time during the first two and a half years of their life in Collioure, Patrick and my mother found it hard to sustain their spirits. Foremost among concerns impossible to overlook was the grinding poverty of their existence, which continued poised on the brink of disaster.

Looking back, five months after their arrival in Collioure their bank balance stood at 600 francs (about 12 shillings). But for the

Patrick and Willy Mucha

unstinted generosity of their neighbours, and occasional contributions from my mother's father, they could not possibly have survived. A year later my mother ruefully noted: 'On Thursday the money had not arrived at the bank, so I borrowed 1000fr. The electricity came & demanded all we had save 5fr. so I went to Tante Alice for another 1000fr.' In April 1951: 'Accounts alarm me much: we spend far too much.' By the end of that month: 'Did month's accounts: 11.000fr odd, much better. Two francs left in the house but will get bread and milk with "j'ai oublié mes sous & money should be at bank tomorrow".'

The year 1952 opened with the anguished query: 'Can we live on 10.500 fr a month until July? We will try.'

For over two years they frequently went hungry. Having cooked a modest feast for St Patrick's Day in 1951, my mother reflected: 'We are so used now to very plain living that we cannot eat much at feasts, we have no capacity.' For everyday diet: 'We live mainly on new potatoes, fried bread & bread-and-marmalade.' Much of their modest shopping was conducted across the frontier in Spain, where prices were much lower. This regularly involved my mother's walking to Port Bou and back: a 34-mile round hike, traversing successive steep rocky ridges.

Patrick's parting words on leaving Wales were: 'if you're going to be poor, it's better to be poor in a warm country'. This was to prove true in some respects, and the couple grew adept at living off the land. On 3 September 1951 my mother 'picked 4 lbs. of blackberries in the river bed, & we made about 5 lbs of jelly'. In the same week they went gathering figs in the mountains at Col de Mollo. The task proved hazardous as well as arduous. 'Got a dozen ripe ones; trees covered in green ones . . . P. in tree and I underneath when a chasseur shot at us: shots spat all round. Coming home met Marraine who said the chasseurs are "très mal élevés", & said Come & see her for some anchovies.'

After a time Patrick, who had been a keen fisherman in Cwm Croesor, took his rod to join men angling at night from the jetty, regularly returning with anything up to half-a-dozen tasty *daurades* (bream).

But this monotonous and erratic diet was largely seasonal, and there were lengthy spans when little or nothing was available to be picked or caught. They might scarcely have survived, had their sustenance not been supplemented by the wonderful generosity of the warm-hearted *Colliourenchs*. Typical entries in my mother's diary read: 'Mlle Margot called me in with great mystery & filled my basket with huge cauli., 4 eggs, a big onion & 6 oranges, all with hideous embarrassment; she could not meet my eye'; 'Tante gave us viande hâchée & bones & pâté & a pot au feu'; 'Mlle Margot brought us 13 fresh eggs & a litre of ? Banyuls "pour demain"' (Easter Day).

My parents never forgot this kindness, and remained lifelong friends with many of their affectionate neighbours, a sadly diminishing handful of whom remain. Within such a tight-knit community, mutual concern and charitable support were taken for granted. Links of family and friendship permeated the town. When the electrician Cadène was electrocuted at work, some 1,500 people attended his funeral. An incomer, having bought a house in the town, sought to eject the tenants on grounds that they had lately failed to pay rent. The husband had in fact always paid, but on falling ill temporarily proved insolvent. The *huissier* (bailiff) arrived, together with a removal van, to enforce their departure. The town rose in anger, and, despite the appearance of gendarmes from Port-Vendres, refused to permit the ejection. The van driver declared that he would not have accepted the employment, had he known it was not an ordinary removal, while the ringleader of the town's resistance was discovered to be gentle Dr Delcos.

The *Colliourenchs* also possessed enchanting natural courtesy. When King George VI died in 1952, 'Women come up & say how sorry about King, tears running down their faces. Tricolor at half-mast in place & at post office.' Women in the shops explained to each other, as my mother passed by, 'c'est son roi à Madame.'

One neighbour remained for some reason dubious about the extent of this Christian spirit, expressing her view with that decisive emphasis that characterizes the true *Colliourencque*. At the time of Odette Bernardi's difficult divorce, my mother 'offered that O. would be happier if F[rançois]. were to remove her from here, Mlle. M[argot]. agreed "parce que c'est un pays de perdition, Collioure". She repeated this many times, saying that we do not <u>know</u> – the terrible character of Collioure, unlike any other village.'

As my mother commented on encountering such baffling pronouncements: 'eh?'

In view of their life of constant privation, it is not surprising that she and Patrick were rarely free from one ailment or another. From June 1950 'medecine' and 'chemist' feature remorselessly in their monthly household accounts. In February 1951, 'P. looked & felt terribly poorly on the 17th'. Dr Delcos paid regular visits, presenting no bill until that May, when additional expense arose from treatment of the dangerous cyst in Patrick's hand. In February 1952 'P's rheumatism very bad'; a few weeks later 'P. went to dr. & had his left ear completely cleaned but it is stone deaf still. The right one hurt dreadfully. He came out with shirt wet through.' A persistent requirement was medicine for his 'nerves'. Similarly, my mother was visited by recurrent afflictions: 'My tum in bad condition'; 'I slept all afternoon – had vile headache'; 'Medecine [M's liver] 530 [francs]'.

Some of Patrick's troubles appear to have stemmed from unremitting mental strain. 'Medicine [P's nervous turn]', reads a characteristic entry in their account book. A bad attack, the nature of which is obscure, occurred in May 1952, when my mother was staying with her parents in England. At dinner with their neighbours the Rimbauds:

> I smoked. In spite of pills I felt the usual trouble coming on, but escaped in time on pretext of seeking Almanach Catalá – on the stairs wondered very much where I was – at home (still on all fours) recovered with dear Buddug's aid (she was very kind on finding that it was not all a great game, and stood quite still, just touching my face) washed, returned in reasonably good form, and was able to finish the evening without, I hope and trust, throwing any damp.

About this time Patrick compiled a six-page essay, perhaps with a vague view to publication, entitled 'How to make the best of poverty'. The advice is pragmatic, being based on daily experience:

> If you have to go a month on x p[ennies]. you <u>must</u> make do on $\frac{x}{31}$ fr. the first day, and on each day after that. Never rely on any bank, friend, publisher or business person to send money on a given day
>
> Do not ever pretend to be rich, with the lower classes. Be as affable as can be with them, but always use a good deal of ceremony

– M. and Mme., and formal greetings always.* If you have to borrow money, do it before you are destitute. Once you have no money at all (literally none) your mind, your values, are terribly distorted.

Careful instructions are given providing advice on giving up smoking: 'The first few days are hard, but your increasing sense of smugness will carry you through. You end up on a wonderful moral pinnacle, and if you ever start to smoke again they taste exceedingly good.'

When the worst comes to the worst, 'Exceedingly weak tea without milk is a good drink, if you take it piping hot.' Even Buddug's concerns were taken into account: 'If you have a dog, feed it before your meal begins. You will find it comes too hard at the end.'

With regard to making ends meet:

The food that you can afford when you are very poor needs a great deal of care and preparation to be anything but sickeningly dull. With very great care it can be surprisingly good – garlic, herbs (especially thyme and parsley) flour and a little oil rightly used can give plain potatoes soul and substance.†

If there are two of you, you would be better advised to leap off a cliff than to allow wrangling to begin. As soon as you are wretched your subconscious, unsavoury mind begins to look about for a scapegoat: you must stop it from picking on the object nearest at hand – the almost invariable object, the loved one.

Furthermore, in a time of poverty you usually have little to do

---

* On 30 May 1952 Patrick wrote: 'the Tante (who, I think, has cottoned on to our dislike of Christian names) gave me a pâté – so good – and Mlle Margot a dish of sardines.'

† The recipe appears to have been inspired by *The Way to get and to save Wealth, or the sure method to Live Well in the World; being the pleasant art of Money-Getting* (London, 1788). Patrick generously gave me his copy for my birthday in 1972.

– you do not shop, you do not go out much, paid amusements stop, the sight of your acquaintance is unpleasant – so once quarrelling starts it goes on.

Regular daily routine was essential for preservation of morale:

It is important to maintain the appearance of ordinary life – regular meals (even if they consist of nothing at all but the thinnest tea), an afternoon walk. One has a tendency to stay in bed very late, to stop washing, not to shave . . . In extreme cases you must give in and go to bed but even then it can be done with a sort of decency. It is platitudinous to point out that you are much richer when you have reduced your needs to a minimum!

A poem written in the same notebook suggests the black despair which at times gripped him:

> Sink: down in the grey sea
> slowly down. The layers
> silent, of depression. Down.
> Through them.
> No irritation, anger left
> no hint of red
> all grey dull and silence welling
> up past your ears.
> You sink your head
> Down. Breathing slow
> Down. Eyes unfocussed
> One tear creeps down the bent
> ash dying face.

As in North Wales during the summer of 1949, the prospect of death returned to haunt Patrick. At the end of April 1951, 'P. said after yesterday's tennis he gets partial black-outs while playing, which connect with feeling of other-worldness – of playing at being alive: a game which might be stopped at any moment.'

On 20 October he 'wrote his death dream', and about that time composed this grim verse, entitled 'You will come to it':

> Do not suppose their motions pantomime
> Because the thing they dig is dark, unseen
> The mattock and the shovel swing in time
> A near approach will show you what they mean.

On 11 May 1951 my mother, more buoyant by nature, experienced a remarkable vision:

A Dream: I died, & arrived on a shore that struck me as being like Lundy, from across a big grey sea. I worried about P coming, & he arrived soon after.* Was filled with immense feeling of relief because of two things: permanence in this existence, & continuence of free will // I am not aware of ever having felt unhappiness from the impermanence of this life, nor of regretting the loss of free will in the usual pre-conceived notion of Heaven. Have worked backwards & am now fully aware of both, though much comforted by the exceedingly vivid dream. The dream had no sequence of events, but was like a state of being. (That life there would go on for ever). (In the manner of owning a house instead of renting it).

Lundy is the island in the Bristol Channel where my mother spent many happy holidays when living as a girl in North Devon. What I am sure she did not know, is that it was regarded by the pagan Celts as a location of the Otherworld, where the souls of the dead are received.†

---

* When eventually the time came, Patrick died just under two years after my mother's death.
† Lundy was the home of Gweir, mythical First Man and primal ancestor of the Britons.

The couple endured this extreme poverty for well over two years. It was on 2 May 1952 that their affairs suddenly altered dramatically for the better. Publication of *Three Bear Witness* had proved a material disappointment, both in reviews and sales. But good news was on the way.

'I was scrubbing the black hole floor', wrote my mother,

when P. came in almost breathless saying 'Such news, M'. It was S.C.B.'s [Spencer Curtis Brown] letter to say Harcourt, Brace want TBW [to be called Questions & Answers over there] for 750 dollars. Quite knocked up, both of us . . . For the first time on such an occasion we are not wild: no rushings out & spendings, nor the desire to do so. Could eat but little lunch, anyway . . . We walked to P. Vendres after tea, feeling upset & disturbed with our wealth. Saw wirelesses, but spent nothing.

Six days later Curtis Brown sent news almost as exciting. The American advance was to be sent direct to France, which, with a modicum of discretion, meant they need not pay the penal British income tax! 'We are so happy & settled in our economy that this wealth worries us,' exclaimed my mother. Charming prospects opened up on every side. 'We plan a 3000 mile round trip of Spain & Portugal'; 'Take many turns around Collioure in a day, to look at cars.' As concerns the latter, it is fortunate that they were not able to anticipate just how premonitory was to prove a sight glimpsed by my mother, given their alarming proclivity for experiencing traffic crashes: 'On way home [from the dentist in Elne] saw vast car turned on its side in ditch, eh?' Patrick did not as yet possess a driving licence, being content for the present for my mother to take the wheel.

Excited plans began for purchase of a car, while Patrick further contemplated buying a sailing boat which was for sale in the harbour. The latter disappointingly turned out to be in too poor condition to be worth even the modest 8,000 francs demanded, but a car they had to have. The noisy and crowded little streets of Collioure appeared ever more unbearably claustrophobic, and they longed for means of occasional escape. Friends in England offered them their Opel for £100, an offer so enticing that my mother travelled to London in July to bring it back, but from the moment she arrived, everything began to go wrong. Additional expenses mounted by the hour: garage bill, ferry fare, tax, French import duty . . . my poor mother was in despair: 'I think my heart is breaking & I never want to see the Opel again, and how I love P. and am utterly lonely.'

Eventually the Bank of England prohibited the Opel's export, and the same afternoon another car rammed the wretched car, breaking an indicator and smashing a window.

Altogether my mother totted up that she had spent a precious £35 on this fruitless errand, and her despair was only alleviated when her father, with whom she stayed in Chelsea, gave her £20. Battered and exhausted, she returned to Collioure, accompanied by Patrick's son Richard, who was now to spend his first summer holiday with them, camping in Andorra. After his eventual return to England my mother noted despairingly: 'Street noises formid-able', and a week later she and Patrick returned by bus to Andorra in the hope of completing a house purchase they had planned during their visit to that country. In the event a pied-à-terre was sadly to prove beyond their means.

Life looked up in the latter part of the year, but even in their days of direst poverty they rarely allowed themselves to feel down-cast for very long, no matter how heavily the dice appeared loaded against them. They swam, walked, sunbathed on the plage St Vincent, and when they could afford it played tennis on the baking-hot hard court in the moat of the Château Royal. The plage in particular provided an ever-present refuge from their claustrophobic little *apartement*, although it had its own occasional hazards – noisy tourists, rowdy children, and (for Patrick that June): 'A disagreeable day . . . A gull shat all over me, the rug and Thos. Mann.'

Odette and Buddug on the plage St Vincent

Odette Boutet (then Bernardi) recalls an occasion when my mother and she swam the *traversée* across the harbour, from La Balette on the south side of the bay to the plage St Vincent opposite. It being the first swim of the season, and the water icy, on emerging they found they lacked strength for the return swim. Accordingly they walked back past the town and Port d'Avall in their bathing costumes. It was an unusual sight in those days, and the contrasted attractions of the two brown-limbed young women – Odette dark-haired and olive-skinned, and my mother fair-haired and blue-eyed – drew much attention from the (chiefly male, I assume) inhabitants along the way.

In the evenings they read, played chess, or engaged in an improvised form of bridge for two. Although an enthusiast for both games, Patrick was (like Stephen Maturin) but a middling achiever at such pastimes, who more often than not found himself beaten by my mother. Once, after a particularly hard-fought contest, Patrick wrote defiantly on the score-sheet: 'Bridge, a silly game. BY ORDER P. O'BRIAN. SEPT 1951'.

Ever adventurous, from time to time they escaped the town to explore the mountains. Their close friend Odette, who was quite as audacious, frequently accompanied them. In June 1951 the three of them (five, including Buddug and Odette's dog Rubill) travelled on foot to the forest behind the Tour Massane, where they camped beside the wood. That night boars could be heard grunting close by. Peering from their tents at the moonlit glade, they were alarmed to discover a large female boar leading her offspring, and quickly clasped the dogs' muzzles to prevent their alerting the irascible parent. The expedition was voted a great success on their return, despite Odette's temporarily losing her voice from exhaustion.

Next month they set off on a much more ambitious expedition, camping for nearly seven weeks in and around Andorra. As ever, they found the little Pyrenean principality entirely beautiful, and largely untouched by the modern world. After a week they were joined by Odette and Rubill. The latter was promptly attacked by four fierce dogs, from which she was barely saved by the two courageous women. So far from displaying gratitude, Rubill constantly eyed their provisions, only to be as regularly forestalled by the vigilant Buddug. Prices in Andorra were much lower than in France, farmers hospitable to the campers, and the weather benign. Their diet was supplemented by wild strawberries and trout from mountain streams. Buildings were picturesquely medieval, and transport off the few main roads was conducted by cows drawing haycarts, while on steep slopes mules dragged loads of hay on angled wooden platforms.

Fortunately the dauntless campers were hardy, and carried on their backs tents, sleeping bags, cooking utensils, and even a heavy wind-up gramophone and collection of records. Odette remembered their dancing under the moonlight to Bach and Beethoven. It was on this or another of their expeditions that she recalled their getting lost one day in a heavy mist. After hours of more and more anxious wandering, they stumbled at last on their camp, having unwittingly strayed in a wide circle. Despite their hardihood, femininity persisted. Venturing beyond the camp to relieve themselves one day, the two young women were startled by a large snake, and fled shrieking back to safety.

In the meantime my parents' concern was aroused by distressing news from Richard. As described earlier, Patrick was delighted when his son expressed ambition to join the Royal Navy. Nothing had been heard from him for some time, when on 23 May 1952 Patrick received what he described as 'a sickening letter from Richard'. The news was indeed bad. He had failed the examination to Dartmouth, and the longed-for career was denied him. 'I am very disappointed as I had worked hard and got nothing for it,' he explained sadly. He possessed considerable natural aptitude for mathematics, and was skilled with his hands, but as he freely confessed was all but hopeless at exams. Regrettably, Patrick's response has not survived. Given his own comparably abysmal experience, together with his understanding attitude towards similar disappointments on other occasions, I feel confident his reaction would have been supportive. Moreover, he knew that Richard was additionally occupied on Saturdays by such work as he could find to supplement his mother's meagre income.

In July, as was mentioned earlier, Richard returned with my mother from London to Collioure, where he spent the summer holiday from July to September. (As the court judgment had ruled that Richard was to spend half of each summer holiday with his father, his mother clearly approved the extended arrangement.) This time he brought with him a good school report, and showed keen interest in joining the Merchant Navy. My parents had made extensive preparations, requiring further dangerous inroads into their ever-strained finances, to ensure that he had the most enjoyable holiday they could provide.

Tents, lilos and other camping gear having been purchased, on 8 August the little party set off crammed into an excursion bus full of excited boy scouts. Arrived once more in the mountains of Andorra, they encamped in pine forests. Here the modern world impinged barely at all. The first person they met was a cowherd, with 'his woolly dogs; his cows are all round, many with bells'.* Richard and Patrick went fishing in a nearby lake, and returned to one of my mother's wonderful improvised meals: 'Fries very successful; lunch today was chops, potatoes, garlic, onion & tomato stew. Dear Budd seems happy & eats heartily.' She was on heat, but fortunately the herd's dogs were all bitches, save one male incapacitated by age. After a swim in a nearby river, they returned to camp, where 'golden eagles flew right over us, being mobbed by choughs or crows'.

Next day my mother went to obtain milk from the cowherd, who 'was asleep under a rock with his arm round his pet lamb who had its head on his shoulder'. The excitement grew briefly too much for Richard, who was sick at supper. Next morning, however, he proved right as rain, and after lunch went on a further fishing expedition with his father. In their absence my mother picked bowls of bilberries and raspberries for lunch.

The herd proved to be guardian of the sheep of the commune of Encamp. Patrick asked whether a hut could be found for them to sleep in. While the cowherd enquired with the Consul of Encamp, Patrick set off to buy food and change money in the town of Andorra. Meanwhile, as my mother wrote in her diary that evening, 'R. & I did nothing but laze, & we played piquet.' The journey to Encamp was pursued along very rough forest tracks, and the next day Patrick succumbed to a bad attack combining fever and

---

* I still have one of these large sonorous bells brought back by my mother.

diarrhoea, which proved to be dysentery. For several days he remained in acute distress, the pain eventually alleviated by the local remedy of boiled rice, together with Entero-Viaform pills obtained from an Andorran chemist.

Richard, who continued in rude health, went off fishing again, and on his return was 'very cheerful, keeps roaring from his tent'. Before long they were installed in primitive beehive huts used by the shepherds of Encamp. 'R's hut: how he worked at clearing & levelling the floor. P. crept over to look at it: it looks dangerous about its roof, is exposed & draughty but very, very beautiful.'

On 19 August my mother left Patrick, who remained sick in their camp, and obtained a lift to Andorra from a pleasant Frenchman. Arrived in the sleepy capital, she enquired about buying a home in the principality, as a refuge from the turmoil of town life in Collioure. By chance it was to the Consul of Encamp that she was directed for information, having been given a paper explaining the law on foreigners owning land in Andorra, together with a letter of introduction. After one and a quarter hours' walk, my mother arrived in Encamp. At the Consul's house, nine of his assembled relatives read the letter in turn: 'some aloud'. This protracted introduction concluded, the Consul himself read the paper and letter, murmuring benignly: '*Benez, Madame*' – but could not be pressed to name a price.

A visit afterwards with Patrick to inspect a suitable site involved a hair-raising drive by an accommodating local up a mountainside. My mother, normally immune to vertigo, confessed that she had 'never been more frightened in my life as when we swerved fast round corners that cambered away into 10000 feet of abyss, on the outside of the road'. '*Vous n'avez pas peur, Madame?*' enquired their driver solicitously. Frustratingly, it proved necessary to postpone the elusive question of the proposed purchase until after their return home, and they returned to camp 'depressed, to fold & carry up tents'.

The great holiday adventure was drawing to a close: 'Felt very sad to leave Andorra.' After erratic journeyings by bus, they picked up the delightful touristic yellow train (it still runs) offering spectacular views of the Pyrenees, until they arrived at the picturesque fortified town of Villefranche de Conflent, in the narrow defile of the Têt. Finally, late on the evening of 23 August they arrived in Collioure, by which time even Buddug was exhausted.

Next day there was great excitement, when a massive backlog of correspondence awaiting their return at the post office was retrieved to be studied over breakfast. It included a parcel of complimentary copies of *Testimonies* from the USA, together with 'Wonderful reviews from N.Y. Times & N.Y. Herald Tribune, Harper's Bazaar wanting short stories'. Spencer Curtis Brown wrote to report that requests for foreign rights to the novel were pouring in – from Italy, Germany, Norway.

Despite his continuing ill-health and exhaustion, Patrick plunged back into his neglected writing. The holiday had been a brilliant success – if dangerously expensive. There remained but 55,000 francs (about £50) in their account. Nevertheless, he and my mother had decided that Richard, being now fourteen, should receive a quarterly allowance to spend as he chose. 'Yesterday P. told R. about his £52 a year: R. much impressed & so pleasant about it.' Naturally he could have had little idea of the sacrifice involved. A week later my worried mother 'Went to P[ort]. Vendres & paid tax. So depressed.'

During the remaining fortnight of the holiday, Richard spent his days swimming, playing tennis, watching the *sardana* danced in the square, attending divine service at the old church by the harbour, and revelling in my mother's rich cooking. 'Made enormous rice – moules & sèches & all. Mme Oliva made us an ailloli. Dear R. likes everything.' He made friends with Odette's young son Robert, and travelled one day to Perpignan to buy a new chain for Buddug; on another he went to Port Bou on a shopping expedition with my mother: 'pleasant morning'. Willy Mucha invited him to stay with them whenever he liked. He made friends on every side. There was work, too, for him and my mother. At dawn on 4 September they were invited to assist René Aloujes with his vendange. They toiled from 6 a.m. until 9, paused for a hefty breakfast until 10.30, and continued until noon: 'R. worked very well. Grapes not very good. A very steep, difficult vigne to work.'

In the evenings after supper the three stayed up playing endless games of racing demon and 'prawns' eyes', in the company of Buddug, Pussit, and a new member of the family: 'Kitten comes in to play; a very good, clean kitten.'

Eventually, the sad day arrived for Richard's departure on 7 September. He was given a lively send-off, loaded with exciting gifts. The garrulous Willy Mucha bustled up, bearing a dried flying fish as a parting token. Finally, 'R. got 7 pm train, so sad P & I: the house is dreary.'

A few days later they were rewarded with a letter, bubbling over with enthusiasm:

Thank you very much for a wonderful holiday; the boys will not believe my experiences, especially the golden-eagles. What a good time we all had. Thank you so much.

Andorra was about the most marvellous country that I have ever been to. What fishing it was! What fun it was in the camp . . .

Very [sic] thing was in tact and whole when I got home: even to scorpion and flying-fish and mostofall my porron.* I have a huge collection now dominated by my banderilla. Every-body shrinks from the scorpion, believing it to be alive. My precious [Andorran] flag is now the envy of all the boys at school who are extremely jelous . . .

The whole form, one and all and dumbfounded when I produced the [clasp] knife.† One boy produced a 'sharp knife', he skinned

* A glass wine pitcher, in Catalan *porró*.
† A traditional fisherman's knife, still available in Collioure shops (I retain mine, given me by my mother during my first visit in 1955). Patrick once told me that they were employed by local smugglers in the mountains, for the charitable purpose of stabbing unwary customs officers.

his arm but did not cut hair, all he succeeded in was cutting himself.

In addition, Patrick had concealed a sophisticated fishing reel in his luggage at departure, which further excited his friends' admiration. As Richard explained, this was 'a pleasant and exciting surprise', especially as 'Finn and Atkins, both seized with fishing mania have reels, not of my superior type . . . I am very much envied in that way to.'

With the reticence characteristic of schoolboys in those distant unsentimental days, Richard omitted to report a distressing aspect of his otherwise triumphant return to Cardinal Vaughan School. As before, I am indebted to his friend Bob Broeder for this revealing account:

When we returned to school for the autumn term, our English teacher set us the task of writing a composition about what we did in the summer holidays. Most of us wrote the usual mundane contents but Richard wrote a masterpiece, describing his journey to the South of France and how he and his father met and spent some time with El Cordobes a renowned Spanish bullfighter.*

Having read it myself I admired his descriptive narrative, his English was marvellous, remarkable and interesting, his father had taught him well. The next time we had English, the teacher handed all the exercise books back to all the pupils except Richard. In front of the whole class the teacher made the announcement that he had asked for a factual essay, not an imaginary one – holding Richard's up to the class. This, he declared, was the work of a fertile imagination without an ounce of reality. I stood up to protest – saying I had postcards to prove that in no way did imagination play any part in his beautiful essay but was

---

* This detail, if Bob Broeder's memory be accurate, represents a pardonable schoolboy embellishment. As my mother's diary shows, no such meeting took place. Possibly Richard's imagination was inspired by the banderilla my parents gave him.

told in no uncertain terms to shut up and to sit down, if I didn't obey the outcome would be a trip to the Discipline master with the inevitable thrashing. It goes without saying that Richard was distraught and very angry. I clearly remember that both I and several classmates tried to console him but the anger had never left him during the rest of his time at the school. I remember his mother was also very upset.

Richard's indignation was fully justified, but his exceptional capacity to harbour resentment may also be noted.

Back in Collioure, Patrick and my mother had resumed their daily struggle. There were compensations to their existence, however. Much of the physical structure of the town stems from medieval times, and among the population there breathed memories of a picturesque past. While most of the inhabitants are Roman Catholics, there has long been a sizeable Protestant minority, who congregate at their Temple above the Château Royal. Relations between these two branches of the Christian religion have traditionally long been cordial. The only hint of disparagement I heard of occurred in the name of a local pastry, known as a *jésuite*. Gazing through the window of the *pâtisserie* in the Port d'Avall, Patrick explained to me that when you bite into one – it proves to be hollow!

At the time he and my mother arrived in the town, there survived numerous customs and practices redolent of beliefs older even than the conversion to Christianity. Popular theology could be a trifle speculative – as this exchange recorded by my mother on May Day 1954 attests:

When I arrived at Mimi Choux's this morning she was in the middle of condemning someone for stating that angels are bald. 'N'est-ce pas, Madame O'Brian, que dans toutes les reproductions les anges ont toujours les cheveux bouclés?'*

---

* 'Isn't it true, Madame O'Brian, that in all reproductions angels always have curly hair?'

A generally equable syncretism between the Church and pagan practices and beliefs survived locally well into the middle of the twentieth century. It was quite common for brides to appear in an advanced state of pregnancy at their weddings. 'About the number of marriages with the girl pregnant', my mother was told, it is 'quite natural, people rigole [laugh] and joke but are not méchants with the girl; there is no onus [blame] on the man at all.'

A curious custom which might have suggested anticlericalism or simple hooliganism was evidently neither, and bore a significance now possibly lost:

Also asked Rimbaud about the bands of youths banging on curé's door. He says it is 'sans méchanceté' & has always been done (he was v. active in his time) & nobody really minds. They bang on the doors of their young women. If dégâts [damage] result, complaints are made to mayor & youths pay up, but it doesn't go to the police.

A practice of having a sprig of hawthorn blessed by the curé taken to the fields to ensure a good harvest presumably reflected the archaic folk belief that its prickles repel witches, ever prowling abroad with the malign intent of blighting the crops of honest Christians.[3]

Not all magic was benign, however:

Mme Rimbaud's tale: yesterday, she alone in the house, a woman selling lace. I don't want any lace. And why don't you want any lace? Because I don't want any lace. Then the woman said if she would not buy any lace, she, who knew how to tell the cards, would put a 'malédiction' on her. That evening she had such a head she did not know whether it was the result of the malediction, or what.

Fortunately there existed magical cures, as well as curses. The Rimbauds 'had an old woman in to cure [their daughter] Martine with a herb cataplasm'. An interesting ritual efficaciously removed headaches. On 10 July 1953, completion of a difficult piece of writing left Patrick with an acute migraine. Next day their landlord, M. Germa:

> told us Georgette [his wife] was having the sun taken out of her head by her mother, with water in a bottle, & prayers. We demurred, & he said <u>he</u> believed it because Jaquie had had it done (bubbles rose in the bottle of water) & three days after his sick headache had gone.

On another occasion Mme Rimbaud similarly had the sun removed from her head by a cousin. When my mother enquired how this was done, she mentioned not only the bottle, but 'a handkerchief folded in a certain way, "*et certainement qu'elle en a dit des prières. Je ne sais pas, moi.*"' The disclaimer suggests that the '*prières*' may not have been altogether Christian in character.

A particularly potent author of cures was the martyr St Blaise, who, as a consequence of his miraculous survival of strangulation or decapitation (accounts differ), specialized in healing sore throats.[4] When my mother was confined to bed with a severe cold, 'Mimi Chou kindly gave me a packet of lump sugar & pastilles blessed on St Blaise's day.' On another occasion she regaled her with a detailed account of the healing process. Saint Blaise being outside Collioure for a stroll one day with Our Lord, the pair bumped into Satan, who coolly informed them: 'I'm off to strangle someone.' 'Nong, Nong, Nong!' exclaimed Jesus and Blaise together, in pronounced Catalan accents: 'You're not doing that!' This pious narrative acted as preface to the charm that effected the cure: a formula strongly characteristic of pagan ritual, in which Christian figures were frequently substituted for their heathen predecessors.[5]

The calendar year was marked by a succession of colourful festivals. On 27 February 1952 Patrick was delighted by the Mardi Gras carnival, which he observed from their balcony winding joyously along the rue Arago, and then descended to follow it to the Place de la Mairie. There were fine floats, followed by men disguised as bears and monkeys:

I saw them pass down the boulevard and then arrive in the Place: immense crowd, charmed: Diego lost in delight. Music – a band to each float. Funny remarks on floats all written in French. Attention Ours méchants et singe vicieu ['dangerous bears and vicious monkey'] . . . Remarkable dancing of 2 pairs of mariés [married couples]. Immobility of masks: singe (sacking? young Germa) probably making singe faces underneath; but quite invisible – vast addition to general effect. Mlle Margot convulsed by bears – pointing, laughing, red in the face with pleasure. M. le Curé not visible – no wonder – Ash Wednesday. Religious aspect quite lost to view . . . Many children dressed up – rouged, powdered – some in Catalan dress – attractive – some as F[airy]. Queens or some such – less attractive.

Each year on Ascension Day an assemblage of small children, beautifully dressed, gathered outside the church to attend their first Communion. The *quatorze juillet* was in contrast a comparatively modest bucolic occasion. 'Procession has just passed up the rue,' noted my mother, 'small boys carrying torches or tricolors, with the garde-champêtre [local policeman], followed by local band.' In the evening there was dancing in the Place, and a display of fireworks in and around the bay. The cheerful informality of the occasion delighted Patrick, who another year was gratified to record: 'Fête Nationale: very scruffy procession except [Dr] Delcos in his tricolore sash.'

Patrick made notes on customs and other items of local interest, such as this recipe for ridding a child of worms: 'Le bon vermifuge[:] frot the child's bosom with garlic and hang a necklace of garlic round the child's neck ça les étouffe.' He further compiled a list of 'Sobriquets' of local families, some of which feature in his novel *The Catalans*. Thus one bore the surname 'L'Empereur – because when he was a baby the Emperor dandled him'. Patrick told me this occurred when Napoleon III was passing through Collioure. At the other political extreme was the family *Cravatrouge* (Catalan *En cravat rougt*), one of whom had been 'le premier radical' of the town. Another is of mysterious provenance: *Piétine dans la boue* ('Trample in the Mud'): Catalan *Pitg a fangc*.

The French Republic being a relative newcomer in Collioure's ancient history,* the town's major annual celebration is the Feast of St Vincent, Collioure's patron saint, on 16 August. Until the beginning of the last century, when it was prohibited by the atheist administration of President Émile Combes, a boat bearing the saint's relics plied from his little chapel on the rock across the harbour, to be ceremonially received on the beach by the curé with a ritual exchange conducted in Catalan.[6] A bullfight in the town's arena by the railway station was one of many celebrations marking the festive occasion. In 1953 my mother passed 'Picasso visible in café des Sports – merry, pink, active. He was président of this year's corrida.' The evening's firework display is especially magnificent, usually surpassing that of the *quatorze juillet*. On one such occasion in the early 1960s, we ascended the ridge above the house to obtain a panoramic view of cascades of fire erupting high into the night sky from the beach, as also from fishing boats moored about the harbour. The highlight of the evening occurred when the French Army, then occupying the Château Royal, blew up with one mighty roar what appeared to be their entire reserve of high explosive. From an invisible vineyard above us echoed an answering primitive bellow of approval from a solitary enthusiast, which greatly pleased Patrick.

---

* The Revolutionary dictatorship was widely resented in the independent-minded Roussillon as an oppressive alien power, to be resisted at every opportunity – even to the extent of welcoming the Spanish army of occupation which attacked Collioure in 1793–4.[7] Even in the early decades of the twentieth century, 'The Roussillon does not talk about Paris. It talks about Barcelona'.[8]

It was not just innate curiosity which led him to conduct careful observation and recording of traditional ways in Collioure. Just before he left England in September 1949, it was seen earlier that he had agreed to write a book about Southern France for submission to his publishers, Secker & Warburg. Although he kept the project in mind, over two years were to pass before he hit on the idea of utilizing the knowledge he had acquired for the alternative purpose of writing a novel. Before that, the indications are that he planned a descriptive account of the life and landscape of the Côte Vermeille, and it was to that end that he noted its more colourful aspects, and encouraged my mother to record observations in her diary. Naturally gregarious, consorting daily with shopkeepers and neighbours, and being more proficient in French and Catalan than Patrick, she was the more productive worker in this field.

It was during the summer of 1951 that the idea of writing a novel with Collioure as its picturesque setting had germinated in Patrick's mind. He and my mother had become concerned with, and to some extent involved in, the divorce of their good friend Odette. On 2 March 1951 my mother accompanied her and her father to lend support in a hearing at the court in Céret. Odette's husband François Bernardi, a successful sculptor and painter, had deserted her for an older but extremely beautiful woman. Next day Patrick sketched a plot based around the affair. Although his initial plan seems to have been to produce a short story, the scheme is sufficiently detailed to suggest the possibility of fuller treatment.

His initial reaction was one of indecision:

It sounds a commonplace little romance. Perhaps I could lift it out of the rut by showing the gradual development of Odette's character – she should be mature at the end, and at last spiritually free of the [her] family's domination – and the parallel development of François' to something like unselfishness and honesty. The moral being that you have got to be free of domination (by cant or by family) before you are any good.

A great difficulty would be the presentation: it could hardly be done from outside (the all-knowing observer) and I hardly know whether I could manage it from inside each character.

Patrick does not appear to have been at all troubled by the possibility that informed readers might identify the protagonists. (His friend Walter Greenway was similarly concerned lest people in Cwm Croesor discover the extent of their potentially embarrassing portrayal in *Three Bear Witness*.) Nor, more surprisingly, does this thought seem to have worried my mother. It seems they generally espoused the view that Patrick's literary work stood apart from the material world: connections between them hardly mattered. Equally, they may not unreasonably have assumed that no one in Collioure was likely to read the book.

In October my parents assisted in bringing in the grape harvest. 'Vendanged for Vincent Atxer', noted my mother. 'Too long, did not like the V[incent].A[txer].s. O[dette]. was there, objectionable. Told us the équipe [working party] in the plains was very grossier [coarse]. Youths rolled women in the dust, took girl's trousers off.'* Next day there was a further vendange, at which my mother was evidently annoyed by 'O[dette]. horseplay moustissing the men.'† On the third day my mother and Patrick 'Worked from 8.30 a.m. to 4.30 p.m. Beastly children. Very, very fatigued.' My mother was far from being a prude, and it is possible that she objected to Patrick's observing their beautiful friend behaving in so wantonly provocative a manner. The sultry Odette was a lissom creature of

---

* This reads uncommonly like a survival of the pagan practice of actual or simulated sexual intercourse to ensure fruitfulness of crops (Frazer, *The Magic Art and the Evolution of Kings*, ii, pp. 98–104).

† 'Moustisser' may be a neologism coined from 'moustique', meaning something like 'teasing or provoking the men like a mosquito'. Whether it was my mother's invention, I do not know.

the South, who amid the grape harvest under the burning sun appeared almost an elemental being.*

Four days later, Patrick 'sketched out vendange tale'. It seems likely that this was the basis of chapter VIII of *The Catalans*, with its vivid depiction of the exhausting physical labour and pain incurred in gathering the grapes, together with the erotically charged relationship between the intellectual outsider, Alain Roig, and the lovely Catalan girl Madeleine, who has been deserted by her painter husband Francisco. The episode builds up to a heated climax, with Alain's symbolic rape of Madeleine:

> With a quick pace he was up to her. He knocked her to the ground. She fell on her knees, and crouching over her he gripped her hair and ears, pressed his teeth hard against her forehead, and in the surrounding cries and laughter he crowed three times, loud like a cock.

Patrick appears at first to have remained undecided precisely what use he might make of these possibilities, until on 18 December he took my mother for a walk up to the Madeloc tower. It was a beautiful day: passing the old barracks (which at one point they envisaged as a permanent refuge from the town), with partridges flying around, they collected wild daffodil bulbs to plant in their window box. Buddug cavorted, madly hunting and catching nothing. As they walked, Patrick for the first time unfolded his idea for a novel on the theme of life among the local Catalans.

Patrick, toying with various approaches to his novel, was struck down yet again by one of his nervous attacks and retired to bed, where he received the usual medication. So bad was the bout on this occasion, that he had to force himself not to think of the book

---

* A lurid claim ('The secret life of Patrick O'Brian', *Sunday Telegraph*, 1 March 2000) of an unconsummated love affair between Patrick and Odette (at the time of my writing this, an astonishingly youthful ninety-year-old) continues even now to arouse her indignant *colère*.

lest the pangs recur. Not until 9 January 1952 did he recover sufficiently to begin working on it. At the end of the month my mother called on Odette to collect information about the social structure of the town, a factor which was to be vividly delineated in the novel. On 6 February 'P. showed me first chapter of novel: terribly impressed & happy.' With my mother's enthusiasm buoying him up, Patrick now found the book advancing with increasing satisfaction. Despite intermittent setbacks and misgivings, he worked throughout the summer, until he finally laid down his pen on 12 September. 'Much fatigued & terribly pale, kept lying on bed feeling faint,' as my concerned mother noted.

However, the task was completed, and both were enthusiastic over the result. In May Patrick had toyed with the title *Interested Motives*, but eventually settled on *The Catalans*. My mother threw herself into typing the text, and on 2 October copies were sent to Harcourt Brace in New York, and Rupert Hart-Davis in London.

No sooner were the parcels despatched, than an anticlimactic reaction set in. On 5 November 'Nervous tension over Catalans suddenly overwhelming. It matters so hideously.' Might it suffer the same distressing fate as the collection of short stories, on which such high hopes had been pinned?

Three weeks passed by, during which they attempted to distract themselves with household improvements. 'Wait, wait, wait, for post.' Finally, on 26 November 1952, came news as good as might be hoped for. A telegram arrived from Naomi Burton at Curtis Brown in New York, announcing that Harcourt Brace had offered to take *The Catalans* at the same rate as *Testimonies*. Since the book was complete, they would shortly receive a second time within the year the princely sum of $750, tax-free!

Exultation reigned in the little *apartement*. 'Very, very happy,' rejoiced my mother. Patrick promptly wrote to Andorra concerning the building plot for which they had been negotiating. Then they jumped up, and 'walked to P[ort]. Vendres without noticing the way'. My mother was 'unable to resist giving P. gloves, camera (whose shutter won't work & Patau [the photographer] is shut) & pineapple in tin. All these were for his birthday' on 12 December. Three days later the contract arrived.

The book represents in many ways a tribute to the rugged land he had come to love, and its lively inhabitants. Among them they now had many fast friends, and were accepted as honorary *Colliourenchs*. It is the more fortunate, consequently, that the novel was not translated at the time into French or Catalan, since it included matter that must surely have provoked offence and dismay in some quarters.

The greatest pleasure I derive from Patrick's novel lies in the exquisite evocation of Collioure (barely disguised as 'Saint-Felíu'), and its stark hinterland of vineyards and mountains. Here is enshrined forever the old Collioure, before the destruction of ancient customs, language, clothing, music; the end of the fishing industry, and the building of rank upon rank of *lotissements* on the skirts of the town. Fortunately, enough of the old town survives in physical form for it to be possible to people it again in imagination, viewed in the light of Patrick's loving recreation in *The Catalans*.

Several of his extended pen portraits are taken from the life. The account of the vendange in chapter VIII, with its vivid depiction of the toil involved, culminating in Alain's climactic 'rape' of the lubricious Madeleine, drew extensively on Patrick's own experience during those three backbreaking days in October 1951, when Odette's provocative behaviour privately scandalized my mother.* Again, the festival in the central *place* of the town, recounted in chapter IX, echoes the Carnival witnessed by Patrick in February 1952.

For the biographer the book contains much of interest. The

---

* Patrick also utilized a five-page description of the previous year's vendange, which he compiled at the beginning of 1951. It appears intended for one of the short stories he hoped to have published about that time, which in the event never attained print.

figure of Dr Alain Roig, returning from long exile in the Far East to resolve a domestic crisis at home, stands (like Pugh in *Three Bear Witness*) in material respects for Patrick himself. A detached, reflective outsider, he is concerned to observe and dissect the psychological turmoil by which he finds himself surrounded. At one point he ascends the town rampart, where he contemplates from on high the tumbled confusion of houses below:

> He passed it carefully over in review, looking for changes and for known, personal landmarks. It was exactly as he remembered it, as he thought of it when he was away, exactly the same and yet with an additional strength of life, a vibrant immediacy: his memory, however sentimental with the distance, might not have provided the shrilling of the cicadas in the oleaster that grew tortuously from a crevice in the wall below, the play of the dancing, shimmering air, the flick and dart of the lizards, and the distant sound of men hauling on a boat.

This was what Patrick himself enjoyed, observing (at times with binoculars) the world from an inaccessible vantage-point, like the peregrine falcon in his adolescent short story of that title.

Familiar, too, from Patrick's own experience are the internecine intrigue and feuding which Alain encounters among his family. The Roig family members represent in varying degree a dysfunctional collection, an affliction largely originating in the character of Alain's deceased uncle: 'an evil-tempered man, powerful, domineering, and restless; a ferocious domestic bully. It was not that Alain blamed his Uncle Hercule then; he accepted him as a force of nature and hated him without forming any judgment.'

All this is too close to Patrick's experience of his oppressive father Charles Russ for coincidence, and the damaging effect he exerted in varying degrees on his offspring.

Alain's return to Saint-Felíu arose from a summons to save his cousin Xavier, Uncle Hercule's son, from what leading members of the family regard as a wholly inappropriate marriage. Alain himself 'was sorry for Xavier . . . There was something very moving, in those days, in the sight of that proud, cold young man being humiliated and bully-ragged, and bearing it with a pale, masked fortitude.'

There can be no doubt that Xavier is a figure similarly deriving from Patrick's character and experience, and the relationship between the dead father and his young son mirrors closely his own experience.

Perhaps the most damaging aspect of the bullying father figure is the way that the distorted relationship repeats itself in succeeding generations. Despite (or rather, because of) his harsh upbringing, Xavier in turn replicates the tyrant in his relationship with his own son Dédé. Although resolved at first to treat the child with the kindness his father never gave him, Xavier grows more and more dissatisfied with the boy, finding him intolerably weak, inadequate and sly. He tries educating Dédé himself, but the child's foolish frivolity and sullen impertinence goad him into subjecting him to repeated beatings. While acknowledging that he had become the oppressor he so loathed in his father, Xavier confesses himself now incapable of acting otherwise.

This unsavoury episode unmistakably reflects both Patrick's assessment of his own nature as a child, and his treatment of his son Richard, when he rashly attempted to tutor him in Wales in 1948–49. In this respect the experiment proved miserable for both father and son, as Patrick himself appears to have acknowledged following his arrival in France. What persuaded him to revisit that unhappy time, above all making Xavier excoriate his son in repellently disparaging terms? The explanation is, I suspect, that here as elsewhere Patrick utilized his writing on occasion as means of exorcizing his own shortcomings. He possessed no confidant beyond my mother, and even with her it seems unlikely that he found himself able to enlarge on actions he had come to regard with profound shame. He successively employed his three autobiographical novels (*Three Bear Witness*, *The Catalans* and *Richard Temple*) as vehicles for such confessions. The approach was presumably effective, as thereafter he appears to have felt he had effectively exhausted the theme.*

The extremity of Xavier's cruelty, and the inadequacy of his justification, are so hyperbolical as to suggest that Patrick expected readers to find the first as repugnant as the second was implausible. I suspect that, by grossly exaggerating his own misconduct, Patrick privately acknowledged it as indefensible. Its function was plainly cathartic. From a biographical point of view, the section in question (chapter IV) should be read in context. Xavier's savagely frank account of his neglect and ill-treatment of his wife and son is set in the form of a confession, accompanied by expressed desire for absolution. Finding his formal confession to the town priest inadequate, he confides his lack of humanity and consequent fear of damnation to his sympathetic cousin Alain. Alain himself represents an alternative personification of Patrick: the gentle, inquisitive, sage adviser, which is how I for one found him when he confronted problems affecting those close to him. Chapters VIII and IX of *The Catalans*, recounting events from Alain's perspective, derive almost verbatim from Patrick's own experience.

Thus, one underlying function of *The Catalans* is to provide Patrick's own confession. More than once in conversation with me he adverted to the *Confessions* of Jean-Jacques Rousseau, laying sardonic emphasis on the writer's ingenuous account of his callous treatment of his children. Unsurprisingly, my mother observed that, on completion of Xavier's bitter self-examination, Patrick found himself emotionally drained. 'P. finished Chapter IV & got terribly depressed.'[9]

The one person whom Patrick clearly would not have wished to understand the reality behind the father–son divide in *The Catalans* was his own son Richard. Equally, he must have appreciated the likelihood that the boy would read the book. As has

---

* While Jack Aubrey's father, the wayward General Aubrey, clearly owes something to Dr Charles Russ, he is portrayed as foolish and irresponsible, rather than despotic or brutal.

already been seen, he followed his father's literary career with filial pride. On learning in October 1953 of the book's completion, he supplied a practical suggestion:

> I am very glad to hear that you are having a holiday after completing the book. It seems to me that no sooner is one book out than you have finished another. Instead of writing with your hand why not get a tape machine or some such gadget or would that wreck everything? I do hope it comes out as you would wish it.

Next July, he enquired of my mother:

> Has Dad heard anything of the last novel, and what is the title. Over in one shop (bookshop) I was peering round and I heard a customer ask for The Frozen Flame [the title of the British edition of *The Catalans*]. It was a terrific thrill to hear that, especially when I know my father wrote it.

His friend Bob Broeder remembers the sensation this aroused at school: 'Richard brought in a book written by his father, the book was called "The Frozen Flame" by Patrick O'Brian. Richard was very proud of this and the whole class were now more than happy to be associated with a boy whose father was an author.'

As has been seen, once Patrick had renounced the ill-considered scheme of acting as his son's teacher, a renunciation which coincided with Richard's arrival at years of discretion, their relationship became unremittingly warm. The boy proved more and more capable of appreciating the literature that Patrick loved. In January 1952 he sent Richard copies of Thackeray's *Henry Esmond* and W.H. Hudson's *Green Mansions*. It is scarcely conceivable that in 1953 he would have published anything he believed likely to prove wounding to the boy. It seems he was confident that Xavier's confession would be read purely as a literary construct.

Regarding the element of savage exaggeration in Xavier's confession, it is further worth considering a linked episode (what Patrick himself terms 'the parallel disaster'), in which his morbid concern to exaggerate the heinousness of his sin becomes yet more evident. Xavier acquires a dog, which proves disobedient and ill-behaved: so much so, that he thrashes it until he eventually 'reduced it to a cowering, hysterical, incontinent, useless cur'.[10]

Both Patrick and my mother were fond of dogs, and adored their own Welsh hunt terrier Buddug. In the early summer of 1952, while he was in the midst of writing *The Catalans*, my mother was obliged to visit England in pursuit of the disastrous Opel car. Always uneasy in her absence, Patrick became increasingly on edge as the days went by, and when after three weeks on the day of her expected return he received a telegram announcing its postponement to the following day, he found himself 'feeling very much the pathetic poor one and generally angry. Poor Budd chose this one day to be bad, and I whipped her sore.'

The nature of her crime and the harshness of the punishment remain undisclosed. Two aspects are, however, clear. In the first place, Patrick was confessedly in an exceptional state of tension. Secondly, this was almost certainly the sole occasion on which the faithful Buddug was ever 'whipped'. Not only is there no record in my mother's diary of such an occurrence at any other time, but I am confident she would not have permitted it. It was surely this uncharacteristic episode that inspired Patrick's awkwardly obtruded account of Xavier's sadistic treatment of his dog. Patrick was deeply ashamed of having lost his temper with Buddug, and inserted the passage in his novel as a further form of exorcism or self-castigation.*

Finally, on this significant topic, there remains Patrick's passing allusion to the formal act of confession, which Xavier finds

---

* This recalls the conclusion of the short story 'A Minor Operation', discussed *supra*, in which the frenzied Patrick-figure is driven to assault the only two creatures he loves in the world: his dog and his wife.

inadequately emollient when he repairs to the town curé, Father Sabatier. What he required was not a bland rite of forgiveness, but surgical exposure and extraction of the moral cancer of which his conscience accused him.

In 1960 he and my mother spent several months in London, coming every day to see me in hospital, where I was confined after a severe back operation. Despite the bitter circumstances of her divorce, my mother remained throughout her life deeply attached to the Russian Orthodox Church, in which she had married my father, and my sister and I were baptized. During this time she and Patrick became regular attenders at our Russian church in Emperor's Gate, where they came to know and admire the parish priest. Father George Sheremetiev was a remarkable figure. Head of one of Russia's greatest aristocratic families, he had previously been a cavalry officer in the Imperial Army. More importantly, he possessed a truly noble character: wise, perceptive, and holy in the truest sense. I regularly confessed to him, and like his other parishioners invariably found his admonitions perceptive and inspiring.

So impressed were my parents by Father George, that they asked him to marry them – their civil union of 1945 being unrecognized by the Church. Since Patrick would have appreciated from my mother how beneficial was the rite, it seems possible that he himself engaged in confession at this time – perhaps of an informal character. In the Aubrey–Maturin novels, Stephen Maturin is consistently portrayed as a Laodicean Catholic, verging on deism. However, after a particularly sumptuous dinner at Ashgrove Cottage, he congratulates Mrs Aubrey, adding jocularly: 'When next I see Father George I shall have to admit to the sin of greed . . .'[11] That Maturin had a confessor at all comes to the reader as a surprise, and that the latter bore so apparently English a name seems further anomalous (one would expect him to have been Irish or Catalan). On the one hand, we never read of Maturin's participation in a Catholic service, while on the other numerous instances attest to Patrick's pleasure in assigning the names of his acquaintances to characters in his books.

Is this what happened here? Did Patrick eventually make the confession he had sought to express through his early novels?

I have dealt with the confessional element in *The Catalans* at some length, as it would be dangerously easy in the absence of knowledge of Patrick's emotional state of mind to take Xavier's rant against his son Dédé as a reflection of his own attitude towards his son Richard.[12] In fact, given the warmth of their relationship at the time of writing, such an assumption appears wholly implausible. Furthermore, even had Patrick perversely decided to blackguard his own son in print, my mother would have registered the strongest objection. She loved the boy almost as much as she did his father. In December 1952, she wrote fondly: 'Horrid letter from Mrs. Power [Elizabeth] about poor R., & letter from the school . . . Started V necked jersey for R. One of school complaints is that he wears my jersey, & Mrs P says he has lived in it since he got it. Cannot help feeling pleased.'

The year 1952 ended on a note of cautious optimism. My parents entertained high hopes for the success of *The Catalans* in the USA, and with luck in Britain too. Contemplating his next project, Patrick returned to notes he had compiled in the British Museum before the War for his planned book on medieval bestiaries. Hitherto the scheme had barely left the drawing board, but now as Christmas approached he completed a 10,000-word draft, which he planned to send with a synopsis of the remainder to his US and British publishers. In the event, it seems that their newly gained wealth allowed pleasurable distractions to interrupt the work sufficiently long for it to be abandoned permanently. It is a pity the draft has not survived, since his notes and provisional chapters in my possession indicate that Patrick could have produced an entertaining work on the subject.

All this is, however, to anticipate the book's publication. It would be a year at least before *The Catalans* appeared in print, and what was to be done during the agonizing months of anticipation that lay ahead? Christmas drew near, with nothing happening as it should. On 19 December my mother was dismayed to find they had spent that year more than 60,000 francs on entertainment alone. The 22 of December proved worse: it was the 'Black Day', when they learned that the *New Yorker* had after all turned down the collection of stories submitted with such high hopes six weeks earlier. On Christmas Eve they received Richard's school report: it likewise proved damning, provoking further depression. Christmas cards arrived, including one from Patrick's stepmother Zoe, of whom he was very fond, and kind neighbours called with gifts. The festival was quietly enjoyed, but they decided they could not afford to give each other the customary presents.

Although the need for economy was pressing, they had managed to amass sufficient funds five days after Christmas to purchase for 100,000 francs a Citroën 2CV, popularly known as a '*deux chevaux*'. This was in due course to prove an even greater asset than the alternative prospect of an Andorran bolt-hole, which they now found themselves reluctantly obliged to abandon.

III

New Home and New Family

I descended a little on the Side of that delicious Valley, surveying it with a secret kind of Pleasure (though mix'd with other afflicting Thoughts) to think that this was all my own, that I was King and Lord of all this Country indefeasibly, and that I had a Right of Possession; and if I could convey it I might have it in Inheritance, as completely as any Lord of a Manor in England.

Daniel Defoe, *Robinson Crusoe*

After more than three years' stressful poverty in their little flat in Collioure, early in 1953 Patrick and my mother found their financial situation greatly improved by the warm reception his publishers accorded *The Catalans*. Since it had been submitted complete, substantial advances of $750 from Harcourt Brace in the States, and £100 from Hart-Davis in England, arrived at the beginning of the year.

Reviews proved encouraging. As a biographer I am primarily concerned with autobiographical aspects of the novel, but as a literary achievement it has gained high esteem. In 1991 the American novelist Stephen Becker wrote to Patrick:

I never told you how I enjoyed meeting an early (if older) version of Stephen [Maturin] in Alain Roig — and allow me to state that I found The Catalans not only first-rate but wise and moving . . .

It is spacious and rich, and all of life is there – land and sea and sky, arts and sciences, food and drink, body and mind and spirit.

Constricted living conditions and the incessant cacophony of the narrow rue Arago had for some time made the couple long for a refuge in the countryside. Attempts to buy or build in Andorra had been frustrated, and despite encouraging praise for Patrick's latest novel, their income remained too unpredictable to accumulate any capital of substance.

However, these unexpectedly large advances had at least enabled them to buy a car, which afforded means of escape from their stiflingly constrained existence. In the New Year, they found themselves in a position to fulfil this dream. They bought their little *deux chevaux* in Perpignan, which filled them with delight. Patrick noted that the number-plate included an M for Mary, and my mother ecstatically confided to her diary: 'Car dépasses all our expectations in every way.' Kind Tante Alice, the butcher, let them use her abattoir for a garage, and that day they drove the car up to the rim of the castle glacis, where it was formally photographed. Proud Buddug perched inside, no doubt foreseeing further camping expeditions.

The *deux chevaux*

If so, she was right. After a couple of days spent motoring happily around the neighbourhood, the three of them set forth on their long-deferred major expedition around the Iberian peninsula. On 21 January 1953 they drove over the Pyrenees by the pass at Le Perthus, arriving in Valencia two days later. Patrick was concerned that precious memories of a journey from which he hoped to profit might fade, and began keeping a detailed journal.

The moment they entered Spain, they were confronted by the homely ways of that then picturesque land, when solicitous customs officers asked them to take a stranded woman with them as far as Figueras. At Tarragona, Patrick was delighted by the prospect of the cathedral by night: 'It was very much bigger than I had expected, and far nobler. Wonderful dramatic inner courts all lit by dim lanterns – bold low arches – theatrical staircases.'

He experienced an uncanny sensation, which was not new to him: 'But I had, probably quite unnecessarily, the disagreeable impression of being stared at.' This persistent fancy conceivably originated in his troubled childhood, when he never knew when the next thunderbolt might strike, whether from his moody father, or one of a succession of harsh governesses.

They took photographs with their new camera, of which I retain the negatives. Unfortunately, health problems continued to dog them. My mother suffered from a stomach complaint causing loss of appetite, and Patrick painfully twisted his ankle while photographing the Roman aqueduct.

The car, however, proved a sterling success: 'A 2 CV. is certainly the car for Spain. Quite often the roads are fairly good (or have been so far) and then they suddenly degenerate into the most appalling pot-holed tracks as they pass through villages: there was one hole this afternoon that must have been a foot deep.'

In Tortosa, their progress was impeded by a 'shocking assembly of carts: tiny donkey carts; carts drawn by one or two mules tandem – even three or one horse and a donkey in front: carts with barrels slung deep, carts with hoods and bodies made of wickerwork and carpet, all milling slowly about Tortosa.'

Nor did the Guardia Civil please Patrick: 'nasty, impudent, over-dressed, over-armed fellows, with a tin-god expression all over their faces'. However, as Patrick tended to view the British police with almost comparable distaste, his disparagement need perhaps not be taken over-literally. In any case, before long he encountered cause to moderate his view: 'The Guardia Civil are strange souls: one whom we asked the way grew excited: he had the appearance of a man about to have a fit. Others seem normal enough, and even cheerful.'

Although largely apolitical by nature, Patrick, like many young people in the Thirties, had nurtured sympathy for the Republican cause in the Spanish Civil War, and corresponding distaste for the regime of General Franco. While he never altered this view, he was frequently obliged to adjust his condemnation of the regime to the languid realities of everyday life in contemporary Spain.

He was greatly intrigued by remarkable contrasts with France, which struck them at almost every turn of their exploration. It used to be said that 'Europe stops at the Pyrenees', a dramatic contrast which both frustrated and intrigued Patrick:

> I have not mentioned the countryside at all. There hardly is any, properly speaking. The country and the village are English inventions. Here there are plantations, barren stretches, small towns. There is something wrong with it all. I wish I could put my finger on it. The little towns and their inhabitants are shockingly rude, hard and brutal.

At the same time, Patrick admired the 'vast plantations of olives (magnificent ancient trees on pink and grey soil) and carobs, and there are charming orange groves – much lower bushes than I had expected, much closer together and carrying twenty times as much fruit – as well as patches of good-looking plough.'

The people likewise appeared to belong to a distinct, all but timeless world. Stephen Maturin's Catalan homeland would not be difficult to evoke, after glimpsing such vignettes as when they encountered 'between Tortosa and Vinaróz the two old tall men in blue knee breeches, one smoking a pipe, with a black handkerchief round his head and white stockings, the other in blue stockings: Catalan espadrilles worn as far as here . . . gipsies, barefoot, with long gold earrings.'

Continuing southwards, it became apparent how few houses in the country possessed piped water: 'We have found the reason for the amphorae. They are for taking water to houses, and they have no bottoms because they never stand up – always in baskets or stands. A terrible number of houses have no water. There is a cart with a barrel and a great many cruches: that is the mains.'

At Sorbas they came upon a community apparently living in caves tunnelled out of the soft rock. It being Sunday, thousands of them were moving along the road in their best clothes, 'girls (some of them) with flowers in their hair, a young man bicycling with a guitar'.

Undisguised curiosity evinced by crowds in the town at the strangers' arrival in their midst predictably angered Patrick, but the kingdom of Granada delighted him, with its exotic Moorish castles and 'charming little red houses with red tiled roofs'.

Patrick's childhood fascination with the exploration of exotic lands was constantly gratified. Arrived at the summit of a pass south of Valencia, 'we could see an enormous moon-like country bare light green-gray rock in dusty white soil, jagged, arbitrary mountains in all directions, and below us a deep valley, terraced in swirling curves.'

Now, on the coast east of Malaga, they came upon Motril:

with its Moorish castle, perhaps the finest we have ever seen. And the backward view of Motril and the great headland beyond it, with the sky and the sea (lateen sails upon it) bluer than one can describe, with bits of the Sierra Nevada in the lefthand corner of the field of vision, that is a view, all right.

At Gibraltar they were briefly separated from Buddug, who was placed in quarantine in kennels at the end of the town. The friendly policeman who escorted them there also showed them HMS *Vanguard* lying in dock, and then took them to a pleasant hotel: 'That evening we walked about until we were quite done up. It is an astonishing place: Spain still predominates, in spite of a very strong element of pre-war England with a dash of India.'

Unconscious seeds of Patrick's future literary creations were being sown. He found *Vanguard* 'very rosy and youthful', admired the Georgian houses, and noted with approbation 'Cheap Jack and Cheap John's Stores', together with Oxford marmalade.

While staying on the Rock, Patrick and my mother paid a brief visit to Tangiers. Crossing the strait, they saw dolphins, while 'A kind mariner pointed out Cape Trafalgar.' On disembarking, they found themselves in a world still more enticingly exotic than Spain: 'We wandered up a street where everybody seemed to be going, a crowded street. But crowded with such people. Moors in djellabahs and slippers, pale Moors like Europeans but with fezzes, slim veiled women veiled [*sic*], blue or white . . .'

Delighted with their brief but memorable visit, they returned to be regaled by affectionate dolphins: 'Not only did they skip and play, but they came right into the ship and swam immediately along the cutwater, having immense fun with the rush of the water. They kept pace effortlessly, turning, rolling, jostling one another.'

Details of these and other curious encounters are frequently accompanied by Patrick's sketches in the margins of his journal. Back in Gibraltar they spent a whole afternoon searching for a birthday present for the growing Richard, before they eventually succeeded in hunting down a leather-cased shaving kit. At dusk they climbed the Rock to view the apes, and next morning set off for Cadiz – which regrettably proved 'the rudest town so far, the ugliest and the dirtiest'. Patrick's resolve to drink sherry at Jerez was frustrated, when a café could only provide him with 'something just as good'. In fact the mysterious beverage proved 'quite good', while an awkward confrontation was narrowly avoided:

> While we were drinking it up – precious little there was – I had my back to the street, facing M. She told me afterwards that all the time there were men, respectably dressed men, leering at her from behind my back, and making gestures of invitation. Perhaps it was as well that I did not see them, because I was feeling profoundly depressed and bloody-minded, and there would have been a scene.

After exploring the region around Malaga, they returned to Motril. By then they decided they had endured all they needed of Spain: 'It is impossible to say how agreeable Collioure appeared in the sordid brutality of Motril.'

Patrick invariably grew restless and ill-at-ease when away from their snug home for long, but buoyed up by the prospect of return 'we began to hope that we were mistaken and that the inland Andalusian was a decent creature'. A visit to the Alhambra aroused Patrick's 'surprise at the extraordinary good taste of the Spanish authorities'. Crossing the mountains en route for Cordoba, he enthused over the presence of a number of magnificent red kite, noting too that: 'Here the little irises began all along the side of the road, on the hill leading out of Jaen, and for hundreds of miles after.' Cordoba's mosque 'was utterly dull from outside . . . but inside – dear Lord, what grandeur'.

Even this splendour was eclipsed on their return to Seville:

> We did see the Cathedral at once, and that was a glorious sight: it seemed to me profoundly religious, and very, very much more important than Córdoba. The severe, clean austerity of what we might call the furnishings was intensely gratifying. No geegaws at all, except Columbus' tomb. (And that, being alone, was impressive too, in its way).

After a night in 'the cheapest (and rudest)' hotel in town, they revisited the cathedral, where Patrick observed the relics, including 'a piece of Isidore' (the seventh-century Spanish scholar), about whom he had intended to write when preparing his book of bestiaries before the War.

After obtaining paperwork from the Portuguese consul, they drove to Huelva and crossed into Portugal by boat across 'the brown and yellow Guadiana, heaving gently, with tremendous rain beating down upon the mariners and dribbling through the hood'. On disembarking, 'The rain stopped suddenly and a complete double rainbow stood on the Spanish side of the river: an omen, I trust.'

It appears to have been, for within hours they found Portugal more congenial than Spain:*

All the way we kept remarking the extraordinary difference the frontier had made – little ugly crudely painted houses, blood red and ochre or raw blue, perforated chimneys like cast iron stoves, ugly, barefoot people, intense cultivation, comparatively dull country, no Guardia Civil, no Franco Franco Franco (spontaneous enthusiasm in durable official paint), no rude staring, no excessive poverty. Even the gipsies . . . looked different: they had not that pariah air, and they wore skirts to the ground and wooden, heel-less slippers. But the greatest difference was at Lagos: not only was there no wild-beasting at all, but when we were walking on the sand we said good-day to some ordinary youths. They took off their caps and bowed.

In Lagos they were taken to watch the masquerade taking place in various clubs. So great was the crush, that they were obliged

---

* Patrick must be allowed to speak for himself and my mother. For myself, I believe some allowance should be made for their detestation of Franco, together with regrettable manifestations of curiosity on the part of the lively Spanish population. This in particular was anathema to the hypersensitive Patrick.

to hover in doorways. But Patrick found the masks 'very funny indeed, almost all of them'. They learned that the clubs were graded according to social status: 'The last was the top, and there, it is true, there were some solemn old gentlemen dancing with masked females. It was unbelievable that so many people should inhabit one small town, or rather village.'

That afternoon they paid their respects to one of England's great naval victories, sitting in a shelter overlooking Cape St Vincent, an 800-foot cliff plunging sheer below them. On the way they passed a working windmill. Ever fascinated by technology of the past, Patrick stopped to photograph it. 'The miller, a rough-looking but kind and sensible man, invited us in, and explained his mill, made us plunge our hands in the flour, moved the top, stopped the sails, and did everything he could to be agreeable – went to a great deal of trouble.'

Patrick sketched careful diagrams of the workings of the sails and internal machinery. During a digression to Faro he likewise drew some fishing boats, being particularly taken with the prophylactic eye (with splendid eyebrow) painted on each boat's bow, a mysterious mop of wool adorning the prow.

The Portugal visited by Patrick appeared little changed since Wellington's day. Patrick noted with pleased surprise: 'No advertisement posters yet in Portugal. None at all.' On the road to Lisbon:

As soon as we passed out of the Algarve the hideous man's hat (black) worn over cotton scarf began to vanish – women here wear velour hat, flattened, with broad coloured ribbon or wide straw hat. Shoes rare – stockings cut at ankle for bare foot. Men in woollen stockings caps dangling to neck. Pleasant boy's faces under black hats (bow behind).

Lisbon proved well up to expectation: 'The sudden view of the Tagus with Lisbon the other side was as grand as anything

I have ever seen.' After strolling into the centre, 'we wandered along the river and admired a square-rigged Portuguese naval training ship'. Amid the capital's architectural glories, my mother was rewarded by a glimpse of 'a windscreen wiper for sale called Little Bugger'.

Making their way across country to the northern frontier, the travellers encountered weather and countryside less congenial. Back in Spain, Patrick attended mass at Santiago, but was strangely unimpressed by town or cathedral. Passing Corunna, they became alarmingly trapped for a while in a snowdrift beyond Villalba. Fortunately the summit of the hill proved not far, and Patrick stumbled behind on foot as my mother gingerly enticed the car towards it. 'When we reached the sea at Ribadeo (a very pleasant looking place . . . hundreds of duck down on the water; tufted duck mostly – and every promise of trout, if not of salmon too) we suddenly saw the Cordillera, pure white with deep snow.'

Passing through Basque country, where 'the red berets were worn quite naturally', they came to Guernica, scene of an infamous German air raid during the Civil War – 'and a melancholy sight it was – every building new, almost, and still a number of ruins'. Driving as fast as they could along precipitous coastal roads, frequently blocked by landslides, they finally gained the frontier at Irun. 'A toll-bridge, and we were in France again. French customs pleasant, sensible – Budd's utter fury at their touching sacred car and even prodding food parcels.'

The fine French roads sped them across country, and on 18 February 1953, 'in spite of the snow we were home at half past five, with an enormous post'. The news was generally good, especially a welcome cheque for £100 from Rupert Hart-Davis. Their neighbours the Rimbauds were warmly welcoming, as was their cat Pussit Tassit (who had managed to become pregnant). 'How pleasant it is, our own place, and how queer the familiarity.' Patrick calculated that they had travelled 3,674 miles, at a total motoring cost of 17,236 francs (about £15).

They had been away from home for a month, the longest foreign tour (not counting England) in which they ever engaged. Although there is little direct evidence of the use to which it may have been applied in his literary work,* there can be no doubt that Patrick's extended immersion into the dramatically archaic world of Spain and Portugal as it was then played a significant function in conferring the astonishing gift for immersion in past worlds which represents so marked an aspect of his historical fiction. Nearly thirty years later he came upon his diary record, noting wistfully: 'I read abt our journey in darkest Spain 1953 – forgotten or misremembered details – how it all comes to life!'

At the time, however, it seems that Patrick was pondering further work on contemporary themes. Shortly after their return, he reverted to his planned series of short stories. In March he wrote 'The Walker', and on 7 April my mother 'Sent off The Walker, The Crier, The Silent Woman & The Tailor to C[urtis]B[rown] New York.' Unfortunately, the last three tales have not survived.

Although the journey around the Iberian peninsula had proved both entertaining and (it was hoped) an inspiring source for future writing, before long Patrick and my mother found themselves reverting to continued frustration over their mode of existence in their cramped quarters in the rue Arago. During a brisk March walk up to the Madeloc tower, they 'Agreed on discontent with present way of life: sick of peasants so close to our life, need garden & hens & bees so as to be able really to save mon[ey].'

Time appeared slipping by, without adequate achievement to slow its passage. In April Patrick received news from his family in England that his once-dreaded giant of a father had suffered a stroke. Patrick, who throughout his life kept in regular touch with

---

* I suspect Patrick to have been author of an anonymous survey of the delights of Spain published in the American journal *House & Garden* later in the same year. I am indebted to Terry Zobeck for a copy of this article.

his family, must already have been aware of his declining health. A profoundly formative era of his past, wretched though it had largely been, appeared to be approaching extinction within the vortex of vanished years. It was at this time (1953) that he began work on an autobiographical novel, which in its final form completed years later evoked years of childhood and adolescence, filling him with a complex amalgam of nostalgia, resentment, and shame.* His work on this project, which preoccupied him inter-mittently over the next two years, will be recounted in due course. As ever, my mother played a strongly supportive role in the writing, and was deservedly gratified by Patrick's heartfelt acknowledge-ment: 'P. gave me immense pleasure by saying he values me most as critic.'

Further matter for concern arose again concerning Patrick's son Richard. Poor reports from school, together with a 'horrible letter' from his mother, persuaded Patrick and my mother to 'decide to take R. & have him work for the school cert. with us, by a corre-spondence course'. The project was, however, postponed for the present, until July when Richard arrived for his summer holiday at Collioure.

Enterprising as ever, he ignored his mother's apprehensive objec-tions, cycling all the way from Dieppe, to whose Poste Restante my mother transmitted 5,000 francs for travelling expenses.† Equipped only with a school atlas as guide, Richard arrived cheerful and excited at the beginning of August.

Collioure proved particularly lively and sociable on this occasion. Within days of Richard's arrival he made a memorable contact.

---

* As my mother noted in her diary, 'P. told idea of Chelsea novel, then retired all morning working.'

† In view of ill-natured assertions that Patrick provided Richard with no finan-cial assistance, it is worth noting the state of his and my mother's finances at this time. A month earlier in her diary she recorded: 'Sad accounts: 29000 instead of our allowed 17.500. P. says he must find him another occupation: writing makes him feel too ill.'

Two schoolmistresses from England came to stay in the town, accompanied by four of their pupils. One of the pair, Mary Burkett, met my parents and became a friend for some years (she had an aunt living near Collioure). It was not long before Richard became friends with the schoolgirls, and one in particular attracted his close attention.

One evening my mother invited the girls to dinner, after which Richard and another boy named Pat entertained their new friends:

All day preparing dinner (Spanish rice). V. successful, whole school. They are wonderfully pleasant young things. After dinner Pat came, & he & Richard escorted Susan, Wendy, Anne-Louise & Jill to fair. R. home at midnight. He prefers Susan, & Pat Wendy. Susan is the best.

Thereafter romance blossomed, and Richard and Susan were together every day until 26 August, when sadly the school party returned to England. No sooner had they been waved off at Perpignan railway station than 'R. wrote to Susan: says he is going to see her the day after he reaches London.' They continued in touch, until on 10 September Richard himself returned to England:

R. had one [letter] from Sue & ever since (2 pm) has been writing back to her. P. took R's bike to P. Vendres & sent it off. Saw R. off at Port-Vendres very sadly, in great wind & with black & purple sky. R. said this has been his best holiday. The house is so sad without him.

Richard had always loved his holidays in Collioure, but this time there had been especial reason for enjoyment. On his return to London, he wrote: 'Thank you both so very much for the best holiday that I have ever had. And it really was the best.' He and Susan had now become fast friends:

The [Cardinal Vaughan] school's secretary stopped me and asked whether the Mr O'Brian that had written The Catalans* was my father. With huge pride I said 'Yes'. Susan has shown me a revue of the Frozen Flame [the book's British title] and it looked very good . . .

Now I am going to begin. Susan sent me a card saying that would I like to hear a lecture on 'Everest'. Well Susan brought her two brothers and there [sic] two friends to hear the lecture . . . Her brothers are extremely pleasant to say the very least. And the lecture given by Hunt, Edmund Hillary and Low was absolutely superb . . .

Susan also invited me down to their house for lunch and tea. Was I scared, as at the last tea-party I sat down on the tea-pot. Her parents are wonderful, they really are. Their house, gee. Susan had told me that it was a small thing. Sixteen rooms and grounds that have a tennis court, flower garden kitchen garden, goat-house and hen house and a tool shed.

Susan's father, Paul Hodder-Williams, a director of the publishing firm of Hodder & Stoughton, was editor of Sir John Hunt's best-seller *The Ascent of Everest*, which he was shortly to publish. The parents' wealth and status in no way inhibited their friendliness to the shy but enthusiastic sixteen-year-old boy. As for their pretty daughter:

Seeing Susan again was terrific only her hair is a bit darker. She has gone back to school today. Ah. I asked her parents if I could take her out during the Christmas holidays, and to my delight they immediately said 'Yes', so that's quite all right. Quite where to take her I don't really know. Please could I have every suggestion however mad? She likes her bracelet. Soon she will be sending some of those

---

* The US title of the book (the true first edition), which was presumably that sent to Richard by his father. It was also the edition retained by my mother. My parents besides preferred it for its jacket design by their friend Willy Mucha.

photos that the girls took of her, they should be marvellous. She is
still the same. What a wonderful girl she is.

In December my mother stayed with her parents in Chelsea,
when she saw much of Richard. For him the outstanding moment
was when she took him to see Richard Burton and Claire Bloom
acting in *Hamlet* at the Old Vic. This was Richard's first visit to
the theatre, and he was enraptured by the 'perfect' production.
Two days later he took my mother to the cinema, and a couple
of days were spent in hunting down his first grown-up suit.

At Christmas Susan sent my parents a copy of Hilaire Belloc's
Cautionary Verses on behalf of her friends and their two schoolmistresses, thanking them again for their kindness throughout their
stay at Collioure. Nothing more is recorded of this charming
romance, which graphically illustrates my mother's and Patrick's
talent for empathy with the young, especially in their amours.
Within a few years they were to evince similar sympathy for me
and my occasionally troubled youthful love affairs.

It was in August 1953 that 'Mary [Burkett] took photographs
of P for H[arper's].B[azaar]. (only one came out, but it is very
good).'

Eventually, as tended on occasion to occur, Patrick took mysterious
offence at something Mary Burkett may or may not have done. In
later years I came to know her, when I was able to reassure her
that it was unlikely to have been in consequence of any particular
offence on her part. Patrick's writing was not going well at the
time, and it was clearly in large part the strain which frequently
made it hard for him to sustain close friendships at a remove. A
chapter of Mary Burkett's privately published biography is devoted
to their friendship. Unfortunately, it includes much factual misrepresentation, despite the fact that when in August 2005 I stayed at
her lovely home Isel House in the Lake District, we talked nostalgically of those long-departed days.[1]

A gift Mary had brought from England to Collioure long

Patrick, photographed by
Mary Burkett in 1953

outlasted their friendship. On 21 July 1954 my mother cryptically
recorded that 'Mary Burkett arrived about 10, she brought us
book-binding stuff.' This was a parcel of early legal documents,
which she had saved at a solicitor's office clearance. Patrick tended
to make heavy use of his beloved leather-bound books, with the
result that their spines often became badly worn. In later years he
replaced the damaged ones with strips cut from the sturdy paper
used by seventeenth-century lawyers.

Books so repaired, reposing comfortably on the bookshelves
looking down upon me as I write, include his much-loved set of
Johnson's *Lives of the Poets* (1824), Camden's *History of The
most Renowned and Victorious Princess Elizabeth, Late Queen
of England* (1675), Cowley's *Works* (1681) and Thomas Stanley's

History of Philosophy (1743). Of particular interest is Patrick's copy of William Burney, *A New Universal Dictionary of the Marine* (London, 1815), upon which he largely relied for his understanding of the workings of the Royal Navy in the eighteenth century, before he subsequently acquired the yet more apt Falconer's *An Universal Dictionary of the Marine* (1769). Normally such amateurish repairs would detract greatly from the collector's value of the books. However, in this case I find them enhanced, being constantly reminded of the pleasure they afforded their impassioned owner.

The year 1954 opened with an accruing worry inflicted on the hard-tried couple, whose financial situation remained precarious as ever. Patrick's son Richard had always encountered difficulty with academic work. He would be seventeen in February, and the time had approached when he must consider a career. His ambition to enrol at the Royal Naval College at Dartmouth having proved sadly abortive, it became essential to find a satisfactory alternative. It was a worrying prospect, not alleviated when on 15 January my mother noted: 'R's report came: very sad.'

However, their overriding concern was with his well-being. Richard and his friend Bob Broeder had become cycling enthusiasts, which involved them in many adventurous exploits – of which their parents fortunately remained unaware. On occasion they would ride as far as Brighton, a hundred-mile round journey, and took to recklessly hurtling at some 60 mph down precipitous Reigate Hill, after removing their brakes. Bob recalls that:

One of our many dangerous [feats] and in retrospect foolish to the extreme, was to slip stream motor vehicles on our bicycles – normally lorries. Our favourite was to sit in wait for a BOAC coach coming from Heathrow to the air terminal in Gloucester Road. We would tuck in behind it and travel the length of the Great West Road at great speed and then overtake it at the Chiswick roundabout!

Eventually Richard became involved in a serious accident. Cycling home one day in the rain from games (a mode of transport conveniently enabling them to pocket their bus-fare allowance issued by the school), he crashed when making an awkward turn in the middle of Hammersmith Broadway. Skidding, he shot beneath a car 'and cut myself to ribbons'. His prime concern was for the precious bicycle, whose frame was badly bent. The insurance company proved uncooperative, on grounds that the car was stationary at the moment of impact.

The repair was estimated at £10 13s. What could he do? Without his bicycle, he explained, he would have to start spending money daily on buses: could he possibly be sent £10? Patrick despatched a cheque by return of post, but the worry about Richard's school progress – or lack of it – remained. Along with the cheque he sent practical advice to his son on mending his ways: he must apply himself consistently to his studies, answer correspondence by return, and generally become more self-disciplined. Richard responded with touching promises to mend his ways.

Although his intentions were good, school progress continued its downward slide. Towards the end of April, a letter arrived from his mother 'enclosing a complaint from school about poor R'. By June he was agonizing over the imminent School Certificate examination (GCE), as his work became increasingly demanding and difficult. Alas, struggle as he might, the task proved too much, and he failed disastrously.

This unhappy news was not altogether unanticipated, and Patrick and my mother urgently discussed what was to be done. There was also the question of which branch of national service (the compulsory two years' military service) would be suitable. Richard suggested: 'Perhaps the Marine Commandos but one has to volunteer for five years and my mother does not like that. Then a friend suggested the engineering side; there to learn about mechanics. But please send your advice, because in the past it has always worked out well.'

Having himself, through little fault of his own, failed miserably in his own school studies, Patrick was determined that Richard should not suffer likewise. By the end of July my worried mother noted: 'R. breaks up: what to do about him?' As early as his return from holiday in Collioure in the previous year, Richard had urged that 'if Dad is willing, I would like him to teach me Latin and Greek so that I could pass in them. I have got to pass.'

A swift decision was made that Richard should indeed come out to Collioure, where he could work undistracted to retake the examination. Hitherto the required subjects had comprised history, geography, and two English papers. They were not his strong fields, and he now enrolled in a correspondence course focused on mathematics and science, for which he had much greater aptitude.

On 12 August my mother and Patrick, accompanied as ever by Buddug, drove across France, camping on the way, to meet Richard at Dieppe. A week later they were back home in Collioure: 'Got R's hair cut & bought him respectable trousers. Dear R.' There was no rush for the boy to begin work, since the examinations would not take place for a year. Initially, pleasant weeks were spent as before, swimming, walking, flying Richard's new kite, and playing cards and draughts. My mother told him about her own children, to which Richard replied that 'he saw Nik. at The Cottage [her parents' house in Chelsea] & that he is good-looking and tall'.* Hitherto my mother had not seen any photographs of my sister and me subsequent to the time when we were small children living at her parents' home in North Devon during the War.

A modest upsurge in their finances about this time spurred my parents to think seriously about buying a house in England or Wales. In February my mother lamented: 'Oh for a quiet home for P: it is a shame.' Now they received particulars of a house in

---

* This was one of the two occasions when Richard and I met. This lack of contact arose entirely from chance, and I particularly regret that my visit to Collioure in the following year did not overlap with his.

Cornwall, which sounded perfect for their needs. On 30 September 1954 they departed, together with Richard and their pets, 'after sad and tearful goodbyes' to all their faithful Collioure friends. So confident were they of finding a new home, that they had decided never to return.

Alas, the expedition proved one of those disasters by which they were intermittently afflicted throughout their lives. From the moment of their landing in England, everything went wrong. On disembarking, they attempted to smuggle the sedated Buddug and Pussit Tasset through customs in a suitcase. Unfortunately, a passenger informed on them, and the animals were impounded in quarantine. From Dover they drove seventeen hours through the night to Boskenna, in deepest Cornwall. Once installed there, my mother found that 'Slugs got down St Loy taps & into marmalade. No beach, only sinister, slippery great rocks with bits of wreck everywhere & one crushed fish . . . Hated Boskenna . . . Cold, foul weather.'

The little family settled into dreary lodgings, ceaselessly battered by winter gales and drenching rain. They were cold, miserable, and badly missed their pets. Although Patrick tried to cheer Richard with tales of smugglers and a proposal to buy a small boat, the reality was too grim to be lightly overcome. A brief visit to my mother's parents in London also went badly for some reason ('Very, very painful week'), and by December they had had enough. On the 8th all three embarked at Dover for the return journey to Collioure.

Their troubles were not over. At Dover their trunks disappeared, and they missed the Boulogne boat. They finally caught a train ferry to Dunkirk, where their animals were returned to them. Then they experienced a 'Nightmare drive from Dunkerque to St Omer instead of Calais through dark & rain & mud & detours & sugar-beet'. Near Toulouse the radiator fell off, and the car seized up. They left it at a garage, and continued the disastrous journey by train.

Back at last in Collioure, the family appreciated what they had nearly lost. So far as their house-hunting expedition was concerned, 'England was bad, we got too unhappy to keep up diary.' In striking contrast, 'Home looking perfectly beautiful & the most welcome thing I've known I think. Village so pleasant – everyone welcomed us.'

The Mediterranean climate helped, too: 'For two days now it has been too warm for the Mirus [stove] even in the evenings – & in England there are tempests & snow-storms & hideous cold. We lunch daily on the beach.'

Normal routine was resumed at once, to everyone's satisfaction. Patrick returned contentedly to his writing, and 'R. works hard too'. At the end of the year Patrick had written to the Ministry of Labour and National Service in Penzance, requesting that Richard be permitted to postpone his national service until he had taken his GCE in June of the following year. Fortunately, this was granted.

That Christmas (1954) little presents were exchanged, but sadly the festival was marred by the underlying burden of 'Horrid anxiety for money'. The lost luggage finally arrived, but there were hefty bills – including a couple of unexplained punctures to new tyres. As will grow more and more clear as their story unfolds, cars and my parents were not always happily matched.

Shortly after their return Patrick wrote his short story 'The Thermometer', which under very thin disguise depicts his unhappy childhood relationship with his father.[2] On 15 January 1955 he recorded in his diary:

I finished a story – broken thermometer – 5000 [words] nearly – very heavy going. It felt dubious – a little embarrassing; self-quaintery is always to be feared in anything at all autobiographical about childhood – approving self-quaintery – <u>own</u> head on one side – oh so unconscious simper – poor one. M did not like it. This makes me hate her, which is monstrously unfair. Dread of losing grip.

My mother, who I do not doubt appreciated its autobiographical character, was indeed depressed on reading the story. However,

Patrick now turned to a synopsis of a book for children based on Anson's voyage around the globe from 1740 to 1744. This my mother found 'quite beautiful and very exciting'. Three days later it was posted to his literary agent Curtis Brown, accompanied by high hopes.

On 2 February Richard's eighteenth birthday was celebrated in style – the last they would ever enjoy together. Presents were bestowed, after which they set off for a jaunt in the car. The weather was beautifully sunny, and they ate a delicious picnic ('stuffed olives; Tante's pâté; camembert; cake [baked the previous evening by my mother]; meringues; lemon-curd tart') in an olive grove beyond Banyuls. After supper at home, they went to the cinema in the square, where they watched *The City under the Sea*, dismissed by my mother as 'an idiot film', but which probably appealed to the youthful Richard as much as it did to me about the same time.*

Life had belatedly begun to look up. A few days earlier a local peasant named Azéma had offered to sell them 300 square metres of vineyard and garden for 125,000 francs: i.e. about £110. Hitherto this would have been well beyond their means, but the final payment for *The Road to Samarcand* (of which more in the next chapter) and now an advance on signing the contract for *The Golden Ocean* could now be imminently counted upon.

My mother enquired of a neighbour whether the price was fair, and was reassured to learn that more had recently been asked for a similar parcel of land, which in contrast lacked a water supply. Everyone was very obliging. Azéma agreed that the money could be paid in instalments, beginning in April. Meanwhile they could work the property. In the event they managed to pay the whole sum in April.

After the disastrous two months wasted in Cornish house-hunting, they now found themselves landowners! On 12 February

---

* The 1954 Hollywood film of Jules Verne's *Twenty Thousand Leagues under the Sea*.

my mother wrote triumphantly: 'We lunched on our earth.' Patrick had longed for this moment ever since their arrival in France. He loved the sense of security and self-worth which came with ownership of even so modest a parcel of land. Despite unfortunate consequences of his initial insistence on following the advice of his seventeenth-century guide to agriculture, his four years' gardening in Wales had afforded him considerable experience. Finally, the ability to grow their own vegetables and fruit promised a material saving on monthly outgoings.

As ever concerned to be master of his own trade, Patrick bought for 350 francs a practical builder's manual by Pierre Certot, *Pour construire ou réparer vous-même murs et bâtiments: Enseignement manuel en 12 leçons. Construction d'une pièce de cottage, de la pièce principale d'une petite maison rurale, d'une petite porcherie. Conseils divers, etc.* (Paris, 1952). His battered copy is spattered with characteristically self-interrogatory notes, such as '* nonsense: it should be 120k – I beg his pardon; I read kilos for litres', and 'It is easier to pump with a wide pipe than a narrow one.'

Instructed further by friendly neighbours and assisted by Richard, with some old tools and borrowed shears they set to work pruning vines and fruit trees, and clearing the ground on the 'aprons' (terraces). Although their finances remained precarious, the world was becoming a better place. Advance copies of *The Road to Samarcand* arrived, and for just over a fortnight Patrick abandoned writing in order to assist in putting the vineyard in order, after which he established a regime of walking over from the town after breakfast to inspect their little estate, and again after lunch to take part in the labour.

Richard proved a pillar of strength, travelling with my mother to the Port-Vendres rubbish dump to collect stones for the ten terrace ramparts, shifting soil, planting vegetables, and watering. Their dog, whose seventh birthday was celebrated at this time, also felt called upon to play her part: 'Buddug dug up the existing parsley.'

At this juncture Patrick suffered a personal blow. News came from his family that his father, who had long been failing, had died of pneumonia at his home in Ealing. While their relationship had been only intermittently happy, he was unexpectedly moved by this melancholy intimation of mortality. As my mother confided to her diary: 'Poor P., his father died. He went aller et retour to Paris to see his [step]mother & brother [Bernard, known as 'Bun']. R. was very sweet to me.' This scarcely suggests that the melancholy news was malignantly withheld from Richard, as has been conjectured by one amiable critic.

The sorry tidings cannot have come as a total shock. In April 1953 Patrick had been informed (presumably by a member of his family) that his father had suffered a stroke, and in the following month Richard passed on a message from Patrick's sister Nora that 'your father is ill and has been taken to hospital'. Other allusions show that Patrick continued in regular contact with members of his family, several of whom evinced sympathetic interest in Richard.

Nevertheless, it is clear from my mother's words that the final departure of this terrifying figure of Patrick's youth had moved him. In the previous month he had written his short story 'The Thermometer', which described the fear and resentment with which he had viewed his harsh and distant parent as a small boy. There are clear indications that, as late as 1949, he had regarded his father's grim persona as largely responsible for his increasingly paralysing bouts of depression and writer's block.

Equally, it has been seen that he finally shed this inhibiting factor after settling in distant Collioure, where he managed to recover his equipoise. Nor should 'The Thermometer', which I have little doubt provides a realistic picture of his childhood experience, necessarily be regarded as an expression of his continuing feelings for his father, who had for two years languished a helpless invalid. At this stage of his literary career, Patrick continued deeply reliant on personal experience as matter for his fiction.

There were other memories on which he could draw, and death frequently has the effect of diminishing the bad and resurrecting the good. Charles Russ had enthusiastically supported Patrick's early literary endeavours, negotiating their acceptance by publishers. He penned a glowing introduction to his precocious first novel *Caesar*, and Patrick in turn dedicated his next book *Beasts Royal* 'To my father'. During the troubled days of his late adolescence, he found an apparently contented refuge in his father's and step-mother's house at Crowborough in Sussex.

My mother's 'poor Patrick' confirms that Patrick was distressed by the news, since he would not have disguised his true feelings from her. Furthermore, he must unquestionably have been concerned for his stepmother, who had been consistently kind to him as a boy, and of whom he remained extremely fond.

It is important to appreciate Patrick's reaction to this emotional occasion, not least because it has been misinterpreted to his lasting disfavour. A biography of Patrick devotes several pages of specu-lation to the event, the gist of which is that he:

> never introduced his son to his father. He never spoke of his father to Richard, and he did not even tell Richard now that his grand-father had just died. The amazing thing is that a man of O'Brian's insight not only was incapable of repairing his relationship with his father but fostered a similar father–son breach in his own house.[3]

No evidence is cited to support these unpleasant charges, the burden of which is profoundly misleading.* Poverty and distance, coupled with wartime travel conditions, might (we do not know) have precluded Patrick's taking his son to Crowborough before his departure with my mother to Wales in 1945, when Richard

---

* I should emphasize here that Dean King's apparent resentment towards Patrick extends only to his personal character. He is, in marked contrast, both admiring of his literary achievement, and not infrequently perceptive in his judgements of individual books.

was seven. While little communication appears to have passed thereafter between Patrick and his reclusive parent, Patrick's siblings have confirmed to me that Charles Russ rarely corresponded with any of his children or grandchildren.

Although it is not impossible that Richard's grandfather never communicated with him, other members of the family were concerned with the boy's welfare. 'Grandmother Russ' (Patrick's stepmother Zoe) visited Richard and his mother at their flat in Chelsea, as did Uncle Victor and other relatives. Richard unselfconsciously passed on family news from them to his father in France, and it is evident that there were no 'forbidden areas' in family discussions.

Unfortunately, Patrick was unable to travel to England for his father's funeral, almost certainly in consequence of acute lack of funds. At the time of Charles Russ's death, my mother wrote in her diary: 'Despairing thoughts of no money to meet car's lettre de change at end of month.' However, Patrick's brother Bun, a successful lawyer in Canada, had flown over to attend. It seems that Bun (as he certainly did on other occasions) generously paid for Patrick's journey and hotel room in Paris, since my mother's accounts record only trifling expenditure connected with what must have been a costly expedition.

It is frankly incredible to suppose that Patrick kept all this secret from Richard. Why on earth should he have done so? Besides, secrecy would have been all but impossible, closeted as the three of them were in the tiny flat in the rue Arago. The further charge that Patrick 'fostered' a breach with Richard himself will in due course be seen to be demonstrably unfounded, and confirms the extent to which such accusations represent no more than ill-natured conjecture.

A month before news arrived of his ailing father's stroke, Patrick told my mother of an idea which had come to him of writing his 'Chelsea novel'. More and more gripped by the concept, in May she observed 'P. internally working on next novel', and by June 'P. is too deep in new novel to go back.' It seems unlikely that it was coincidence that led Patrick to turn to such an introspective theme at a time when he was becoming aware that the once-daunting parent figure was slipping from the scene. Was he unconsciously afraid that his father's death might deprive him of an identifiable explanation – or even pretext – for his continuing inability to realize his ambition?

In the event Patrick made little attempt to tutor Richard during his long stay at Collioure in 1954. Not only was the boy enthusiastic enough about the subjects he had chosen to apply himself to without any necessity for supervision, but throughout this time his father had become immersed in writing *The Golden Ocean*. My mother, who taught her stepson French on the beach, was delighted to learn that 'R. gets excellent reports on his course.'

With the arrival of warm weather, much time was spent beside the sea, taking long walks, exploring neighbouring places of interest such as the magnificent castle of Salses north of Perpignan, and entertaining a stream of friends. Richard began learning to drive, but sadly expenditure on the purchase of the vineyard eventually compelled the sale of the much-loved *deux chevaux*. On 25 April my mother drove to Perpignan, sold the car for 210,000 francs (about £200), in a rare fit of indulgence enjoyed 'an immense lunch' at the Duchesse de Berri restaurant, and took the train home. As has been seen, she and Patrick went straight to the Azémas, and paid the full price of the vineyard. '*Vous voilà propriétaires défini-tifs*,' declared Madame Azéma. My mother triumphantly inscribed the joyous words in the margin of her diary.

Apart from benefiting from the strip of land to make the family self-sufficient in fruit, vegetables, wine and honey, their plan was to construct a small stone chamber beside the road at the top of the vineyard, where Patrick could write in peace, away from the hurly-burly of the rue Arago. Such cells, known as *casots*, are scattered about the nearby hillsides, being used by cultivators of *vignobles* to store their tools and provide shelter from the burning sun during breaks from cultivation.

In order to accomplish this, it was first necessary to excavate a recess at the top of the rocky slope, which could only be accomplished by means of explosives. After obtaining the requisite permit, Patrick bought a quantity of dynamite and detonators. These being required to be kept separate, the dynamite was kept under Richard's bed. In later life Patrick proved less circumspect. Nearly half a century later, not long after his death, I looked into the high shelf of a cupboard in the narrow passage next to the bedroom where my mother and Patrick slept. There I discovered a brown paper parcel which proved to contain two sticks of dynamite together with a detonator.

No wiser than Patrick, I assumed they posed no danger, since their explosive power must surely have long ago dissipated. Some years later I recounted my discovery to an old school friend, a retired Army officer. He impressed on me that the explosive was undoubtedly *more* dangerous, having become unstable after the space of half a century. This alarmed me, and it was arranged for it to be removed and exploded by the gendarmerie. I still feel qualms when I think of my parents blithely sleeping for decades with their heads three or four yards from a package capable of blowing up the entire house.

Returning to 1955, Patrick and Richard travelled beyond Port-Vendres to Paulilles, where they purchased the explosives. Unfortunately they missed the return train, and trudged the weary miles home, each carrying a 10-kilogram load. Next, holes were prepared with pickaxes and sledgehammers, and faggots gathered to restrict the effect of explosions, after which mining began.

Patrick was convinced he could handle the detonations himself, until a massive explosion discharged a load of rock perilously close to him and Richard. Henceforward he grudgingly employed a pair of burly Catalan miners, Cardonnet and his friend Juan, who completed the work with professional skill. This was the limit of assistance required, and the family's daily toil is recapitulated in detail in Patrick's gardening diary he kept that year. Mining completed, there succeeded the arduous labour of shifting stones out of the recess created. Although he and my mother worked themselves to the bone, the satisfaction at finding themselves at long last working their own land was boundless.

My mother with Buddug at the well

The work continued throughout July, when thundery weather made the heat all but unbearable: 'we drip and pour,' recorded my mother: 'I plunged naked into the basin [by the well] yesterday after stone-shifting.'

Patrick was anxious to keep bees, as he had done successfully in Wales. By June the first hive was installed, and before long they were enjoying their own honey. Over the years complaints arose from inhabitants of the Faubourg below that they were persistently being stung. When suspicion turned to the outskirts of the town, Patrick shifted the hives out of sight onto the flat roof of the house. To a policeman calling to enquire whether they kept bees, he blithely denied the fact. However, this arrangement proving inconvenient as well as risky, in 1965 the hives were reinstalled by arrangement with a neighbour in a vineyard at the foot of the ridge of the Saint Elme above the house.

Eventually, the sad moment came when Richard had to depart. On 29 June he took the train to Paris, whence he sent back cheerful postcards. He left behind farewell presents of sweets and cigarettes, took with him a basket of presents for my mother's parents in Chelsea, and posted parcels to her small nieces and nephew.

Save for the disastrous weeks in Cornwall, which had dampened the spirits of all three, there is every indication that Richard had enjoyed a particularly happy time throughout his long stay. Acquisition of the vineyard provided rewarding occupation, while his correspondence course kept his thoughts almost as busy as they had been with pretty Susan Hodder-Williams. Back in England, he successfully sat the examination at Cardinal Vaughan School. A month later, he wrote to say that he had joined the Royal Navy.

Richard's departure left a tincture of sadness over the little household. Clearly, his service in the Navy would allow him small opportunity to return to Collioure during the two-year spell. Such leave as he would obtain was most likely to be spent with his mother in Chelsea. What neither they nor Richard anticipated was that he would never return. As will be seen in the next chapter, this was not in consequence of any specific decision, but arose from a constant lack of funds, together with Richard's determination to forge a way for himself in the world. Patrick had good reason to be proud of him, but much distress lay in the offing.

A few weeks later Richard had settled contentedly into the service, enjoying the company of his comrades, and nurturing a fresh ambition to become a Fleet Air Arm pilot. Never a frequent letter writer (like many young men), he found himself so preoccupied that his correspondence grew more and more sporadic.

Meanwhile, having for the present lost a 'son' to whom she was devoted, my mother was about to resume relations with her real son, whom she had last encountered as a small boy at her parents' home on the North Devon coast.

Throughout my schooldays there had been no communication between us, save my mother's abortive attempt to resume contact on my sixteenth birthday. After leaving Wellington College in the summer of 1953, I enrolled in the Army as a regular soldier. After completing basic training in the Buffs (my local regiment) at Canterbury, I entered the Royal Military Academy at Sandhurst. By then I had developed an increasingly painful back ailment, which caused me to be invalided out of the Army in the spring of 1954. In June my mother sent me out of the blue a cheque for my nineteenth birthday, and we began exchanging letters.

In August of the following year she invited me to stay at Collioure. My stepmother had never disguised her dislike for me, and my father rarely showed me any affection. The time had come when I resolved to see the mother of whom I retained a bare half-dozen infant memories. That month I joined my father and stepmother for a typically strained holiday in northern Spain, and from there I journeyed at a leisurely rate in Spanish trains to Port Bou on the French Mediterranean frontier, and thence up the coast the three stops to Collioure. It being impossible to predict the precise time of my arrival, my mother remained on tenterhooks for two days. On the 29th she received 'Letter from N., apparently woken up to the foolishness of going back to England before coming here, so he will reach Irun at 8 pm tomorrow en route for Collioure. I called on O[dette]., told her . . . Called on Tante & Marinette & told them: how they stared.'

Two days later: 'Met trains all day, home beautifully neat under usual strain, but no Nikolai.' Finally, on 1 September, I arrived at Collioure and made my way to the rue Arago. I climbed the steep staircase, knocked on the door, and there was my mother. I vividly recall Patrick standing a little behind, in that characteristic attitude which was to become so familiar, smiling with his head a little on one side and hands clasped before him.

My own emotions were confused, my mother being for me effectively a stranger, of whom I retained only the most fleeting of images. However, in consequence of my unhappy relationship with my father and stepmother, I found it exhilarating to find myself at home with contrastedly interesting and affectionate parents. My mother was understandably in raptures:

> I had taught [her pupil] André his English, & P & I were sitting at tea when there was a knock, & it was N. Actually I am writing this on the 12th, being too excited before to write. I did not know how wonderful it would be to have N. again – Lord, Lord, I am so happy with P. & him, and so thankful. I would that R. were here too: he wrote to say that he is an Ordinary Seaman in the R.N., sounding very happy.

With hindsight, I fancy the visit might have gone better had Richard indeed been there, providing companionship of my own age. For the first fortnight all went well. My youthful enthusiasm for history overlapped closely – perhaps too closely – with Patrick's own tastes. I browsed contentedly among his eclectic collection of books, which stood ranged against the wall in boxes he had carefully constructed to house them. We were a stone's throw from the beach, and there was much to excite my passion for the Middle Ages in the ancient town. We travelled by bus to explore Andorra, still a wholly unspoilt medieval principality in the mountains.

By the time of my arrival, the walls and roof of the *casot* were all but completed. Like Richard, I assisted in my turn with the labours, my more modest contribution being attested to this day by a cement buttress beside the door bearing my initials. It was an exciting time for all, and my mother wrote exultantly: 'We already plan next storey.' (I am, incidentally, baffled by a writer's claim that Patrick 'built the hut by hand, something that O'Brian ironically would be ashamed of and very touchy about in later life when he became more established'. In reality, he was immensely proud of the fact that he had contributed so much of the labour, to which he regularly drew visitors' attention when they called throughout the years that followed.)

I learned much about Patrick's writing, and remember being particularly delighted by his good-humoured short story 'The Virtuous Peleg'. His other writings were less to my adolescent taste, which was disinclined to stray beyond current obsessive enthusiasms. Unfortunately, those of his own works which would have appealed to me at the time remained inaccessible, since no copies of his early books published under the name Richard Patrick Russ were to be found in the house. Equally, the robustly exciting boys' books *The Road to Samarcand* and *The Golden Ocean* had yet to be published.

It is hard for me now to be certain how far my faded image of those memorable three weeks remains entirely accurate. However, I do recall that after a week or so I began to find Patrick increasingly didactic and irritable, to an extent which swiftly became all but intolerable. Referring to himself on one occasion as 'a writer who has been compared with Dostoevsky' (which may conceivably have been true), he was openly contemptuous of my preferred reading: old-fashioned favourites such as Harrison Ainsworth, Charles Lever and R.D. Blackmore. Oddly enough, so far as I am aware Patrick had not read the one 'good' writer whose works I also loved – Walter Scott.* However, he possessed the 1839 ten-volume edition of J.G. Lockhart's classic biography of his father-in-law, which on discovering my enthusiasm he presented to me during my stay. Glancing at it now, I suffer once again an acute pang of nostalgia, fancying myself back in the snug little flat at 39, rue Arago.

---

* This could explain why no one in the Aubrey–Maturin novels is represented as even mentioning such immensely popular contemporary works as *The Lay of the Last Minstrel* (1805), *Marmion* (1808), or *The Lady of the Lake* (1810). On the other hand, in a piece written for radio about music aboard ship in Jack Aubrey's day, Patrick observed: 'I have the impression that only a very few of the most advanced [naval officers] would have had anything to say to the early Romantics.'

Today I remain shamefully conscious of the fact that the growing coldness which developed between us during my stay was very far from being Patrick's sole responsibility, as I then believed it to be. I still recall with painful embarrassment how prone I was at the time to faults not uncommon among young men of twenty. Uncompromising political views, assertions of belief as incontrovertible fact, and related failings made me no more tolerable to my elders than many another immature youth awkwardly poised between adolescence and manhood.

On 13 September my parents' old friend and colleague from their wartime service with Political Warfare Executive, the American academic Jack Christopher, came to stay. Lodgings were found for him with the Azémas, while he spent each day with us. A tall, mild-mannered scholar, he was co-author of a recently published two-volume *History of Civilization*. I recall Patrick's humorously condemning the work, on the grounds that it omitted to mention a battle between the O'Tooles and the Danes – a joke repeated from a passage in *The Golden Ocean*, which he had just completed. While Jack was a model of discretion and politeness, Patrick at times used his presence to 'punish' me in a manner he not seldom employed when irritated, deliberately excluding me from conversations, in the course of which he occasionally let fall none too subtle allusions to my deficiencies.

Recollection of this first visit still pains me. Indeed, I was for long inclined to accept almost the entirety of blame for the mutual ill-feeling which increasingly pervaded my stay, until many years later I came to read my mother's diary account of my visit: 'N. left on 19th: when it started going bad I do not remember. Only I do remember being in the middle of it & trying & trying to think of something to bring things back to pleasantness.'

As her normal reaction to any such awkwardness was to support Patrick, right or wrong, I am inclined to infer that she sensed the faults were not all on one side. Long afterwards, I was told by their friend Mary Burkett that Patrick angrily declared on my departure that he would never allow me in the house again! This was the only such occasion of which I am aware when my mother put her foot down, insisting she would continue to see me regardless.

Fortunately the unpleasantness blew over, and the letter I wrote back after my return reads as though all had been warmth and light. Over the decades to come, I confess that Patrick and I continued at times to find each other difficult, or even downright insufferable. But each in his own way was, I believe, conscious that blame lay not all on one side, and such unpleasant clashes were invariably overcome and dismissed – lessening considerably, too, as the years passed by. However, there is no escaping the certainty that, had I not been my mother's son, I would never have been invited to Collioure again.

IV

Voyages of Adventure

From tho yles that I haue spoken of before in the lond of Prestre
Iohn, that ben vnder erthe as to vs that ben o this half, and of other
yles that ben more furthere beyonde, whoso wil pursuen hem for to
comen ayen right to the parties that he cam fro and so enviroune
alle erthe; but what for the yles, what for the see, and for what strong
rowynge, fewe folk assayen for to passen that passage, all be it that
men myghte don it wel that myght ben of power to dresse him
thereto, as I haue seyd you before. And therfore men returnen from
tho yles aboueseyd be other yles costyng fro the lond of Prestre Iohn.

M.C. Seymour (ed.), *Mandeville's Travels* (Oxford, 1967), p. 223

By 1954 Patrick's inspiration appeared to be flagging. Many
authors will recognize the symptoms, when we find him turning
to revisiting old notes and uncompleted earlier ventures. Among
the latter was a novel for boys, which he felt might prove worth
reviving. On 15 December 1945, not long after their arrival in
Wales, he wrote in his journal:

I have just re-read that Samarcand tale. It is better than I had supposed,
and it is well worth finishing. Suffers from want of central plot. It
is hardly more than a series of incidents, more or less probable,
fortuitously connected. M. is typing the rehashed novel. I hope it
may not prove a disappointment, but it was poor stuff to begin with.

This indicates that the manuscript was among those efforts which he wrote in a flurry of creativity just before war broke out. However, the debilitating attack of writer's block which assailed him during their four years' stay in Wales obstructed any further endeavour in that direction, and eventually he found himself unable to progress beyond chapter six.[1]

Under pressure, he tended to look back to those exhilarating pre-war days, when inspiration apparently flowed unhampered by doubts. In November 1952 my mother observed that Patrick was 'thinking of Samarkand'. Once again, nothing came of it, and a further year passed by when 'P. took out Samarcand & looked at it.' This time he experienced a sudden flow of inspiration, and on 26 January 1954 'P. did 2000 words of S.' He was sufficiently pleased with his progress to write next day to his literary agent Naomi Burton at Curtis Brown in New York, enquiring whether Harcourt Brace might take the completed work.

By the beginning of February 1954 the book was well under way, when Naomi responded to my mother with a 'fine misunderstanding about me leaving P[atrick]., & she says send Samarcand to her'. This appeared encouraging, so far as it went, and Patrick raced ahead to the conclusion. Ten days later he came to bed at 1.30 in the morning, 'having finished Samarcand. He could not sleep, & looks so poorly today. S. posted . . .'

They had sent their sole typescript of the text, and an agonizing wait culminated on 24 April with a letter from Naomi containing the dispiriting news that Harcourt Brace was not interested. The precious typescript itself did not return until 6 May, when they forwarded it to Spencer Curtis Brown in London. Their relief and excitement may be imagined when, on 17 June, they learned that the publishers Rupert Hart-Davis were '"very enthusiastic" about dear Samarcand & suggest £100 advance'. On 24 June a contract was signed for 'a Juvenile work by the Proprietor at present entitled "THE ROAD TO SAMARCAND"', with the advance payable in successive tranches of £50 on delivery and £50 on publication.

The money was welcome (though as ever slow to arrive), and high hopes were pinned on the novel's success. However, when *The Road to Samarcand* was published in February 1955, the outcome proved disappointing. Reviews were sparse and varied. While the naval historian Oliver Warner gave it a cautious thumbs up in *Time and Tide*, the *Times Literary Supplement*'s anonymous reviewer tartly derided its conclusion – 'as absurd politically as it is geographically'. The criticism may have been directed against the protagonists' dramatic escape from Tibet in a Russian helicopter, discovered intact in a snowdrift. The story comprises many exciting adventures, of a character familiar to readers of early boys' journals such as *Boys' Own Paper* and *Chums*, wherein a daring English lad, customarily accompanied by an excitable Irishman and laconic Scot, survives a succession of hair's-breadth perils at the hands of sinister foreigners. Patrick's contribution to the latter is an evil Bolshevik agent named Dimitri Mihailovitch, who has his neck deservedly broken by the youthful hero's uncle Sullivan. Evidently Patrick could not resist according this scoundrel my unfortunate father's Christian name and patronymic!

The pre-war genesis of *The Road to Samarcand* represented a throwback to Patrick's earlier success with children's stories. However, while *Caesar* and *Hussein* were delightful original creations, it is hard not to concede that *Samarcand* represents something of a pastiche of the boys' books that he loved during his lonely and imaginative childhood.*

Derrick, the boy hero of *Samarcand*, is an orphan assigned to the custody of his uncle Terry Sullivan, master of the schooner *Wanderer* plying the China Sea. Sullivan and his Scottish companion Ross are the protagonists of Patrick's three immediately preceding

---

* When republication of the novel was suggested by Norton in 1995, Patrick responded: 'As for The Road to Samarcand it had no merit apart from the title, and its republication would do neither of us any good.' This seems a little harsh, and I suspect the schoolboys for whom it was clearly intended would enjoy it today.

published short stories, the third of which ('No Pirates Nowadays') is effectively prefatory to the events recounted in the novel.* The crew includes a comical Chinese cook Li Han, whose exotic English provides a lively source of humour. Together with the eccentric and resourceful archaeologist Professor Ayrton, the friends survive perilous adventures in China and Tibet, battling Chinese warlords and Bolshevik agents, eventually coming through against all odds and acquiring the customary treasure.

I suspect that Patrick's voracious reading as a boy in Willesden Green or his Devonshire preparatory school included *Under the Chinese Dragon: A Tale of Mongolia*, published in 1912. The author, Captain F.S. Brereton, was a prolific creator of rousing boys' adventure stories. The hero of his tale is a brave orphan boy, David, who outwits dangerous Russian anarchists, and afterwards joins Professor Padmore on the China Station. Among the crew is an excitable French cook Alphonse (who must in turn be derivative of the more celebrated comic cook Alphonse in Rider Haggard's *Allan Quatermain*), whose quaint speech is juxtaposed with that of faithful Chinese attendants. They are attacked by pirates, undergo stirring adventures in China and on the Mongolian frontier, and conclude by finding a hoard of valuable objects, including documents which enable David to recover the inheritance of which he had been cheated.

Although well written and fast-moving, *Samarcand* may perhaps be regarded as a retrograde step in Patrick's writing at this time. To do him justice, I think it likely that the novel represented a distillation of half-remembered early reading, rather than overt plagiarism. In any case, much of it, as has been seen, was written at an early stage of his literary evolution. Although it was published at the time in Germany and Sweden, a publisher could not be found in the United States until 2007.

Nevertheless, 1955 was to prove a pivotal year in Patrick's life. It was purely fortuitous that his son Richard's final departure

---

* I am grateful to my friend Terry Zobeck for reminding me of this factor.

coincided with my first arrival in Collioure. As has also been seen, it was in this year that my mother and Patrick established themselves permanently at Collioure, buying the vineyard at Correch d'en Baus, and beginning work on building the *casot* and upper room of the home they would inhabit for the rest of their lives. Finally, January 1955 saw what may be regarded as the inception of Patrick's enduring contribution to world literature.

Here I would emphasize that nothing in the unhappy contretemps arising during my first visit (described in the previous chapter) stinted one of Patrick's most amiable characteristics: his unfailing generosity. I had returned to England laden with presents, ranging from an open razor and leather strop, which I used for years, to a precious copy of *The Trial of James Stewart in Aucharn in Duror of Appin, for the Murder of Colin Campbell, Esq* (Edinburgh, 1753). This is the now rare book which inspired Stevenson's *Kidnapped*. When Patrick bought it in early 1945, he noted in his diary:

> Before reading Catriona [the sequel to Stevenson's *Kidnapped*] I went through James Stewart's trial, which was very good, if somewhat repetitious reading. Unfortunately I chanced to see the result before reading it, which rather spoilt the suspense for the last speeches, but before that it was positively exciting. It is impossible to see it objectively, having read Kidnapped but I am sure I could never have made such a tale of it.

Despite this rueful acknowledgement, while being fortuitously in a position to compare it with its prime source, Patrick's diffident self-criticism provides a premonition of his eventual mastery of one of the most difficult (yet oddly underrated) of literary achievements, the historical novel. In 1945, a month after reading *Catriona*, he had skimmed through:

> Dr Goldsmith's History of Rome [1782], abridged by himself, as a preparation for Gibbon. A poor piece of work, I think, though I

liked 'through desarts filled with serpents of various malignity'. All somewhat Little Arthur-ish.[2] One gets the impression that the Romans were an appallingly bloody-minded lot – true maybe – but what is far worse, and quite false is the impression that they were modern men (insofar as they were men, and not names) acting in an incomprehensible way in a vacuum. It is not history – hardly chronicle. It seems to me that works like the Hammonds' English labourer are worth more than a dozen such works, as far as inculcating an historical sense goes.

This trenchant criticism might be levelled at all too many historical novelists. Indeed, the indications are that it was about this time that Patrick himself came to shed his earlier jejune concept of historical fiction. In January 1940 he had written a melodramatic short story about a crusading knight, John of Bellesme, which owes more to the romantic novels of high adventure written by the Sussex novelist Jeffery Farnol than to anything actually occurring during the Middle Ages. Although Patrick preserved the manuscript, he must surely have been relieved in later years that it was never published.[3]

His only other transitory attempt at historical fiction appears to have been written about the same time. Published in *The Last Pool*, 'The Trap' is much inferior to its fellow tales set in Patrick's own day. Although as ever well written, its tale of a daring youth who fares forth to poach in the grounds of a tyrannical squire is too reminiscent of the stock characters and standard predicaments of juvenile fiction to carry much conviction.[4]

Following a flurry of creativity over the momentous winter of 1939–40, it seems that Patrick's wartime employment, first as an ambulance driver in the Blitz, then as an operative with Political Warfare Executive, effectively diverted him from writing. Finding himself, for the first time in his life, unexpectedly in possession of a settled income, he bought many books, chiefly in the second-hand shops of Cecil Court. These he read and clearly absorbed, but it was only as the War drew inexorably towards its close over the winter of 1944–45 that his authorial ambition became reawakened.

The fact that there is frustratingly little documentation for this period of his literary life is in itself suggestive. He began keeping a pocket diary on 1 January 1945, and the care with which he preserved his diaries thereafter makes it unlikely that earlier copies have perished. In it, as well as in memorandum books compiled about the same time, Patrick began entering comments on his reading, together with suggestions for books he contemplated writing. The indications are that, although the war years provided him with a period of respite from creative work, they were also a time of protracted parturition. His perceptive condemnation, on the one hand, of Goldsmith's trite Roman history, and on the other his unqualified praise for Stevenson's masterpiece *Kidnapped*, indicate his dawning understanding of the realities of historiography, together with its glamorous offspring, the historical novel.

Mention of Stevenson's two great books leads me incidentally to wonder whether Patrick may not also have been unconsciously influenced by the Scottish author's creation of paired contrasted characters (David Balfour and Allan Breck), their attitudes reflecting disparate political and social aspects of the age: an antithesis which at the same time enriches a memorable friendship.

Again, I wonder whether his new-found propensity for imbuing his narrative with humour – grotesque and farcical, light-hearted and ironical, at times cheerfully vulgar – had lain submerged beneath a long-held conviction that *adult* literature represented an essentially serious business. His natural sense of humour, ironical and exuberant, took long to emerge in his work.* At times I put this belated development down to the influence of Somerset Maugham, whom Patrick like many of his contemporaries rated

---

* Occasionally Patrick's humour has sailed over a reader's head. His ludicrous use of a passage in the *Spectator* of 1710 for the preface to *Lying in the Sun* has been gravely interpreted as 'a caustic jab at an innocent public' (King, *Patrick O'Brian*, p. 183).

high in the literary scale. But there can surely be little doubt that the enduring precarious state of his finances played its part in producing an entrenched state of gloom.

After *Hussein*, only his sparkling short stories 'The Green Creature' and 'The Virtuous Peleg' fully revealed Patrick's propensity for laughter in court. However, an observant follower of his literary career would have noted how his anthology *A Book of Voyages* (1947) reproduced specimens of choice rococo passages which afforded him perceptible delight.

As was mentioned in the last chapter, the theme Patrick selected for his fresh venture was Commodore Anson's celebrated voyage around the globe in 1740–44. One reason for this choice was almost certainly the fact that his library was well equipped for the purpose. He had first grown familiar with the story from the concise account included in Beatson's six-volume *Naval and Military Memoirs of Great Britain*, which he bought before the War.[5] Subsequently he acquired the Reverend Richard Walter's account of Anson's voyage, published in 1762, together with its accompanying (now rare) handsome quarto volume of maps and plates.[6]

For the social, literary and political history of the time he profited greatly from a present fortuitously given by my mother. In February 1945, 'M[ary]. very civilly gave me the Gentleman's Magazine 1743-4–5. Masses of information, both solid and (what is more in some ways) ephemeral. Handsome panelled calf. Vilely printed – hard to realise that any verse can be good in such a dress.'*

---

* The care with which Patrick perused these volumes is shown by a slip inserted at p. 165 of vol. xv, where he notes references to subsequent promotions of Lieut. Justinian Nutt and the Rev. Richard Walter, who had participated in Anson's expedition. In February 1945 Patrick read a biography of Anson, which did not enthuse him: 'Life of Lord Anson, by Captain Anson Kirker c. 1910. Horribly disconnected. It is not enough to be a naval officer and a descendant to be a good biographer.'

In the following month Patrick read the latest Hornblower novel, on which he commented in his diary:

> Forester's The Commodore is, I think, the first new novel I have ever bought. It seems much more extravagant than paying a guinea for, say, the learned job. It's a good tale, but not as satisfying as the other Hornblower stories. Smacks a little of formula and wants design. Also, it has not a great deal of meat, or if it has, a greater length is required to give it body.

Patrick could not have dreamed that he would one day write his own novel *The Commodore*, which I imagine most readers would concur entirely avoids the faults he ascribes to Forester's work.

Patrick's criticism of Hornblower seems not unjust. However, as his comment on Stevenson's *Catriona* indicates, he did not at the time feel sufficiently confident of his own abilities to attempt a 'meatier' historical novel. It was not until nearly a decade later that inspiration struck quite suddenly. On 4 July 1954 my mother wrote in her diary: 'I typed fourth story,* & P. thought of Anson juvenile.' It is intriguing to note that Patrick remained caught up by the notion that exciting adventure stories were exclusively appropriate to a youthful readership, despite his having appreciated *Kidnapped* and *Catriona*, which enthral readers of any age.

The remainder of the year was taken up with house-hunting, concluding with the disastrous visit to Cornwall in October and November recounted in the previous chapter. By the New Year of 1955, however, Patrick with a flash of clarity grasped the way forward. It was on the cold evening of 19 January that:

> P. wrote boy & thermometer tale & I got so depressed. But today he showed me wonderful notes & pieces of Stag⁷ & synopsis of

---

* For the published collection *Lying in the Sun*.

Anson which are quite beautiful & very exciting . . . P. wrote to Phebe Snow who answered that yes, Hart-D. might advance on synopsis of Anson.

Rupert Hart-Davis had already proved happy enough with *The Road to Samarcand* to agree a contract for 'the next Boy's book to be written by the PROPRIETOR following "THE ROAD TO SAMARCAND"'.

The 'boy & thermometer tale' to which my mother referred is the indignant autobiographical account of Patrick's childhood terror of his generally grim, authoritarian father. 'The Stag at Bay' seems also likely to reflect some aspect of Patrick's psychological breakthrough. The story concerns a self-righteous, priggish author unwittingly cuckolded by his young wife.

The protagonist Edwin is portrayed as suffering from an attack of writer's block. He has been commissioned to write a piece on marriage for a women's magazine:

> The article was proving much more difficult than he had expected. It was not for lack of raw material . . . and it was not for lack of experience or thought. Marriage was a subject that he had thought about a great deal, deeply, and he had supposed that the profound part of the article would be the easiest: yet although he was in the right mood, costive and solemn, the words would not form themselves into an orderly and harmonious procession. They remained in his head, swirling in grand but indeterminate shapes; or if they had any concrete existence at all it was in the form of scrappy notes, odd words jotted down . . .

Meanwhile, as he struggles with an article intended to define the high ideals of marriage amid the squalid débris of a neglected flat, Edwin's wife has engaged in an affair with an elderly playboy cousin – not from love or lust, but merely 'to know, to really know, what adultery was like': 'She sloughed the anxiously contriving housewife, dropped ten years from her appearance, and responded to his cheerful obscenity with an assured impudence that no longer shocked her inner mind.'

The moral of the tale is clear. Life is overtaking the drudgery of the laborious author, who writes with ponderous difficulty about an institution which has in his case atrophied, while his amoral young wife instinctively grasps at fleeting pleasure before it becomes too late. The writer's block is plainly Patrick's own. The 'pink, virginal and inviting' young wife was doubtless suggested by the ever-present figure of my mother, while the customary pristine neatness of the flat in the rue Arago happened at the time of writing to be uncharacteristically chaotic, owing to the need to dry and iron quantities of dirty clothes brought back from their extended trip to Cornwall. As my mother acknowledged, 'place looks like inferior old clothes shop'. The fictional wife's flighty enjoyment of a sensual affair possibly suggests a metaphor for Patrick's dawning realization that successful writing should be *fun*. Certainly nothing suggests that Patrick ever suspected – still less, had reason to suspect – infidelity on my mother's part.

It is nevertheless a measure of Patrick's commitment to the ideology of high-mindedness that he regarded rollicking adventure stories as essentially immature: 'Anson juvenile', as he termed it. This derogation may indeed have proved fortunate, enabling him to cast away inhibition, writing from the heart. His cheerful tentative opening passages have survived in a notebook:

At half-past eight on the drizzling morning of Tuesday May the 22nd, 1739, the uproar outside the rectory of Ballynasaggart reached its height; for at that moment Peter . . .

The Rev. Mr Septimus O'Toole behaved extremely well in the troubles of 1715; he was also a very considerable scholar – his commentary upon the Stoic philosophers of the Lower Empire had given him . . .

When the troubles of 1715 broke out upon the land, the Rev.

Mr Octavius Murphy published a little small pamphlet entitled The Idea of an Expedient King in favour of the Hanoverian succession; and this did more for him, in the matter of worldly success, than the three octavo volumes of his Commentary upon the Stoic Philosophers or the square quarto of his Pelagius Refuted . . .

All three drafts were discarded, possibly because Patrick came to realize that in reality the Jacobite risings of 1715 exerted little impact on repressed Ireland. He further toyed with the idea of 'Funny lower deck character who spells with a wee [substitution of w for v] and patronises Irish person on a/c of he don't speak English proper or at least not wery.' Eventually, he decided to open *in medias res*, with Peter Palafox riding away to Cork and high adventure across the glimmering billows of the western sea. Almost at once the writing began to flow with wonderful facility. As my mother happily observed, 'P. wrote beautiful beginning for *Golden Ocean* after days of pain.'

On 22 January 1955 she posted a synopsis of the novel to Curtis Brown. A week later: 'Things go well. Rupert will . . . give advance & contract for The Golden Ocean.' So inviting was the encouragement from all sides, that progress continued unchecked. As my mother excitedly commented on 2 April, 'P. is back at work since 31st: Golden Ocean is perfectly splendid.' The book was completed in July, and posted to England with high hopes. On the 27th my mother returned from the doctor after tearing a muscle when working on the foundations of the new house. 'P. met me, Oh Joy bringing kind letter about Golden Ocean from Ruth Simon (H[art-] D[avis]). She thinks too that it is quite lovely.'

Changes to chapter I were proposed by the publisher (did the original version begin with one of the trial opening paragraphs?). Patrick was happy with the suggestions: 'P. & I worked on G. Ocean, P. cutting & substituting, I reading for a list of sea-terms. It is such a LOVELY book,' enthused my mother. By the end of October, 'P. finished beautiful diagram of Centurion for Ocean, I typed list [of sea-terms] he made.' Both diagram and sea-terms drew extensively on Patrick's copy of Dr Burney's revised edition of Falconer's *Universal Dictionary of the Marine*.[8] It was not until 1971 that he obtained a copy of the original (1769) edition, which was more apt for the chronological setting of his novels. Burney, however, served him well – so much so, that the spine came clean away from overuse, and as has been seen was eventually rebacked by Patrick in vellum in 1989.

The Golden Ocean is indeed a wonderfully happy book: lively, good-humoured, exciting, and convincing as a vision of a past era to an extent which only a tiny modicum of historical novels ever attains. At last Patrick had succeeded in weaning himself off gloomy and introspective themes, and thrown himself into a creation which displayed to marvellous effect his natural genius. Like Dumas recounting the grandiose excesses of Porthos, he subsequently recalled that 'I wrote the tale in little more than a month [between *Testimonies* and *Richard Temple*], laughing most of the time. It made no great impression, nor did I expect it to do so; but it had pleasant consequences.'[9]

And all composed in that little crooked nest above the rue Arago, permeated by the sounds and smells of the south!

Reviews were generally laudatory, the most perceptive being that of the academic T.J. Binyon in the *Times Literary Supplement*, who described it as: 'wholly absorbing and wonderfully funny, like the best children's books it can be appreciated fully only by adults'.*

In 1970 Patrick confided to his diary that 'I am childishly attached to the book', and seven years later he described it to his editor Richard Ollard as 'a book I look back upon with affection – it was such fun to write, & it came flowing out in a month or

---

* Looking back in 1992, Patrick remarked that 'what I wanted to write was a book for readers of no particular age (after all, one can delight in <u>David Copperfield</u> or <u>Kidnapped</u> at 12 or 72)'.

two'. As has been seen, 'a month or two' represents no more than pardonable exaggeration, for it is clear that his pen did indeed run happily away with him.

There followed a German contract for the novel, for which he received £40 advance and royalties. Much more rewarding was its acceptance by the John Day Company in America, whose contract provided for advances totalling $750 and royalties.

1956 proved a generally quiet and unproductive year. None of the family came to stay. I was preoccupied during the summer with preparations for my entrance examination to Trinity College Dublin, while Richard was absent from home beginning his national service in the Royal Navy. However, in January 1957 exciting news reached the little house in Collioure, which had by now been accorded the Catalan name Correch d'en Baus. On the back of an envelope containing one of her stepson Richard's letters, my mother has written: 'R is at Toulon! Patrick goes in eight days (on the first of Feb.) to see him, and perhaps I go also. Do I take my beautiful robe with me please?'

Unfortunately, nothing more is recorded of this event, though the happy expedition was presumably undertaken. On the other side of the envelope my mother wrote further: 'Hurray Hurray Hurray', and jotted down train times for travel between Collioure and Toulon. Relations could not have been closer between Richard, his father, and his stepmother, despite their enforced separation.

Throughout this time building work continued on the first-floor living room and kitchen above the *casot*, which among other benefits would provide room for Richard and me when we came to stay. Although Patrick concealed himself when writing in the *casot*, in order to avoid being distracted by the exuberant discourse of the workmen above, it was unfortunately impossible to escape them altogether, as this indignant note shows:

May 8th or 9th 1957. I am sitting here – a dark, coldish spitting late afternoon – waiting for the Men to go, so that I do not have to go up & say anything myself. Allez, bon soir. A demain – à demain, eh!

And this stupid situation (I would rather go back now for tea. I would rather have gone back some time ago) this silly indeterminate stuffed state comes from old Oliva's ill-temper this morning which (its effect continuing) makes it impossible for me to be there watching him crépir [roughcasting] & occasionally helping without truckling.

I had thought of making some observations about all this but they are rather muddled & it really does not seem worth while. I am terrified of the English, French & American income tax people: less the people than the Thing, of which they are the righteous & I am sure complacent powerful hands. Blind but percipient tentacles, slow, slow, ridiculous; & then terribly fast & efficient.

If the English do not send the rebate we are destroyed: as it is can we ever pay for all this ghastly house? It engulfs material: and now it no longer belongs to me at all: I am, at times & on sufferance, a dull kind of labourer, while the capable ones – Oliva's rough capability is depressing, very – while they walk about & spit & piss on the walls.

Now the silly, silly little man is peering about outside. I pretend not to see him. He is looking for the saw. I still do not see him. Enlightened self interest. He was not looking for the saw but the marteline & the marteau. Just how silly can one get?

Fortunately Patrick's elder brother Bun in Canada came to their aid with a generous 'loan' (seemingly intended as a gift) of several hundred dollars. Despite this, Patrick underwent bouts of restlessness and discontent. In November my mother wrote sadly to Richard, saying that his father and Willy Mucha had taken to sitting up late, complaining about their common lack of inspiration.

Fortunately, it was shortly after this that Patrick's literary career revived. In due course, the commercial success and gratifying critical acclaim of *The Golden Ocean* led to a request for a sequel.

Patrick breakfasting on the balcony of the *casot* in more contented mood

On 30 December 1957 Rupert Hart-Davis signed a contract with Patrick for a novel to be entitled 'THE VOYAGE OF THE WAGER'. As with its predecessor, the stipulation was for £100 advance, half to be paid on signature and half on delivery.

In the course of researching Anson's voyage for *The Golden Ocean*, Patrick had come across the extraordinary plight of the crew of a ship of the fleet, which he had found no occasion to mention in the novel. On 14 May 1741 the storeship *Wager* was wrecked on the coast of Chile, a terrible storm preventing the crew's rescue. The survivors underwent appalling hardships during their protracted struggle for survival in that desolate region. Eventually, a remnant managed to reach Valparaiso, whence they sailed to England, arriving in February 1745. This fortunate group included Midshipman (later Admiral) John Byron, grandfather of the poet. In 1768 he published a vivid account of their ordeal, which drew great attention then and thereafter.

While Peter Palafox, engaging Irish hero of *The Golden Ocean*, reappears in the tale, Patrick introduced two fresh protagonists. These are the dashing historical Jack Byron himself, and his fictional comrade Tobias Barrow. Tobias is the adopted son of a wealthy squire, Mr Elwes, a neighbour of the Chaworth family, with whom Jack and his sister live. While Jack and Tobias become fast friends, as a malevolent Whig Mr Elwes was regarded with disfavour by the well-born Tory Chaworths.

Mr Elwes had acquired his riches from successful practice as a surgeon and dubious investment in South Sea stock. He adopted Tobias, with the dual intent of bringing him up as his apprentice, and indulging a hobbyhorse project of educating him to become a marvel of omniscience. As the system involved almost unceasing daily toil and 'the most severe whippings', it did not prove a happy home for the boy. Moreover, while he achieved a considerable hoard of knowledge, principally in Latin, Greek and the physical sciences, in addition to an encyclopaedic understanding of natural history, in other respects he failed his oppressive patron's expectations dismally. Nor was his situation likely to be improved by the imminent arrival of a stepmother, 'an odious woman with a dark red face', who 'hated Tobias at first sight'. Faced with this distasteful prospect, he attaches himself to Jack, accompanying him to serve with Anson's squadron in the great expedition to harry the Spaniards.

Tobias is an eccentric solitary, a boy-man with an obsession for collecting and studying exotic creatures: 'he had spent all his days in that strange, dark, unsocial house, with odd, unsatisfactory servants perpetually coming and going.' Hopelessly absent-minded and inattentive to appearances, he all but falls overboard on boarding ship.

It is not hard to detect the original of Tobias. As a boy, Patrick led a lonely and unloved existence in various grim and silent homes. There he was subjected to the harsh whims, including it seems severe beatings, of his cold and selfish father – likewise an eccentric medical man – who engaged in desultory attempts to instruct his young son. Again, the extent to which Mr Elwes's Whig principles antagonize his better-bred Tory neighbours recalls Dr Russ's attachment to the Liberal Party, which Patrick came to believe accounted for their isolation and supposed ostracism at Lewes by the local Tory nobility and gentry.*

Dreamy and impractical, Tobias sought refuge in varied fields of esoteric learning – just as had Patrick, during long periods of abandonment to his own devices. While Patrick was fortunate to avoid having an unpleasant stepmother, he was regularly tyrannized by a succession of largely ill-qualified governesses. Again, at sea Tobias resents the rough pranks of his youthful messmates in the cockpit of the *Wager*. His ordeal most likely echoed the stiff and awkward Patrick's own unhappy experience during his brief service as a cadet in the RAF, later (as I have suggested) recalled in his short story 'The Happy Despatch'.[10]

Towards the end of the book, Jack and Tobias receive an invitation to dine with the Spanish admiral at Valparaiso, when Jack expresses dismay at the tattered condition of their clothing. At this point Patrick uncharacteristically adds his own comment: 'Even in this century, when clothes mean comparatively little, it is very disagreeable to find oneself in an ordinary jacket when everybody else is in tails . . .'

Some ten years had passed since Patrick underwent just such a mortifying experience, when, invited to dinner by Clough Williams-Ellis at the manor house in Cwm Croesor, he found himself the sole guest not wearing evening dress. Neither time nor distance could eradicate his embarrassment.

Many of these characteristics are correspondingly shared by Tobias with Stephen Maturin, the former being an unmistakable prototype of the latter. Jack Byron's description of his friend is revealing:

---

* Patrick's niece Gwen has suggested to me that 'Elwes' may be an anagram of 'Lewes', which certainly seems possible.

He is a little cove, ugly, with light green eyes and a pale face: wears an
old black coat and sad-coloured breeches . . . He has an odd fashion
of staring about him and jerking his head, and you might think he was
simple; but he is a very learned cove indeed, and must be civilly used.

While identification of some of the sources of Patrick's creation
is of interest to a biographer, it can in no way detract from his
achievement. *The Unknown Shore* (the title replacing *The Voyage
of the Wager*) is a worthy successor to its predecessor, recounted
with comparable vivacity, humour, and historical verisimilitude.
Patrick's imaginative creation flowed with remarkable speed. His
pocket diary shows that he completed chapter 3 within twenty-four
hours, the next four chapters within nine days, and the remaining
seven over a further fortnight.

Turning the page back a little, it was in the autumn of 1956
that I went up to Trinity College Dublin, where I was to enjoy
some of the happiest years of my life. They swiftly resulted in a
love of Ireland generally, and Celtic studies in particular. It was
curious chance that led both Patrick and me, neither of whom
possessed a drop of Irish blood, independently to succumb to the
same infatuation. In the summer vacation of 1957 I returned for
my second visit to Collioure, when the holiday there proved altogether different from my first disastrous visit two years earlier.

An upper room had by now been added to the *casot*, in which
we enjoyed what were often hilariously convivial evenings.
Generous provision of their good *vin du pays* from the previous
year's vendange, together with a decanter of Patrick's favourite
cognac or Banyuls, played their part in the jollification.

Patrick was particularly interested in my news from Trinity
College Dublin, where I had established an elegant retreat in my
spacious Georgian two-room suite on the first floor of number 2,
Front Square. Recitations of poetry, conducted by each in turn,
provided part of our festive entertainment, following my mother's
delicious suppers. I remember how we particularly relished the

With my mother in 1957 (Willy Mucha's portrait above)

American boys' book *Rival Bicyclists* by Captain Ralph Bonehill, published in Chicago in 1897 (where Patrick picked it up, I do not know). The climax of the tale lay in the young hero's outspeeding his unscrupulous rival, who bore the unusual name of Lemuel Akers. The author's constant emphasis on 'spurting', as practised by the speeding protagonists of the tale, evoked much lubricious mirth. Years later, when announcing his arrival in England, Patrick sent me a telegram signed simply 'Lemuel Akers'.

Life appeared sparklingly full of promise at this time. In the following summer of 1958 I brought my girlfriend of university days to stay for a month. Patrick and my mother were greatly taken with beautiful auburn-haired Susan Gregory, whom I described in advance as my 'dauntless female companion' (a description demurely applied to Maid Marian, in one of my favourite Robin Hood comic books). Her good humour, gentle tact and lively enthusiasm won them over completely. One day Patrick watched her through his binoculars returning along

Susan Gregory

the *passerelle* below the castle, where a dashing young Frenchman tried to engage her in conversation. Patrick much admired the gracious way in which she deflected his advances. On another occasion, when I was unwell, he took her to see a corrida at the bullring beside the railway station (now sadly demolished). No bulls were killed at Collioure bullfights, and what Patrick particularly enjoyed were what he described to me as 'spectacular exhibitions of cowardice' evinced by local youths seeking to impress their girlfriends, by descending into the arena to snatch a flower placed between the agile creature's horns.* At a critical moment, demure Sue delighted Patrick by rising from her seat and, placing her fingers in her mouth, emitting a piercing whistle of encouragement.

Later that year Patrick travelled to visit me in Dublin (his first visit since 1937), where he entertained us to a fine lobster dinner at the Shelbourne Hotel. At his departure he slipped me a generous £10 to take Sue out to dinner tête-à-tête. Visits to Ireland always tended to bring out his youthful optimism and engaging good humour.

---

* I have to say that on those occasions when I attended the spectacle, the youths appeared to me remarkably courageous.

V

In the Doldrums

My Melancholy increases, and every Hour threatens me with some
Return of my Distemper; nay, I think I may rather say that I have
it on me . . . Dear *Pope*, what a barren Soil (to me so) have I been
striving to produce something out of! . . . I find myself in such a
great Confusion and Depression of Spirits, that I have not Strength
enough even to make my Will . . .

> John Gay to Alexander Pope, October 1727
> (C. F. Burgess (ed.), *The Letters of John Gay*
> (Oxford, 1966), pp. 65–6)

While my mother was married to my father she threw herself
with enthusiasm into the world of Russian culture. She was
happy to see my sister and me baptized into the Orthodox Church,
attempted (with some success) to speak and write in Russian, and
enthusiastically supported my father's determination to ensure that
I grow up bilingual. Despite his continuing resentment towards
my father, Patrick shared this fascination, and my mother and he
each seized the opportunity to visit the then mysterious 'forbidden
territory' beyond the Iron Curtain. In the spring of 1959 my mother
paid her first visit, when Patrick instructed her: 'You will have to
bring something growing from Russia, of course, as well as bags
of the holy earth.'

On 10 April she travelled first to visit her family in England.

As was all too often the case, I fear her stay with my grandparents and me in Kent proved not altogether happy, as Patrick noted that: 'She has never mentioned Nikolai, horde [her brother Binkie's children], holiday.'

On the other hand, she managed to see Richard, who as ever displayed much affection to his stepmother. 'Darling P,' she wrote:

> I had such a happy time with our dear Richard. He is so affectionate & confidential & handsome & properly dressed & short-haired. He is as good as gold. We spent five hours talking without a pause, & he told me lots about the Navy (they still have the 18 inch space for each hammock as in Nelson's time) & frightened me terribly by darting me about swiftly in his car & took me to a coffee-bar. He has not changed, except that he has fined down immensely, & his voice is a deep <u>man's</u> voice. He hopes to have a month for Collioure this year. Lord, I love our Richard. We talked so lovingly of you P., & agreed that we are vastly proud of being your family.

Patrick was delighted with the news.

A fortnight later my mother embarked in a state of high excitement on the Russian ship *Baltika*, sending Patrick the first of a succession of long letters describing her adventure. Although conditions on board were fairly spartan, she swiftly came to love the attendants and sailors for their kindness and good manners. She was proud, too, of the extent to which she found herself able to communicate with them in their own language. 'Lord, what an adventure,' she reported. 'How unbearably loquacious shall I not be on my return.'

In Copenhagen she was shown the sights by their old friends Charles and Mary de Salis, Charles being now attached to the embassy. As with all O'Brian expeditions, the purpose was as much to acquire useful information as for enjoyment. So far as the latter was concerned, my mother found it hard without her soul-companion. From Helsinki she wrote plaintively:

P dear, it seems many years since I left home. I shall be shy. Lard, how happy I shall be if I ever do get home again which seems improbable in this utterly foreign & utterly unaccustomed life of mine. Glorious though it is, it will not happen again. In future I shall never desert Mr. O'Brian.*

However, she was so entranced by the romance of finding herself for the first time in Russia, that she declared: 'We should live in St P. I think. It is so inciting.' During a trip on the Moskva, she piously dropped a piece of paper into the river bearing in Cyrillic letters the names of 'Patrick and Mary O'Brian and Buddug'. Despite her romantic enthusiasm, however, she was not blind to relentlessly grim manifestations of 'Big Brother' attendant on the dourly regulated May Day festivities, combined with many signs of lamentable poverty. Compensation was provided by attendance at a crowded Easter service, the piety of whose congregation was patent and touching.

For his part, Patrick kept her au fait with detailed accounts of domestic affairs in Collioure, and conveyed encouraging news of the imminent publication of *The Unknown Shore* in the United States. At home he had resumed work on *Richard Temple*.

My mother's Russian voyage comprised the longest period of separation from her beloved Patrick during their long life together, and brought about a uniquely voluminous correspondence. It comprises a succession of deeply affectionate love letters, faithfully preserved by Patrick in my mother's original STEWART BROWN TRAVEL CO. folder. On rereading them now they appear at first glance hard to associate with a couple who had lived together for twenty years, and been married more than ten. But as an old friend of mine, John Yeowell, remarked on reading the first volume of this biography: 'it is as much a great love story as the life of a great writer.'

---

* In fact they could not have afforded to travel together on so expensive a journey, while Patrick was besides immersed in refashioning his novel.

Patrick and my mother standing proudly outside their home

My mother's eventual happy return to the little house in the vineyards was marked by the arrival the week before of the first copies of the British edition of *The Unknown Shore*. Patrick was gratified by its appearance: 'The Unknown Shore came. It is not a very pretty book, but perfectly acceptable and it has such pleasant things about [The Golden] Ocean on its back – Times Lit Sup etc – which is opportune, welcome, encouraging.'

Sadly, this time reviews were to prove sparse and generally unenthusiastic. It is hard to see why, given the chorus of approval which greeted *The Golden Ocean*. As Patrick conceded, it lacks something of the élan and inventiveness of its predecessor, but surely not to the extent of being unworthy of praise. Despite Patrick's initial high hopes, it was not to be published in the USA until 1995.

This lack of interest must undoubtedly have dampened his spirits at the time, and conceivably accounts for his own less than enthusiastic reaction on rereading the book nearly forty years later. The new edition had been proposed by Norton in the United States, leading him to undertake a fresh assessment:

> I finished the Shore (not without pleasure). It owes much more to the historical Jack B[yron] than I had remembered – indeed some important events (Cheap being marooned) were quite forgotten, perhaps because I did not invent them. It is not a v good book, but not discreditable either – perhaps rather dull.

Nevertheless, at the time one admirer's lavish praise for the book gave Patrick particular pleasure. From his mother's home in Chelsea (to which he had returned, following completion of his national service), his son Richard wrote:

> Thank you a thousand times for my copy of the 'Unknown Shore', secretly I have been hoping for such a copy for a long time. Now I am immensely pleased and delighted with it; I have read it twice already and shall do so again for the book improves the more one reads it.

In his long letter, Richard volunteered practical advice about buying a boat, which my parents apparently contemplated at the time. He went on to enthuse about his new car 'Chloe', in which he had overtaken a Morris Minor speeding at 50 miles an hour, and explained that he was presently engaged in a six-year course for a degree in engineering.

By 1959 Patrick's initially promising venture into seafaring fiction had ground to a disappointingly abrupt halt. Nearly ten years were to pass before circumstances would cause it to be unexpectedly resumed. Meanwhile, my mother's Russian expedition had cost a formidable (for the penurious couple) £42 9s. However, as Patrick toiled intermittently at *Richard Temple*, she was able to supplement their income by continuing her tutoring of young people in the town for their examinations. One of these was Danielle Banyuls, a teenage girl requiring tuition in English literature in order to enter the University of Montpellier. She was taught by Patrick and my mother twice a week for two hours each afternoon. The course required mastery of three difficult texts, including Carlyle's *Sartor Resartus*. Their teaching proved as ever highly successful, and Danielle gained her place. Describing this to me in later years, she was astonished to learn that Patrick himself had never attended university, having found his exposition of the texts more profound even than that of her university lecturers.

At the outset of 1960 Patrick's career appeared to be undergoing another fretful period in the doldrums. Financially, *The Unknown Shore* had proved only moderately successful, and for the present it seemed that he had exhausted the congenial theme of naval fiction. The only work he had on the stocks was *Richard Temple*, but that was still proving hedged about with difficulties. It was as long before as March 1953 that he first conceived the idea of the 'Chelsea novel'. Behind that in turn lay his story 'William Temple', written in 1951. The autobiographical element in the latter version was slight, reflecting little more than Patrick's disappointment at having been unable to engage in active service with the French Resistance. Although the story is exciting and vividly written, it was never published – possibly on account of its awkward length, being too long for a story and too short for a novel.

It does not appear that any manuscript or typescript trace of Patrick's writing of *Richard Temple* has survived. This is unfortunate from the point of view of a biographer, since the story is profoundly concerned with his own evolution as an individual and an artist. Its writing involved much agony of spirit, which makes the persistence with which he pursued the task against all odds the more impressive. I think it safe to assume that the fresh work was autobiographical from the start: a conclusion supported *inter alia* by the substitution of his own first name Richard for the

'William' of the earlier version. The completed work is imbued with a deep sense of shame at perceived inadequacies of his former self: his lack of formal education, his early abject poverty and social inadequacy, the failure of his first marriage, and his jejune attempts to achieve success as an artist (in the story he becomes a painter, rather than author).

It is equally clear that the dogged persistence with which Patrick conducted his long and frequently agonizing struggle to complete the work, in face of his own underlying revulsion at the prospect, combined yet further with discouraging responses from publishers, reflected the intensely purgative function of his task. The story is told in the form of Richard's reflections on his earlier life while incarcerated in German-occupied France. His recurrent physical humiliations at the hands of brutal Nazi interrogators add to his sense of worthlessness. Despite this, he doggedly manages to withhold the information sought by his captors, and the story ends with Richard's liberation by the French Resistance, and his dazzled emergence into a bright new world.

Fortunately, my mother's diaries provide revealing insights into the novel's prolonged and arduous gestation. It was in March 1953 that Patrick hit on the concept of the 'Chelsea novel', after which he spent three months 'internally working'. It was not until the end of June that 'P. wrote those fatefull words "Chapter I", & began the book.' Three days later he 'showed me perhaps ¾ of Chapter I of Temple novel: immensely impressed'. Although Patrick greatly valued my mother's judgement, within a few days: 'P. says he must find him another occupation: writing makes him feel too ill. He is looking terribly pale. Book has reached about 4000 words.'

Ten days later, Patrick himself recorded that he 'Worked spasmodically towards the end of Ch. 1. Is it any good? Even if it is (which I doubt) it is little more than a kind of preface.' The struggle continued over the next two months, when in desperation he decided to send the completed chapter I, together with a synopsis of the planned whole, to his literary agent in the States. It must have seemed a forlorn hope, until a week later my mother delightedly recorded: 'Wonderful post: Naomi to say dear H[arcourt].B[race]. will advance $750 for new novel (to be called Richard Temple): $500 when contract is signed, further $250 on completion of the book.'

The contract was signed and the initial payment received . . . but the momentary excitement became as swiftly abated. 'Walked after lunch round Cap Dorat; poor P. in despair when he thinks of <u>having</u> to write R. Temple.' The ups and downs continued day after day: 'P. steadily working now, morning & afternoon'; 'Home, to find P. in despair: worry about Chap. II of book . . . After tea I read what is done of Chap. II'; 'Poor P. worries about his size as a writer.' Eventually, though, Patrick got into his stride, and on 16 January 1954 'P. finished typing R. Temple this evening.' The typescript was despatched to America, with what high hopes may be imagined. By June they were summarily dashed: 'Such bad news of Temple: poor P. HB want a book of short stories instead, & Collins put a ps on Naomi's letter with advice to offer Temple elsewhere.'

The cloud hanging over the rue Arago was partially lifted by a generous proposal forwarded by Patrick's literary agent from the American publisher: 'C[urtis]B[rown] to say Harcourt scraps Temple contract & will produce $500 advance on short stories.' Yet the fact remained that all his hard work and mental torment had seemingly gone for nothing. *Richard Temple*, which in some ways meant more to Patrick than any other of his work, was it seemed doomed to remain stillborn.

Yet its necessity to Patrick's inner well-being would not go away. Five years later, in March 1959, 'I begin Temple again.' This time, at any rate at first, it seemed to go smoothly. Within two months he had completed four chapters. His agent liked the work, which she passed in its truncated form to his current American publisher, John Day. Now hopes were raised higher than on the previous occasion, as Day evidently exchanged contracts and paid an advance.* However, disappointment loomed yet again:

> John Day have done the dirty, as I rather expected they would. A man who begins a sentence with too, meaning also, is capable of anything. Naomi is very indignant, won't repay the advance and thinks that Little, Brown might buy . . . It undermines my confidence a little . . .

Although Patrick momentarily toyed with the idea of resuming work on *Richard Temple*, it seemed that his career as a novelist had come to a premature close. By good fortune, it was at this very time that an alternative source of literary income presented itself. Nine years earlier his agent Spencer Curtis Brown had approached the publisher Fred Warburg with the suggestion that Patrick was well equipped to undertake translation work from French into English. Nothing came of the proposal at the time, but now out of the blue Weidenfeld and Nicolson invited Patrick to provide a translation of Jacques Soustelle's *La vie quotidienne des Aztèques à la veille de la conquête espagnole*.

A biographer asserts that Patrick disliked 'the inglorious and underpaid labour of translating'. In reality, nothing could be further from the truth on either count. Apart from being happy with the increasingly regular income it provided, as a consummate craftsman he was fascinated by the fine-tuned skills required to transform subtle nuances of writing from one language to another, producing a text in fluent English, while at the same time preserving the full intent of the original. He noted in June 1978: 'A man at Chatto would like to commission a book on the Merchant Adventurers: well, maybe, though I should prefer a quiet good translation in a way.'

---

* This is clear from what Patrick wrote at the time, but my mother did not preserve the aborted contract.

He was gratified when reviewers singled him out for praise as a translator, and told me once that Harrap had invited him to provide corrections or additions, where he came across them, to their authoritative French dictionary.

Nor (in Patrick's case at least) was translating at all 'underpaid'. In 1958 he received a £200 advance for *The Unknown Shore* (then known as *The Voyage of the Wager*), half on signature and half on delivery. In 1960 he received comfortably more than that for translating Soustelle's book, and two years later an increased rate of payment per thousand words gained him £913 for translating *A History of the USSR* by Louis Aragon.

Patrick completed the Soustelle translation in May 1960. It was his promptness of delivery as well as his professional skill that drew publishers to engage his services on a regular basis, thus providing my parents for the first time with a reliable regular income. Eventually, between 1960 and 1988 he would complete thirty-two translations.[1] By the time of the last, Jean Lacouture's hefty two-volume biography of de Gaulle (of which Patrick translated the first), he was being paid £32 for every thousand words. With much satisfaction he was enabled to devote himself to working alongside my mother in their garden and vineyard throughout the remainder of May and June.

At this point it is necessary for me to digress a little to obtrude a few words about myself. On leaving school in 1953, I had entered the Army for what was intended to be my career as a regular soldier. After basic training at Wemyss Barracks in Canterbury, I arrived in the New Year at the Royal Military Academy at Sandhurst. Hitherto I had been extremely fit, having represented Wellington at athletics, and on leaving spent the summer of 1953 digging drains on mountainsides for the Forestry Commission at Glendoll in the Scottish Highlands. However, as the winter of 1953–54 drew on, I began to suffer increasingly from back pain. This was eventually diagnosed as spondylolisthesis, an ailment arising from a vertebra's moving out of place, causing acute pain from pressure on adjacent nerves. Military and civil medical experts found my problem to be congenital, subsequently exacerbated by the pressures of military service.

Invalided out of Sandhurst, within a year I unexpectedly gained a recovery which lasted until the beginning of 1960, when I was in my fourth year of study at Trinity College Dublin. The pain had returned with increasing severity, until it was decided that my condition required an urgent operation. In July, when the summer term was concluded, I was admitted to the National Orthopaedic Hospital in Great Portland Street.

My mother, deeply concerned about my operation, at once arranged to fly to London to be by my side. On 7 July I underwent a protracted operation which she described immediately afterwards:

> One vertebra [had] slipped outwards; pain is caused by the stretching of the tissues (nothing to do with the bone). They take a piece of his hip & use it to continue the straight line of his backbone: they remove no back bone & neither do they move it. Danger? Of the piece of hip cracking.

Recovered from the anaesthetic, I was lowered onto a bed of wet plaster which swiftly dried to provide a cast in which I lay immobile for nine or ten weeks. The pain in my back continued excruciating by day and night, when the slightest movement on my part caused the nerves at the base of my spine to contract. The distress was exacerbated by permanently bleeding sores in my buttocks caused by unrelenting pressure from the edges of the plaster cast. However, this was in some ways a pioneering operation, and in view of its eventual success I certainly cannot complain.

On receiving news of the operation, Patrick at once flew to join us in London. Care of the house and garden at Collioure was entrusted to Danielle Banyuls, since it was clear that I would not be released from hospital for some considerable time. Throughout this period they visited me every day for as long as was permitted, their cheerful and solicitous company affording me great consolation. Patrick brought select books – only P.G. Wodehouse had to be banished, as even a suppressed chuckle darted a hideous spasm through my spine.

My parents' financial situation at this time was far from satisfactory. For the present Patrick had not been offered another translation, nor was any novel under commission. They managed to find a refuge above an antique shop at 8, Jubilee Place in Chelsea. The owner was Edward Marno, a neighbour of my grandparents during their time at The Cottage in Upper Cheyne Row, the house where my parents before them had lived during the War. In return for Marno's hospitality, my mother helped in the shop.

This enforced stay clearly aroused in Patrick and my mother strong feelings of nostalgia for their dramatic wartime years in Chelsea. Almost every street evoked some memory of those exciting days of yesteryear, when the borough was nightly racked by fearful explosions. Not only this, but they now saw much of Richard, who in the latter days of the War had been a cheerful schoolboy living at his mother's house around the corner in the King's Road. So strong were their feelings, that my parents for a time contemplated abandoning Collioure and returning to live in London.

Among buildings they passed frequently at this time was the Chelsea Registry Office, where they were married in 1945. Both being religiously inclined, they had never been satisfied with a purely civil ceremony.* My mother, who was I believe baptized into the Russian Orthodox Church after her marriage to my father, remained strongly attached to our faith, into which I was duly baptized in 1935. Now she and Patrick took the opportunity to attend services at the Russian émigré church in Emperor's Gate,

---

* '. . . Diana Villiers was what he [Maturin] usually called her in his own mind, for their marriage aboard a man-of-war, with never a priest in sight, had convinced him no more than it had convinced her' (Patrick O'Brian, *The Letter of Marque* (London: Collins, 1988), p. 121).

just off Gloucester Road. There they came to revere Father George Sheremetiev mentioned in an earlier chapter.

Before long my parents decided to be married by Father George. A handful of old friends attended the ceremony, among them Barbara Puckridge and her son James, who as a boy had stayed with my parents in Wales, where he became friends with Patrick's son Richard. Barbara had driven ambulances in Chelsea with my mother and Patrick during the Blitz, which further evoked nostalgic memories of those dramatic days. As James later told me:

> When they were over [in London], my mother would nearly always ask us [James and his wife Stina] round . . . so we kept contact with them through my mother . . . I suppose we must have been having a drink together, and they said 'we're going to get married' – frightful excitement, in the Russian Orthodox Church, and they mentioned this wonderful guy, the Russian priest . . . and they asked us if we would like to come along to the wedding, and we said 'yes, we'd love to come on to the wedding'. There were no children there! And then Patrick said: 'would you like to be a crown-bearer?' I don't know who the other one was . . . There were five of us there: Edward Marno, your parents, my mother, Stina and I – there might have been one other couple, if that. I can't remember anybody else there . . .

James remembered Marno (as do I) as 'tall, gaunt, dark-haired . . . All I know, he was a roaring poof . . . his manner of speech, and Patrick and Mary had told us that he was a poof beforehand, so that we wouldn't be surprised, I think. But they were very friendly at that stage, and Edward gave the wedding party . . . in the shop, just off King's Road.' Eventually Marno's flamboyant homosexuality came to irritate Patrick, and he and my mother moved for a time to the flat of my great-aunt Maroussia in Kensington. However, my mother, whose attitude was more complaisant, continued to help in Marno's shop when not visiting me in hospital. This minor contre-

Patrick and my mother on the day of their wedding

temps was later introduced by Patrick into his fiction, when a dead convict named Edward Marno on board the *Leopard* is committed by Jack Aubrey to the deep – his death having originated in part from 'a vicious habit of body'.[2]

My parents' enforced stay in London, and Chelsea in particular, powerfully influenced Patrick's literary career at this critical juncture. Their close association with Barbara Puckridge inevitably resulted in much nostalgic recollection of heady wartime days, just as their belated marriage brought back to mind the passionate romance which blossomed at the time.* Although he had returned to London two years after the Blitz, Patrick's son Richard shared many of these fond memories. The familiar streets and buildings in and around King's Road, which had changed little since 1945 (save for rebuilding on bomb sites), served to revive many a long-forgotten incident.

Patrick had wrestled to an extent unparalleled in the creation of his other books with the text of his novel *Richard Temple*. First, there was the novella 'William Temple', written in 1951, the manuscript of which I possess. Unfortunately almost nothing is known of the content of the first two revived versions which followed, which I imagine Patrick destroyed. The description 'Chelsea novel' indicates the period of Patrick's impoverished pre-war life when married to his first wife Elizabeth, while the switch in Christian names from 'William' to 'Richard' (Patrick's first name, and his son's) confirms the increased autobiographical aspect of the book. At the same time, a note jotted down in April 1959 indicates that the French Resistance theme still played a significant part in the story: 'in the morning I had what I thought quite a good idea for Temple – to inject pieces of the present (Germans blowing up bridges in their retreat, miliciens killing hostages) by way of counterpoint and a perhaps rather obvious irony.'†

What I suspect happened is this. 'William Temple' is broadly a vigorous action hero, while the two abortive 'Richard Temple' versions accord him considerably more depth of character by allotting him an earlier seedy existence in Chelsea, from which he is eventually emancipated by his subsequent paramilitary exploits. It was when he came to live in Chelsea in the late summer and

---

* Terry Zobeck informs me that 'several years ago I bid on a proof copy of *Richard Temple* inscribed by Patrick to Barbara. I lost. It is one of my great bibliophile regrets that I didn't bid more, which is only exasperated now that I know how close the association was between them.'

† I imagine Patrick had in mind the clean break between Temple's unsatisfactory past and imminent transformation.

autumn of 1960 that he hit on the idea of depicting in fictional form his earlier unsatisfactory life as an immature youth. No longer an heroic adventurer, Richard Temple is largely Patrick himself, whose real or fancied faults are laid bare with brutal candour. The result is an intensely introspective work, vividly depicted with much of Patrick's best descriptive prose.*

For me the picture the novel provides is almost painfully evocative. In 1945 my grandparents took over the lease of Patrick's and my mother's house in Upper Cheyne Row, where I regularly stayed as a schoolboy and young man. For me *Richard Temple* conjures up that vanished world as does no other of which I am aware. That this version represents a radical improvement on its predecessors is suggested by the contrasted alacrity with which Macmillan moved to commission the work.

Following my release from hospital, Patrick (followed shortly afterwards by my mother) returned for a few weeks to Collioure to harvest their grapes and set the garden in order for the winter. By the time of their return to London in September, Patrick had all but completed the novel, and on 23 February 1961 the decade-long project came to fruition with a contract that included a welcome £150 advance. My parents' selfless decision to remain beside me throughout my ordeal meant that everything now hung on a financial shoestring. As my mother had reported to Patrick: 'Poor little shop: I have sold nothing, but nothing, except that one lamp for £6·10·0. And a bill has come in for the half-yearly rates.'

However, willing assistance was at hand: 'Dear Richard came in yesterday, & wafted me home in his van. He gets £13 a week: it is not much when he has to pay for van out of it. He is a kind pet. He is coming tonight to do some delivering with me.'

* Terry Zobeck reminds me that, very unusually, 'there is barely any dialogue at all in the novel'. Could this derive from his drawing to an exceptional extent on personal memory? Also worth consideration is the fact that meditation and dreams frequently contain little or no dialogue.

Not only had Patrick given me his unfailing support, but their prolonged stay had brought him closer to his own son.

In view of the book's overridingly autobiographical nature, I have examined this aspect in some detail in the first volume of my biography, which covers Patrick's pre-war years in Chelsea. So important was its purgative function to Patrick, that I suspect the self-indictment to be considerably harsher than deserved. Both Patrick's first wife Elizabeth and my mother feature recognizably in the narrative, but disappointingly I can find no record of my mother's estimate of the final version of the novel. All in all, there can be little doubt that it served to rid Patrick of painful feelings of guilt which had troubled him over the years.* When he and my mother reappear as Stephen Maturin and Diana Villiers in the Aubrey–Maturin series, the picture is altogether sunnier.

When my parents returned to London in late September 1960 they rented a comfortable ground-floor flat at 6, Chesham Street in Mayfair until June of the following year. It seems that they continued temporarily beguiled by the notion of living in London permanently. Among their motives would, I assume, have been a desire to be close to their respective children, Richard and me.

Both Patrick and my mother remained in many respects very youthful in outlook, and among other things proved wonderfully understanding – and helpful – during crises attendant on my own youthful affairs of the heart. As has been seen, they were very fond of my longstanding university girlfriend Susan Gregory, whom they had come to know in both Collioure and Ireland. To my distress

---

* While Dean King is mistaken over the dating and circumstances of Patrick's writing of *Richard Temple*, I would endorse his judgement on the work: 'Dealing with many issues that were clearly of personal relevance, *Richard Temple* appears to have been a cathartic work for O'Brian. Literarily, at least, it seems to a great extent to have emptied him of bile and severe introspection and, perhaps for a time, of motivation. He did not publish another novel for seven years. Nor did he ever write another set in the twentieth century' (*Patrick O'Brian: A Life Revealed* (London, 2000), p. 195).

Sue had proved uncharacteristically unsympathetic during my operation, visiting me only once in hospital. Furthermore, her course at Trinity now required her to spend the Michaelmas term studying at the Sorbonne in Paris. With the heightened emotions of youth, I became at first resentful of her inexplicably cool attitude, then reconciled by a brief *tendresse* for her pretty friend Alison Wingfield, until I found myself finally unable to continue without my 'dauntless female companion' of three years' standing. At every stage of this impassioned drama my parents* provided wonderful support, happy to console and gently advise. Eventually I wrote an appeal to Sue in Paris, asking whether we might not make it up.

Her favourable reply transported me into an Elysium of joy, and I vividly recall that day in January 1961 when she arrived from Paris on the doorstep at Chesham Street. Her beautiful auburn hair had been tastefully dressed by a Parisian *coiffeuse*, and after being warmly welcomed with a drink by Patrick and my mother, they tactfully withdrew. Sue and I then joined a couple of Trinity friends in a nearby pub, where the pact of amity was delightfully restored.

Sue and I remained as close as might be for the remaining two terms of our four years together at Trinity. I also continued fascinated (or maybe obsessed) by historical problems connected with Dark Age Britain in general, and the elusive figure of King Arthur in particular. I had been engaged throughout my time in Dublin in preparation of a massive book on the latter, which my mother kindly typed and retyped in addition to her arduous work for Patrick. (Fortunately for my scholarly reputation, this premature work never saw the light of publication.) Patrick was highly amused when Sue once privately confessed at Collioure that she felt my one failing to be that I was 'rather too keen on ye olde folks'.

In May I was invited, unusually for a student, by the Irish

---

* Although I always addressed him as 'Patrick', his diaries show that he regarded me as his son, and subsequently my children as his grandchildren.

Historical Society to give a lecture on early Irish history. My mother flew to Dublin to attend the event. This was her first and only visit to Ireland, and she sent excited postcards to Patrick describing her delight when Sue drove us to Tara, Clonmacnoise, and other evocative sites. Patrick's virtual adoption of Ireland as his spiritual home (a passion independently espoused by me since my arrival at TCD in 1956) served to redouble my mother's raptures.

'Votre pays est merveilleux,' she exclaimed on a card showing the round tower at Ardmore in County Waterford. To those obsessed by the curious desire to prove (in order to disprove!) Patrick's fanciful intimations of Irish birth, this might appear to provide strong confirmation of his deception. In fact, a moment's reflection indicates that it is the diametrical opposite. My mother, who was naturally more familiar than any beyond his own family with the authentic circumstances of Patrick's birth and parentage, is scarcely likely to have absurdly endorsed a claim both knew to be false, in a message shared by themselves alone. What she unmistakably intended was that 'Your *spiritual* (or *adopted*) homeland is wonderful' – an assertion which might at the time equally have been ascribed to me, enthused as I was by comparably besotted Hibernophilia.

For the rest of the year Patrick was engrossed in the now remunerative work of translation, creative writing having for the present deserted his muse. He spent the summer months completing a history of the Massacre of St Bartholomew by Philippe Erlanger, followed after the vendange by another book in the 'Daily Life' series, this time Henri Daniel-Rops, *Daily Life in the Time of Jesus*. Both books were published in the following year, receiving acclamation that confirmed not only Patrick's skill as translator, but his reliability as a punctilious deliverer.

VI

A Family Man

'Never mind, my Vasia. True, our son has broken away from us: he is like a falcon – he has flown here, he has flown there, as he wished: but you and I, like lichen in a fallen tree, are still side by side, we are not parted . . . And I shall ever be the same to you, as you will be the same to me.'

Ivan Turgenev, *Fathers and Sons*, ch. xxi

Richard Temple, the last of Patrick's three largely autobiographical novels, was followed by several years' abandonment of creative writing. Although its melodramatic plot was of his own devising, the setting of *Three Bear Witness* (1952) in almost every other respect represents a vivid recreation of his more and more frustrated existence in North Wales in the late 1940s. *The Catalans* (1953), although a generally sunnier work, depicted with equal perception and exquisite Mediterranean colouring the Collioure he and my mother had come to know and love over the following decade. The book also drew extensively on aspects of Patrick's troubled family relationships, which continued to arouse in him disturbing sensations of shame and guilt.

Now *Richard Temple* had been completed after some ten years' gestation, being of all his books that which he experienced most difficulty in writing. It is also the most profoundly autobiographical. It was rare for him to acknowledge his faults to others (even,

I suspect, to my mother), so that a literary approach provided his sole effective means of confronting and exorcizing what he considered unpalatable aspects of his past.

The novel is couched in the form of a protracted confession, throughout which Temple excoriates his former 'silly' and 'weak' self. All this takes place within the symbolic confines of a Nazi prison in France, where he is constantly bullied and tortured by his gaolers. Finally, his internal confession completed, he is freed by forces of the French Resistance:

> . . . with his blind white face straining towards the door he cried out, 'What? What is it?'
> 'Come out, come on out,' they bawled. 'This is the liberation.'

With hindsight, Patrick's two brilliant historical novels *The Golden Ocean* (1956) and its sequel *The Unknown Shore* (1959) appear as bright precursors of his greatest literary achievement. However, while he continued to express pride in both works, at the time Patrick does not appear to have accorded them the esteem they deserved. They were commissioned and marketed as children's books, a category which he had come to regard with some embarrassment as a phase in his literary life he was now concerned to supersede. Only later does it appear that he came fully to accept that the best children's literature transcends the genre. Besides, he had exhausted the possibilities provided by Anson's great voyage in the 1740s, to which his naval researches had largely been confined.

Patrick was certainly not alone among talented authors in being regularly tormented by fears that he had 'written himself out'. Fortunately, this relatively infertile phase of his career coincided with continuing commissions to undertake translations. He prided himself on rendering the original French of his translations into fluent English, while adhering as closely as possible to the style and approach of the original. He was deeply conscientious in his approach, being also a stickler for meeting contractual deadlines. In consequence, he became widely regarded as a model translator. Reviewing his translation of Soustelle's *Daily Life of the Aztecs*, Geoffrey Gorer wrote in the *Observer*: 'The translation, by Patrick O'Brian, is impeccable, so fluent that for pages at a time one forgets that this is a translation.'

Calculating ahead how many words in a working day were required to achieve this goal, he would settle down contentedly to his daily task.* Since publishers could be confident of receiving texts of a high standard promptly delivered, he rarely found himself short of a commission. This also ensured that he was well paid for his labours. With translation providing a respectably predictable income, he was relieved of much destructive worry. Thus, in 1963 Patrick earned £20 1s 4d in royalties from his fiction – and £1,765 19s 3d from translations!

Such royalties were well earned. Working rigorously to a structured daily programme, between 1960 and 1966 Patrick completed no fewer than fifteen translations. Some, like Louis Aragon's *A History of the USSR*, a turgid apologia for Soviet Communism, must have appeared wearisome indeed. Its companion volume, André Maurois's *From the New Freedom to the New Frontier*, a history of the United States over the same period, although in contrast accurate and enlightening, required much additional research, chiefly arising from the need to track down the original texts of passages translated by the author from English into French.

---

* Dean King claims that Patrick's approach 'often' included 'starting to translate about a third of the way into the book to catch the author's language and rhythm in stride. Later he went back to the beginning' (*Patrick O'Brian: A Life Revealed* (London, 2000), p. 191). So convoluted an approach would be very unlike Patrick's *modus operandi*, and it is clear from extensive references to translation work in his diaries and correspondence (as well as his conversations with me) that it is doubtful he ever adopted this curious approach in reality.

I saw much of Patrick and my mother at this time. On completion of my honours degree in Modern History and Political Theory at Trinity in the autumn of 1961, I entered upon an in some ways unproductive period of my life. Initially I returned to live with my ever-generous grandparents in Somerset, where I had obtained a post at nearby Millfield School. I naively anticipated spending all my spare time completing my magnum opus on King Arthur, a solitary scholar surrounded by an already substantial library. A brief romance with another attractive Trinity graduate had led me still more misguidedly to break off my longstanding love affair with Susan Gregory. Not long after, I belatedly came to realize that the life of an eremitical scholar was not for me, and I abruptly abandoned Millfield for London, where many of my university friends were living. On my journey I called at Sue's home to try to mend bridges with her. To my dismay I found that she had had enough of my shilly-shallying, and sweetly but firmly explained that all was over. The rift proved permanent: she married a more reliable spouse, bore two children – and was eventually tragically drowned while deep-sea diving in the West Indies.* Although I experienced a couple of further fairly serious (if unfortunate) romances during my bachelor years, I could not get over my longing for darling Sue. It was not until I met and married my equally beautiful and clever wife Georgina a decade later that I eventually found happiness.

My kind grandparents were too far removed in their generation to be able to advise and console me in intimate matters of the heart, and it was to Patrick and my mother that I regularly turned for comfort and advice during this troubled period. I remember once, when telephoning my mother with news of my latest daunting setback, she laughed and said: 'You always ring us when you're in trouble!' When I began muttering an apology, she interrupted: 'But of course we like that!' I think it was partly because their

---

* On 14 March 1979 Patrick noted in his diary: 'A pleasant letter from Nikolai, but with the quite shocking news of Sue's death.'

own romance remained fresh in their hearts, that they were able to empathize so closely with lovelorn youth.

In January 1962 they drove for a holiday in the Ariège, unusually without (so far as I know) any accompanying literary purpose. Returned to Collioure, the most exciting event of that year was the long-hoped-for acquisition of the strip of land adjacent to their southern boundary. As my mother wrote at the end of the year:

> I only started the accounts again from September inclusive. We had a very rich, very spending year, and spent a thousand pounds on new property. We end the year with practically nothing at all in France and minus one penny in England, though for three weeks now Hart-Davis has owed for the Tazieff translation.[1]

In June 1963 Patrick came to London for a short stay, when he treated me to a splendid lunch at Prunier's, then the best fish restaurant in London. He was in high spirits, and I remember his delight on overhearing a middle-aged businessman inform his young female companion: 'My wife doesn't understand me.' Hitherto, he explained, he had assumed that this line only occurred in bad novels and music-hall patter.

That summer Patrick's elder brother Bun brought his wife Fifi and two children Elizabeth and Charles from their home in Canada for a four-month tour of Europe. Elizabeth later recalled the occasion for me:

> My first meeting with Uncle Pat in 1963 was arranged by my Dad. He and I and my birth mother and brother were travelling through England and parts of Europe that summer. I remember meeting Dad's [and Patrick's] stepmother Zoe at her home (in Ealing – what a place! Small but unbelievably cluttered. You had to wind your way through piles of books and newspapers and such like to get about). She, by then, was quite deaf and rather feeble minded, altho very sweet and kind. She gave me an antique coin which, sadly, I

lost. When we reached Paris Dad and I stayed in a hotel and Pat came up alone to meet and visit with us, have a meal and a 'walk about'. The photo in Dad's book was taken during that visit altho King got the year wrong. Mind you, I don't mind being mistaken for 10 years younger now! I believe Pat stayed in the same hotel as us but, sorry, I don't remember the name of it. I do remember him being very formal and polite, dressed nicely, but friendly and smiling and genuinely glad to see my Dad and to meet me. I was very impressed with his fluent French. My mother and brother had gone on to Italy and were not present.

Bun and Patrick in Paris

I went to stay at Collioure for four weeks in August and September. I was accompanied by my old friend Jonah Barrington, whose family had since childhood provided me with a happy welcoming home at Morwenstowe on the rocky coast of north Cornwall. Jonah had in due course joined me at Trinity, but, finding the academic workload somewhat of an imposition, and the pubs of Grafton Street and its environs too much of an attraction, he was politely invited by the University to pursue a career elsewhere. Although not a very assiduous student, Jonah was in every other respect lively and intelligent, his principal forte lying strongly in sport.

After pleasant days spent at his parents' home in Cornwall, Jonah and I made our way to my parents' home in the south of France. We hitchhiked all the way, our passage to Southampton being facilitated by an accommodating lorry-driver. On being informed of the country of our destination, he remained silent for a few miles, then mused laconically: 'I been there once – excitable lot.' Our days were spent in swimming and walking, while Patrick joined us for energetic tennis matches under a baking sun in the court set in the dry moat of the Château Royal. Casting an expert eye, Jonah was admiring of Patrick's natural skill and energy at the game.

Jonah and I fulfilled (to our own satisfaction at least) the singularly pointless ambition of becoming the two brownest men in Collioure. On the beach he fell passionately in love with curvaceous Christine, a charming young friend whom my parents had tutored before her admission to university. Unfortunately Jonah could speak no French, but like many of his compatriots was persuaded that speaking loudly and emphatically in English with a foreign accent facilitated understanding. Once, desperate to communicate, he held up a pebble on the beach, explaining ponderously: 'In Eengleesh we call thees "stone".' To which the Sorbonne student responded brightly: 'Yes – in Old English it is declined *stan, stanes, stanum*'! On another occasion Jonah nearly floated off the beach, when Christine with true French insouciance confided her fear lest the lapping waves remove the top half of her decidedly skimpy bikini.

A nocturnal mishap provided further cause for mirth in our little household. Whether it was the wine or the grapes, Jonah awoke one night in the small hours with an acute stomach problem. Not wishing to disturb anyone's slumbers, he made his way swiftly out of the house and up the lane, where at a respectable distance from the house he squatted down to do his business. Next moment, however, a car came winding unexpectedly up the hill, whose headlights became swiftly focused on the bare buttocks of the naked Jonah. All he could do was flee up the hill, but the drystone walls on either side obliged him to race ahead for a hundred yards or so before he found a gap through which he could scramble into protective darkness. The car was that of an amiable neighbour, who lived in the only house above us. A couple of evenings later we were invited up for drinks, after which Jonah was much teased by Patrick, who wondered whether General Sobestre had recognized whose backside it was that his headlights had so embarrassingly illumined.

Sadly, romance with Christine failed to materialize, and Jonah and I returned to England. With my parents I had often discussed my ambition to become a professional historian, and with characteristic generosity Patrick now offered to fund an academic course. I was accordingly enrolled to study for a doctorate at London University, where he paid the fees.

That November Patrick followed in my mother's footsteps with a visit to Russia, that mighty and mysterious country which fascinated them both. Violent seasickness marred his faring forth, but on arrival he was delighted by almost everything he saw. At the Novodevichy Convent in Moscow: 'I set up candles (pure bee's wax, surely) for M[ary], N[ikolai], aunts M & L [my great-aunts Maroussia and Lily], & with a general intention towards F[athe]r George: though with an uneasy feeling that they might not be pleased.'*

Like my mother four years earlier, Patrick was intensely moved by the Russian Orthodox service, this time at the Nikolsky Cathedral in St Petersburg (as he firmly termed the city):

---

* Presumably on account of his presence in the Soviet Union, which Aunt Maroussia scornfully termed 'Bolshevia'.

Enormous crowd, mostly middle-aged & elderly women, but with many young & men. Several carried babies, mostly over on the corner of the trancept ready to be brought forward at the end (perhaps for some particular blessing). Very moving service – candles passing up continually – chanting by congregation – my neighbour in tears. Ancient beautiful white-bearded priest.

In the Hermitage Patrick particularly admired the Cézannes and Matisses: 'a Matisse Collioure was almost the first thing I saw – oh for reproductions'.*

Throughout Patrick's visit to Russia my mother remained in England, visiting our family in the West Country, and comforting me in my latest *crise d'amour*. It was not only in matters of the heart that she and Patrick retained their empathy for the young. For a year I had lived in a large Kensington flat at 34, Redcliffe Gardens with close friends from Trinity. After a cheerfully irresponsible year, this admirable arrangement concluded in the summer of 1962, when two of my closest friends departed: David Robertshaw to be married, Jo Xuereb to lecture at the University of Benghazi. After a glorious summer spent once again with Jonah in Cornwall and Collioure, I returned to settle in London.

It was when I eventually acquired a place of my own that there arose a grave crisis. The tenancy of the Redcliffe Gardens flat had passed to another set of Trinity graduates. My old flatmate Jo Xuereb had bequeathed me his bed, which I now sallied forth to recover. Accompanying me was Patrick, who offered to help me move it. However, the current owner-occupier, George Green, asserted that Jo had assigned the bed to him. We Trinity men being then a sadly pugnacious lot, I threatened to knock him down if he did not give way. 'If you touch me, I'll call the police!' he exclaimed. Patrick interposed scornfully: 'I never thought to hear

---

* My account of Patrick's 1963 Russian trip draws on the fifty-page journal he kept throughout his visit.

a Trinity man decline a fight!' He himself appeared ready for a fracas. However, George held a trump card in the form of my precious library, which I had left behind locked in a large cupboard. It could not readily be removed, nor could I risk any depredations on the books. In the end my parents paid for a new bed.

In the spring of the following year, 1964, Patrick suffered a personal blow, which I feel certain affected him for the remainder of his life. Ever fearful of personal betrayal, a dread amounting at times almost to paranoia, was now fulfilled in a particularly wounding and (as will be shown) undeserved manner. In the first volume of this biography I devoted considerable space to describing Patrick's disturbed relationship with Richard. Although Richard, by his own admission, was as a boy inclined to be idle, unresponsive, and even on occasion impertinent, it is equally manifest that Patrick was ill-equipped by nature to play the role of instructor to a growing child. Many faults, real or fancied, which he condemned in Richard when a boy, unconsciously reflected his own acknowledged inadequacies at the same age.

It is hard not to believe that it was awareness of his own infantile failings that impelled Patrick's desire to 'purge' similar lapses he perceived in Richard. I had frequent opportunity to observe how Patrick, who was often tense and apprehensive in company, was particularly susceptible to a fear of those qualities of spontaneity and unpredictability which are so marked a feature of childhood. Furthermore, in his own infancy Patrick gained solace by inwardly mocking those harsh adult figures – his father, together with a succession of inept and unsympathetic governesses – by whom his solitary existence was governed. With hindsight, I suspect that, with this experience in mind, he in turn may have come to harbour fears of being covertly ridiculed by children.*

---

* Patrick's aversion to spoiled children (or what he regarded as such) was shared *inter alios* by Jane Austen and Lord Byron (cf. *Sense and Sensibility*, chs 7, 21; Leslie A. Marchand, *Byron: A Biography* (New York, 1957), pp. 1037–8).

Patrick O'Brian: A Very Private Life

One or two reviewers of my previous volume, belonging to a very different generation, expressed horror at Patrick's occasional recourse to caning as punishment for his son during his well-intentioned but misguided attempt to act as his teacher in Wales. However, there is no suggestion that this exceeded what was normal practice in almost all British schools and many families at the time.* Moreover, it will be recalled that such chastisement occurred uniquely during the relatively brief period when Patrick undertook the experiment of removing Richard from school in order to teach him at home. As Richard himself recalled:

From my point of view he was teaching me mainly useless things. Arithmetic was OK. English was fine. But I couldn't see the point of Latin. He was a pretty rigorous teacher. He didn't like mistakes. If I made one, I would be told to put it right, and if I went on getting it wrong, he would cane me, but not heavily – don't run away with the idea that it was sadistic.

I got on much better with Mary, my father's second wife. She was a fine person – good fun, pleasant, an excellent cook and, on top of that, extremely good-looking. In the holidays I would go back to my mother, who was now living in Chelsea, and my boxer dog, Sian. I missed my mother terribly when I was away from her. The dog used to sleep on my bed, and I missed the dog hugely, too.

This went on for two years. I was living in a very remote area, and I didn't mix with other children, but a little boy out in the countryside can find his own entertainment. I didn't feel that I was missing out on a more conventional upbringing because I had no yardstick. Children are very resilient.[2]

---

* I was regularly beaten at school, and occasionally at home by my father. Although I naturally disliked the experience, like many of my contemporaries I accepted corporal punishment as an unpleasant fact of life in a generally pretty spartan existence.

Prevented from seeing her own son between the ages of five and twenty, my mother did indeed become deeply attached to Richard, and he to her. Without doubt, her presence considerably ameliorated what, it must be stressed, was a brief period of strained childhood relationship with his father.

However this may be, relations between father and son undoubtedly changed radically when Richard arrived at adolescence. He was twelve when my parents left England for Collioure in 1949, following which his affinity with his father became quite suddenly warm and unstrained. For this it is not necessary to rely solely on consistently amicable sentiments expressed later on in their extensive correspondence – a medium which may after all be suspected of containing an element of pious artificiality. Richard's eagerness to visit Collioure for regular holidays, culminating in his stay for nearly a year during 1954 and 1955, suffices to show that the family relationship had become established on an affectionate basis by both parties.

After his departure in the summer of 1955 Richard never returned to Collioure. The severance arose from purely practical considerations. His service in the Royal Navy, combined with lack of funds and the arduous and low-paid employment in the years that followed, meant that several years passed by without any opportunity arising for another family reunion at Collioure.

Despite this, relations continued cordial during ensuing years. Richard's letters are full of the excitement of serving in warships with the Mediterranean fleet, together with eager questions concerning Collioure and glowing expressions of pride in the continuing success of his father's publications. As has already been seen, there was almost certainly at least one joyous reunion in January 1957, when Richard's minelayer HMS *Manxman* put in at Toulon.

That August when he was discharged from the service, Richard wrote eagerly from his mother's flat in Chelsea to enquire after every detail of life in the house at Collioure, which by now boasted an upper floor with spacious living room, small kitchen, and terrace overhanging the vineyard below. He was immersed in Patrick's collection of short stories *Lying in the Sun*, and longed to return to Collioure, but regrettably he was inextricably 'tied up in England trying to get a decent job. Thus, although I really want to, I cannot come out. It would have been so pleasant. Please write soon, as I want to know how things in the property are going.'

Patrick responded with sympathetic advice on career possibilities. As I have reason to know, his was invariably a profoundly warm and perceptive attitude to such problems. Richard promptly replied, explaining further complex difficulties facing a young and unqualified job-seeker, and concluding: 'Thank you very much for writing, it is a wonderful feeling to have a father that backs one up in such a way.' Thereafter correspondence continued affectionate, if sporadic, as is frequently the case in such relationships. As Richard concluded a subsequent letter to my mother: 'I am sorry this [is] so brief, with evening classes and other things, I have no spare time.' However, he was conscious that his father was also encountering problems at this time: 'How is Dad? and has he started writing again? In your last letter you say that both he and M. Mucha lack inspiration so they talk every evening.'

Eager to raise his father's spirits, he continued: 'Recently I reread "Lying in the Sun", and it becomes even more wonderful each time it is read again. Its amazing to think that one man could produce such a book.'

A month later Richard sent Patrick cheery birthday greetings, accompanied by the filial reflection: 'I wish you were more accessible; there are so many things I would like to ask you; in a letter they would sound funny. Once you started on reincarnation, after a meal, but you never finished the subject for some reason or other.'

However, he had aspirations of coming over in the summer, when he hoped to indulge an enthusiasm for underwater exploration: 'I was hoping to persuade you into using an aqualung and the rest of the equipment. You would be very interested, despite the excuse of grey hairs and old age that you used some time ago.'

As time moved on, Richard wrote of the acquisition of his car Chloe, in which he hoped to drive to Collioure, in addition to a companionable if 'rather fierce' girlfriend. In the spring of 1959 my mother seized the opportunity to see him on her way to Russia. She wrote an enraptured account of their meeting to Patrick:

> Darling P., I had such a happy time with our dear Richard. . . R. kept making our old family jokes & each time I responded he said he was glad I hadn't forgotten. He was so kind to me. He said why was I not wearing a short skirt & when I said Because I am too <u>old</u>, he said very earnestly: 'No, Mary. You don't look a day over thirty-two [she was in fact 44].' He takes his exam about the 26th & I shall see him, Pat, on my return from Russia & the Scandinavian ports . . . how is that Temple, my dear?

However, financial straits and an arduous workload continued to preclude Richard's oft-planned return to Collioure. On the other hand, in 1960–61, when they came over to attend on me in hospital, he saw my mother and his father almost every day. By 1961, he was still living with his mother in King's Road, while encountering worrying obstacles to attaining a worthwhile career. Keen to attend university, he learned dispiritingly that two or three years' work would be required to pass even the preliminary examinations required for entry.

On the credit side, his girlfriend, Mimi Parotte, was proving an affectionate and loyal companion. Unhappily, the poor girl suffered from a debilitating nervous affliction (apparently some form of narcolepsy):

> Mimi is not any too well. Now and again it seems that she suffers from nervous and physical exhaustion, when this happens she hibernates; literally, she goes to sleep and does not wake up. On this

occasion she is only half asleep; she does things but is not really sure of what she is doing. If she sits down she promptly goes to sleep.

At the end of 1962 Richard sent their combined best wishes for his father's birthday. In the following March he apologized for a delay in thanking him and my mother for their Christmas present, explaining that 'work and study take up an average of a hundred hours a week'. Still, it was never too late: 'Thank you both very much indeed for the cheques. Mimi and I blessed you for an extremely good supper and we drank your health almost to excess.'

Increasingly concerned by Richard's Sisyphean struggle to achieve a career in engineering, Patrick entered into correspondence with my mother's cousin Sir Richard Paget, a Fellow of the Institution of Professional Engineers. Sir Richard provided detailed advice on various avenues open to the boy, and suggested he get in touch with him directly if there were more he could do to help.

Everything shows that these affectionate family relations continued unabated, when in October 1963 Patrick and my mother paid a six-week visit to London. One evening I was invited to call for drinks at the flat they rented in Chesham Street in order to meet Richard and Mimi, who had now become engaged.

As it happened, Richard and I had met only once before, when I was a boy staying at my grandparents' house in Chelsea after the War. However, there were others present on that occasion, and the encounter has left no trace in my memory. Obviously we had talked about him over the years at Collioure, but this little gathering in 1963 represents our sole personal contact after the fleeting childhood meeting.

It is for this reason, I imagine, that I retain a particularly clear recollection of the occasion. Dean King, who obtained his information from Richard and Mimi over thirty years after the event, describes the occasion as follows:

It was probably in late 1963 that Patrick and Mary met Richard's fiancée . . . despite the special occasion, the evening with Patrick and Mary at a London apartment was strained. For one thing, Mimi found Patrick cold and intimidating. She was probably not unbiased, for by this time Richard had come to realize fully what a mess his childhood had been and how it had scarred him. 'My father had been very, very bad to my mother,' he concluded. 'You just don't do this to a woman. And you hope like hell it does not happen in your family.' In fact, Richard had delayed marrying Mimi for several years to make sure that they would not make the same mistake his parents had.*

For what it be worth, my own recollection of the little family gathering is quite different. I found Richard tall, pleasant-looking and friendly, while Mimi appeared attractive and intelligent. As ever, Patrick was generous in plying us with gin and tonic, and the atmosphere was cordial throughout. I sensed that my parents wished to draw me and Richard together, which if so would have been natural. Of course such impressions are subjective, many years have passed since, and Mimi might have interpreted Patrick's somewhat formal manner as cold and distant. That this was really his attitude, however, seems improbable, particularly in view of the fact that he and my mother had gone out of their way to invite me to meet the future bride. In my case, too, my parents were invariably favourably – I would almost say, uncritically – inclined towards an offspring's loved one. Nevertheless, whatever the case, Mimi clearly formed an uncompromisingly hostile view of him.

---

* Dean King, *Patrick O'Brian: A Life Revealed* (London, 2000), pp. 196–97. It seems odd that it took some two decades for Richard to appreciate almost overnight the effects of his father's desertion of his mother, when he had lived with the latter for much the greater part of the previous twenty years and more. Others have expressed further puzzlement as to how Richard's delay in marrying Mimi might be expected to ensure 'that they would not make the same mistake his parents had'.

Furthermore, she naturally saw much of Richard's mother throughout their courtship, which may well have confirmed her hostile view of Patrick's character.

So far as my parents were concerned, it is clear that throughout this time they continued blithely unaware of any alteration in Richard's attitude towards them. Whatever Richard came to believe about his father originated, as he himself asserts, in angry reflections by his mother subsequent to her discovery of his infidelity during the War. She had been badly treated by her alcoholic second husband, and after his abrupt departure remained afflicted by poverty and ill-health. She did not marry again, and it would have been natural for her at times to ascribe her continuing tribulations to Patrick's desertion. Richard has confirmed that Patrick himself never discussed the issue with him, so that inevitably his assessment was altogether partial.

That Christmas my parents sent Richard their usual cheque, followed by another for his birthday in January. Since what follows has been seized upon by critics concerned to destroy Patrick's reputation, it is important to establish what occurred as accurately as possible.

Dean King, drawing exclusively on Richard's subsequent version of events, describes the unhappy rift as follows:

In the spring of 1964, Patrick and Mary received a letter from Richard, now twenty-seven years old, telling them that before the wedding he planned to change his name back to Russ. Richard did this, he later said, 'for the sake of honesty'. He reasoned that he was born a Russ, and he wanted to be married a Russ. He did not make the change out of anger to spite his father, he insisted. Nevertheless, as he had matured, Richard had come to better understand the nature of the breach between his parents, and, in the absence of any conversation with Patrick regarding it, he had drawn his own conclusions. He had not so much sided with his mother as condemned his father's behaviour in leaving the family . . .

Reverting to his earlier surname allowed him to distance himself from his father's illusion and separate himself from this painful episode in the family history. Mary wrote to Richard, saying that she understood . . . But Patrick did not respond at all, and he would disown his only child. Inability to express emotion, to work through anger, to swallow pride and then to heal had caught up with the family once again.

Richard married Mimi Parotte on 1 July that year. Elizabeth had said she would not attend if Patrick did, so Richard and Mimi did not invite Patrick and Mary to the wedding. The breach was complete. Patrick and Richard never spoke to each other again. In this regard, Patrick relived the sad history of his sometimes perverse family, where injured pride all too often clogged the lines of communication.[3]

Four years after the publication of King's biography, Richard himself returned to the topic, in an interview timed to coincide with the premiere of the film of *Master and Commander* in London:

I had met a man at work, an ordinary Battersea guy, who had been in the army. I asked him how he could settle down in civvy street after all the excitement of war. He said he had three youngsters and that he had come home to find his wife dying of cancer. So he buttoned down and got on with it. He didn't walk away. And I thought, 'Good on you. That's how a man should behave.' It suddenly hit me that not all men behaved in the manner that my father had done. It gave me a big push to changing my name back to Russ before I got married. I was born a Russ and I wanted to be married a Russ. I didn't want to be part and parcel of a sham . . .

When I changed my name, I wrote to my father. Mary wrote back . . . She said she fully understood, and she apologised for writing my old name of O'Brian on the envelope through force of habit. She said it wouldn't happen again and it didn't, because that was the last time I heard from them. I made no attempt to get back in touch with them myself. It was a clean cut.[4]

Since Patrick declined to be interviewed by King, and equally refrained from discussing his private life with anyone save presumably my mother, Richard's version of events is of necessity one-sided.* Moreover, he was speaking nearly forty years after the event, which presumably explains striking variations in his story. It was not his fault, consequently, that his understandably partial accounts led to Patrick's being described in the press as 'a monster'. Most unfortunately, such vituperative attacks have exercised a lasting effect, leaving a lingering public impression that, although a brilliant writer, he was personally despicable.

Were this the only evidence available, some might consider it reasonable to accept it as an accurate representation of the facts, if tinctured by emotional considerations. Fortunately, it is far from being the only evidence, as will now be seen.

This is the text of the letter Richard wrote to my mother on 8 March 1964, set forth here for the first time:

Dear Mary,
I apologise most humbly for not writing before now.

Since many things are happening all at once nothing has been decided upon [with regard to his wedding]. Dates are non-existant since I may be in the middle of changing my job. Mimi's parents seem to be travelling, or confering, quite a bit, but events are in a constant flux. The provisional date is the first week in July. Mimi wishes to visit some place that neither of us have been to before, for many lengthy and valid reasons. The upshot of this is that, unfortuneately, we cannot state any concrete dates, and, as a result,

---

* Shortly after Patrick's death, I telephoned Richard to suggest our meeting for a drink. He responded brusquely that he wished to have nothing to do with me or my family.

we are unable to fit in with your plans. Both of us feel rather low, since we would have liked very much to come to visit you.

Mimi wishes to thank both of you very much for her beads, she seems to wear them more than any other necklace she has. Thank you also for the gloves, most comforting in the snow which comes and goes so often; thank you also for my birthday present, now turned into two text books, a drafting pen, and a very good supper, Mimi enjoyed it too.

When you were in London last, Mimi and I called on you one evening. Time went so quickly that there was no opportunity to mention one subject that is of importance. For some time I have wished to change my name from O'Brian back to Russ, since marriage is round the corner this was accomplished a little while ago. There are two reasons for this, both of us felt that an Irish name was not suitable for two people who were not Irish, whereas Russ is neutral; also, it is difficult to get a job with an Irish name, there seems to be some predjudice against Irish names, now I find that firms are replying to applications more than before. This is not a question of independence, but one of practicality. I hope I have not put this down too bluntly.

I do apologise for not writing before. Both of us thank you most kindly for offering to have us, and we feel sad to have to refuse.

Richard.

As the letter was not posted until nearly ten days after it was written, it seems that Richard pondered his explanation with some care. He acknowledged subsequently that he appreciated the decision would displease Patrick. On the other hand, it may be questioned whether the example of the 'Battersea guy' was as decisive as he later came to believe. In his interview with Dean King, he appears to have made no mention of this factor, stating merely that his impending marriage made him wish to resume his original family name – a recollection which accords with the content of his letter. It may be noted, too, that Patrick did not desert his wife, as Richard's account implies, on discovering that his daughter was diagnosed with a terminal illness, but severed relations over two years after that event, following the poor child's death.*

On the other hand, the reasons Richard gave in his letter to my mother cannot be altogether rejected out of hand as tactful prevarication. He was indeed searching for work at this time. He was now twenty-seven, and his employment continued temporary and precarious. For at least two years he had been working as part-time commentator to tourists on Thames launches, while in the evenings he served as barman in a Soho pub.

Nevertheless, nothing supports the conjecture that Richard's failure to invite my parents to his wedding so angered Patrick that 'he relinquished his paternal role'.⁵ By curious chance Richard and Mimi's predicament was effectively replicated ten years later, when my sister Natasha married. She was obliged to explain to our mother and Patrick that she could not invite them to her wedding, as our father had refused to attend should they do so.† Although this doubtless caused disappointment at Collioure, my sister's explanation had no adverse effect on their affection towards her.

While it may be that his mother objected to Patrick's presence, Richard never in fact informed his father and stepmother of such a contingency.‡ Patrick may well have resigned himself to the fact that a meeting with Elizabeth would be an embarrassment to both of them. Indeed, it appears for some time previously to have been tacitly accepted by all parties that he and my mother would not attend the wedding. Far from contemplating a journey to London

---

* See Appendix B.

† Natasha, having been only two when our mother left us, retained no childhood memories of her, and consequently remained closer than I to our father and stepmother.

‡ Richard's letter to my mother of 8 March 1964 represents his sole communication throughout this time. He had last written to her in the previous March, well before any question of marriage had arisen. In 1964 my parents had yet to install a telephone at Collioure, and there was no other effective means of communication.

in July, they had arranged to receive guests at Collioure throughout the whole of that month. Their old wartime friend Barbara Puckridge was arriving with her son James, followed immediately by my mother's cousin Brigid and her husband Michael Roffe-Silvester, who were putting in for a stay at Collioure in their yacht *Merry Harrier*. Lastly, I was expected once again with my friend Jonah Barrington on the 26th.

As an enjoyable alternative, my mother and Patrick invited the bridal couple to spend their honeymoon at Collioure, where Richard had spent successive happy holidays in the past, and which would cost the indigent couple nothing.* He states that my mother replied sympathetically to his letter, saying she fully understood his decision to change his name. Clearly, it was *not* this that primarily caused the rift between Richard and his father, but the former's decision not to answer my mother's letter, nor make any further contact for the remainder of their lives: 'I had been mulling it over for years. I found I was not very impressed with my father. I decided not to spend my life with dishonesty. I decided never to speak to him again. When I stopped, so did he.'[6]

My mother's response to Richard's letter was as ever warmly sympathetic. Although he declined to reply, she had no reason to anticipate any lasting rift: indeed, she promised to employ his resumed surname of Russ in future correspondence. That there was no further communication was primarily Richard's decision. It was he who decided not to continue it, by rejecting the invitation to spend part of their honeymoon at Collioure, and then declining to answer my mother's response. Patrick's failure to respond at the time signifies little, since it was my mother, who effectively regarded Richard as her son, who chiefly conducted their correspondence.

---

* There would have been no problem over accommodation in the little house: Brigid and Michael slept on board their yacht, while Jonah and I were accustomed to camping in my tent.

However, as Richard later explained to Dean King, he anticipated that Patrick would resent the implicit rejection and, given his highly sensitive nature, was likely to take grave offence. It is clear from his own account that this is precisely what Richard wished to occur.* After all, he might readily have tactfully concealed his change of name. He maintained little or no contact with his other Russ relations, and there was no reason why Patrick should have discovered the change. Richard's sudden overriding attachment to his natal name seems unaccountable, too, in view of his continuing lack of communication with his Russ relations.

In view of these considerations, it seems not impossible that Richard's abrupt decision to initiate a rupture with his father, after long years of unremittingly cordial relations, owed something to his fiancée's influence. As has been seen, she took an instinctive dislike to Patrick at our meeting in Chesham Street, finding him 'cold and intimidating'. It was she, too, who rejected the invitation to stay at Collioure after the wedding. The fact that she suffered from some form of medical condition conceivably played an ancillary part in her hostility.

While it is impossible to see into the hearts and minds of others, it is tempting in part at least to associate Mimi's visceral dislike of Patrick with her own upbringing. Her father was Jean Parotte, a senior diplomat at the Belgian Embassy in London. Bob Broeder, Richard's friend from their schooldays, saw much of Richard and Mimi at this time. From them he learned that her father was something of a domestic tyrant.

In view of this, it would have been only natural had the 'tyrant' objected, at least initially, to his daughter's choice of indigent fiancé. Did Mimi envisage Patrick as a similarly oppressive father figure?

---

* 'The feeling built up inside me that the false name represented my father's falsehood . . . It was a crunch time. I felt a deep resentment at the way he had treated us. He changed his name to chop out the past. I changed mine to bring the past back. We never spoke again – and that was 37 years ago' (*Mail on Sunday*, 16 January 2000).

Her account of their sole meeting in Chesham Street may suggest this. Possessed only of a partial (in some respects untrue)* version of his treatment of Richard and his mother, and being by all accounts a strong character possessed of a high standard of morality, might it not have come easily for her to believe the very worst of her future father-in-law?

Patrick in contrast continued to nurture deep affection for his son over the years to come. Some ten years later he recorded this intriguing dream:

> In the night . . . a dream of a mountainous desert, a large salamander (2 ft long) hurrying down a cliff, lost to sight behind a rock & on being approached found to be a pair of furry ostriches. They were startled by a band or pack of ~~brown~~ yellow spaniels, & one bird, seeing me withdraw a little as they came back to this rock, assured me, with some reference to the 'one sweep of powerful wing' that it would not kick. We spoke of diet: I wondered how they could live in such desolation but did not like to stress their being birds: the ostrich said it needed so much to put on a pound as opposed to our requirements; but I forget the figures. A civil bird, but rather absolute & not particularly likeable. Richard, abt 12/14 was in this dream: at first he thought they were gazelles.

The most touching indication of Patrick's painfully continuing affection for his son is provided by a charming photograph, which he preserved in a pocket diary kept beside him in his study until his death. It shows a cheerfully grinning Richard, aged about nine, perched on a plinth of the Albert Bridge in Chelsea, with his beloved boxer Sian.

---

* Cf. pp. 312–13 of the first volume of this biography. Richard acknowledged that he retained almost no memory of his parents' relationship during his infancy.

Richard, aged around nine

There can be no doubt that Patrick remained deeply wounded by his son's peremptory decision to break off relations. He and my mother doubtless felt that expansion of their little family through Richard's marriage would if anything bring them closer together, and this I felt was also their purpose in inviting me to meet him and his fiancée in the previous autumn. Had they come to Collioure in July, when I was staying there with my genial friend Jonah Barrington, we might all indeed have become close. Life is full of such sad mischances.

Constrained by the isolated and vulnerable circumstances of his own childhood and adolescence, as in other instances Patrick built a defensive wall around his unhappiness. When his niece Elizabeth Russ visited him at Collioure in 1989, she was surprised to find that 'He denied Richard's existence!' I do not know how much Patrick spoke of the tragedy to my mother, who was undoubtedly deeply distressed by the mystifying rift. As Patrick jotted down about this time: 'one does not expose: the [Jerusalem] Temple had a veil. So all but very shallow creatures speak in tropes.'

In April, a month after the rupture with Richard, Patrick was struck by another personal tragedy, when news reached Collioure of the death of his stepmother Zoe. In marked contrast to his frequently bullying and unpredictable father, she had acted as a markedly affectionate parent: effectively the only mother he could remember. He entertained the fondest memories of her, who had so often shielded him from his father's erratic tyranny. It was out of concern for his health in London that she took him for the years 1926 to 1929 to live in Lewes, where he enjoyed the happiest period of his troubled childhood.

Patrick spent a week in England attending the funeral, where he encountered a number of his rarely assembled relatives. Among them was his younger sister Joan, who had been the close companion of his boyhood. Bun (also called Barney) had flown from Canada to join the gathering, and recalled the occasion long afterwards in a letter to Joan:

> . . . I expect you will recall our going from London to Staffordshire by train for our step-mother's funeral and that the little town of Stone was delightful in the Spring. I recall drifts of daffodils and other Spring flowers on our way between the station at Stafford and the churchyard where the funeral took place.

Dispersed as the family was, this melancholy occasion was to prove the last occasion that many of them were enabled to meet. In particular, Patrick never again had the chance to see those to whom he was closest: Bun and above all Joan. Dean King, once again at pains to emphasize how chilling was Patrick's relationship with his siblings, asserts that:

> After Zoe's death, O'Brian reached almost complete emotional detachment from his Russ family. When Joan tried to initiate a correspondence with him, he wrote back saying that he would rather not be reminded of his youth. Joan's pride was injured, and they

never communicated with each other again. If not for Barney's persistence, Patrick most likely would have forever severed ties with his family at this time.[7]

This extraordinary charge is in fact completely untrue. Furthermore, it is implicitly utilized to bolster the claim that Patrick went out of his way to shun his own son. A number of reviewers of King's work and the first volume of my biography have uncritically swallowed the accusation whole, using it to besmirch Patrick's character.

Broadly speaking, communications between members of the Russ family were as intermittent as is the case with many families in the modern world. In their instance this was much exacerbated by geographical separation, combined with the usual preoccupations that characterize busy family lives. Patrick himself was an exceptionally industrious man, who for much of his life struggled to make ends meet. Living abroad, and lacking time and opportunity to meet his relatives on any sort of regular basis, communications tended to be restricted to relatively rare occasions, such as Christmas and birthdays. An exception was provided by Patrick's elder brother Bun in Canada, who on his retirement maintained an extensive correspondence with his surviving brothers and sisters.

As has just been seen, King writes of Patrick's younger sister, who had been the closest to him in early days: 'When Joan tried to initiate a correspondence with him, he wrote back saying that he would rather not be reminded of his youth.' Joan's original letter lies before me, together with a copy of Patrick's reply. Dated 14 November 1979 (not *c.* 1964, as King implies), she explains that her letter was instigated by reading his biography of Picasso, which Bun had sent her. This was the first communication between either of them since they had met at their stepmother's funeral, and Joan had discovered Patrick's address from Bun – which incidentally indicates that she had made no attempt to contact him since at least 1949, when Patrick moved to Collioure. After congratulating him on writing such a 'fascinating' book, she went on to tell him of her family life in Birmingham, and concluded with the cheerful admonition: 'So. Regard this as a fan-letter and answer it as you will or not. My, by now, sepulchral voice from the past is only concerned with saying Good Show.'

Ten days later Patrick responded with an affectionate letter, in which he expatiated on shared childhood memories of their successive parental homes at Kempsey and Crowborough. After discussing points Joan raised about the Picasso biography, he concluded: 'And so with many thanks for your letter and with my love. Yours ever Pat.'

There the correspondence ceased, until more than two years later Joan took up the exchange again, this time to send Patrick a copy of a pencil drawing of himself as a baby sketched by his brother Victor, together with a copy of a portrait of their elder brother Mike beside his Lancaster bomber during the War. This instigated further nostalgic memories of Patrick's and Joan's life together at Lewes and Crowborough, and Patrick replied promptly on 20 March 1981. After describing his feelings on paying visits to both of their former homes in 1967, he concluded with this poignant reaction on viewing the latter: 'It fairly went to my heart, and I did not go down the leafy lane into Ashdown Forest as I had intended but turned the car and drove away into the present as fast as ever I could. And so these [memories], my dear, I leave you With much love and many thanks Pat.'

Further correspondence passed between them. However, as she grew older, Joan became according to family accounts increasingly cross-grained, and in 1987 responded to Bun's latest complaint about Patrick (whom Bun does indeed appear to have regarded with a comical degree of jealousy) with the assertion that he 'has been consistently blocking all communication with one and all'. However, this was clearly a reaction to Bun's complaint, rather than any reflection on her own lack of contact with Patrick. After all, a few months earlier Bun had reminded her:

I am very pleased to know that you did receive a letter from Pat.
He is not a good correspondent, but for one who writes so much,
I should have thought letter writing would have come very readily
[authors naturally have so much time off from their writing!].
Anyway, he has done his bit and for this I am glad.

As will be seen in due course, in 1989–90 there occurred a brief
severance of relations between the brothers, in consequence of
Bun's publication of his privately printed family memoir *Lady Day
Prodigal*. Despite Patrick's plea to be excluded from his eccentric
work, Bun insisted on including allusions to Patrick which the
latter found embarrassing. Nevertheless, despite this setback it was
not long before good relations were once again resumed.

Thus, the accusation that Patrick severed relations with his
family in 1964 is entirely untrue. He maintained correspondence
with Bernard and Joan into old age. They were the two closest to
him, both in age and shared childhood memories. Among his other
siblings, Godfrey and Michael were long dead, Nora had become
a nun and from the 1950s made her home on the other side of
the world in remote Vancouver Island, Olive had left the family
home when Patrick was still a small boy at Lewes, and Connie
had become largely distanced from the entire family in the 1920s.

Patrick maintained especially warm feelings towards Victor, who
had found him and his family the Suffolk cottage where they lived
during the early years of the War. When Victor died in 1985,
Patrick recorded in his diary: 'At last I wrote to Bun about Vic's
death: strangely painful.' Victor's widow Saidie told me that Patrick
also wrote to her after his death: a letter which included the
acknowledgement that: 'Victor was a very good brother to me –
much better than I was to him.' The extent to which Patrick
maintained communication with him and others of the Russ family
is unknown. What is clear is that the slur on Patrick's memory is
entirely groundless, and the extent of its uncritical acceptance
strange, if not unaccountable.

Returning to 1964, in July and August Jonah Barrington and I paid an even longer visit to Collioure than in the previous year. This time we were accompanied by Timothy Heneage, a mutual friend from Somerset. Patrick and my mother were greatly taken with Timothy, whose name Patrick adopted in his novels as that of Jack Aubrey's particular friend Heneage Dundas.*

At the same time, my parents were becoming increasingly concerned by Jonah's failure to discover his métier in life. His decision to forgo studies at Trinity had led to his premature departure without a degree. Ever active, he had by this time been gaining a precarious living from such varied activities as heaving sacks for a Cornish coalmerchant, acting as groundsman at Bude Recreation Ground, and painting houses (with me) for the gloomy little local poet Ronald Duncan – with whose pretty daughter Bryony I had become romantically involved. No doubt recalling his own peripatetic youth, Patrick sought to identify some professional activity that would suit Jonah's talents. During both our visits he admired Jonah's prowess on the Château Royal tennis court, and when Jonah mentioned that he had heard of a clerical vacancy at the Squash Rackets Association in London, Patrick and my mother enthusiastically urged him to take this up. As I recall, Jonah was at first averse to the prospect of accepting a deskbound job, but eventually succumbed to my parents' encouraging pressure, and submitted the application.[8]

Fortunately, it proved successful, and on his return he found himself for the first time with a regular job – albeit a rather modest one. Eventually, however, Jonah's talent on the courts caught the attention of influential figures in the sport, and in due course he

---

* There was a real-life Captain the Hon. George Heneage Lawrence Dundas (James, *The Naval History of Great Britain* (London, 1837), iii, p. 113), but the context suggests that the fictional Heneage Dundas's friendship with Jack Aubrey arose from Patrick's affection for Timothy. This is further indicated by Dundas's skill at mathematics (*Master and Commander*, p. 343): at the time Timothy taught mathematics at Millfield School.

went on to gain international acclaim as the world's greatest squash player, winning the British Open no less than six times in seven years. Many potent figures in the world of sport were to help him along the road to fame and success, but as he freely acknowledged it was Patrick and my mother who had given him that vital initial spur.

The New Year of 1965 opened with severe financial problems at Collioure, which *inter alia* required my mother to spend the ten days before Christmas frantically typing Patrick's current translation *Munich, or The Phoney Peace*, by Henri Noguères. However, after some juggling of their finances, on the last day of 1964 my mother defiantly wrote: 'I have a strong feeling that 1965 will be a very happy year for us & ours.'

Throughout February and March they spent much time toiling on the neighbouring strip of land they had acquired in 1962. Having learned that rigorous restrictions had been imposed on building in the vicinity, they set to work making the land productive. Apparently oblivious to his previous perilous experience when preparing ground for building the *casot* ten years before, Patrick now bought fresh explosives in Perpignan in order to create terraces for a vineyard. Although a local builder was employed to undertake the work, Patrick could never resist discharging explosions where opportunity offered. As my mother recorded: 'Cardonner finished on 18th but yesterday poor P. blew away a piece of the new wall with a vine-hole mine. Still, C. said today never mind he will come one day and do it.' Patrick was suffering from a severe ailment of the eyes at the time (which may account for the erratic behaviour of the mine), so that much of the labour fell on my mother, who wrote: 'All day in vineyard perfect sun & no wind. Finished mines & making places, & planted 44 racines. I carried stones, had a bonfire & finished weeding entire vineyard.'

In January 1966 she noted: 'I must try to record last year, though it was so crowded we have both lost all sense of chronology. It really was a good year, though at times we felt battered. Work:

Marie Mancini finished, then La Douceur de Vieillir & Une Mort très douce none of which are out yet.'

The references are to Patrick's continuing work on translations, on whose financial support their modest though increasingly comfortable income depended.[9]

My mother seems to have regarded 1965 as a potentially formative time, when she compiled a detailed journal for this and much of the following year – the first and last since she gave up keeping her earlier annual diaries in 1955. A week into the New Year she reported exciting news from Patrick's literary agent: 'C[urtis] B[rown] wrote to say MacMillan keep asking when P is coming up with another novel. Dear Lord I feel so deeply about P's writing.' Ten days later 'I am in that blessed state of living in the present & enjoying every moment & every thing.' Towards the end of the year she received a premonitory glimpse of the revival of Patrick's creative writing: 'The most important happening for us in 1965: P wrote a splendid tale for my birthday. He said it came easily, freshly, unspoiled by translating so much for so long. I had been terrified his gift might have been eaten away. It is what really counts.'

Unfortunately, the story has not survived, and some time was yet to pass before Patrick's muse returned in earnest.

His translation work continued to provide a regular income, subsidized by my mother's modest private income and her private tutoring. Nevertheless, relative poverty remained a pressing reality. On 28 January my mother noted: 'I put vast patches on P's corduroy trousers.' A week later: 'Poor P. found that if he had joined the London Library some years ago it would only have been about £50 & now it would be £107. I wish he would have it though.' A change of scene momentarily attracted them. 'We found an advert. for a furnished cottage on Loch Corrib for £50 for three months & got very excited.' The image of Ireland as a romantic haven from a fretful world regularly recurred to Patrick's mind. But as on other occasions this came to nothing.

In the summer I paid my annual visit to Collioure, which was as ever greatly enjoyed by the three of us. I am glad to find my mother writing afterwards: 'Nikolai 29th [July] for only a fortnight because of PhD: he was delightful the whole time.'

At the end of the year she and Patrick travelled to England, where they stayed for the second half of December with my mother's parents in Somerset. A highlight of their visit was a stay with my mother's cousin Brigid and her husband Michael Roffe-Silvester, who lived in a ramshackle but exceedingly picturesque farmhouse in the valley of the Culm. Michael was Master of his own pack of foxhounds, 'Mr Roffe-Silvester's Hounds', while his brother Peter was Master of the Exmoor Staghounds. Rural England is today being subjected to a tidal wave of uncontrolled building which appears set before long to extinguish forever the traditional countryside, which will eventually become accessible only through the evocative imagery of such resources as Hardy's novels and Constable's paintings. At the time of my parents' visit, however, much of the traditional world continued little changed from that of Surtees and Trollope a century earlier. They enthusiastically attended the hunt: 'Prettiest meet in the world, with Michael really stunning, lots of cherry-brandy. Sun all day & we saw 3 foxes.'

Such glimpses of a world so close in many ways to his beloved eighteenth century enhanced Patrick's ever-brimming imagination, and are found transmuted into fiction in the opening chapter of *Post Captain* and elsewhere in the series.

Although little of solid moment had been achieved in 1965, it appeared largely a year of promise. Indeed, so ebullient had they become, that they indulged in a major extravagance during their visit to England, buying four silver plates for £137 10s, off which they regularly dined thereafter.

Like so much else in the cosy living room at Collioure, the plates found their way into Patrick's literary creation. Early in his career Jack Aubrey decides to emulate Lord Nelson: '. . . I dare say I described those elegant silver plates he has? . . . Please could you go ashore and order me four . . .?' When Stephen Maturin brings them into his cabin, Jack exults: 'Here's elegance, damn my eyes. How they shine!'Much later, when fallen into temporary financial difficulty, he exclaims with feeling: '. . . nobody could be poorer in reality than sailors in a ship without any stores – what crusts you may scrape together eat with more relish in handsome silver.'*

Unfortunately, unlike the silver, the generally optimistic outlook of 1965 proved short-lived, and 1966 was to prove something of a nadir in the couple's fortunes. Superficially, the outlook appeared promising. Commissions for translations continued to provide a dependable income. The first five months of the year Patrick spent working on *The Quicksand War*, a well-informed history by Lucien Bodard of the French war in Indo-China. Patrick admired the author and his book, for whose translation Little, Brown paid well: $1,000 on signature and $1,500 on delivery. Completion was due by 1 September, but Patrick characteristically despatched it at the beginning of June. At the publisher's requirement he skilfully abbreviated the two-volume original, and provided an excellent introduction. A week later he learned (in my mother's words): 'Bodard received with applause / relief, relief.'

The next commission was finished even more speedily. On 20 June he began work on Michel Mohrt's novel *The Italian Campaign*, which he finished on 17 July. However, the speed of its completion did not reflect any enthusiasm for the task. As my mother sighed after its despatch, 'Mohrt is the rottenest book we've done.' Next came an improvement, in the form of a well-paid American contract for translation of the two-volume memoirs of Clara Malraux. Patrick's remarkably disciplined approach to his work is exempli-fied by a note he wrote on 29 June: '120000 [words] at 1,500 a

---

* *Post Captain*, pp. 378, 381; *The Yellow Admiral*, p. 215. Two years later my parents bought a further two plates to make up a set.

day is 80 days. In August, September & October there are 79, counting Saturdays & perhaps I shall have 10 in July.'

In the event he finished the work on 5 December, which was still good going. The payment was good, and by the end of the year they were respectably in credit.

Although there were many pleasant interludes, and work within and without the house continued unabated, my parents were both plagued by physical ailments. My mother was also beset by bouts of depression hard to avert, as well as the occasional frightening dream. In March: 'Horrid nightmare I had. Nikolai was desperately ill in a foreign hospital & I could not find him.'

Translation of the execrable Mohrt upset Patrick, to the extent of triggering a momentary coldness between him and my mother. On 23 June (when she recorded my birthday), they enjoyed a convivial dinner with neighbours. However, my mother sensed that all had not gone well: 'I irritated Patrick at dinner though. I MUST TAKE CARE AND WATCH OUT. So nervy & upset we are.' As a precaution she headed successive weekly pages of her diary with the watchword: 'REMEMBER TO SAY YES.'

This may sound unduly obsequious. In reality, however, I had long been aware that each intuited the other's mood through a sort of osmosis. She perfectly sensed the underlying causes of Patrick's withdrawal, which was his characteristic mode of dealing with real or fancied setbacks he could not for the present handle. As she continued in her diary: 'I hate P having this inferior chap Mohrte [*sic*] – and I suppose the bulldozer does really affect us.'

Her reference was to the nearby construction of one of the regimented *lotissements* which continued remorselessly creeping up the valley. In the previous month my mother fretted that she 'felt low about whether P should not have been in London all these years & whether he is happy here. Very low.'

What appeared more and more unjust in view of the tasteless building programme in the valley at the time was that an application on 28 September to build a garage and spare room on their newly acquired land was eventually rejected by the *Mairie*. They still had no bedroom for guests, nor anywhere to house their car. Their purchase of the adjacent land had been in large part motivated by a desire to make their little home more habitable. For the present they had had to be content with constructing a paved terrace beside the house. Furthermore, their financial predicament was once again dire. In July my mother had recorded with alarm: 'I wrote to Barclays again for mon[ey]. We are so short. We went to P[ort]V[endres] & I got the last 25000 until mon[ey] gets through.'

However, the situation improved as the year wore on, largely owing to the diligence with which Patrick completed his translations. In September my mother spent ten days with her parents in Somerset. Unfortunately 'It was a dreadfully sad time in England.' This, I fear, arose from the fact that her parents tended to find her persistent well-intentioned attempts to assist them in their old age more of an irritant than a help.

Despite this, she returned with Patrick to stay in Somerset for the last three months of the year. This time they sensibly lodged for the greater part of their visit at a nearby pub, the Rose and Portcullis in Butleigh. There Patrick was able to continue his translation of Clara Malraux's memoirs in peace, while they enjoyed the congenial company of my mother's cousins the Slacks and Roffe-Silvesters. Another friend from the past was George Turner, head of classics at nearby Millfield School, who lived close by. A shy but friendly soul, he had nurtured a secret passion for my mother during her teenage holidays on Lundy Island.

Finally, the year ended on a promising note. Despite the expense of their stay in England, they found themselves some £850 in credit at the bank, despite having spent £285 on their protracted jaunt to England. Nor was their time entirely profitless from a literary point of view. Although Patrick was yet to know it, the time was drawing near when his familiarity with timeless aspects of English country life would be put to striking use. His observant eye was ever open, noting such delicate touches as 'a strong frost & now in a dead calm the leaves fall, one by one or in little showers'; 'A cock blackcap ate asparagus berries outside my (or rather Nikolai's) window' at my grandparents' house.

VII

Master and Commander

When I cast my eye on the expanse of waters, my heart bounded like
that of a prisoner escaped. I felt an unextinguishable curiosity kindle
in my mind, and resolved to snatch this opportunity of seeing the
manners of other nations, and of learning sciences unknown in Abissinia.

Samuel Johnson, *The History of Rasselas,*
Prince of Abissinia, ch. viii

After three months in England of enforced abstention from
literary work, Patrick and my mother prepared to return to
Collioure. Before their departure he experienced a bout of nostalgia
for the days of his childhood. It was recollection of homes in the
countryside which drew him, rather than those in town.

As has already been noted, it was in January 1967, on their
way home from Somerset, that the couple drove from London to
Ford Field Cottage at Crowborough, the last of Patrick's boyhood
homes, to which three decades earlier his parents had withdrawn
following the failure of Charles Russ's erratic medical career. There
Patrick and his sister Joan had enjoyed a considerable measure of
happiness.* The previously fraught relationship between Patrick
and his father had by that time mellowed. Charles Russ appears

---

* After Patrick's eventual departure, Joan's life became more and more lonely
– indeed wretched.

to have reacted sympathetically to Patrick's abortive attempt to gain a career in the RAF, regarded his promising literary successes with parental pride, and subscribed to a clipping service to ensure that he obtain a full set of book reviews. In 1934 Patrick dedicated his second book *Beasts Royal* 'To my father', while during his subsequent impoverished existence in Chelsea the cottage continued to provide a welcome haven.

Next they drove to Lewes, where Patrick and Joan had earlier lived as children with their stepmother from 1926 to 1929. Patrick and my mother had arranged to stay the night with a friend, but having arrived early they strolled in the water meadows by the Ouse, where as a boy he had whiled away spells of gentle contentment immersed in the natural world. Lewes had provided the happiest interlude in his otherwise largely monotonous and at times frightening childhood. His compensating affinity with nature made the countryside a secure and rewarding refuge, while his father's regular absences at his distant London surgery can only have been a relief.

It would be fascinating to know what he told my mother about his youthful existence during this poignant visit. Could the grievous pang of nostalgia he experienced at Crowborough have arisen from a sharp contrast between blossoming hopes of early days and his current bout of creative stagnation? By 1940 he had published three books and a continuing succession of short stories, and entertained high hopes of pursuing a brilliant literary career. Then the War disrupted his creativity, although it provided compensating excitements. After that followed the four increasingly frustrating years in North Wales, with their mounting accretion of writer's block and the depression it entailed.

That dark period seemed for a time largely banished, following their removal in 1949 to sunny Collioure. For several years Patrick's books and short stories continued to be well received, and although disappointingly none had proved a bestseller, they were accorded considerable praise – at times by reviewers whose judgement Patrick respected.

These achievements had culminated with the publication of *Richard Temple* in 1962. For Patrick, that book and its predecessors *Three Bear Witness* and *The Catalans* were defining works: each well received by reviewers, and apparently foretokening an assured literary future.* Yet something had gone astray. Sales had been respectable, but not so extensive as to set publishers pressing for further work.

The character of the three books suggests an explanation for Patrick's impasse. Each in its own way represented a work of purgation, and was in consequence overlaid with gloom. The travails which afflicted him in North Wales and Collioure were successively depicted through the eyes of world-weary, misunderstood and ultimately betrayed protagonists, whose real-life prototype is readily distinguishable. Finally, *Richard Temple* dissected the Patrick whose memory the author sought to expose and banish altogether: the penurious failed artist, who had deserted his wife and then been betrayed by his real love. Although the latter disaster never occurred in actuality, it nonetheless loomed as a fitful irrational fear.

Dimly recalled pronouncements gathered during my first stay at Collioure in 1955 suggest another unconscious influence on Patrick's writing at that time. High tragedy was a staple of the works of great writers, he indicated, and I received dampening snubs for favouring authors who relied on rollicking characters and high adventure. At the impressionable age of nineteen, Charles Lever, Harrison Ainsworth and Rider Haggard ranked high among those lively writers whose works I devoured, but . . . 'Nikolai, we do not call that *literature*.'

My subjective impression may be borne out by Patrick's initial acceptance (he was later to revise this view) that his own adventure novels, *The Golden Ocean* and *The Unknown Shore*, were expressly intended for a juvenile readership (they are described as 'for children'

---

* Here, as elsewhere, I cite the book titles preferred by Patrick.

on the dustjacket of *Richard Temple*). At the same time, although commissioned on this basis, it seems that a relaxed Patrick wrote them in the first instance, as do many good writers, for himself. In common with other readers, I still fail to find them generically distinct from the *Master and Commander* series. Like *Treasure Island*, *Kidnapped*, and Conan Doyle's *Adventures of Gerard*, they are just as absorbing for adult as for juvenile readers. Patrick generally produced his best books at a publisher's suggestion, while others composed on his own initiative often proved less successful. It seems he had yet fully to discover his true métier.

Richard Temple, that intensely autobiographical work, did not afford any avenue for a sequel. Nothing suggests that he seriously contemplated writing a further work of fiction during the half-dozen years that followed. He appears to have felt that he had exhausted all possibilities in that line.

Moreover, a further disincentive was afforded by the alternative course of accepting commissions for translations, which had happened to recommence at the time of publication of *Richard Temple*, and was proving a healthy source of income. In January 1967, Patrick had been commissioned to translate a second work by Simone de Beauvoir, *Les Belles Images*, which he completed at the beginning of March. This was followed in quick succession by an undistinguished biography of Louis XVI, and a work on Easter Island.[1] Neither of the latter books appealed to him, and in July he noted with relief that he had 'finished disgusting E Island'.

As though to emphasize the drudgery of this relatively unde-manding work, the weather in the early months of 1967 continued unremittingly grim ('foul tramontane: the weather has been horrid this year,' Patrick recorded as late as 19 May), and on the day he finished the de Beauvoir translation he wrote: 'Depression: I note it to see whether it has any pattern, cyclical pattern.'

However, it was at this seeming nadir of his career that events combined to launch him onto an entirely fresh and absorbing departure. On 8 April 1967 he received a 'remarkable suggestion'.

Robert Hill, editor-in-chief of the prominent US publisher J.B. Lippincott, had read and admired *The Golden Ocean*. C.S. Forester, whose Hornblower novels enjoyed enormous success on both sides of the Atlantic, had died a year earlier, and Hill perceptively singled out Patrick as a writer eminently qualified to fill the void. He invited him to submit an outline for a novel about an eighteenth-century naval commander – Hornblower's successor, if not epigone, as it might have seemed at the time.

Patrick responded swiftly. On 6 May he 'Wrote long & careful letter about projected book to C-B [Curtis Brown, his literary agent] for Lippincott.' In the meantime, by odd chance, he received an invitation from Marni Hodgkin, an editor at Macmillan in London, who was preparing the fourth number of their Christmas annual *Winter's Tales for Children*. She suggested that Patrick write a short story for inclusion in the coming Christmas edition. For this, he cleverly adopted the device of composing what is effectively a missing chapter from *The Unknown Shore*. Characters and setting thus being ready-made, he began writing on 20 April, and laid down his pen on 25 May.

The story, to which Patrick gave the title 'The Centurion's Gig', slots seamlessly between chapters 5 and 6 of *The Unknown Shore*. (It is perhaps surprising that, so far as I am aware, no publisher has thought to do so.) Given the picaresque nature of the novel, interpolation was not difficult. The *Wager* is discovered tacking in a placid and all but windless ocean, some 20 leagues off the coast of Morocco. After a close encounter with an inquisitive whale, the heroes of the story, having become detached from their vessel in the visiting gig of the *Centurion*, escape an attack by Barbary corsairs, whose menacing polacre is driven off in the nick of time by the arrival of the *Wager*'s sister ship, the *Tryall*. (This encounter is echoed in Jack Aubrey's repulse of an Algerine galley in chapter 4 of *Master and Commander*, written in the same year.)

However, interest is primarily sustained by lively and humorous dialogue, together with the happily contrasted characters of the protagonists. The similarity between Jack Byron's companion Tobias Barrow and Jack Aubrey's friend Stephen Maturin becomes more apparent in the short story than it was in the novel, as this extract illustrates. (It is also intriguing to note that the story brings Jack and Toby from *The Unknown Shore* together with Peter Palafox from *The Golden Ocean*.)

'I will just hurry downstairs and bring up my little net and a jelly-bag,' said Toby. 'With so placid an ocean it is possible, just possible, that we may light upon yet another pedunculated cirripede.' 'Would he be making game of us, now?' asked Peter Palafox, who was very quick to resent anything like an affront. 'Never in life, upon my word and honour,' said Jack. 'You would never believe what a learned cove he is – reads Greek for the joy of it, has filled our cabin with curious flayed monsters in spirits of wine, and has never spent five minutes of daylight below since we left the chops of the Channel in case he might miss some sea-fowl, in spite of being as sick as a dog every time we meet the slightest hint of a sea. And now ever since we have reached these latitudes he has spent every night in the long-boat, staring at the things that light up, like a cat at a vase of goldfishes.' 'Well, I honour learning, the Dear knows,' said Peter. 'So he's not the great seaman, at all?' 'Lard no. He had never seen salt-water, never smelt the bilges of a ship, till I brought him to Portsmouth at the beginning of this commission. He is my particular friend, you know – you should see his prodigious collection of serpents at home – and I have brought him into the Navy by way of making his fortune. But I should never call him a seaman: no. He looks upon the whole ocean as a museum of natural curiosities; why, the other day he desired the first lieutenant to put the ship about because he fancied he spied a turtle. I try to keep an eye on him and make him understand our ways, but he's in the moon three parts of the time, parsing his Sanskrit verbs.'

Here unmistakably may be glimpsed Maturin's erudition, unworldliness, and ignorance of sailing. Yet to come are his character as doctor, intelligence agent, disenchanted outsider, uneasily married man, and duellist. The amiable extrovert Jack Byron provides but a pale premonition of the full-blown Jack Aubrey, but again the genesis is nonetheless evident.

Marni Hodgkin received the tale with enthusiasm: 'One thing I am certain of – The Centurion's Gig is the best story in my collection by quite a long chalk . . . In fact an almost embarrassing chalk.' As the other contributors included such well-known writers as Richard Garnett, Leon Garfield, Ted Hughes and Noel Streatfeild, this was invaluable praise.

Although she later sent him a photocopy of the published story, Patrick neither preserved it, nor included any reference to it in the list of his published works he provided for Arthur Cunningham's Festschrift in 1994. I can only suppose the omission to have been deliberate. The writing is well up to the standard of *The Unknown Shore*, a book to which he remained attached. On rereading the latter 'not without pleasure' in January 1995, he remarked: 'It is not a v good book, but not discreditable either – perhaps rather dull.' These moderate strictures were in any case provoked less from disparagement of its literary merit, than by his consciousness of the extent of the novel's dependence on the historical record for its plot.

It is possible that Patrick's reticence arose from concern that the public should not nurture any suspicion of the genesis of his magnum opus in his earlier writing for children – a misgiving he expressed openly at the time. Like many of his fears, it appears groundless, but for him it presented jeopardy.

Reverting to Patrick's state of mind in 1967, with the beginning of summer developments fast combined to suggest that the world was becoming a better place. On 21 May he rejoiced that the weather was 'Warm, warm, for the first time almost', while within the week: 'The tax is all right Joy / I was irrationally worried.' (In fact, Patrick appears ultimately to have proved more than a match for both British and French tax authorities.)

On 5 July he received the American publisher's reaction to his draft: 'Lippincott want book – amazed & rather cross, put out.' Whatever the cause of these reservations, two days later he 'Wrote to C[urtis]-B[rown] accepting Lippincott's offer of $7,500.' The contract was signed on 15 September, the book being described simply as 'Untitled novel about an 18th Century naval adventurer'.

A delighted Patrick plunged into preparatory reflection and research for a work perfectly attuned to his tastes and talent.* His two earlier naval novels had employed Anson's celebrated voyage around the globe in 1740–44 as their setting. Having exhausted the possibilities of that momentous theme, he now fastened on the apogee of the Royal Navy's achievement, Britain's twenty-year struggle against Revolutionary and Napoleonic France. Conditions of shipping and seamanship at that time were not radically different from those obtaining in the 1740s, so that his extensive researches provided him with a solid grounding for the work.

As a model for his '18th Century naval adventurer', he required a young and enterprising officer, exercising an independent roving command. Browsing through William James's six-volume *Naval History of Great Britain* (1837), which he had bought during the War, Patrick at some point fastened upon the striking figure of Lord Cochrane. One of the most dashing and resourceful frigate commanders of the Royal Navy during the war with France, his deeds and (in part) character provided an exemplary prototype for a fictional hero.

Further to Cochrane's skill and daring, as also his recurrent conflicts with higher authority, Patrick appropriated a succession of his exploits in the brig *Speedy* in 1801, throwing in for good measure his capture of a battery on the Spanish coast in 1808. As he pointed out in his introduction: 'When one is writing about the Royal Navy of the eighteenth and early nineteenth centuries it is difficult to avoid

---

* It is likely that he had been toying with a version of the project for some time. Fifteen years earlier my mother recorded in her diary 'P. has talked for last 3 days of "Martin" novel.' 'Martin Joyce', as will be seen shortly, was the original name he chose for Stephen Maturin.

understatement; it is difficult to do full justice to one's subject; for so very often the improbable reality outruns fiction.'

In addition to attentive study of the narrative chronology provided by James, Patrick acquired invaluable material from Cochrane's autobiography, as well as the works of Frederick Marryat, who served under Cochrane and introduced his heroic commander's exploits into his fiction.*

From Cochrane, Jack Aubrey derived his exemplary seamanship, tactical cunning, courage, and resentment of higher authority, wherever he sensed (rightly or wrongly) incompetence or injustice. In the previous volume of this biography, I advanced reasons for believing that Patrick's depiction of Jack's qualities of leadership in action also owed much to his admiration for the skills of Captain Jack Jones, Gallipoli veteran and Master of the Ynysfor Hunt, which Patrick and my mother had followed enthusiastically among the mountains during their time in North Wales.†

Other aspects of Captain Aubrey's character and his physical appearance owe nothing to Cochrane or Jack Jones. A shrewd conjecture comes from Keith Wheatley, in his account of an interview with Patrick:

> Might not 'Lucky' Jack Aubrey, hugely strong and fit, a superb shiphandler, and brave as a lion and a natural if unreflective leader, be seen as the author's aspirational alter ego? Stephen Maturin is

---

* Patrick did not own any of Marryat's works, and some years ago I publicly questioned whether he ever read them. However, I had overlooked telling allusions among his preparatory notes for *Master and Commander*. They include a reference to 'Marryat's book on the press', an allusion to the author's *Suggestions for the Abolition of the Present System of Impressment in the Naval Service* (1822), while another note records that Patrick ordered a copy of his novel *Poor Jack* from the London Library.

† 'Jack [Aubrey] had a great respect for a man who could show good sport with a pack of hounds' (*Master and Commander*, p. 197), while the exhilaration experienced in combat was 'like fox-hunting at its best' (*The Ionian Mission*, p. 185).

half-Irish, slight, clever, a gifted linguist (O'Brian is fluent in French, Spanish and Gaelic and has won praise for his translation of Colette's letters)* and an obsessive amateur naturalist. He is also a spy and O'Brian reluctantly concedes to having spent the second world war working in British intelligence. Are the parallels not obvious?[2]

There is little doubt in my mind that Jack Aubrey did indeed represent in significant respects the man Patrick would have liked to be. As a child, he was small, nervous, prone to occasional bouts of debilitating illness, alternately neglected and harshly treated by his bullying giant of a father. How many in such circumstances have not longed to become a physically impressive leader of men?

In addition, his elder brother Mike provided just such a figure for emulation: tall, strongly built, and supremely self-assured. He had emigrated to Australia as a young man, where he pursued an adventurous life in the outback. Like the rest of his family, Patrick followed his adventures with avidity, which were transmitted home in regular correspondence. He was only twelve when Mike departed, and he met him again in profoundly affecting circumstances. In 1941 Mike joined the Royal Australian Air Force, and early in 1943 he was posted with his squadron to England. One day he called on Patrick and my mother in Chelsea, on whom he left an indelible impression of a bold, genial giant of a man. His impressive height actually required the cockpit roof of his bomber to be raised. A few weeks later he was killed in a bombing raid over Germany.

In another interview Patrick denied any projection of himself into the characters of Jack or Stephen: 'I am fond of them both, but I am in no way identified with either.'[3] This is true up to a point, since like all rounded literary characters they reflect a compound of elements, and, once created, independently evolve

---

* '. . . the Colette letters are in Goudeket's book (the <u>New Yorker</u>, by the way, said "the translation is perfect")' (Patrick to Arthur Cunningham of the British Library, 24 August 1993).

personality traits. Nevertheless, the substantial debt Jack owes to Patrick's own outlook and experience must be plain to those who knew him intimately.

Thus, we learn that Jack Aubrey's mother died during his early childhood, while his reprobate father plunges from one reckless financial disaster to another, causing Jack himself to fear and shun the taint of poverty. Jack's brief and unsatisfactory schooling is marked by bouts of flogging (which Patrick also endured while at school in Lewes), and such learning as he possessed was largely self-induced. His preferred pursuits include enthusiastic riding to hounds, a pronounced taste for good music, and astronomy. All these factors find close echoes in Patrick's own experience.

If substantial aspects of Jack Aubrey derive from Patrick himself, there can be no questioning the extent of his parallel identification with Stephen Maturin. The latter's physical appearance represents an amusingly unflattering image of Patrick, while their shared obsessive interest in natural history and other aspects of the exact sciences are too evident to require comment. His medical practice almost certainly derives from Patrick's father's profession, and his scientific enthusiasm doubtless owed something to his uncle Sidney, Professor of Physics at the Middlesex Hospital Medical School. Thus, it is a work of supererogation to emphasize the resemblances between Stephen Maturin and Patrick. I cannot resist evoking Maturin's physical stance on being harangued by a troublesome bore: 'His voice ran on, low and urgent, and Stephen stood with his hands behind his back, his head bowed, his face gravely inclined in a listening attitude. He was not, indeed, inattentive; but his attention was not so wholly taken up that he did not hear Jack cry . . .'[4]

So minutely does this posture correspond to one regularly adopted by Patrick himself, that to me at least it provokes the question how far Maturin reflected Patrick, and to what extent Patrick in turn came to model himself on his creation.

At the same time, Patrick drew on appropriate historical characters for his portrayal. First, and most obvious, is the ship's surgeon James Guthrie, with whom Cochrane enjoyed a close friendship, and who served on every ship he commanded as captain.[5] At the beginning of 1979 Patrick further noted 'Byam Martin's secret agent, a gentlemanlike man, P Cummings'.[6] He remained on the lookout for real-life models, commenting in 1988: 'Humboldt tends to be rather absolute & he is something of a bore, but he is the true natural philosopher through & through. I wish I had read him before, for SM.'

In the summer of 1967 I paid my customary visit to Collioure. Together with Michael Brereton, an old university friend, I had visited Greece, camping on the islands of Tinos and Mykonos. There we parted, I having booked a passage on what the Turkish owners assured Thomas Cook's in London was a pleasureboat, on which I had reserved what was described as a 'deck berth'. The description proved to be quite literal, and for three nights I lay alone in my sleeping bag under the stars, woken before sunrise each morning by the sailors' assemblage on deck for prayers towards Mecca, following which I had to keep shifting my resting place to dodge powerful hoses employed in swabbing the decks. The other passengers, who at least possessed the luxury of cabins, were outraged by the primitive conditions, and a petition to the captain was got up. In the event the Turkish passengers declined to sign, while the French and Spaniards could not agree on which was the language of high culture appropriate to such a measure. In fact this would have proved wholly immaterial, since the captain as I learned was a monoglot Turk. No food was provided for the solitary deck passenger, and when eventually the ship docked at Barcelona on 29 August I was consumed with hunger.

Patrick and my mother had arrived to collect me, and promptly plied me lavishly with fine food and wine, which swiftly restored my spirits almost to excess. Three days later Patrick confessed in his pocket diary: 'Too much bouillabaisse at Port Vendres Too much white wine.' We spent the days swimming, walking in the mountains, and working in the vineyard. As ever, there were long and stimulating conversations, and they displayed lively interest in my experiences in the Aegean.

We naturally talked much of Patrick's exciting commission from Lippincott. Regrettably, almost all that I now recall of those distant discussions was his concern to discover what, if any, conspiratorial activity by United Irishmen is recorded to have occurred aboard King George's men-of-war during the French Revolutionary wars. I had studied Irish history at Trinity College Dublin (which Maturin likewise attended), and well before that had succumbed to a life-long fascination with every aspect of the late Georgian period. Despite the substantial number of Irishmen serving in all ranks of the Royal Navy at the time, there is in fact scant evidence of seditious activity among them.[7] In the event, Patrick relegated this factor to Maturin's abandoned past experience, and currently that of the *Sophie*'s First Lieutenant, James Dillon.

We also canvassed a suitable name for the Irish protagonist of his story. Patrick explained that he wanted an Irish name, but not one that was too self-evidently so. Years later he noted that 'S Maturin was called Martin Joyce for the 1st few chapters', but this evidently left him dissatisfied. He envisaged a character standing largely outside national and social stereotypes, so that Stephen was finally cast as a half-Irish, half-Catalan bastard, not ostentatiously attached to the Roman Catholic faith of his upbringing: indeed, an opponent of religious and political bigotry of any kind – like Patrick himself.*

I recall suggesting the name Considine, featured in one of Lever's novels, but eventually Patrick came to prefer that of Maturin. I do not now remember his telling me where he originally found

---

* It may be wondered how, as a Roman Catholic, Maturin was admitted to the staunchly Protestant foundation of Trinity College Dublin. In Patrick's prepara-tory notes (although not, so far as I recall, anywhere in the printed works), Martin Joyce (as the Doctor was originally named) describes himself as 'nominally Protestant'. On the other hand, Catholics were formally admitted to the College from 1793, and had in individual cases been admitted even before that date.

the name, which already features in his novel *Three Bear Witness* (1952), but Dean King's suggestion that he adopted it from a reference in Somerset Maugham's *The Razor's Edge* may well be correct. Patrick held Maugham's work in high regard, and in the context the latter's reference to 'a bishop in the family, and a dramatist and several distinguished soldiers and scholars' would undoubtedly have appealed.

In due course I returned to England, and am glad to note that my parents enjoyed the visit as much as I did: 'Farewell to Nikolai – sad, but never such a pleasant stay Summer's ending.' The auguries appeared generally good at Collioure that year. From the moment my parents bought the narrow strip of vineyard on which they built their house, they had set their hopes on acquiring the adjacent vineyard on the northern side, whose proprietor they nicknamed Naboth, after the biblical landholder whose vineyard was coveted by king Ahab. 'Naboth' was a proper Collioure character, who adored animals. Beside his *casot* he kept some much-prized rabbits in hutches, which he regularly invited me to inspect when passing up and down the lane from our house. There was also a pet fox, and, most striking of all, a handsome mule. This beautifully brushed glossy-haired creature lay luxuriantly stretched out on a bed of straw beneath an open-sided extension. We could see it from our balcony, where it reclined immobile save for an occasional languid flick of its tail. Meanwhile Naboth toiled ceaselessly under its placid gaze, bearing baskets of earth or grapes, according to the season, up the steep slope. The mule disdained any form of labour, and appeared the true owner of the *vignoble*.

Now, after fourteen years, Naboth had agreed to sell. On 22 September 1967 Patrick recorded: 'M bought Naboth's vineyard for a million [francs] We are as amazed.' A fortnight later 'M began weeding Naboth, at a great pace, which makes it real.'

Although their financial position did not allow further spending at this time (nor indeed for long after), their extended property now permitted expansion of the house when finances should allow. Patrick had long entertained the idea of constructing a quasi-monastic cloister on the southern adjacent vineyard, which they had bought in 1962. This would provide a comfortable outdoor space sheltered from the baking sun of high summer, while warding off the maddening force of the seasonal tramontane winds which seasonally bedevil the district. Furthermore, they would be concealed from the inquisitive stares of walkers passing on the track before their front door, which irritated Patrick beyond measure. For the present, however, he was obliged to be content with construction of a plywood model of the planned cloister, as he had done in 1952 when imagining a design for their original humble *casot*. I possess both models, which continue to imbue me with a melancholy nostalgia.

It was at this time too that the contract was signed with Lippincott for *Master and Commander*, and two months later the first instalment of $2,500 (£812) was lodged in their bank account in London. Pleasingly, this more than covered the purchase of Naboth's vineyard.

Meanwhile Patrick was engaged in translating Joseph Kessel's *The Horsemen*, a book he came to admire. It was completed by the end of October, which finally enabled him to concentrate exclusively on his naval tale. On 24 November he and my mother set off by car for England, visiting among other places Lourdes (where my mother attended vespers), La Rochelle ('delightful'), Nantes ('peu sympathique cruelly bored in museum. Wonderful donjon Le Gd Fougeraye'), and Mont St Michel ('lovely green mud'). Arrived in London on the 30th, they dined with friends, and Patrick began researches at the London Library and Greenwich.

Next, they repaired to Somerset to stay for ten days near my mother's parents, Howard and Frieda Wicksteed. On a visit to Wells, Patrick lighted on a book which more than any other was to provide an invaluable vade mecum when compiling his naval tales: 'Rather more snow. To Wells – doubts about Faulkner's Dic., extreme beauty of square snowy fields, bare Breughel trees – [Glastonbury] Tor.'

Patrick hesitated for a week before returning from a visit to

Bath to clinch the deal at Heap's Bookshop. He already possessed the 1815 edition (edited by William Burney) of the book in question* – William Falconer, *An Universal Dictionary of the Marine* (London, 1769) – but clearly the 1769 edition provided a safer guide for his purpose. Above all, it plainly could not include anachronistic allusions to matter introduced after 1801, the year in which *Master and Commander* is set.

Regular visits to my mother's family in Somerset continued to afford Patrick lively images of aspects of English rural life, which were not difficult to extrapolate into his image of late Georgian England. Both my grandparents at Barton St David, and their neighbours the Slack family (Joan Slack was my grandmother's younger sister), belonged to the old school of country gentry in speech, manner and tastes. Patrick appreciated the fact that no more than three generations or so stood between them and their Regency ancestors, while the material contents of their homes were readily assimilated into his evocative image of rural England in the opening decades of the nineteenth century. Thus, the elegant furniture from Jack's mother-in-law's house, crammed into Ashgrove Cottage in *The Mauritius Command*, echoes almost exactly that found in my grandparents' home at Barton St David, even to the graceful satinwood 'cane settle' in their drawing room whose fragility prevented its practical use.

It was my eccentric uncle Austin Slack who unwittingly supplied one of Jack Aubrey's endearingly familiar traits. Readers will recall the latter's contortions and ill-suppressed guffaws when repeating one of his well-worn jokes. Just so Uncle Austin, a benignly simple soul, in manner and appearance a bluff nineteenth-century squire straight from the pages of Surtees, would shake with pleasure when erupting into a prized (frequently salacious) witticism, his broad ruddy features dissolving into a delighted grin that suffused his

---

* In his preparatory notes for *Master and Commander*, Patrick reminded himself 'Working a ship – Burney'.

Uncle Austin and Aunt Joan, summer 1960

face. One lunchtime at the Rose and Portcullis in Butleigh, Uncle Austin and I were seated with Patrick and my mother's old friend and admirer from Lundy days, George Turner. George was a classical scholar, and he and the rather prim (in company) Patrick were plunged deep in some abstruse philological discussion. All at once Uncle Austin felt inspiration arise within him. Winking at me, and grinning with anticipatory delight, he cryptically blurted out 'FART!' A startled Patrick was halted in mid-flow. He himself rarely swore, resented interruption, and was as I could see uncertain how to react. However, when George smiled and I burst out laughing, his apprehensive expression changed, and he too chuckled good-naturedly. Now, when I read of Jack Aubrey's jejune attempts

at wit – 'The spreading merriment, the relish, the thunderous mirth
. . . Jack . . . wiping the tears from his scarlet face'[8] – I see again
my dear old Uncle Austin's ruddy features float before me.*

Finally, I cannot help wondering whether the circumstances of
Jack Aubrey's initial meeting with Stephen Maturin at the celebrated
concert in Port Mahon may not have owed something to Patrick's
and my initial unhappy encounter at Collioure in 1955. Our
disparate natures had then aroused mutual resentment, which
however evolved into a lifetime's affection – albeit marred at times
by testy exchanges.

During their return to London in mid-December, my mother and
Patrick called at Portsmouth to see Nelson's flagship: 'A wonderful
morning aboard the Victory, great kindness from CO; entrancing
museum.' Back in town he conducted researches in the Public Record
Office. From his literary agent, Richard Scott Simon, he received
further encouraging news. Not only was Macmillan now offering a
contract for British rights to the naval novel, but they wished in
addition to republish *The Golden Ocean*! On New Year's Day Patrick
was invited to lunch by Marni Hodgkin, the editor at Macmillan's
Puffin imprint who had commissioned 'The Centurion's Gig'. She was
delighted by the prospect, subsequently writing to him: 'Reading
slowly and carefully through THE GOLDEN OCEAN, cover to cover,
has been an experience of purest enjoyment. Law, how I did laugh!
I do think it's the best novel of this period that I have <u>ever read</u>.'

Contracts (which continued to categorize the novel as 'Juvenile')
were exchanged in May.

Patrick's own judgement of his earlier work was more measured.
On 4 June 1969 he recorded his tentative misgivings:

I finished my revision of the Ocean, & really with all its faults I
am quite pleased with it. There is a richness of texture, a multiplicity

---

* At Christmas 1963, I had reported to Patrick that 'Austin was in great form,
and his jokes were even more feeble and vulgar than usual'.

of incident, & a strength of narrative (not mine, of course) that carries its sometimes embarrassingly false notes & curiously smug (almost mouthing) righteous conformity. And its clichés too, I hope. Lord, how little I knew of maritime life then! At least I have cut out a great many shameful errors.

The period 1967–69 was to prove the major turning-point of Patrick's career. The plot and leading characters of *Master and Commander* had been germinating ever since he received the invitation from Lippincott, and his researches over Christmas at Greenwich, the Public Record Office and the London Library provided him with a wealth of material relating to life at sea in Nelson's time, which he was now preparing to bring to life with a matchless authenticity and vigour.

Soon after their return to Collioure, Patrick was offered by Collins a new translation by Simone de Beauvoir, *The Woman Destroyed*. He appears to have worked on this during February and March, after which he launched himself into the delayed novel.

It is clear that he sensed something momentous stirring within him. Soon after his return from England at the beginning of 1968, he began for the first time since 1945 keeping a regular diary. Previously, he had jotted intermittent memoranda into pocket diaries and notebooks, but now he evidently decided that a detailed sequential record of his activities and thoughts was required. I doubt whether it be coincidence that he makes Stephen Maturin a diarist: certainly, the justification for his activity in the novels reflects Patrick's own viewpoint:

> For many, many years he had been unable to open his mind fully to any man or woman at all, and at times it seemed to him that candour was as essential as food or affection: during most of this period he had used his diary as a kind of surrogate for the non-existent loving ear – a very poor surrogate indeed, but one that had become so habitual as to be almost necessary.[9]

In *Master and Commander* Stephen's journal is carefully inscribed in code: a precaution necessitated by crowded life aboard ship, and in subsequent books by his function as an intelligence agent. This precaution was superfluous to Patrick's own requirement, since there could be no difficulty in concealing his diary in a home visited only by close friends and family. I am at times inclined to think that it was not read even by my mother, whom Patrick occasionally criticized to an extent I imagine he would not have wished her to discover. On the other hand, it is possible that he employed it on occasion as an oblique means of alerting her to issues provoking his irritation or distress. Apart from a lacuna for the three years 1971 to 1973,* he continued to record his activities every day up to the eve of his death thirty-one years later.

It is deeply regrettable, therefore, that journals for what were possibly the most significant years of this period have been stolen. They are the first and last of the series: those covering 1968 and 1999. As their disappearances occurred in distinct circumstances, I leave aside for the moment the fate of the diary for 1999.

There can be no doubt that each was independently stolen. In the case of the 1968 diary, the theft occurred many years after its compilation, and was planned with considerable ingenuity. Obviously I know much more about this than may safely be published (I have some experience of English libel law), and here confine myself to recording the fact.

The first theft was most likely motivated by the diary's exceptional interest and financial value as a collectors' item, describing as it does the genesis of *Master and Commander*. As first of the series, too, its disappearance might have been hoped to pass unnoticed. This could indeed have proved to be the case, but for the

---

* It appears that he did not keep a record during these years. In 1993 he noted: 'Unhappily I do not seem to have anything for 1971–/2/3, the probable years of their [onions'] planting.'

fact that the thief was clearly unaware that Patrick employed his diaries as journals of record, to which he regularly referred when checking information ranging from dates for planting orchids or vegetables, to previous levels of medication and records of tax returns. Like most diarists, too, he occasionally found himself browsing through earlier numbers from general interest. Nor had the thief reason to anticipate the care with which I have been obliged to sift the diaries when preparing this biography.

What has been lost to literary appreciation by the disappearance of the 1968 diary is indicated by this chance allusion on 4 July 1989:

> It was our [wedding] anniversary, which I tend to forget: & looking back into my diary of 68 to see what we did then I found the whole history of M[aster] & C[ommander] & many other things – how we swam & walked! Some I had quite forgotten such as the whiteness of Jean le blanc preening himself somewhere up by the Astrabol,* others are as lively as though they had happened yesterday.

For the foreseeable future, therefore, we possess only fragmentary indications of the fervour of inspiration which gripped him at this time. In April he and my mother sailed to Minorca, where Patrick built up that unforgettable picture of Port Mahon and its environs which affords one of the most celebrated openings in the annals of fiction. So far as I am aware, the sole accessible evidence for this expedition survives in two chance references.

My mother's accounts for April include this terse entry: 'Voyage . . . Barcelona-Port-Mahon boat 13,994 [fr]'. And in a letter written in 1974 to my uncle Ivan, she mentioned: 'Minorca. It is such a beautiful island, so unspoiled compared to the other Balearics. We took an archaic steamer to Port-Mahon at the time of Master and Commander, and absolutely loved it.'

---

* In the mountains above Collioure.

Judging by the plenitude of detail provided in successive descriptions of the port and its narrow entrance from the sea, he made extensive diary notes at the time. It was not until 1995 that he paid a brief return visit to the island.

Driven by an inspired enthusiasm which seemingly never flagged, Patrick wrote the novel during the summer months of 1968. Although the theft of his diary for that year appears not to have occurred in his home, it is ironical that in July the peace of the little household was disturbed by a burglary. For convenience my parents occasionally stored sums of money at home, often hidden inside a hollowed-out copy of *The Golden Ocean*, ranked unobtrusively among other books on the shelves. Wherever it was stored on this occasion, the raiders helped themselves to 65,000 francs (£55). Ancillary beneficiaries were the voluble Collioure guardians of security: 'We gave the police a dozen vin vert,' noted my mother. Given the then isolated situation of the house, and extended periods when it was left empty, it is surprising that this was the only burglary experienced from its initial construction in 1955 to the present day. A burglar would in any case have been unlikely to have discovered the diaries, which were carefully hidden. Even had he chanced on them, it is unlikely that a French thief would have been able to read them, nor in any case would he have any means of appreciating the financial value of a particular volume among so many.

In October and November Patrick and my mother drove across France for a month's stay in England, where once again they spent much of the time with my grandparents and the Slacks in Somerset. As the novel was not yet completed, the visit may in part have been for the purpose of conducting final researches.

Many intimations in *Master and Commander* attest to the extent to which it represents an intensely personal work. Patrick enjoyed introducing familiar material objects from his home into his tales, such as the whale's tooth young Babbington was concerned to save should the *Sophie* be sunk.* His friends were likewise granted brief appearances. The American ship *John B. Christopher*, which Aubrey is ordered to search for two fugitive United Irishmen, bears the name of Patrick's colleague during his wartime service in London and continuing friend, the historian Jack Christopher. An American sailor, Plimpton, punished for drunkenness during Thanksgiving at Port Mahon, is named after Sarah Plimpton, another longstanding American friend. It has been seen that Patrick similarly fastened on the name of our Somerset friend Timothy Heneage as that of Jack Aubrey's intimate friend Heneage Dundas.

Patrick's extraordinarily painstaking preparations for the book are apparent from his detailed notes in my possession, covering chapters 1 to the start of 5. These comprise a melange of material, ranging from details of ships (a sketch of the interior of the *Sophie*[10] illustrates how very small she was) to extracts from conversations between the principal characters. The latter echo Patrick's long-established practice of interrogating himself in mental soliloquies, extensively recorded in his diaries, notebooks, and even odd slips of paper used as bookmarks or posted around the house.

From his notes we learn that Jack was born in 1773, and was accordingly twenty-seven in 1800. Martin Joyce (as Stephen Maturin is initially named in Patrick's notes – he only becomes 'Stephen' by chapter 5) is described as 'unbelieving, disseminated sense of sin, at the most a deist, unaccepted outside'; 'MJ a detached spectator' – just like, of course, Patrick himself. In a snatch of dialogue, on explaining

---

* *Master and Commander*, p. 319. In *The Golden Ocean* (pp. 224–27, 225) Commodore Anson presents Peter Palafox with William Winstanley's quaint anthology *The New Help to Discourse* (London, 1716), of which Patrick possessed what I like to consider the copy owned by Peter. Patrick's favourite silence-breaker from Winstanley's guide during conversation was 'Who was the most famous Whore in her time?' (p. 27). Both tooth and book are now in my possession.

that he is 'nominally Protestant', he is asked by Jack: 'What do you mean <u>nominally</u>?' Martin: 'Just as you people are nominally abs [able seamen] with 5 yrs sea-experience – so as to get the post. Just the same. Is it – dubiously?' The disparate outlooks of Jack, 'Martin' and James Dillon are carefully established: 'the thing is that they are all (though they think themselves so old) malleable & still forming their definitive personalities'. A common bond is established between the otherwise markedly differing personalities of 'Martin' and Jack: 'they both perceive order in music'.

The indications are that these notes were compiled before, during, and after Patrick's stay in England at the end of 1967. Following those for chapter 5, they become very cursory. It was some time after his return to Collioure in early 1968 that he set down, with what it is hard not to believe was a gratified flourish, the title 'MASTER & COMMANDER'.

By Christmas 1968 the completed typescript was sent to Richard Scott Simon at Curtis Brown. As inevitable days followed by less explicable weeks went by without attracting any reaction from the publishers, Patrick became increasingly disquieted. From Lippincott across the Atlantic delay was to be expected. However, Simon had agreed a British contract at the beginning of the year with Macmillan, which included the substantial advance of £1,000, to be paid in customary instalments.

On 10 January 1969 Patrick began to express concern: 'I expect Lippincotts, Macmillans' response (I am probably very anxious about these).' By the 16th: 'I am beginning to armour my mind for a thumping disappointment about <u>M&C</u>.' Nothing seemed to be going well. On the 29th he learned that 'There is a post-office strike in England. This has happened before just when we have been very anxious for news.' Next day, however, came the great breakthrough:

Such a pleasant letter from Lippincott. We were charmed having (I find) been very much afraid; but it ruined our digestion & put us into such a hurry of spirits that we were obliged to go early to bed, with a pill. It would have been morally & financially disastrous if Lippincott had disliked the book – a really blushing crow.*

Patrick need not have worried. As his editor at Lippincott, Tony Gibbs, later recalled:

the publishing house I worked for signed up Patrick O'Brian, on the basis of his highly regarded historical novel for teenagers, *The Golden Ocean*. I'd never heard of O'Brian, but I was asked to take a look at his new manuscript because I was the only editor on staff who owned a boat.

So *Master and Commander* landed on my desk. I picked it up without enthusiasm. I was a confirmed aficionado of Forester – a skillful weaver of plots and a careful scholar with personal experience of sailing vessels and the sea. In Horatio Hornblower he had created a seafarer with whom readers could empathize: a cerebral hero (aren't we all?) who was prey to the same fears that weekend mariners recognized all too well.

Long before I'd finished *Master and Commander*, I realized that O'Brian had leapfrogged over Forester. O'Brian wasn't writing about the early 19th century; he seemed to be writing from within it – and with a sense of humor entirely lacking in historical novelists. Further, O'Brian peopled his universe with delightful, three-dimensional characters, especially his two protagonists – Captain Jack Aubrey, a skillful lion afloat though nearly helpless ashore, and Dr. Stephen Maturin, physician, secret agent, and unhappy lover.[11]

Thus far, all was as good as might be, but a fortnight later Patrick received:

* The spoonerism at first escaped me.

A most disappointing letter from Macmillan. 'Book delightful, but' & that but includes lack of drama & 'tension between the characters' – presumably J[ack]A[ubrey] & J[ames]D[illon]. We had expected a series of more or less piddling objections, but nothing like this fundamental taking apart. Qu. is he right? If so to what degree? Walking very swiftly in the freezing wind to the milestone . . . I decided to wait for Simon, Cushman & above all [?]; & if they concur to go to London & talk to James Wright [at Macmillan]. Even if they do not I probably ought to do something if I want to stay with Macmillan. Do I? They have been the book's bane. But I am very vulnerable.

Racked with doubts, Patrick began to wonder whether:

the book (M & C) might concentrate more on the disagreement between JA & JD, omit the voyage to Alexandria, & end with the (enhanced) Cacafuego action – no capture, Algeciras, court-martial. It would be more of a piece, better from the point of view of construction & thus perhaps of atavistic tension: less episodic, less rich, too. But then I should have those remaining chapters as a dash-away start for an eventual 2d vol.

Fortunately, these authorial misgivings were brushed aside almost at once by a renewed intimation of his American publisher's enthusiastic endorsement:

Lippincott's total of changes required is that I should identify Port Mahon. As for Macmillan, Richard Simon is showing MS to Collins with the idea of changing publishers . . . A curious feeling of great relief. Why? The situation in London is still quite tense.

As ever, the natural world served to soothe Patrick's frayed nerves:

We went to see whether there were snowdrops yet – yes, just beginning. Snowy forest road with innumerable tracks, boar, genet, fox, badger. Heavy going, but the alp was delightful. A probably golden eagle, 2 uncertain falcons. I think lanner & merlin & a buzzard. Home very tired, & M did not sleep . . . She said I snored too, but this was an illusion, for I did not – was awake.

Finally, on 26 March came further exciting news, which put everything at rest. Collins had accepted the novel!

Letter from Richard S[imon] with most agreeable, <u>soothing</u>, tranquillizing (& totally unexpected) news that Macmillans yield up £500 as unreturnable, so that when the Collins advance is in we are £250 up. This, from yesterday's supposed position, is a gain of £500; a real one of £250. Calmness rather than joy; & a suspicion that Macm. are willing to pay the 500 to go away. Or is it James Wright being good & kind?

Richard Scott Simon's switch from the unenthusiastic Macmillan was to reap dividends extending far beyond any current concern. The editor at Collins whom he approached was Richard Ollard, who had been a King's Scholar at Eton, and a talented historian in his own right. He had served in the wartime Royal Navy, where poor eyesight prevented his participation in active service. While he never pulled critical punches, he was appreciated as a fair and penetrating assessor of other men's labours. It is hard to conceive of an editor better qualified to give Patrick's work its due.

Ollard read the text of *Master and Commander* with avidity, providing the formidable Sir William Collins with this ringing endorsement:

This novel was jointly commissioned by Lippincott in the USA and Macmillans here. Lippincott are delighted with it but Macmillans were tepid, so Richard Simon, wanting him to be published by someone who would put some punch into it, offered the novel to me.

I did just mention it in a letter to you dated March 12th, from which you will have gathered that it is a novel of the C.S. Forester/ Dudley Pope type, done with originality, gusto, and a really astonishing knowledge of the sources. Indeed, very occasionally the author's expertise in the technicalities of sailing ships or his fondness for parodying 18th Century turns of phrase leads him into faint tiresomeness, but these are the most minor of blemishes, easily removed. What he has got is first class narrative power. This is a book which is extremely difficult to put down, and the descriptive passages, particularly of naval action, are thrilling. He is also a more than competent hand at characterisation except that his women do not seem to be up to much, but that doesn't matter in a book about a Nelsonic naval officer as the women appear for strictly utilitarian purposes.

After a summary account of the book's plot and principal characters, Ollard concluded: 'This is a book of high literary quality and I think we could set it very well . . . I would therefore most emphatically recommend taking this novel . . .'

On 3 April the contract was signed, and Patrick's literary career now appeared firmly settled on both sides of the Atlantic. While Tony Gibbs was shortly to leave Lippincott, Ollard continued as Patrick's editor until 1993. It swiftly developed into the happiest of collaborations. A tall and authoritative figure, Ollard was decisive, occasionally acerbic, in his judgements. However, they were invariably sensible, and in Patrick's case sparingly applied. In Ollard he had acquired a sympathetic editor, whose learning and judgement he came profoundly to respect. Ollard's combination of gentlemanly courtesy, impressive physical appearance and perceptive acumen combined to allay the easily irritated author's generally dismissive view of the comments of critics and editors alike. He it was who contributed all the subsequent dust-jacket 'blurbs' for the Aubrey–

Maturin series, which he recalled as having invariably been submitted to Patrick for approval and occasional alteration.

Ollard was not the only scholar-editor working at Collins. He amusedly passed on a plea from Philip Ziegler, the biographer, who was 'deeply disturbed that you should speak so harshly of the future William IV (whose biography he is writing) as you do on page 232, but I will leave you to fight that out with him . . .' The allusion was to the fact that Aubrey 'had been shipmates with that singularly unattractive hot-headed cold-hearted bullying Hanoverian'. Patrick provided this spirited (and surely justified) response:

> . . . it grieves me to speak roughly of the Duke of Clarence. But H[is] H[ighness]'s treatment of Schomberg, Byam Martin, the officers of HMS Andromeda ('Shd any officer or gentleman be reprimanded by the capt, it is expected upon these occasions no answer is given'), naval uniform, American painters, George III, & Mrs Jordan make it difficult to love him.*

Patrick felt well served by his publishers, save in one significant respect. At the end of July 1969 he received the 'Draft of a jacket from Collins. Embarrassing, but better than Lippincotts'. The American jacket depicted an agitated and bewigged Aubrey, yelling aimlessly at a fiery ocean. 'Horrible Lippincott jacket,' commented the author. 'If I had written a book it matched, I really should have prostituted myself.' The Collins version was little better, where Aubrey features as a diffident youth crowned with twentieth-century haircut and sheepishly clutching an anachronistic percussion-hammer

---

* Ziegler himself came to acknowledge that 'there is no doubt that Prince William in 1787 was bad-tempered and even sometimes brutish' (*King William IV* (London, 1971), p. 59). In subsequent novels Patrick came to portray him in a more favourable light, corresponding to his improved character after leaving the Navy.

pistol.* My mother was so disgusted with it that she threw it away, subsequently replacing it with the more tasteful design by Arthur Barbosa introduced for a later edition.

Just before Christmas: 'Collins M & C arrived, to my astonishment: it was all right, apart from the lamentable blurb actually inside the book: but I don't care for it.' It is difficult to see what there was to dislike, but his correspondence suggests that he took exception to what in an earlier version he regarded as excessive emphasis on his writing for children, as also to comparison with C.S. Forester. (Setting aside filial prejudice, I can only concur that there is no realistic comparison between the two authors. But such judgements are best left to the reader.) Ten days later copies of the US edition arrived. They had been held up by the customs, and in fact this appears to be the first edition, if only by a few days.†

While the objectionable blurbs were concocted by the publishers, Patrick devoted particular care to the wording of his introduction. Ever fearful of rancorous criticism, he was particularly 'unwilling that any envious worm with gnawing lips should spring up on his hind legs in the TLS and cry "This chap has been cribbing".' He was at pains to explain that he had indeed drawn extensively on works of contemporary naval historians like James, and was inspired by the real-life heroics of 'the Cochranes, Byrons, Falconers, Seymours, Boscawens' and others who distinguished themselves during the epic conflict. At the same time, he had not hesitated freely to reorder events and characters with dramatic licence.

I remember Patrick's once affirming the best moment in an author's working life to be the receipt of page proofs. There the

---

* Patrick was further dismayed by the Collins paperback cover, whose protagonist he described to me at the time in a letter as 'a left-handed gentleman, of markedly simian appearance'.

† The delay accounts for the fact that my mother retained the Collins edition as her personal copy. Patrick himself appears to have regarded the Lippincott edition as the first. When visited by the journalist Mark Horowitz in 1993, Patrick noted that: 'He had brought . . . a 1st ed (Lippincott 69) of M&C to be signed.'

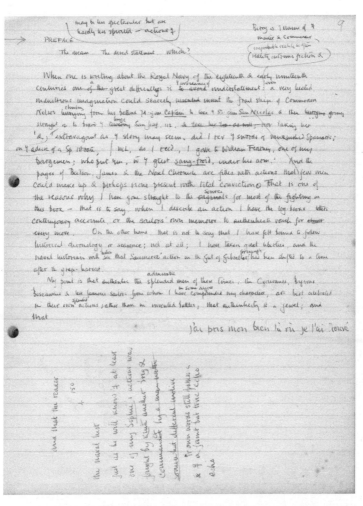

Patrick's original draft preface to *Master and Commander*

work appears for the first time in book form, while opportunity remains for correcting surviving solecisms. Now, however, it was too late for further correction. On this occasion natural caution, combined perhaps with a sense of anticlimax experienced by many authors, led him at first to harbour grave doubts about the book's literary quality. Five days after receiving his first copy, he went so far as to confess: 'I am much depressed by M & C.'

Fortunately, the initial acclaim which greeted its appearance rapidly swept away his doubts. In January he received 'Such a kind, generous letter from Mary Renault in S. Africa: very difficult to reply to, but I like it extremely.' Author of a succession of highly regarded historical novels, Renault remained a regular corre-spondent and admirer of Patrick's work over the years that followed. Richard Ollard wrote 'to congratulate you on your outstandingly successful debut as a historical novelist', while Philip Ziegler declared himself delighted that 'Master And Commander has got off to so good a start. 25,000 words of my William IV whitewash are now on paper!'

So satisfactory were sales, that as early as 9 February Richard Ollard wrote to Patrick, informing him: 'I am delighted to say that we have to-day put in hand an immediate reprint of Master & Commander. It should be through in about 3 weeks. I do congrat-ulate you on your success & hope that it will encourage you to further labours.'

The judgement of reviewers was, however, oddly mixed and strangely muted. Inevitable, but surely inapt and largely pointless, comparisons with Hornblower featured, as feared, with monoto-nous regularity. In the *Irish Press* H.J. Poole dismissed the book as 'not, I think, memorable, at least in the Hornblower way', while David Taylor in the *Library Journal* patronizingly suggested that 'mourning Hornblower fans may prefer to read a good if disap-pointing book rather than to reread one of the master's epics'.

Fortunately there were more perceptive assessments to set against these dismissive comments. The naval historian Tom Pocock extolled Patrick's achievement: 'It is as though, under Mr. O'Brian's touch, those great sea-paintings at Greenwich had stirred and come alive.'

Martin Levin, in the *New York Times Book Review*, provided a careful appraisal, in which he declared that *Master and Commander*:

re-creates with delightful subtlety, the flavor of life aboard a midget British man-of-war plying the western Mediterranean in the year 1800, a year of indecisive naval skirmishes with France and Spain. Even for a reader not especially interested in matters nautical, the author's easy command of the philosophical, political, sensual and social temper of the times flavors a rich entertainment.

However inept, peevish, or unfair he considered it, a poor review never failed to dash Patrick's spirits. More than once he humorously cited to me an aphorism he ascribed to Mae West: 'Don't give me criticism – all I want is unstinted praise.' Setting aside a few trifling inconsistencies (Jack Aubrey cannot have been stationed in the West Indies throughout the Irish uprising of 1798 *and* engaged in the battle of the Nile in the same year), Patrick displayed an encyclopaedic, yet at the same time *comfortable*, mastery of historical detail unmatched since Scott or Stevenson.

In time he was able to consider his most famous book from a dispassionate perspective. Five years after publication he reread it, concluding with an assessment most readers would I imagine strongly endorse: 'The beginning of M & C is as good as anything I ever wrote: there is a freshness that I doubt I shall ever recapture.'

Later still, in 1988:

I spent the day with M & C, correcting some mistakes & making alterations. Some of the book's liveliness comes from the fact that this was my 1st adult encounter with the RN – I could describe many things that could scarcely be described again, or not often, in later books – but although I like what I have read (only 100 pp) I may have over-rated it. The last 2 [books] have perhaps more weight & depth.

VIII

The Green Isle Calls

> 'I am of Ireland,
> And the Holy Land of Ireland,
> And time runs on', cried she.
> 'Come out of charity,
> Come dance with me in Ireland.'
>
> William Butler Yeats,
> 'I am of Ireland'

The years 1969 and 1970 saw major shifts in Patrick's literary and household situation. His perennially precarious financial position had been improved by completion of his translation of the celebrated memoir *Papillon* by Henri Charrière, a convicted criminal who effected (so he claimed) a dramatic escape from the notorious French penal colony of Devil's Island. On 14 August 1969, Patrick's literary agent Richard Scott Simon negotiated a contract with Rupert Hart-Davis which accorded terms exceptionally favourable to the translator. Patrick was to receive 'a fee calculated on the basis of £5. 0. 0. (five pounds) per thousand words . . . and a royalty of 1% (one per cent) on all copies sold after 20,000'. From the following year the book swiftly became an international bestseller, eventually adapted into a major feature film starring Steve McQueen and Dustin Hoffman. However, despite the welcome income received in consequence of the terms agreed with Hart-Davis, the US publisher's choice of a different translator deprived him of a much more substantial revenue that he would otherwise have obtained.

Patrick began by being impressed by the book, but eventually:

> I finished [reading] Papillon with some contempt for his easy sentimentality, hypocrisy & really <u>silliness</u>, which was a pity. But on reflection I see that there was a good deal in the earlier parts: a picture of some value; & as the pte or post-face says, a remarkable récit linéaire.

When the book was published, Patrick was invited to meet the author in Paris. To me he confided afterwards that he found Charrière shifty and untrustworthy – a shrewd assessment, since borne out by evidence.

By now Collioure, though still a gem of the western Mediterranean, was changing – not, alas, for the better. Strolling through the town one day, Patrick observed with a pang:

> Desolation on the plage des pêcheurs – I went on, to the jetty having posted letters. They are making a port de plaisance, which is reasonable, perhaps, but they have seen fit to smash three beautiful fishing-boats, allegedly to make room. People standing about, silent. Py [Patrick's barber] nervous, conscious, apprehensive. Impiety.

It was not long before a philistine *Mairie* blithely ordered the remaining fishing boats to be destroyed in a huge bonfire on the beach. Fishing was henceforth banished from Collioure after untold centuries of colourful life, to be conducted henceforward by a vast grim vessel emerging from Port-Vendres, which indiscriminately gorged up everything living within the violated deep.*

---

* In 1948 Raoul Dufy had written in the *livre d'or* at Les Templiers restaurant: '*Collioure sans voiles, c'est un ciel sans étoiles.*'

Melancholy as the prospect appeared to Patrick, he at least was able to immerse himself in loving re-creation of another in many ways for him more congenial world. He had written *Master and Commander* in a high flush of inspired enthusiasm. Despite this, he found himself encountering problems with its sequel. The first work had been germinating off and on for many years – as has been seen, possibly from as early as 1955. After the tremendous surge of energy and imagination that resulted in *Master and Commander*, Patrick at first entertained grave doubts as to whether he could make a success of a renewal of his heroes' exploits. This apprehension had arisen before, when he gained lasting delight from *The Golden Ocean*, but reckoned its sequel *The Unknown Shore* somewhat lacklustre and over-reliant on the historical record.

Nevertheless, in July 1969 Patrick noted that 'I have a rough idea of about ½ the next book THINK Privateering? Piracy?'. Within a few days he had:

> finished Chapter I & typed nearly all of it: about 5000 [words]: showed it to M but am afraid she does not like it, or at least has strong reserves. Sad. If I ask for praise I shall get it (& any Qu. is a request for praise) & know it is worthless; & if I do not I shall never know for sure. There are other relationships very like this . . . No sleep. So depressed about the book. It is pretty trivial, I know. Drop it? Press on alone?

Such was the initially uneasy genesis of *Post Captain*.

I do not know what induced my mother's lack of enthusiasm. Had she detected the obvious affinity between herself and the strong-minded but scarcely moral Diana Villiers? Then again, there was the unpleasant figure of Mrs Williams, who removes her beautiful daughter Sophia from Jack Aubrey's company on learning of his descent into poverty. The character plainly draws on my mother's own mother Frieda Wicksteed, who continued throughout her life in some degree disapproving of Patrick. For the purpose of his narrative Patrick endows Mrs Williams with characteristics of meanness and vulgarity, neither of which was remotely applicable to my intelligent and elegant grandmother.

Other problems assailed Patrick around this time. His right hand was recurrently affected by Dupuytren's disease – a particularly

Patrick's little study in the year of his death

unpleasant affliction for a writer. Bouts of depression came and went. Then again, the household was far from providing a restful literary refuge. In September 1967 he and my mother had finally managed to buy the vineyard on their northern boundary, which they had long coveted, for a million francs. A year later they obtained the *permis de construire* from the *Mairie* to extend the house onto the new property, and on 20 March 1969 the bank at Port-Vendres 'promised eventual support in the neighbourhood of 500,000 without formality'.

In due course a handsome bedroom with adjacent bathroom was constructed, and beyond it a substantial garage. Extension of this structure allowed for opening up below a *cave* in the rock for storing wine, together with an outer gallery which was to become Patrick's study for the remainder of his life. A lavatory was conveniently – if a little obtrusively – installed beside the open entrance to the *cave*. Although these added facilities would transform their home life, for the present their peace was shattered for months. Apart from enthusiastic builders constantly banging on the roof and adjacent walls, while shouting to each other in exuberant Catalan, creation of the *cave* and gallery below required deployment of mines and pneumatic drills. At times evasive tactics were required: 'Very stupid this morning. Beautiful sun, breakfast out[side]. Down through the dew, along the correch to avoid the workmen (small talk in short supply, & continued rather servile admiration probably vexes them). They were not there.'

It was not until 2 April 1970 that Patrick recorded with relief: 'Chairs painted, & gallery: house nearly done: this is the 8th month.'

He celebrated this near-completion with a brief restorative trip to his beloved Ireland.* From Dublin he toured the south from County Wexford to Dingle, whence he gained a 'splendid' view of

---

* Terry Zobeck reminds me that, 'given the closeness between him and Mary, he certainly took a good number of trips by himself'. This is true, and I assume arose from a combination of shortage of money, the requirement for someone to remain looking after the house and vineyard, and (I fancy most likely) Patrick's occasional need to detach himself entirely from his workaday routine. However, I have not found the reason specified anywhere in his diaries or correspondence.

the Blasket Islands. He was also gratified to see men fishing from currachs. Destructive changes looming over Ireland's matchless countryside were yet to come. At Ennis he:

> Was set upon by pure beggar-woman with blanket & then – 'I'm an Irish person, your honour. & a Catholic, & would not tell a lie'. She was going to hospital tomorrow to have a baby; & she would pray for me. She was also the 7th daughter, she observed. gave her 3 1/-. On, rather pleased. Many asses, turf stacks. Marvellous [round] tower between Crushen & Gort.

Having gazed from the towering cliffs of Moher onto the Aran Islands, he returned to Dublin by 'splendid Clonmacnois all to myself' and Maynooth, visiting along the way 'Carton's splendours, shown round by kind owner'. After concluding his round trip in Dublin with a poor dinner at Jury's restaurant, he penned a heart-felt: 'Dear Dublin. Quando te aspician?'

Aside from such material interruptions, Patrick continued finan-cially largely dependent on translation work. Over the winter of 1969 to 1970 he translated Robert Guillain's *Japon: troisième grand*. This he fortunately found 'exceedingly interesting & literate', although 'very hard to put into running English'. Nevertheless he completed the 110,000 words within three months: 'In 2 bouts I finished Japon: it was a very heavy task indeed.'

No sooner had he completed this than he was commissioned to provide his third translation of a work by Simone de Beauvoir. Patrick fortunately entertained a high respect for her reputation, and was concerned to do her work justice. A meeting in Paris was arranged in April, which led to a continuing friendship. However, even this three days' separation from my mother distressed him, and he wrote in a letter he gave her on his return:

> Dearest M. You brood dark unhappy thoughts: they are essentially baseless & they arise from the old, unfounded impressions of

disseminated guilt that your childhood was bathed in – unscrupulous, insecure people can easily make the sweet-natured young feel bad & inadequate, & those feelings can come to the top in moments of stress. I am not much of a creature, whatever in your kindness you may say, but such as I am, with all my faults, I am yours P x.*

Throughout this time he also continued working on *Post Captain*, for which he signed a contract with Lippincott in the US in February 1970, and with Collins in England in April. Despite this, he suffered from continued misgivings, lamenting in June: 'PC is sadly twee & knowing – pastiche, too sub-Austen. But how can I tie in the new beginning? I sat down to write it, but ran aground on technical triv-ialities. What was the armament of a 28 gun frigate in 1801? 9lbers?'

Recurrent bouts of writer's block plagued him. It was probably in an attempt to deflect this, that at the end of May and beginning of June 1970 he and my mother paid a visit to Vienna, where they came to know two charming elderly aristocratic Austrian ladies, the Princesses Schönburg and Auersperg. Close friendships devel-oped, and shortly after their return to Collioure Patrick returned a fortnight later to stay as a paying guest at Princess Auersperg's magnificent Schloss Goldegg outside Vienna. His hope was that the change of scene would serve to detach him from pressing worries and distractions at home, enabling him to break the back of the still troublesome novel.†

Unfortunately, although he applied himself with wonted dili-gence, further unexpected considerations arose to disturb him. His

---

* Everything I know indicates that my mother had in reality been very much a favourite of her parents, both as a high-spirited teenage girl and following her marriage to my father. I fear it was not her childhood that was bathed in disseminated guilt, but rather her abandonment of my sister and me five years after her wedding. But Patrick of course knew only what he learned or sensed from my mother.

† My own experience echoes that of Patrick: viz. that changing the location of one's writing rarely induces any lasting renewal of inspiration.

account of the incipient love affair between Stephen Maturin and Diana Villiers owed much to the troubled days of his own furtive romance with my mother on the eve of the War. As he confided to his diary on successive days in July: 'I am tempted now (10 pm) to start the piece with D[iana]V[illiers] & S[tephen]M[aturin] at the ball, but I need to be on top of my form'; 'I wrote the piece about the ball quite well I think'; 'M[ar]y obvious parallel to DV: a temptation to push it too far (facility etc) must be resisted.'*

To my mother he wrote: 'Is my DV credible? Can you speak of naked motives without making your character odious? Is the technique of never seeing her from the inside valid? Is the use of SM's diary a solution of facility, weak?' It seems that relations between Maturin and Diana Villiers were so enmeshed in Patrick's mind with his own clandestine relations with my mother in 1939–40 that he was not entirely able to disentangle the two. 'I have mucked up the SM–DV intrigue, probably, but at least there is something to work upon.'

Before long Patrick was finding the separation from my mother all but intolerable:

No word from M. This seems to me inhuman & I wrote her a pretty ignoble blackmailing letter. Spirits extraordinarily up & down – mostly down – a strong sense of ill usage . . . I read M & C, perhaps too quickly. It seems poor thin stuff to me.

Patrick's 'pretty ignoble blackmailing letter' survives, and is worth citing for the insight it provides into a surprising aspect of their intensely close relationship. Although the couple were now in their mid-fifties, Patrick clearly continued as much in love with my mother as he had been thirty years previously – or indeed would be thirty years later:

---

* This provides a unique but tantalizingly cryptic glimpse of Patrick's initial relationship with my mother just before the War.

Saturday

You said you would not write, and I did not believe you: when I found no word here after those days and days of driving I was strangely shocked, and your one, cold dutiful note of the 22nd disturbed me even more. The lunchtray came up just now, and when I realized there was no letter on it I pushed the whole thing aside: all the more since yesterday was the only moderately cheerful evening I have spent for God knows how long – shopping with Heinz and Eve, playing bridge with Princess Schönburg – and since I spent this morning sending you a bauble for our silver wedding day. It seemed impossible that our minds should not have crossed.

Sometimes you have said that I do not speak clearly, and it is true: I distrust words and I value indirection too highly. But I will say this as directly as can be – if you think my writing worth a straw, do not keep me in this state. While expostulations, harangues and pleading drift between me and my paper I can do nothing but hack work, and that only with a grinding, inefficient labour.

Our relationship is vital to me. Write kindly if you have kindness left: tell me plainly if you have none.

My mother's side of the correspondence has not survived, so one can only surmise what led her to respond in so apparently perfunctory a manner. Could his cheerful and chatty correspondence have led her to think that he was enjoying himself rather too much without her? Did she herself suffer from depression in his absence? Was she ill, as was all too often the case?* Fortunately, harmony was restored when they were eventually reunited, and Patrick found their 'House so much prettier than I had remembered.'

Although he applied himself undeterred to his current literary

---

* The torment inflicted by a loved one's failure to communicate provides a recurring motif in Patrick's novels: e.g. *The Surgeon's Mate*, pp. 37–38; *The Far Side of the World*, p. 119.

commissions, he continued over ensuing weeks assailed by misgivings and bouts of depression. In February *The Golden Ocean* had been republished (with Patrick's minor corrections) by Macmillan, and in October Penguin Books agreed on paperback publication. Unfortunately, however, sales of neither proved satisfactory. Macmillan in consequence declined to republish *The Unknown Shore*, and eventually Patrick received disquieting news that their remaining copies of *The Golden Ocean* were being pulped.

While in the summer of 1970 much of this remained in the future, Patrick himself expressed dissatisfaction with *The Unknown Shore*, which as has been seen he regarded as too derivative from the historical record, and generally less inspired than its predecessor. This in turn may (at least in part) account for what most readers will surely consider exaggerated doubts about the merits of his sequel to *Master and Commander*. In September he noted: 'We decided to go to Minorca when the money comes.' Nothing came of the project, which conceivably reflected an additional scheme for the recovery of inspiration.

Further signals of Patrick's continuing low spirits very likely account for the abandonment of his diary for the three years covering 1971 to 1973. It was his regular tendency to preserve a careful record of his activities when his affairs appeared promising, and to abandon it when they did not. Thus, he kept a lively journal for the first nine months of his and my mother's stay in Wales. Their withdrawal to the mountain wilderness presented so exciting and promising a project that Patrick was concerned to preserve a detailed account of their adventures. This he did, and most entertaining reading it affords. However, when after some months a protracted bout of severe writer's block set in, he abandoned the project. It was surely no coincidence that he made his momentous decision to keep a daily journal in 1968, the year he began to fulfil Lippincott's magical commission to write *Master and Commander*. As mentioned earlier, although this invaluable record was regrettably stolen at the end of Patrick's life, we know from a subsequent diary entry that he regarded 1968 as an (if not the) *annus mirabilis* of his life, when he researched and wrote *Master and Commander*.

In January 1971 Patrick was cheered by a proposal from Collins's Children's Books Department to write a brief explanatory account of British warships during the Napoleonic wars. This was naturally a project easy for him to fulfil. He received a welcome advance of £300, but publication was oddly delayed until April 1974, when he noted: 'Men-of-war has just arrived, a pretty little book – pictures wonderfully reproduced but some dreadful blunders, mine or the printer's, that make me really low.'

In March Patrick returned to Vienna, this time accompanied by my mother. Sadly, the change of scene once again proved no recipe for success, as he explained on their return in a letter to Richard Ollard, his valued editor at Collins:

What a long time we have been out of touch; and it makes me feel guilty, because if it had not been for the strike I should have told you months ago that Post-Captain was not coming along as well as we could have wished, and that I should find it very difficult to keep to my contracted date of March 25th.

I was ill in Austria – Vienna was nearly the death of us both – but since we have been back the right flow has returned and I am quite pleased with the chapter I finished yesterday. At this rate the book should be finished by midsummer.

At the moment Jack Aubrey is being harried by tipstaffs: but you know although arrest for debt was so usual, I am sadly ignorant of the essential processes – the rules of the game – I wonder whether you are acquainted with any succinct account of the law as it stood in say 1800.

Austria was not all pills and physic, however, and among other things we heard a most magnificent Fidelio, and a Mozart mass in a perfect little baroque cathedral in the country.

In June I became engaged to Georgina Brown. Patrick and my mother sent enthusiastic congratulations, eagerly inviting us to Collioure. We arrived by train at the end of July to an excited welcome. Georgina proved a great favourite. As lively as she was beautiful, she was for the most part tactfully content to sit demurely listening when the conversation became overly intellectual. However, at one point she glimpsed an opportunity to obtrude her own contribution. Patrick was discoursing about the Indian sect of Jains, who among other customs are said to sweep the ground before them as they move about. 'Oh, I know,' exclaimed Georgie: 'they want to make sure they don't tread on any minute orgasms!' On Patrick's and my mother's looking askance at this odd explanation, she blurted out: 'Oh, no – what I meant of course was "minute organs"!' There followed a moment's mute mystification, followed by much laughter. Although many who met Patrick found him daunting and withdrawn, in private with his family he was a continual source of merriment – not infrequently, infectiously childish.

Another incident I recall from that holiday was distinctly alarming. As I shall have regular occasion to mention, both my mother and Patrick were irredeemably appalling drivers, who on innumerable occasions escaped death by a hair's breadth. One day they took us for a jaunt in their little *deux chevaux* up the mountains to Le Perthus, on the Spanish frontier in the Pyrenees. At one point during our journey we found ourselves climbing a mountainside on a narrow road with a precipitous drop unnervingly close to our immediate left. After a while Georgie, who was sitting beside me on the back seat, whispered that she was convinced there was something wrong with one of the rear wheels. Not being a driver myself, I had noticed nothing untoward and tried to reassure her. Eventually she whispered that she was too frightened to continue, which I promptly explained to Patrick, asking if we could stop to check the wheels. Telling us firmly that there could not possibly be anything wrong, Patrick reluctantly stopped the car, and we gingerly descended. For once he had to admit himself at fault: all but one of the nuts had fallen off the bolts holding the outer rear wheel in place, while the remaining one had also begun working itself loose! After replacing the wheel, we resumed our journey without further mishap.

Following our departure after a happy holiday in Collioure, Patrick received encouraging news concerning *Post Captain*. Both his literary agent Richard Scott Simon and editor Richard Ollard expressed enthusiastic approval, the latter writing: 'I do think it is a superb piece of work and I cannot too much admire the way in which you combine inventiveness with fidelity to detail and, like Raymond Chandler, contrive to criticise ideas and surprise the reader into thought at the same time as you are dazzling him with narrative and descriptive skill.'

This was gratifying, but disappointments continued. The advance from Collins was respectable, but scarcely princely, being £400 on signature and £200 on publication. In the USA Lippincott pointed out that the 165,000-word text far exceeded the contractual length. Equally, the editor accepted that: 'Your book is so beautifully structured he does not feel that large pieces could be taken out without damage to it.' Eventually these frustrating issues were overcome – not least in consequence of a rapturous endorsement by the historical novelist Mary Renault, received in July 1972:

MASTER AND COMMANDER raised almost dangerously high expectations; POST CAPTAIN triumphantly surpasses them. Mr O'Brian is a master of his period, in which his characters are firmly placed, while remaining three-dimensional, intensely human beings. This book sets him at the very top of his genre; he does not just have the chief qualifications of a first-class historical novelist, he has them all. The action scenes are superb; towards the end, far from being aware that one is reading what, physically, is a fairly long book, one notes with dismay that there is not much more to come.

I sincerely hope that reviewers will remit their current obsession with psychopathology, to give this brilliant book the acclaim that it deserves.

Generally speaking, this being a biography rather than a literary critique, I leave evaluation of the qualities of Patrick's writing to his readers, and confine myself in the main to noting intriguing personal touches embedded within his fictional creation. The affectionate Sussex setting at the beginning plainly derives from Patrick's largely happy childhood days in and around the lovely Georgian town of Lewes.* The hunting Dr Vining (*Post Captain* (London, 1972), p. 15) is borrowed from my mother's grandfather Dr Francis Wicksteed, who in the latter half of the nineteenth century was often diverted by the attractions of the local hunt when riding to visit patients in his practice. Patrick was much taken by the tale of the horse's fart (p. 39), which I had once recounted to him. Jack's escape from France by the pass at nearby Le Perthus disguised as a bear (pp. 86–96) doubtless owes something to those participants attired as bears who had delighted Patrick years before at the Mardi Gras Carnival in Collioure. The amiable Captain Azéma (pp. 115–25) acquired his name from the proprietor of the original vineyard bought by my mother for their future home.

The glowing account of Stephen's castle in Spain on page 141 includes details drawn from Patrick's fondly imagined plans for an eventual extension to their house. Although its construction was not to achieve fruition for another fifteen years, he had begun planning it in April 1969. As Jack explains to his tiresome mother-in-law: '. . . the most romantic thing I ever saw was . . . the orange-tree in Stephen's castle . . . this orange-tree was in a court with arches all round, a kind of cloister . . .'

---

* When first considering his new book, Patrick jotted down this cursory note: 'Cold: young man on foot in spatterdashes: is [?] curate (in pursuit of Hawke)'; 'nursery – bread & butter misses'; 'set it all in the Southdown country'.

Such also was one day to be Patrick's ambulatory. Among many characteristics shared with his creator, Maturin is a devotee of apiculture (pp. 339, 353). The Dover taxidermist Griffi Jones (p. 351) acquired his name from the man who drove Patrick and my mother through Cwm Croesor to their little Welsh cottage in 1945. These and other borrowings confirm the extent to which much of Patrick's own life passed into his novels. Obviously many novelists use matter from personal experience, but in Patrick's case I feel confident that this afforded means of inextricably melding his own experiences into his literary creation.

Patrick's Questar (July 1984)

Reverting to 1971, when in July Georgina arrived with me for her first visit to Collioure, I had brought with us a newly purchased astronomical telescope, which we heaved with difficulty in its trunk-sized box from train to train en route. Patrick at once espoused an enthusiastic love of star-gazing. In those days there was little or no light-pollution in our otherwise empty valley at Correch d'en Baus, so that astonishing panoramas of the night sky were always visible save on the occasional cloudy night, with many shooting stars coursing smoothly among their fixed brethren. He proved equally delighted by the opportunity the telescope afforded of gazing into the sitting room of a *lotissement* some distance away. Of course, we could only *see* and not *hear*, which provoked much jocular speculation about the personal lives of our happily unwitting neighbours.

Patrick, like Maturin, was a keen natural scientist. I imagine he had always nurtured curiosity about the night sky, but it was my telescope that kindled his devotion to serious astronomical observation. Not long after our visit he purchased his own instrument in consequence of an advertisement in the *Scientific American*, to which he had long been a subscriber. Powerful as mine was, it was outshone in almost every respect by the Questar. Not only was the new acquisition compact enough to be housed in a modest portable case, but by connecting it to the household electricity it constantly moved to correct the effect of the rotation of the earth. In consequence a single heavenly body might be kept under observation without continual readjustment. However, whatever envy it provoked in me during ensuing years is now sadly stilled, as the faithful Questar eventually passed into my possession. (It incidentally surprises me that Patrick never bought a microscope.) I would emphasize that his enthusiasm for sky-gazing was no dilettante pastime. Thereafter the house became increasingly littered with notebooks and loose sheets of paper covered with baffling equations and cryptic calculations.

In September he was faced with a momentous professional decision, when his agent Richard Scott Simon decided to leave Curtis Brown and set up an agency under his own name. Patrick loyally decided to go with him: a move he never regretted. Writing to Simon, Patrick added his wish, despite the burgeoning success of his naval novels, to continue with translations 'if only as an insurance against sterility'. This further disposes of the suggestion that he regarded translation as mere drudgery, imposed solely by the need for a regular source of income.

Following Georgina's and my return to England, our wedding took place in October, which Patrick and my mother flew over to attend. Fortunately, no problem arose like that attendant on his son Richard's wedding nine years earlier, when (according to Richard's account) his mother had refused to appear should Patrick be present. In our case my father, likewise, firmly declined to appear were my mother or Patrick to be there. Fortunately, a conflict did not arise, since they attended the Anglican ceremony at Georgina's parish church in Radlett on the Saturday, while my father and stepmother were present the next day at our wedding in the Russian Orthodox church in Emperor's Gate, London.

Our wedding at Radlett in October 1971

In 1972 Patrick failed again to keep a diary record, it being a relatively uneventful and possibly unsatisfactory year. In February Richard Ollard and his wife Mary came to stay for the first time at Collioure. Richard was a perceptive observer, and the impression he obtained during this and subsequent visits tallies, in part at least, with my own observations. As my résumé of a later discussion with him records, his:

visits [to Collioure] were always extremely pleasant: Mummy was always a delightful hostess – could not have been nicer. However one always had to be on one's guard with Patrick, but Richard found once he had learned the ropes this was not an insuperable problem. Mary Ollard however felt on the first occasion indignant at the way in which Patrick from time to time rudely corrected Mummy, and felt strongly that he imposed unduly upon her good nature.

Richard was fully aware that one had to remain on one's guard in conversation with Patrick, but given that caveat was able to commune with him quite happily. His impression was that Patrick was concerned to inflict snubs when he felt so minded, but was not really seeking to be offensive, nor to crush his 'opponent' beyond the immediate context. He agreed that Patrick altered very little over the years in character and even looks, and was always very fit. He held himself well, and was an exceptionally energetic walker.

This perception appears to me remarkably shrewd, my chief reservation lying in Mary Ollard's comment concerning Patrick's treatment of my mother. It is perfectly true that he was inclined on occasion to contradict or even ridicule observations she proffered, reproofs to which she invariably meekly submitted. Like Mary Ollard, for long I found this not a little tiresome, or even offensive. However, after many years of observation at close quarters, I eventually came to a differing conclusion – a view incidentally shared by Georgina, after she had also come to know my parents well. We became more and more persuaded that all was not as it might appear. My mother's apparently submissive attitude in large part represented an act (she would even address him as 'sir'!), whereby she exercised a subtle degree of control over Patrick. I realized, too, that she was fully aware of his underlying insecurity, and the concomitant need to sustain his self-confidence. Equally, she herself could on occasion appear sharply dismissive, as when Patrick showed her some piece of handicraft of which he was endearingly proud.

My subsequent immersion in their voluminous diaries, memoranda and correspondence strongly confirms this interpretation. Provided one accepted the 'rules', which once understood were really not difficult to follow, Patrick was the most delightful, interesting, and good-humoured companion one could wish for.

To these virtues must undoubtedly be added his astonishing industry. Unfair criticism and publishers' occasional neglect afforded him disproportionate distress, but were rarely permitted to hinder his productivity. Thus, between January and April 1972 he translated Miroslav Ivanov's *The Assassination of Heydrich*; from April to July he wrote *H.M.S. Surprise*, the 110,000-word sequel to *Post Captain*; and from September until January he translated Charrière's *Banco: The Further Adventures of Papillon*.

In May Patrick paid another of his recurrent brief nostalgic visits to Ireland, which invariably exercised an uplifting effect on his spirits. Having flown to Dublin he drove in a hired Ford Escort to Belfast, then at the height of the Troubles. It was his first visit to the city since his stay in 1937, when he wrote part of his youthful novel *Hussein*. Now, however, 'I did not, do not, remember the town at all – not a single building, street nor the orientation.' Troops and police were everywhere, and 'It was forbidden to stop, that is to leave an unattended car, & the only car park I could find was full.' In the evening he walked for miles through the ravaged city, alert to dramatic insights. However, 'I don't think the people I speak to here tell the truth: they are certainly under great tension.'

Driving to Londonderry, he found the situation if anything worse:

> . . . I walked in the drizzle on the walls as far as I could, which was perhaps three quarters of the way (the barbed wire barriers being set

sideways) . . . a valley below & ¼m away a rise with a poor-looking scattered suburb on it. This was the Bogside, though I did not know it, and I was looking at [the cannon] Roaring Meg (bore about 10 cm) when a soldier crept from his sandbags & said 'You might get shot'. He kept very low under the parapet: his simple anxious young face was not so much black as streaked. I did not know whether he might feel compelled to shoot me & asked him to repeat himself twice. No, it was the Bogside that might let off at a moving head.

After this he drove westwards away from the troubled Six Counties. On his way to Sligo:

a little after Donegal I picked up two wet girls who wanted to go to Galway where they study, so I took them there. One, Grainne, a native speaker from Aranmore, told me delightful things about her island. Sweet, gentle, trusting & rather confiding children longing for <u>experience</u>, quite learned too, & with the right ideas. But I missed Sligo & many another place, as well as infinite miles of country, talking [thinking?] on the other hand, that Grainne was I suppose as pure a piece of the ancient land as could be seen or heard.

I wonder where is Grainne now, and does she recall her long conversation with the obliging stranger?

On his way to Achill Head Patrick ascended Croagh Patrick, where St Patrick encountered the angels:

As stiff a climb as I have known, on a path, sliding back in some places at about 35°. Up to the ridge in an hour, then beyond to the true cone, where I turned & was instantly hailed up so as to sting my ears despite hat. Down, blundering, and to the dear old late Gothic friary, where to my astonishment I found myself within 20 ft of a Cornish chough, nesting I imagine in the top of the wall. It defied me: & in time I realized I had miscalculated the hours – flew back to Oughterard, or tried to fly, would have flown if half Ireland had not been taking its cattle, asses, sheep, lamb, along the road.*

Next day he spent an enjoyable (though unproductive) day's fishing on a nearby lake. 'I feel deeply rested,' he noted next morning, before making his way back to Dublin. On the way he stopped at Loughrea to view 'a 1stC[entury] phallic stone at Turoe. I found it in time, & phallic or not it is a splendid mysterious thing. Grey.'† Back in Dublin, he encountered a disappointing reverse. He had hoped to meet one John de Courcy Ireland, an advocate of various fashionable radical causes, who had also published books on Ireland's maritime history. However: 'arriving here, naively expectant, all I found was a single anonymous typed note wholly concerned with business matters & arrangements: the old familiar depression came straight back – anger – indignation – hopelessness. A quoi bon?'

Quite why he was so eager to meet this relatively obscure figure is unclear, but his excessive dismay at being apparently fobbed off illustrates yet again his extreme fear of being slighted or ignored.

Indignantly, he left Dublin for another tour by way of Galway, Clonmacnois, and the Bog of Allen, before once again returning to the capital. There he was forcefully reminded of his youthful protracted Irish visit in 1937, whose very occurrence has been called in question by his detractors:

Dublin again, & I am strangely reminded of New York:‡ but only by the old-fashioned mouldering squalor of many of the smaller

---

* Patrick commemorated his ascent of Croagh Patrick in verse (Patrick O'Brian, *The Uncertain Land and Other Poems* (London, 2019), p. 36).

† Patrick's reservation was apt. The coy fashion for seeing phallic symbolism everywhere in prehistory has long been exploded, and the stone is now more plausibly considered an omphalos, or marker of a provincial sacred centre.

‡ The comparison strongly suggests that Patrick had at this time paid an earlier visit to New York, of which no record is known to me. Since it cannot have occurred at any time after the outbreak of war in 1939, we must, it seems, look to the sparsely documented period of his life before that.

shopping streets (so like upper 8th Avenue) & the stark nakedness beyond Christchurch; not in the least by the people, the freshfaced pleased-looking creatures, so very polite & helpful, only civilized. (The old ladies in a black & muddy alley who walked back a hundred yards with me through the rain to make sure I did not miss Tailors' Hall: the chambermaid who said No that there were no chemists' shops open after 7 but who fetched me aspirin for my incipient cold.) I love the smokey-eyed girls & shiny clean bumpkin-faced boys . . .

Shelbourne pleasant, & my window looks straight on to the corner of Stephen's Green, diagonally across from the dear Miss Spains of 35 years ago [where he lodged]: a striking contrast & in some ways a sad one.

The melancholy provoked by reflecting on those ebullient days when he was writing *Hussein* was increased by his having succumbed to a severe cold.

Next day he hired a car and 'drove off to veiled Tara – looked respectfully at a figured stone in the mound of the hostages which must, I take it, have been of immense antiquity in the time of the kings'. Driving west, he gave a lift to two students whose company he found tediously dull, and arrived that evening at Currarevagh House in County Galway where he had stayed during his visit in the previous year. 'That evening after dinner I talked with two pleasant, ingenuous brothers from Dublin: we drank port until 12. There is a quality in Irish people that I have seen nowhere else at all.'

He drove on to Galway and thence to the sea. Much of the formerly beautiful coastline near Spiddal was now covered with rows of depressingly monotonous bungalows. Although disappointed, his viewpoint was not blindly romantic: 'Many of the bungalows seem to be the old houses replaced & now inhabited by the original people, which is I have no doubt more comfortable. To live in an externally beautiful rural slum for the sake of outsiders is scarcely right.'

Moving on to wilder parts, he observed with delight many fine seabirds, but while pondering some godwits he managed to get his car stuck in a gateway on slippery seaweed (a valuable fertilizer). Two men in a passing lorry stopped and pushed it free. When he began apologizing for putting them to the trouble one replied to his gratification: 'Sorry, no English.' Some hours later, after passing through fine wild country around Clifden, he managed to get his car stuck again, this time while 'wishing to look into a lough for mergansers . . . few birds give me a greater feeling of rarity & triumph'. Rescued by another helpful passer-by, he drove on successfully for an hour or so, until attempting to consult his map while driving he 'lurched violently into the hedge. Amidst the din I thought "this is it: all is up". But no: car wrenched clear unhurt, hardly scratched & the world continued.'

What with his recurrent accidents and ever-worsening cold, Patrick was now finding his expedition less and less enjoyable. After an abortive attempt (it was closed) to revisit Carton, the palatial former seat of the dukes of Leinster, he arrived in Dublin and retired to his hotel room 'where I lie prudently, soberly in bed'.

Although illness had marred some of his holiday, what shines through his occasionally lugubrious account is his intense love of Ireland and the Irish. Having repudiated his largely unhappy early life, it is evident that from the time of his first liberating visit in 1933 (symbolically, also the occasion of his first deep love, for a beautiful Irish girl) he fastened on Ireland as a spiritual refuge. However, I am sure that he was throughout perfectly conscious that it provided him with a Happy Otherworld of the spirit, not a country to which he had ever belonged in reality. Whenever the possibility of settling there presented itself as a practical opportunity, as in 1945 and 1954, he rejected it without providing any compelling reason.

On this occasion Patrick toyed yet again with finding himself a refuge in the Green Isle of Erin:

On to a point between Glinsk & Cashel, & a notice Site for Sale: a cheerful young woman in a filthy booth (car at the door, however) with a fierce, mute ancient man by the fire ('himself is a hundred years old') & a baby in her arm, said the site might be above or below the road or by the water (a pond) according to one's fancy – half an acre or less & the price about £1200. Bog & rock, but the view over Bertraghboy Bay to the Twelve Pins on so beautiful a day (the mountains three-dimensional & the water right sapphire) was improbably lovely.

Although conscious that critics may elect to regard this as special pleading, I would stress again that his scanty half-hearted claims to Irish origin reflected reluctant awareness that the Ireland he loved was a land of dreams, unrealizable in the harsh world of actuality. As he wrote in his diary at Collioure two years later: 'I . . . read in the Shell guide to Ireland, longing for that almost non-existent country.'

Early next morning he flew back to London, where he met my mother, who had I assume been staying with her parents in the West Country. They lost no time in returning to Collioure, where he spent the remainder of the year reading and working at home. In a marginal note written on a draft letter to Richard Scott Simon, Patrick triumphantly recorded: 'Goody. Have just finished Surprise & will be quite ready to start translating in Oct. Should like to do both (can do Papillon [i.e. *Banco*] at 2–3000w[ords] a day Beauvoir [*Tout compte fait*] slower about 1000) Can schedules be made to coincide?'

H.M.S. Surprise was published in August of the following year. Although I imagine few now would find it in any way inferior to its two predecessors, reviews were mixed, ranging from strongly enthusiastic to what can only be described as painfully obtuse. In March 1974 Patrick noted 'some deeply stupid US reviews of Surprise. Most praise leaves me untouched: most blame too unless it is literate, but the accumulation of these really vexed me.' In the following month he heard from Richard Scott Simon. In his diary Patrick recorded: 'Last Pool sold to *H[ouse]& Garden*: Surprise sold 6000, almost exactly the same as the last 2. I am astonished & rather disappointed. Why no increase?' To this plaint Simon responded sympathetically (and prophetically): 'I too was rather disappointed with the sales of H.M.S. SURPRISE, but I think it should have a long life.'

Eventually the novel received its due from readers and reviewers. To me, what is perhaps the most weighty compliment derived not from a literary reviewer, but a professional sailor and historian. In his scholarly account of the prize system in the Royal Navy, Rear-Admiral Hill extols Patrick's astonishing powers of insight into the technicalities of history:

> Patrick O'Brian in *H.M.S. Surprise* . . . gives a fictional account of a discussion in the Admiralty on this case, which, like all this author's work, is based on historical study and shows deep understanding of the factors that may have governed Their Lordships' decision.[1]

A former wartime naval officer responded with equal enthusiasm to another striking aspect of Patrick's writing. On 6 November 1995 Sir Alec Guinness confided to his diary:

> Spent the evening reading Patrick O'Brian's *HMS Surprise*. The smell of the sea lifts off his pages together with that of tar and the oiliness of so many Mediterranean harbours. His description of a storm in the south Atlantic catches one's breath away with fear and excitement. This is the third of his books I have read (in the wrong order) and I am now resolved to climb up the rigging of all of them.[2]

Finally, we may note a strand of continuity in Patrick's writing. In chapter 7 Stephen Maturin takes in hand a delightful little Hindu girl named Dil, who comes to a sudden distressing end. She surely cannot be dissociated from the impudent, amoral, and wholly charming Sher Dil, 'a lively lad of eleven', who takes service with the author in Francis Yeats-Brown's best-selling work of 1930, *Bengal Lancer*. Patrick had read the book at an early age, when he evidently drew on it for his short story 'Wang Khan of the Elephants' in 1933, as also for his novel *Hussein*. The theme of a homeless bright child's being discovered and protected by a sympathetic father figure can scarcely have failed to appeal to Patrick, whose own childhood had been so lonely and relatively loveless.

IX

Pablo Ruiz Picasso

But I shall little care for censure, as long as the testimonies I use
doe assure and warrant me: since I intend not to describe him
otherwise, either good or bad, but as He really was. Onely where
he holds any doubtfull part, I conceive it will be but just to give a
favourable construction.

> Lord Herbert of Cherbury, *The Life and Raigne of King
> Henry the Eighth* (London, 1649), 'The Epistle Dedicatory'

Despite the acclaim with which the text of *H.M.S. Surprise*
was received by those whose opinions mattered most to
Patrick, its completion provided something of an anticlimax.
Although Collins remained enthusiastic about his naval tales,
sales had continued satisfactory but unspectacular. When he
reported to his agent Richard Scott Simon that he would shortly
be delivering the typescript of the novel, Simon's reply raised
only the possibility of fresh translations and made no mention
of a further sequel. He had two suggestions: the latest volume
of Simone de Beauvoir's memoirs, and the sequel to Henri
Charrière's bestselling *Papillon*.

Patrick was relieved at the prospect of an imminent influx of
income (a month earlier Simon had written gloomily: 'So far no
luck with translations. I am asking around the whole time but
there seems to be nothing which publishers need to have turned

from French into English'), and enquired whether he might obtain contracts for both books.

His gift for flawless translation had long been acknowledged by publishers, and the proposal was accepted without difficulty. Within three weeks Weidenfeld had drawn up a contract for the de Beauvoir book, and (as has been seen) at the beginning of December 1972 Hart-Davis commissioned him to translate Charrière's new memoir *Banco*.

Although it was the second of the books commissioned, and the advance smaller, Patrick decided to begin with Charrière: possibly because, as with its predecessor, the contract ensured him a royalty of 1% on all copies sold above 15,000. On 17 September he assured Richard Scott Simon: 'Have just finished Surprise . . . can do Papillon [i.e. *Banco*] at 2–3000w a day . . .' By 19 January 1973 Simon responded: 'With amazing speed the translation has arrived . . . I don't know how you managed to do it so quickly. You must be quite exhausted.'

Although Patrick enjoyed the skill and predictable income generated by translation work, ideally he preferred to alternate it with creative writing. Since there was now no immediate call for a sequel to *H.M.S. Surprise*, he contemplated undertaking a biography of Lady Craven or Queeney Thrale. He had long possessed copies of Lady Craven's successive memoirs,[1] and conducted research into her life when preparing his anthology *A Book of Voyages* in 1945. The lady enjoyed an adventurous life, divorcing her husband after bearing him seven children, after which she married the Margrave of Anspach, and travelled across Europe as far afield as the Crimea and Turkey. Hesther Maria Thrale, known as 'Queeney' to Dr Johnson and other friends, married Admiral Lord Keith in 1808.* Both ladies were strong characters who led adventurous lives, but Richard Scott

---

* They feature, in a deliberate anachronism, as married in *Master and Commander*, which is set in 1801.

Simon feared that neither was well enough known to appeal to Patrick's American publisher. The project was dropped, but the redoubtable Queeney featured memorably as Jack Aubrey's friend and mentor.

Meanwhile in December my mother received distressing news from England. Her father, who was now eighty-nine, had become seriously ill and was clearly failing. At the end of January she and Patrick drove across France to England, where they stayed at her parents' home in Somerset. In the local cottage hospital she found her father sadly changed from the upright athletic figure she had known all her life. He had grown a beard, spent much of the time sleeping, and suffered long lapses when he had difficulty in understanding his predicament. However, he recognized his daughter, and was to her intense pleasure plainly happy to see her. She visited him every day, cooked for her mother and Patrick, and looked after the house.

Howard Wicksteed died on 19 February 1973, much loved and missed by all his family. At my last visit he murmured: 'Remember me to those who love me.' In my mother's case her natural distress was intensified in consequence of difficulties in their relationship rooted in the disgrace of her elopement with Patrick. These were sadly never entirely effaced with time, as might in other circumstances have transpired. Patrick's awkward demeanour in my grandparents' presence irritated my grandfather, who belonged firmly to a generation that detested any sign of self-consciousness. My mother tended to compensate for her sense of exclusion by at times seeking too ostentatiously to establish herself as a presence in the household. From her diaries and letters I know that she felt woundingly excluded from her parents' affection. It was a tragic situation, arising from mutual misunderstanding and profound differences in character and upbringing.

It is unpleasant to record these family differences, nor would I do so but for the lasting ill effects they exerted in differing ways on my mother and Patrick. As my wife Georgina and I were living nearby, we were fortunately able to see much of Patrick and my mother during this sad time.

A week before my grandfather's death we called at my grandparents' cottage to find my parents in a state of high excitement. Patrick gleefully explained that he had just heard from his literary agent Richard Scott Simon, who reported that his US publishers, Putnam, wished to commission him to write a biography of Picasso. For this they were offering the very substantial advance of $20–30,000.

Negotiations continued over the next three months. By April Putnam's had settled on $20,000 for approximately 200,000 words. Richard Scott Simon managed to persuade them to retract their initial insistence on acquiring UK rights, and a month later Collins in Britain agreed to a further advance of £4,000. Patrick was overjoyed. William Targ at Putnam's expressed his confidence in his ability to produce a book of lasting worth, and like almost every author Patrick was flattered and encouraged by the handsome advances. He was a longstanding admirer of Picasso's achievement, and felt confident that, although he must clearly face volumes of research, he was capable of producing a fuller and more penetrating work than any that had so far appeared.

Patrick possessed a keen appreciation of the visual arts, and in his semi-autobiographical novel *Richard Temple* his protagonist features as painter rather than writer. As biographers will, he developed a degree of identification with the subject of his work. Picasso had risen from relatively humble origins (although this was not the case with Patrick, the unhappy circumstances of his childhood had imbued him with a tincture of irrational shame about his family origins), to achieve the highest artistic success imaginable. Picasso's work had endured obscurantist abuse, but a potent mixture of innate talent, unstinted industry and overriding confidence in his abilities led to his becoming arguably the most admired and successful artist of the century.

At the time Patrick obtained his contract Picasso was plainly nearing the end of his days, and William Targ at Putnam made it clear that he did not expect Patrick to interview him. As it happened, the painter died in the very week that Putnam and Collins began to draw up their contracts.

Despite the acute sense of loss my mother endured at the passing of her father, it was with high hopes and a sense of the beginning of a bright new phase in their lives that she and Patrick returned to Collioure. Not only had he been assigned a task which filled him with enthusiasm, but the generous advances meant that he could pursue his researches as thoroughly as he wished. (In the event he expressed his belief that he could have written a much better book had he been allowed three years rather than two in which to complete it, but this probably reflects more the perfectionism of the professional writer than strongly felt regret.)

Meanwhile a dramatic change occurred in my own life, in which Patrick took sympathetic – indeed, enthusiastic – interest. After leaving Trinity College Dublin in 1961 I had taught at a succession of preparatory schools in London. My ambition since childhood had been to become a writer, with my interest firmly focused on history. During the holidays I had managed to write and publish two books, but with my marriage to Georgina and realization that time was passing by without any notable literary achievement to my name, I decided with her unhesitating support to take the plunge. I would abandon my teaching career entirely, and retire to some country retreat in order to apply myself full-time to literary work. A modest inheritance had unexpectedly come my way from my great-aunt Maroussia, and we set about seeking the ideal writer's cottage.

I was at the time only dimly aware of the circumstances in which Patrick and my mother had moved to Wales after the War. However, with hindsight I can see that our adventurous step, which was understandably regarded with misgiving by members of both our families, would have aroused nostalgic enthusiasm in Patrick. For when it soon became apparent that we could not afford any property in the West Country, the friendly Chaplain at Canford

School (where I was teaching at the time) informed us one day that houses were very much cheaper in Wales than south of the Bristol Channel. When we received particulars of a house in the Forest of Dean seemingly ideal for our choice, Patrick eagerly suggested his accompanying us to view it.

I vividly recall his excitement as he insisted from time to time on taking the wheel of our trusty Morris Traveller (bought for £100 the day before our wedding) on the journey to our destination. He drove at frightening and erratic speed, being particularly delighted with the Severn Bridge. As we wound through the wooded defiles of the Forest of Dean his boyish enthusiasm soared with every mile. The estate agent's description of the house seemed to accord with our fondest dreaming. According to the particulars it was an elegant dwelling set behind wrought-iron gates at the end of its drive, while at the rear the property extended to an acre or more of hillside. Glowing emphasis was laid on what was described as 'the 18th-century wing'.

For some reason the agent was unable to arrange the viewing of the house at the time of our arrival, so we asked whether it was possible to view it without them. 'Oh no,' came the answer over the telephone: 'the main gates are locked, and it would be difficult to see the house from the road.' Despite this we decided to explore, and it was then we learned how great may be the disparity between an estate agent's description and harsh reality. The drive proved to be a stretch of gravel about 10 yards long, separating a rickety iron gate from the front door, while the '18th-century wing' was a dilapidated penthouse attached to the side of the house, bearing the inscription '1718' painted suspiciously brightly in whitewash above its solitary window. From what we could glimpse through the cobweb-festooned windows, the water supply comprised a solitary tap dripping over an old sink. The 'extensive grounds' at the rear, which we had excitedly discussed during our journey (with Patrick proffering much practical advice about conversion into a smallholding), turned out to be an almost perpendicular scree dominated by a gigantic electricity pylon. The disappointment would have been upsetting, but for Patrick's infectious glee on discovering the reality of the eighteenth-century wing and attendant manorial splendours.

Soon after this little adventure he and my mother returned home. Driving back across France they diverted from their route to visit Avignon, where a major exhibition of Picasso's works was being held in the Palace of the Popes. Annoyingly for Patrick, it was being filmed at the time, and he found the great chapel cluttered with screens and cameras, while the film crew was shouting and scurrying about. At least the display of drawings in the sacristy could be viewed in peace. After careful examination, Patrick came away troubled by intimations he saw of the extent to which old age had begun to erode the artist's extraordinary sexual and creative vitality. However, soon after leaving the palace it dawned on him that 'this was a marvellous performance for Picasso at ninety', who in defiance of his advanced years had been energetically planning a further show at the same site.

Ever prone to alarming accidents, my mother hurt herself badly in May. As Patrick explained to Richard Ollard: 'Mary has seen fit to break a rib, and we are all very indifferent.' Fortunately, she recovered in time to accompany him next month on an exciting expedition.

For the first time in his career Patrick was flush with money and faced with the prospect of an inspiring project, into which he threw himself with unbounded enthusiasm. He decided to begin by visiting the United States, which housed many of Picasso's finest paintings. This would also provide him with an opportunity to meet his publisher William Targ and US literary agent John Cushman. Despite an apparent bygone mysterious visit (alluded to in the last chapter), Patrick had always regarded America as an exotic land not altogether real, and an amused Cushman wrote to reassure him that: 'I doubt if you will find any grits available in New York – even in the South restaurant grapes ain't worth the eating – and squirrel may be equally difficult to find.'

In the second half of June he and my mother flew to New York, where they were hospitably entertained by Cushman and Targ. For Patrick the highlight of his visit was provided by hours spent in the Museum of Modern Art, where he gazed with particular rapture at the celebrated mural *Guernica*. They also visited Philadelphia to view several of Picasso's other major works, and returned home well satisfied with their trip. Patrick wrote enthusiastically to Targ after their return that 'we still talk about your charming high-perched nest and of the splendid (and to us wildly exotic) dinner that you gave us in the [Greenwich] Village'.

Apart from my mother's setback, life generally appeared to be taking an increasingly propitious course. In August *H.M.S. Surprise* was published in Britain to generally enthusiastic reviews. Initially Patrick had made enquiries regarding the possibility of hiring a research worker to investigate material on Picasso for him in London, but now wisely thought better of the idea. There was much to be done, but he realized that only he could know what precisely was needed. He wrote to Richard Scott Simon on 23 August: 'I shall be in London on September 7 if our aged 2cv does not burst between here and Le Havre.'

In London he and my mother stayed at their familiar Challoner Club in Knightsbridge, where he spent his days working in libraries and viewing art galleries, while the evenings were passed with visits to Richard Scott Simon, the Ollards, and other friends. Not long before this Georgina and I had finally purchased the home of our dreams, an old Welsh longhouse in the romantic setting of a wooded valley in Montgomeryshire. We were settling into our first home of our own and my career as an author, when Patrick and my mother arrived to inspect the household. It must have reminded them vividly of their very similar situation at the same time of year in 1945, when they arrived in their own wild Welsh refuge in Cwm Croesor. Patrick eagerly inspected the house and grassy area around, citing advice from Cobbett's *Cottage Economy* and expressing infectious optimism for our future.

In January 1974 he travelled to Barcelona, in order to inspect locations where Picasso had lived and painted in his youth, and viewed the collection in the Museo Picasso. His main purpose, however, was to interview Maurizio Torra-Balari, a long-term friend of Picasso. The meeting began with some difficulty, as the old gentleman proved to be deaf and at first suspicious of Patrick's motive in writing his book. However, he unbent sufficiently to provide valuable insights into the painter's character. Jacqueline Hutin, Picasso's second wife, was 'a good devoted soul, utterly destroyed by P'. Picasso himself was 'a monster of egoism (but not to be attacked by anyone else)': i.e. other than Señor Torra-Balari. The painter:

> did not speak Catalan, had no Andalou accent, was highly cultivated, read much (by night) including history, geography, literature, liked children up to the age of about 12, dreaded death (saw it in his big room at Mougins)* would not make a will, though urged by TB, was near with his sous [i.e. stingy] . . . impossible that he should be uncultivated vu [seeing that] his father was a professeur de lycée.

On his return home Patrick at once began writing the first chapter of his book. Before his visit to Barcelona he had noted in his diary: 'My feelings for P vary: a certain antipathy arising (most recently)', and now Señor Torra-Balari's frank account appeared to confirm this initial low estimate of the artist's personal character. However, he could suspend judgement, since for the present all his energies were devoted to providing an exhaustive account of Catalan history, geography and social life, the impact of the Catholic Church on the Spanish *Weltanschauung*, the origins

---

* Picasso's home on the Riviera, where Torra-Balari visited him not long before his death.

(factual and legendary) of Picasso's family, reflections on the psychological relationship between father and son – and finally all that he had discovered about his early childhood. This was Patrick's first book to require such extensive research, and he is far from being the only author in such circumstances to begin by amassing a vast amount of material which readers would find hard to digest.

He worked hard to complete the chapter, which after my mother's typing was despatched to London on the eve of their departure for a second more ambitious journey of investigation in Spain. Not long before he had been much distressed to learn of a disaster striking our newly established home in Wales, which had so excited his nostalgic enthusiasm during his visit at the time of our installation. A workman misguidedly passed the metal chimney-pipe of a stove through a beam in the wall, and one night when we were out the house was burned to the ground. 'The horrible news of poor Nikolai's house burning down', and a day later: 'A brave letter from N: says everything is burnt.' Generous as always, Patrick sent us a handsome cheque, and he and my mother provided us with much consolation during the difficult time that followed.

In March they set out on an extensive expedition to Spain, in search of places and people associated with Picasso. In Barcelona he returned to the Museo Picasso, where he found his perceptions of the master's painting refined and modified. 'I did see with new eyes, many of the things I have been writing about; & I must modify my remarks about religion.'

Patrick was fortunate, and his notes are the more valuable, in that Spain at the time of his visits was physically little changed from the days when Picasso lived and worked there. He visited the Llotja art school where Picasso studied 'and looked again at Merced 3 [where the artist lived], which has a battered, effaced coat of arms over the door. Four storeys & perhaps an attic, facing other houses of the same height across the street 4–5 yards wide.'

Much of the next day was spent driving south to visit the village of Horta de Sant Joan, where in 1898 Picasso stayed at the invitation of his kindly friend Manuel Pallarès, at first to recuperate from a severe bout of scarlet fever. This was the first time the artist had lived in the countryside, and his experiences of the unchanged way of life among the peasantry were to influence him for the rest of his life – an experience curiously paralleling Patrick's years of rural isolation in Wales, and subsequent affinity with the fishermen and peasants of Collioure. In later years Picasso declared: 'Everything I know I learned in Pallarès' village.' It was there that he acquired (contrary to the claim of Torra-Balari) his fluent Catalan, and Patrick's description of Horta itself and the time Picasso spent there is one of the more evocative in his biography.

He found Pallarès' house 'no longer inhabited – was obviously big, rambling, presumably a court in the middle', and sketched a plan. He and my mother found lodgings in the café Augustin, kept by a descendant of Pallarès. There they found old men playing cards and speaking Catalan:

> As we drank, we watched mules. The way they ride them is to perch high on the immense panniers (made in one piece, slung across & held with a ? breastband & certainly a crupper) sitting on the beasts withers. One I saw was shod in front with rubber, perhaps from a tyre.

Patrick possessed an acutely perceptive eye for local life and landscape, and his prodigious memory and detailed notes enabled him to bring Picasso's early days vividly to life:

> Going down to Tortosa by way of Prat del Comte we followed Pic's steps I believe (more or less, because the old road mule-track by the stream can sometimes be seen at a distance from the new good, but enormously winding modern road. It must have been an heroic walk, up & down, but mostly up, rising in all I suppose 1000–1500 ft . . . thro narrow defiles, crossing the stream by fords. The trees

were a curious pine (? Aleppo) & I saw some mistletoe on them, with here and there arbutus, lentiscus, rosemary undergrowth. Even in the least inhabited places, olives, beautifully terraced, & almonds. Some sheep. A large herd of black & white goats, far away, against bare rock by the river.

Quite suddenly we dropped to the Ebro, by a noble dam, & there were oranges everywhere, groves of them, with a good deal of fruit still, a splendid colour in the sun.

Glimpses of local life were jotted down between his notes, suggesting the eye of the artist (Patrick included several rough sketches and plans) as much as that of the writer: 'streets [of Horta] too narrow for cars mason's huge jar as reservoir'; 'small dog riding on mule, master walking'; 'Little brown pigs crossing the road'; 'the abandoned railway, with its stations standing bare – no rails'.

At Peñiscola they stayed at an inn 'which is kept by the rudest ugly fat bastards I have ever seen even in Spain'. As though this were not affliction enough, 'My bed stank of gambas [prawns] all night. At one point I rose in case it should be me, & washed heartily, but no – every time I neared the sheets (the night was cold) the vile reek met me.'

On they drove southwards, much of the journey dull (Patrick noted the lack of birds) and even dangerous, with ill-driven and ill-lit columns of lorries carrying fruit thundering along the roads. However, the dramatic landscape of Andalusia – 'brilliant snow on the S. Nevada' – proved gratifying, and on 15 March they arrived at Malaga. It was here that Picasso was born and spent his early childhood days. Patrick made his usual careful plans and notes, but although he was to make good use of what he saw in his book came away largely disappointed with his visit. 'A poor dinner: early to bed & away from this vile town (& yet I do not dislike it either: but such a waste of hope) tomorrow.'

By this stage Patrick had begun to feel he had seen more than enough for his purpose, and the long drive home was punctuated with complaints about dirt, poor roads, poverty, and alleged examples of Spanish bad manners. He was consoled at this stage by observing many unusual birds, but it appears that his enthusiasm for absorbing the atmosphere of Picasso's youth had palled, and he was anxious to get back to writing.

As ever a considerable amount of mail awaited their return, and Patrick seized eagerly upon letters from Richard Scott Simon and Richard Ollard. Each impressed on him as tactfully as possible the need to make a fairly drastic abridgement of his first chapter. I have the original typescript beside me, and there can be little doubt that their detached editorial view was the wiser one. After living in Catalonia for nearly a quarter of a century, immersing himself in its social life, culture and history, Patrick was able to draw on a massive fund of information which he was at first unable to resist imparting. Despite the considerable amount of labour it was now suggested he should discard, he accepted their advice with remarkable equanimity, commenting only: 'Some objections to the book (I had wanted only praise) but some kind words.'

Meanwhile, during Patrick's visit to our house in Wales I had discussed with him a literary project of my own. The British government, blithely unaware of the hornet's nest it would one day unleash, had begun releasing documents relating to the Western Allies' forced repatriation in 1945 of hundreds of thousands of Soviet citizens and other helpless victims to be killed, tortured and enslaved by Stalin. During my youth within the Russian émigré community I had heard individual stories of this dreadful tragedy, but it was only when a friend now drew my attention to the documents that I swiftly realized that the cruel policy involved numbers of victims and complex political considerations far beyond anything I or anyone else had hitherto imagined. With Georgina's loyal support I had withdrawn our modest savings from the building society to pay for photocopying thousands of documents in the Public Record Office. This expense was primarily motivated by fear lest the government appreciate the dangerous revelations likely to ensue, and withdraw the material from public access. At the time my misgiving might have been dismissed as melodramatic fantasy, but in the event it was proved to be prescient even in excess of my early fears.

Based on these and other preliminary researches, I sent a draft outline of a proposed book on the subject to a literary agent recommended by a writer friend. After the disaster of seeing our house burned down, there now appeared an upward turn in our fortunes. Patrick, who as ever displayed keen interest in our activities, recorded in his diary at the beginning of April:

Nikolai . . . has signed a contract to H[odder] & Stou[gh]ton, an excellent one, I think, and with an advance of £3,500. I am amazed, & very pleased. (And I am pleased not to detect the slightest tinge of jealousy: dismal surprises, so discreditable, often lie within: but not this time at all events.)

Three weeks later he expressed pleasure on receiving a letter from Georgina containing 'a sweet photograph of the old-fashioned child Alexandra' (our little eldest daughter).

All this was good, and 'We worked out the tax returns, from which it appears the writing brought in £6845 last year . . . What would this have meant in [19]45–50, when we really needed it?'

Altogether everything appeared to be improving for Patrick and my mother. As has already been noted, three years earlier he had been commissioned by Collins to write a slim book about the Royal Navy in Nelson's time. This was of course for him an easy task, and in April he finally received his advance copies. It is doubtful whether the general reader would have noticed the errors his mortified eyes discovered, and the book still provides an admirable introduction to be read with profit by adults as much as children.

A venture which concerned him much more nearly was the publication of a collection of his early short stories, which appeared in June. Richard Ollard had suggested the idea two years earlier, and Patrick, who was justly proud of his skill in this genre, applied himself with considerable care to preparing the book. After some consideration, he reported a problem to Richard Scott Simon:

> there is one aspect that worries me: I want this book to be as good as I can possibly make it, both for my own sake and for the sake of the biography [*Picasso*], and now that I have gone through the earlier volumes I find that even with a great deal of re-writing only sixteen or seventeen tales really satisfy me now, and they amount to no more than some 70,000 words.

The extent of his revision shows his concern. He went through the original versions with a fine-tooth comb, effecting minor alterations in some and altering others almost to the point of creating new versions. Particularly interesting is his treatment of 'The Long Day Running', a hunting tale deriving from his experiences with the Ynysfor Hunt in North Wales. Details are added to the description of the unnamed Master of the original version to make him accord yet more closely with the real-life Captain Jack Jones, while his nephew and successor Major Roche (who features as no more than 'the tall soldier' in the original version) is identified as 'Major Boyd'. Clearly Patrick's memory of the man he had so greatly admired thirty years before remained as vivid as ever, and his concern to fill out the figure of Captain Jones strengthens the likelihood that he drew on him for aspects of his own Jack Aubrey.

To bring the book up to an acceptable length he added four stories not included in his previous published collections *The Last Pool* and *Lying in the Sun*. These, which he thought 'pretty good', were 'The Rendezvous', 'The Chian Wine', 'On the Wolfsberg', and 'A Passage of the Frontier'.*

'The Rendezvous' describes frustrating and eventually dangerous experiences encountered by a man travelling by train from some-

---

* The last had appeared earlier in the year in *The Cornhill*, Spring 1974.

where in France via Paris to England. Its themes are unmistakably autobiographical, although probably based on Patrick's fears and fancies rather than actual experience. The station from which the unnamed protagonist sets out can only be Perpignan, and his repeated missing or near-missing of trains reflects a recurrent fear ('oh familiar nightmare') to which Patrick was himself subject. 'Last night I [dreamed I] was naked in the street again, & missed another train – we both missed trains,' he noted in his diary about this time. I am sure Patrick was conscious of the obvious symbolism of missing trains, and used them for the purpose of his tale. His protagonist is to meet a woman in London, and it is clear that his misadventures en route endanger not merely their meeting but their entire future.

Again, there is no mistaking my mother as the woman waiting (or not waiting) at the journey's end, since Patrick goes out of his way to identify her by a hat she habitually wore at the time: 'there could be no Cossack hat at the far end of the platform – did she still wear that hat, or had worms fattened on the Persian lamb?' During more than half a century of marriage Patrick suffered from occasional irrational apprehensions that my mother might lose her affection for him, or even vanish altogether from his life either by abandoning him, or (as the fattening worms suggest) being snatched away by death. This fear arose from ineradicable sensations of insecurity originating in his childhood, coupled with a consciousness that his whole being depended on her affection and comradeship. There was no one else in whom he could repose confidence: the closest of friends, relations or colleagues might at any moment prove treacherous and hostile.

In 'The Chian Wine' an outsider named Alphard has settled in an ancient seaside town named 'Saint-Felíu'. The opening description provides a lyrical evocation of the largely unaltered Collioure of Patrick's early days in the town. This is followed by a lamentation over changes introduced in recent years. Old customs and costumes have all but vanished: 'Pert white houses had sprung up outside the walls, with red-brick well-heads over nothing, gnomes, plastic storks', while 'in high summer the villagers wandered like strangers among the tourist hordes'. Alphard and his friend Halévy, a Jew from Avignon who had opened a small gallery facing the harbour, commiserate with each other over these regrettable changes.

However, Alphard is partially consoled by seeing the village priest: '"There," he said to Halévy, "there is your bridge – one of your bridges. The Church has not changed."' But all is not well in this sleepy and increasingly muddied backwater. The surviving archaisms which console Alphard prove to include a horrifying undercurrent. In his Good Friday sermon in the church of Saint-Felíu the curé dwells morbidly on the responsibility of the Jews for Christ's death, 'and the moment the priest cried "Death to the Jews!" they [the congregation] all burst out "Death to the Jews!"' At this the children rush forth from the church blowing whistles and shrieking, 'leaving the adults to listen to the collect'. Incited by the priest's inflammatory harangue, the frenzied youth of the town focus their collective hatred on the benign Halévy, whose shop is incinerated with him inside it.

When I read this story at the time of its first appearance I found it grotesquely melodramatic. As its whole emphasis is on the survival of atavistic instincts and practices, why had the old priest's sermons not provoked so grotesque an outrage in previous years? Is it likely that parents would have permitted their children to leave the church in the midst of the service, still less run riot in the town? Patrick appears to have recognized the unlikelihood that the townspeople would even have known Halévy to be a Jew, making him identifiable only by donning 'a beaded skull-cap' that very day! Anyone who knew the Collioure of Patrick's day or its kindly curé would find the episode laughable, rather than sinister or tragic.

In fact the germ of the tale lay in a curious anecdote related to him by my mother twenty years before. They had visited Perpignan to watch the annual *procession des pénitents*, which moved them profoundly with its air of ancient majestic piety. Returning home, my mother spoke with their neighbour, who mentioned mysteriously that 'she heard the whistles coming out of church. "Aie mare, je me suis dit, on tue les juifs."' I suspect that this reflected no more than bizarre conjecture on the part of the good-natured but not overly intelligent Madame Rimbaud, which my mother recorded as an example of *Colliourench* eccentricity.

This supplied Patrick with the basis of his plot, but I suspect that its inclusion reflected deep-rooted fears inside his own psyche. The first was his at times irrational aversion to children and adolescents, unruly creatures who might at any time indulge in some uncontrollable outburst. The second was a less evident but nonetheless real fear that ancient beliefs and customs could, among much that was good, preserve a residue of atavistic cruelty. When his car got stuck during a recent visit to Ireland he had been rescued by some monoglot Galway men. Although Patrick loved the ancient language of the country and regretted its passing, he felt impelled to record: 'It is ungracious to say it even privately but together with the kindness I do sense hostility to the stranger here & a savagery.'*

His apprehension in these cases was plainly as groundless as it was idiosyncratic, but anyone who had lived through the Second World War could not fail to be aware of the extent to which cruel and irrational impulses lurk in the depths of the human psyche.

'On the Wolfsberg' is a brief tale of a maltreated woman who has lost her memory, while 'A Passage of the Frontier' recounts a fugitive's flight across the Pyrenees from the Nazis during the War. The latter (if I understand it correctly) is a paradigm of the Passion of Christ,† although its cryptic ending leaves one guessing at some of the symbolism. As ever, the best passages in the stories are their

---

* This is a running theme in Liam O'Flaherty's novel *Skerrett*, which Patrick read at an impressionable age.

† Patrick named the mountain (which is probably in reality the Canigou) under which the fugitive in the story passes 'Malamort': from *malemort*, 'cruel death'.

wonderfully evocative depictions of scenery, and their effect on the emotions of the solitary Wanderer.

However, it was just as everything in their lives appeared at last to be moving on a smooth and prosperous course that a cruel fate, all too often disposed to act against them with preternatural malignancy, struck yet again. In June Patrick was carrying a washed barrel out to drain when he felt a stab of pain in his back. His agonized yell called my mother to his assistance, and he was barely able to creep on all fours to his bed. At first he thought he must have pulled or torn a muscle, but when the pain persisted and the doctor called it turned out that he had slipped a disc.

During the next three weeks the pain remorselessly increased, treatment proved ineffectual, one of his feet lost all feeling, and an acutely painful paralysis began creeping up his leg. Taken to hospital in Perpignan, as he afterwards explained in a letter to Richard Ollard:

> a capital neurosurgeon laid bare my spine, discovered une énorme hernie discale paralysante, removed it & gave it to me in a little bottle of alcohol. Then came 3 weeks in the clinic, 3 weeks that I had hoped to fill with reading about Pic; but alas my wits were very much astray, and although the sciatic pain was gone it was replaced by others so that I still could not sleep naturally. However, all that is receding into the past; I am home again.

It was not until the end of July that he was able to apply himself to his work again: 'Here I am at my desk again 48 days lost.' Even then, he felt weak, suffered from recurrent pain, and encountered difficulty in recovering his concentration. As so often, Jane Austen provided him with a restorative. He reread all her novels, concluding with *Mansfield Park*: 'such a refuge, that comfortable stable world, in spite of its sometimes (I think) false values & cant'.

Patrick displayed his customary courage and stoicism when he became so cruelly and unexpectedly afflicted, and apart from this painful setback 1974 should have been regarded as a successful year. He had made good progress with *Picasso*, both in writing and research, seen the successful publication of his short stories in *The Chian Wine* (a book which meant much to him), and for good measure published the 'pretty little book' *Men-of-War*.

At the beginning of December he still suffered from recurrent back pain and a series of sleepless nights, and was, I imagine, distressed on attaining his sixtieth birthday.* Normally he and my mother celebrated the anniversary with presents and a feast, but this time he left his diary blank for several days. On Christmas Eve he recorded 'Black depression', and a few days later 'mild happiness gave way to depression, I cannot tell why.'

However, although such despondent moments recurred, with the New Year of 1975 Patrick found his equanimity returning. For Christmas I had sent him a copy of the nineteenth-century Irish novelist Charles Lever's rollicking *Charles O'Malley*, which afforded him a contented interlude: 'Dear Nikolai sent a 1st of O'Malley as a Xmas present . . . Idleness, reading Lever: there is an old & charming pleasure in a tale whose conventions (spotless hero &c) one absorbed 50 years ago.'

Patrick in turn was as ever generosity itself. Concerned by my Georgina's responsibilities in having a house to run, a husband working at home, a two-year-old child, and now the imminent arrival of a second baby, he offered to pay for a cleaner – an offer she gladly accepted, and which Patrick and my mother continued to provide for the next couple of years.

The only irritations in his life during the early part of the year were as ever idiosyncratic: 'Hordes of vile sex-cats in the garden: how they anger me.'

A few days later another mishap aroused his ire: 'Absurd trouble

---

* Patrick maintained such contact with members of his family as distance and long separation allowed. He and his brother Bun always exchanged Christmas letters, and his sister Nora wrote at this time to Joan: 'My – Pat is 60 yrs old tomorrow! I must write to him next.'

with a lost button-shank, & now having found it I have dropped it again. Hot, sweaty hot with rage.'

With the approach of spring he decided the time had come for further researches in Paris, where their kindly friends Pierre and Monique de Saint-Prix offered their flat as a base. The day after their arrival Patrick and my mother visited the Musée Nationale d'Art Moderne, where he 'was <u>amazed</u> by the Pic's, particularly by a black & brown still life with a bust (white line scratched on black) & melon, & by a 1929 piece as calm as anything he ever did . . . Many of my ideas are upset, above all those of steady chronological flow.'

Next, Patrick conducted extensive researches at the Bibliothèque Nationale, in what appears to have been his first visit: 'Here I am in the Bib. nat. Much the same atmosphere as the B Mus, the old round Reading-room, but smaller, less nobly domed. And the catalogue is much harder to handle. But on the other hand what active kindness from the middle-aged erudite at Renseignements.'

There he toiled for successive days making copious notes, breaking off occasionally to indulge in a smoke:

> Yesterday I grew v tired of my restless neighbour & stopped work early – stuffed & stupid anyhow by an excess of food & wine (turbot, eaten in a modest little place where people nevertheless pay 2000 + In my smoking walks about the Bourse the gold coins awakened my cupidity, & some marvellous high-relief Greek silver.

He also inspected various houses where Picasso had lived and painted, despite his 'Back destroyed by street-walking'.

The highlight of the visit came on Sunday, when they visited Marguerite and Claude Duthuit. Marguerite was the daughter of Matisse, and had known Picasso well. Patrick and my mother struck up an instant strong rapport with the couple, and Marguerite provided him with a fund of valuable information and anecdotes:

Relation of Mat & Pic far subtler than ordinary jealousy (which was fermented by others, particularly literary gents). Made to understand one another. During the war Picasso came to have his papers stamped near Mat's house Quai St Michel always called, waited late. Though not cowardly had a blue dread of the gendarme.

A close friendship with the Duthuits ensued, from which Patrick gained much of that insight into Picasso's complex character which represents so marked a factor of his biography.

Next month he and my mother returned to a snowbound Paris for further study in the Bibliothèque Nationale and galleries. While these expeditions were intensely rewarding, as ever they were relieved and happy to be back in their little white house in the valley.

Its comforting atmosphere of familiarity and security inspired him to compose a verse in French extolling its qualities as a safe haven in a treacherous world:

> *J'occupe seul cette demeure*
> *blanche*
> *ou rien ne contrarie le vent*
> *si nous sommes ce qui a crié*
> *et le cri*
> *qui ouvre ce ciel*
> *de glace*
> *ce plafond blanc*
> *nous nous sommes aimés sous ce plafond.*
> I alone occupy this white dwelling,
> Where nothing impedes the wind.
> If we are those that have cried out,
> And the cry
> Which opens the sky
> Of ice.
> This white ceiling –
> We loved each other beneath this ceiling.

Inevitably a biographer's estimate of his subject's character fluctuates with continuing absorption of fresh evidence. At the beginning of March Patrick noted: 'I made a tentative attempt at a piece on P's developing often worsening (from point of view of his own happiness) character. Do not know whether it will come off.' While his enthusiasm for Picasso the painter was enormous, he frequently questioned whether his personal nature was altogether admirable. In particular he was concerned by the artist's promiscuity, neglectful and even at times contemptuous attitude towards his successive wives and mistresses, and the bully in him which vied with generous and kindly aspects of his character.

'P the painter is more important than P the prick – though indeed the 2 are inextricably mingled,' he noted. More serious doubts arose from the danger of 'presenting P as injured innocent when some pages back he [Picasso] said what a tough Spanish beast he was in his trampling [on women?]'. In the completed book Patrick tended to opt for charitable interpretations where possible, which seems the fairest approach for a biographer – provided there be no suppression of relevant evidence. There is so much one person can never know about another, however familiar the relationship, that cautiously generous interpretations must generally be more appropriate than the alternative.

Although there were many marked similarities between their early lives and characters, the social milieus inhabited by Picasso and Patrick could hardly have been more different. While the painter was a hugely gregarious and sexually promiscuous figure who revelled in his public image, his biographer concerned himself with women other than my mother only in a playfully amorous way (and that rarely), largely confining his society to a limited circle comprising my mother, a handful of local acquaintances, me and my increasing family, and his publishing contacts in England.

Towards the end of 1974 he had received welcome news. 'Such an agreeable Post. Georgina is to have another baby', and now in April he recorded: 'Such a pleasant letter from Georgina in hospital with Anastasia, who was born on the 17th.'

Local characters afforded him moments of wry amusement:

> Henri Doublier came to lunch, mute & overwhelmed at first, but more confident quite soon. He appreciated the Noah's ark animals: drew in chalk on the floor: told extravagant tales about a boa that approached a cooked chicken & was slain by his mama with an arrow that happened to be lying about – one of the Collioure boas.

While Patrick was often ill at ease with children, he was also capable of actions of much kindness and sympathetic consideration towards them. The allusion to the Noah's Ark provides a striking example of his warmer nature. In the spring of 1974 he had begun an ambitious project on his lathe in the garage, and by 21 April reported with satisfaction: 'I finished turning Ham, Shem & Japhet, 2 hippopotamuses & 1 general-purpose animal, all on the same piece of wood – thoroughly wooden & stupid they look, too.'

The project was the construction of an ark for our two children, on which he toiled during intervals of work on *Picasso*.* The wood came from an old apricot tree in the garden, and the task proved a lengthy labour of love. Each month the numbers and quality of its crew and animal cargo grew. In May 'Hippopotamus legs, fine work indeed' appeared, and the next month 'A fat tiger, larger than the lion alas'. By September he had completed 'A stumpy animal designed to be a leopard: so

---

* The two tasks marched in tandem, designs for lions and tigers appearing on the backs of Patrick's notes on *Picasso*. The ark and its inhabitants now dwell in my library, where they continue much admired by grandchildren and visitors.

like the bear however that painted both brown, & that answered fairly well'. A week later 'Idleness & sleep, though I did rough out what I meant to be a pair of leopards': 'The leopards, which I began to paint, are pitiful things like mice'. As with his writing Patrick was meticulous, and in the New Year of 1975 he completed 'Noah's daughters in law', and next month 'after infinite labour, I glued the 2d camel. This morning I undid the cramps & dreamily sliced off one layer too many from its head: I may possibly be able to recover it by giving the beast a sideways posture.' Patrick was nothing if not resourceful, and by the end of February could report: 'Camels, one, the colour of anchovy sauce, looks flayed: the other is better.'

So the work continued, until at the end of September, after almost as much time and trouble as may have occupied Noah himself, he wrote to me to announce the imminent arrival:

The ark is on its way, borne by Charles and Mary de Salis.* They were staying with us until a few days ago, have returned to England by car . . . and (if they can ever find Parbrook) will bring it over. You will like Charles, I think. We first met him some twenty-five years ago, when he was first secretary in Paris; and since then he has flitted about the world, ending up as something very grand in Rio. If plied with red wine he grows uncommon droll. Noah's family will be found in the deckhouse (the three female figures that are not Mrs Noah are daughters-in-law) and the animals in the hold – the deck lifts off. Please let Georgina take care not to throw away two very small creatures, possibly guinea pigs, it may easily escape her unwarned mind, by reason of their exiguity: there are also some barely-perceptible though necessary doves. The dull purple quadrupeds are bears, and the squat yellow things with green eyes leopards.

* Charles Gay in Patrick's *Richard Temple* is partly modelled on the diplomat Charles de Salis.

Patrick proudly displays his completed Noah's Ark, its crew and passengers*

As may be imagined the delivery was greeted with delight by two-year-old Alexandra. Despite Patrick's derogatory comments, the ark is an impressive piece of work for a self-taught carpenter. While some of the creatures are a trifle quaint, such as the tubular hippos and tigers, the giraffes, elephants, and camels in particular are skilfully rendered.

In his letter Patrick expressed warm pleasure at the news that I had at last completed my book on the forced repatriation of Russian prisoners and refugees – now entitled *Victims of Yalta* – commiserated (no doubt with particular feeling) over extensive cuts required by my sensible editor, and provided invaluable advice and information for my next book. He had earlier suggested my compiling a biography of the second Lord Camelford, episodes in whose short but lurid life he had come across in Marshall's *Naval Biography*. Although my initial researches showed that

---

* Patrick later made a *second* Noah's Ark, for my sister's sons Michael and Robert.

Camelford was a much more colourful character even than we had suspected, my current publisher proved unreceptive to the project. Eventually, by the New Year of 1977 Patrick reported: 'A long affectionate letter from Nikolai – ark v well received – but we are worried by his underlying anxiety, by Hodders not taking Camelford.' Fortunately it was commissioned by Jonathan Cape shortly afterwards.

Reverting to Patrick's work on Picasso throughout 1975: in May and June he travelled with my mother to Barcelona and Antibes in search of material. At the beginning of July they visited the Comte and Comtesse de Lazerme at their ancestral home in Perpignan. They had been long-standing friends of Picasso, who stayed with them in August 1953. They took him to Collioure to see the bullfights and the town's splendid fireworks display honouring the feast day of the Assumption.

The artist was greatly taken with the beauties of the Roussillon, and on revisiting the Lazermes a year later decided to find a house suitable for use as a studio. Unfortunately there proved to be few houses in Perpignan comparable to the Hôtel de Lazerme, and the painter extended his search to Collioure, whose attractions had struck him during his first visit. Like so many other painters, the more he saw of the town the more he loved it. But the houses were small, and the streets narrow and intolerably noisy.

However, above the Faubourg, on the summit of the last shoulder of the Pyrenees overlooking the Mediterranean, is perched the Château Saint-Elme. The castle had been built by the Emperor Charles V when the Roussillon continued part of the kingdom of Aragon, and was after the French conquest provided with star-shaped outworks by Louis XIV's great military engineer Vauban. Together with Madame Lazerme, Picasso ascended the hill and inspected the castle with increasing delight. Here was the perfect combination of a magnificent historic building in a beautiful setting, extraordinary vistas of mountain and sea, space and privacy. Regrettably, every effort to secure it proved unavailing: the castle belonged to the state, whose bureaucratic apparatus apparently blocked each attempt.*

Picasso's visits naturally aroused great excitement in Collioure. On 16 August 1953 my mother noted in her diary: 'Picasso visible in café des Sports – merry, pink, active. He was président of this year's corrida.' A few days later: 'Picasso comes on plage, looks quiet & pleasant', and subsequently 'Picasso solemnly swam about.' Patrick and my mother possessed a close mutual friend in the form of the ebullient émigré Czech artist Willy Mucha. Mucha's relationship with Picasso had its ups and downs, and on 23 September my mother recorded:

> Saw poor Willy – in bed (comme ça) poor Willy having been knocked down by one we think to be Esperiquette by the petit pont last night in front of 20–30 people. Poor W. terribly upset, also because Picasso was cynical & publicity-seeking & generally base, when dining with W. & Pignon etc. two days ago.

Mary Burkett, who saw much of my parents at the time, described to me what appeared to have been Patrick's initial contact with the great artist:

> As to the Mucha episode. I distinctly remember being told by Patrick & Mary. At the time, as I was an art teacher & rather obsessed with Picasso, it was of great interest to me. Picasso used to come to Collioure at least once a year. I know, coz I met him there. The children [from the school where Mary taught] were at the castle & we suddenly saw him walking along the main street with his blonde girl friend. We all, naively thought autographs!

---

* Cf. Patrick O'Brian, *Picasso: Pablo Ruiz Picasso* (New York, 1976), pp. 414, 420–23. I have been told that Brigitte Bardot was similarly frustrated in a subsequent attempt to acquire the fortress.

and bounded across the road to surround him. He took it in good part & signed all their bits of paper, my sketchbook still bears mine! also a sketch I did of him in the next few minutes, as he continued his perambulation. At that point Patrick & M. had not met him. It must have been a year or so later when they told me their story. Picasso had come to visit Mucha & he had asked Mary & Patrick to go round to see Picasso. When they arrived Willy Mucha said that they must not disturb him as he was still finishing a piece in Willy's autograph book, but that they could get around to the back of his studio where the land rose steeply and they could watch him through the skylight window. They all three went round and watched him as he scribbled & scrubbed. He worked so hard on the central part that when eventually Willy inspected it closely, Picasso had made a hole right through the page! They were greatly amused and I think just left. I certainly can't remember their saying they met him to speak to . . . So I can't confirm or deny, but think it's highly likely that Patrick was too shy to meet.

Patrick himself asserts that: 'Even in 1952, when I first met him and when by the calendar he was over seventy, there was nothing at all of the old man about him: he was trim, compact, well-made, his round head burned brown in the sun – age was irrelevant.'* At one time I was myself inclined to question whether Patrick did indeed meet the artist, but in a recent conversation Odette Boutet, who was far better placed than Mary Burkett to know the facts, confirmed to me emphatically that the two met frequently at JoJo Pous's Café des Sports (now Les Templiers). The initial introduction was presumably effected through the good offices of their mutual friend, the affable Willy Mucha.

---

* *Picasso*, p. 126. Patrick's chronology had become a little hazy, as Picasso's first visit to Collioure was in 1953 (ibid., p. 413).

In the high summer of 1976 Patrick's prodigious labours drew to a close. True to form, he had completed his mammoth task within the stipulated two years. Such authorial punctiliousness was customary with him, and further ensured that the family finances were maintained in a healthy state. For the first time they were able to afford a regular cleaner (it is typical of his and my mother's generosity that they had provided us with one long before themselves). Ana, a Portuguese immigrant, proved a faithful support for the remainder of their lives.

Understandably, completion of his task brought flutterings of worry. In August Richard Ollard wrote suggesting that he undertake 'another naval tale after Pic'. Given the wounding rebuff he had received three years earlier this should have been encouraging, but a month later found Patrick assailed by doubt: 'Unpleasant dreams these nights. This one was that Collins liked neither Pic nor a new naval tale: there was nothing to be done. They were indifferent & I was a nuisance. Too logical for nightmare.'

His dreams were frequently disturbing. 'A beautiful dream of a house in a tree, uninhabited since 1925, but habitable. A cross father – dog tamed & loving.' Furthermore: 'I have an odd feeling of playing a role these days, & as if the unconvincing stage on which I play it were all that was left to me. A falsity runs through everything: but I do not mind v much.'

The irate father, recourse to affectionate animals, and an incurable sense of detachment from the world, suggest that even now Patrick could find no complete escape from the daunting shadow of Dr Charles Russ.

On 8 August the task was completed: 'Well. I wrote the end, feeling quite moved: but whether it is adequate, whether it will do or not I do not know. It seems rather slight, & the anti Pic words about the drawings may outweigh the pro-Pic about the paintings.'

First as ever came the judgement of his most valued critic: 'M has read right thro the MS – repetitions, notes, usage etc. Speaks kindly of the book as a whole: encouraging.'

After both had carefully read it through again, the bulky manuscript was despatched to Richard Scott Simon. Patrick found his reaction and that of Richard Ollard initially dampening. Their praise appeared in part to be an emollient designed to stress that the book was too long, and in places too detailed. Ollard strongly advised fewer descriptions of the artist's paintings, and Patrick's initial half-hearted resistance was overcome by Richard Scott Simon's recommendation that he comply.

One cannot help feeling that the publishers were largely to blame in not having decided at an early stage on the question of illustrations. If reproductions of Picasso's work were included, then description would have become largely supererogatory. Equally, the publishers' difficulty is understandable. In the case of so prolific an artist, which works should be included? Given that it was emphatically not designed as a coffee-table book, illustrations must necessarily be few, rendering them in that case so selective as to be effectively arbitrary. In the end, probably wisely, it was decided to have none. At the same time Patrick was persuaded to pare down his perceptive but too detailed comments until they provided a delicate compromise between laborious description and apt analytical detail, allowing the reader to appreciate the intent and effect of Picasso's achievement.

Fortunately, Patrick's compliant acceptance of Ollard's suggested cuts swiftly brought the work to a state where the publishers could freely accord the work its due. Possibly because it had been agreed that Collins should undertake the editing, William Targ at Putnam proved gratifyingly enthusiastic. On 13 October he wrote:

The Garden House
Castle Road, Saltwood
Hythe, Kent, CT21 4QX
Tel. Hythe 69300

PICASSO

by

PATRICK O'BRIAN

Published by Collins

Patrick O'Brian has written much the best biography of Picasso. It is full of information, the judgments both of Picasso as a man and as an artist seem to be remarkably convincing, and it is extremely well written. In particular, the relationship between Picasso and Catalan painters is given its true importance, both in his formative years, and, as friends, throughout his life.

Kenneth Clark
....
LORD CLARK

October 12, 1976

Lord Clark's letter to Patrick

I've just finished reading your manuscript, PICASSO, and hasten to send you my sincerest and warmest congratulations. To Mary, too, my felicitations; I can well imagine how much she contributed to the materialization of this splendid work. It is a monumental work – informative, moving, visual, interpretative – the total biography.

This was just the sort of reaction every author needs, and there was more to come. At the end of the month, after supplying me with fresh information about Lord Camelford, Patrick continued:

Speaking of peers, Ld Clark, Sir Kenneth as was, has just written me the very kindest possible letter about <u>Picasso</u> – says 'a really excellent book – much the best biography of P – very good judgments – very well written.

This pleases me.

Among other admirers whose opinion Patrick valued was Mary Renault, who sent an equally enthusiastic encomium from Cape Town.

When the book appeared a year later reviews ranged from the frivolous and envious to the serious and considered, but overall Patrick felt it received its due. In the letter conveyed within the crowded hold of Noah's ark by Charles de Salis to England, he gave me this overview:

Yesterday's post brought the first review of the English edition of Picasso: the Guardian was rotten (its literary editor is a Trotskyist), the Mail concentrated wholly on Picasso in bed, some others praised foolishly, but John Raymond did the book proud in the Sunday Times, speaking of hard work and corruscating genius. Hard work, yes: but as I snort and wheeze at my desk this morning the corruscation seems somewhat less than obvious. Furthermore, the drains have blocked.

A major criticism that might have been levelled at the book, which many critics continue to regard as the most perceptive biography of Picasso, is its virtual ignoring of the wayward artist's appalling record as a callous apologist for Stalin and Soviet totalitarianism.[2] While Patrick cannot have been unaware of this unsavoury aspect of the artist's character, it probably did not impinge greatly on his area of concern. He himself entertained only marginal interest in politics, and probably took Picasso's besotted admiration for the genocidal regime as the minor aberration of a mind focused on higher things. Above all, he was genuinely persuaded that an artist should be judged by his works rather than his character.

X

Shifting Currents

I hear the noise about thy keel;
I hear the bell struck in the night:
I see the cabin-window bright;
I see the sailor at the wheel.

Lord Tennyson, *In Memoriam*

When *H.M.S. Surprise* was published in England in August 1973 it received what Richard Ollard described to Patrick as 'marvellous reviews'. However, the immediate aftermath proved somewhat disappointing. When the American edition eventually came out in the spring of 1974 Patrick was upset by 'some deeply stupid US reviews of Surprise. Most praise leaves me untouched: most blame too unless it is literate, but the accumulation of these really vexed me.' Nor had the generally laudatory English reviews achieved all that might have been hoped.

The failure to achieve an increase in sales over its predecessors was disappointing, but that it held its ground at least ensured Collins's readiness to publish a sequel. With the typescript of *Picasso* safely in Richard Ollard's hands, Patrick began pondering Jack Aubrey's next adventure. On 16 September 1975 he slept on the sofa upstairs, where he:

spent a wretched night – ruminating a variety of resentments and (I hope a little more profitably) going over the beginning of a naval tale phaps to be called the – Command (Indian Ocean). The reverse of Paradise – domestic joys – better to marry than to burn, but what if one burns married? – no point in living, bringing up children to just the same miserable round – SM[aturin] agrees, no point at all, unless reference to futurity – let us not whine however – here at least the illusion of real purpose (i.e. command) & at least it is between men, more comprehensible. In idyllic cottage, m-in-law, twins (? m in law lost money ? twins wanting [i.e. mentally deficient]) women constitutionally unaffectionate.

In this way the introductory section of the novel came to Patrick almost in its entirety during the course of a single cold, damp and unhappy night. Jack Aubrey's initial pessimism clearly reflects Patrick's own worries about the future, now that he seemed faced by the prospect of uncertain waters. His doubts and fears brought on a resurgence of old demons: the difficulties inherent in marriage, and the burden of a disapproving mother-in-law.

However, peace of mind returned once he began to conceive the main section of the work. Three days after his nocturnal musing the weather at Collioure had changed from sodden grey to 'A bright clear day, with lovely roses in the garden'. Patrick began to see his way ahead: 'Mind full of naval tale. Antagonist to be a role-playing man, the dashing naval officer. It would be useful to have him a peer (Irish or Scotch) playing the part too, but that might lead to too much my-lording.'*

His plan continued: 'His wife wants a lift? Late, purposely left behind. He was JA's senior, but was made [promoted] later – reversal of roles. SM quite likes him, so vulnerable.'

---

* My sole criticism of the book when in due course Patrick sent it to me was that Jack did not sufficiently employ the customary 'my lord' when addressing Lord Clonfert!

Having provisionally arranged his principal characters, Patrick 'looked into James[1] & my Indian Ocean campaign, & find it much less simple than I had remembered'. It can be seen that he conjured up an image of the novel more or less as a whole before checking its historical setting. Even now he continued to focus on the characters and plot, rather than the historical circumstances: 'An idea for the novel. Maturin & surgeon of antagonist's ship (? both United Irishmen but the 2d a drunken though able Presbyterian) to act as chorus pointing out the motives, failings & perhaps fate of the main characters.'

However, there came an unpleasant check when Patrick found that his further reading in James conflicted increasingly with the initial plan:

> Going on to the Mauritius campaign I found to my horror that my memory had been at fault. The island was taken not by the commodore but by an admiral with an enormous force. The first part – his being reduced to a single frigate & then capturing 2 – will do, but the rest will not; & I can hardly use history in one part & abandon it in the next.

Patrick raised his concern with Richard Scott Simon:

> It seems to me that there are three courses open to me. I can scrap the idea altogether, and think of another campaign of a similar nature. Or I can transpose the situation that I had first got hold of to a fictitious milieu as I did in 'Post Captain' and 'Surprise'. Or I can keep all the historical sequence that suits my purpose and change some of the later facts towards the end for the sake of the tale: in point of fact, if I did that I should only have to interpolate one or possibly two actions so as to make the commodore's personal triumph virtually certain before the admiral comes to take it over. The third course seems to me the best . . .

Both Richard Scott Simon and Richard Ollard concurred with Patrick's judgement. His qualms perfectly illustrate the narrow path the historical novelist must tread between excessive pedantry, and flying so free of the facts as to invite the question whether he be an historical novelist at all. As before, he selected his ground with consummate skill. He promptly set to work summarizing James's detailed account: 'So long as I abandon JA's triumph as the climax, the historical sequence will do v well. (Though I shall have to make Willoughby a post-captain straight away).'

What chiefly concerned him at this time was less his ability to write a worthy successor to Aubrey's three previous adventures, than whether continuing relatively modest sales would ensure further commissions in that line. He toyed with the idea of writing a biography of the Marquis de Custine, who visited Russia in the reign of Nicholas I and afterwards published a celebrated critique of the Russian Empire. However, 'it would call for an immense amount of reading all round'. 'We are both very dismal these days': a complaint with which many writers and their spouses will be familiar.

On 18 October 1975 Patrick:

> wrote 1000+ of Mauritius Command with much pleasure & in the evening looked into the other [Aubrey] naval books to catch the tone & to remind myself of what had happened. They were better than I had remembered, though in places too high-flying & the reader is expected to fill too many gaps. I must speak plainer in this one.

This was largely necessitated by the fact that this time his story centred on a major historical event, one which involves Jack in extensive combined operations.

Patrick's literary labours were regularly interrupted by the constant necessity to polish his *Picasso*, engage in extensive correspondence, tend the garden, and press the grapes. In November he planted twenty-one cabbages – no doubt those which Jack proudly shows Stephen at the beginning of the novel. Their beloved tortoise Caroline had disappeared, and Pierrot Camps (a Collioure fisherman, with whom he and his wife Hélène my parents were longstanding friends) arrived with one he believed might be her. It was not, but my mother 'appropriated it quand-même'. Next day the wanderer reappeared, and 'a few minutes after their introduction, Caroline & the new tortoise coupled heartily'. Two days later the testudinous Lothario decamped.

On 25 October an 'excellent contract' for *The Mauritius Command* arrived: '£2000 advance & 12% rising to 15% after 5000'. That afternoon friends called for luncheon with their three-year-old daughter, whose movements Patrick observed much as Stephen Maturin would have those of a Réunion lemur: 'I had not considered that the little girl would be walking, nay <u>running</u> about & vocal. She is a good child, but ½ hour of her would have been enough. A perpetually renewed miracle for the parents, less so for others.'

She appears unwittingly to have contributed to Patrick's description of Mrs Williams's tiresome granddaughter Cecilia.

Pleasanter inspiration came from a visit to an *étang* near Perpignan, where he saw 'Thousands of duck, perhaps flamingoes beyond them. Cormorants! Hunchbacked curlews.' His bouts of low spirits persisted, however:

Is it worth recording my gloomy reflections about loss of faith, loss of music equally desire for unremitting punishment – for continued wound (not to say mutilation) that the inflicter must always bear. Perhaps it was the unconvincing starets [in *The Brothers Karamazov*, which he was reading] who started this train of thought. He speaks of pleasure in clinging to an offence.

My conjecture is that Patrick at times tended to dread unhappiness rather more than he actually experienced it.

It was presumably in consequence of the protracted break after writing *H.M.S. Surprise* that he continued to find it hard to immerse himself in his new work: 'I re-read what I had done of Ch I, &

did not think much of it. It seemed to me contrived, inorganic as it were, with the remarks made on purpose to illustrate various points.'

Two days later he recorded wearily: 'Some work: qu. (& a grave one) am I rather tired of the RN?' Next day: 'I finished Ch I rather abruptly (too long: 11000 +) & am somewhat at a loss how to go on.' This would appear to reflect a temporary despondency, since the account of Stephen's arrival at Ashgrove Cottage is replete with life and colour.

Much of the opening description derives from Patrick's visit in the high summer of 1973 to our first home in wild Wales, with its 'hanging wood on the other side of the valley'. Like Jack Aubrey, I possessed a large astronomical telescope: that which we had earlier taken to Collioure, in order to scan the heavens at night. Again, the passage 'Stephen Maturin had thought of Aubrey as powerful resilient youth itself for so long that this change and the slow, weary motion as the distant figure closed his instrument and stood up, his hand pressed to an old wound in his back' was surely drawn from the foot-long scar across the base of my spine, resulting from the operation I had undergone in 1960, when Patrick and my mother for weeks attended daily by my hospital bed, which recurrently caused me severe pain for years thereafter. However, when Maturin 'saw not only that look of anxiety but also the marks of age and unhappiness', he was, I imagine, drawing on my subsequent appearance a fortnight before he wrote the passage, when he and my mother visited us at our cottage home in Somerset:

> Nikolai welcoming, but drawn & anxious. Will not really tell me about his book. Incapacity? Smokescreen? . . . To the Slacks* . . .

---

* My mother's Aunt Joan and Uncle Austin – the latter I have suggested earlier as another partial model for Jack Aubrey. Of course, Patrick did not draw for inspiration on any one figure, but blended aspects of different people into the finished characters of his own creation.

& we exchanged our anxieties about N . . . Our general impression
(& M's) is that he has bitten off more than he can chew.

The book was my *Victims of Yalta*, which at the time was
proving hard work, in its initial form too long, and delays in
publication continued matter for stressful financial concern.

After some difficulties, Patrick sets Jack and Stephen on their
voyage with the capture of the 28-gun *Hébé* off the Dry Salvages,
for whose topography he turned to that mainstay of his world-
picture, the eighteen-volume *Histoire Générale des Voyages* by the
indefatigable Abbé Prévost (1746).* Now firmly into his stride,
Patrick was able to celebrate his sixty-first birthday (12 December)
in style. My mother had found him an appropriate present, a jersey
from Mauritius made of pure Shetland wool. They drove to
Perpignan, where they enjoyed a fine lunch at Les Antiquaires,
accompanied by a bottle of 1963 Gevrey-Chambertin:

> Then a most amusing film, Le Sauvage: the pretty, spirited C[atherine]
> Deneuve & sympa Y[ves] Montand – no pretensions, great fun,
> lovely scenery, preceded by astonishing Caribbean birds – pelicans
> diving, cormorants, frigate birds. Home in the twilight, quite done.

The year 1975 ended on a propitiously happy note. My mother
invited some close friends to lunch on New Year's Eve. Patrick
noted: 'They all accepted, alas & our only hope is that 1 falls v
mildly ill. 6 perfect, 7 an unmanageable horde.' The day arrived,
with Patrick's apprehension undiminished until he found 'Monique
[de Saint-Prix] had had to cry off – grippe – as if in answer to my
prayer. Not that my prayer included any painful incapacity,
however.' The reduction seemed to do the trick: 'A v cheerful party

---

* On showing his handsome set of Prévost's great work to the American writer
Ken Ringle in 1994, he remarked: 'It's an irreplaceable resource, but it's never
been translated into English, so few people know it exists.' The volumes now
occupy pride of place in my library.

indeed: remarkable quantities of [home-made] gin. Mathilde wonderfully funny . . . We were neither of us much done up until the v end of the day: such a pleasant end to the year.'

Fine sunny weather assisted inspiration in the New Year, when within a few days Patrick brought Jack near the Cape. Four days later a book arrived from Mary Renault in South Africa, describing the detention of a Russian naval captain at the Cape in 1808–9.* This not only provided Patrick at the *moment juste* with a detailed description far in excess of what he already knew, but enabled him to provide the inebriate Captain Golovnin a walk-on part in the story ('I was trying to be droll with Golovnin').

Arrival of the paperback edition of *H.M.S. Surprise* cheered Patrick and my mother, while the proofs of *Picasso* were checked and returned with general satisfaction at the quality of the book. Less gratifying was the state of their accounts. These revealed that they needed £4,000 'for a year's ordinary quiet living', while the 'sea tales' – assuming they continued indefinitely – brought in only about £2,500 p.a., which meant drawing £1,500 from their savings, leaving sufficient only to last a further year. 'But perhaps Pic will do well: how I hope so.' However, an author's life is frequently up and down, every book being a fresh venture. More to the point, within the week came news that my mother's Aunt Barbara had died, leaving her a life interest in her estate which promised to amount to £1,000 p.a. This was followed by the further welcome announcement that a capital payment of £1,500 was due in addition to the income.

Despite this, February proved as so often the nadir of the year. *The Mauritius Command* was moving slowly, and Patrick was troubled by unhappy reflections on 'the mutilation of age'. Once again, he suspected my mother's affections of waning, and 'thought of putting into SM's mouth "Who can possibly tell the failures,

---

* Her Christmas card that year bears a copy of an oil painting of Table Bay by John Thomas Baines, in which she enquires: 'How does this fit your period?'

the deep humiliations, the disappointments & the frustrations in such a relationship!"' Fortunately he did not, but it is worth noting his all but explicit identification with Maturin, and my mother with Diana Villiers. The black mood passed, and 'in bed I snored so that M left me'.

Fortified by their unexpected windfall, Patrick contemplated travelling to Réunion and Mauritius in order to obtain local colour. Before long, however, he abandoned the project, confirming how little he needed beyond his imagination and reading to assist creation. His slow progress was paralleled by my own with *Victims of Yalta*, for which he expressed characteristic sympathy: 'Nikolai, poor chap, is having the same difficulty about length . . . We are anxious for him.'

It was a generally worrying time. Although *The Mauritius Command* was beginning to flow satisfactorily, there seemed no especial reason to hope that it might sell materially better than its predecessors. In addition there was the grievous setback of the sudden loss of interest in the series by American publishers. He contemplated undertaking a biography of Matisse, which with any luck should appeal to the cultivated William Targ at Putnam.

As not infrequently occurred when prospects appeared gloomy, Patrick became concerned about his health. At the end of January my mother had paid one of her regular calls to old Madame Naudo, who had helped fugitive Allied servicemen to cross into neutral Spain during the War.* Sadly she found her frail and blind, unable to distinguish night from day, and hence possessing no notion of time. Patrick found this 'an added horror that I had never thought of', and suffered nightmares of losing his sight. Everything depended on his good health, which caused him to suffer from bouts of what may at times have been mild

---

* My mother had been appointed local representative of the Royal Air Forces Escaping Society, her prime responsibility being assessment of the financial needs of beneficiaries.

hypochondria. In fact his physical powers were to remain vigorous for years to come, and he noted of his regular walk up the steep ridge behind the house: 'To the milestone (& the measured walk, uphill, requires 1992 paces, which leads me to suppose that I am slightly longer legged than the average Roman) on a perfectly sound pair of feet. No panting, either.'

Both my mother and Patrick suffered at times from sudden irrational premonitions of disaster. 'M shocked me extremely by speaking of her illogical morning anxiety, sometimes so great that she can hardly walk,' Patrick recorded. A fortnight later he was gripped by the same uneasiness: 'Quite often I wake with a sense of some undefined catastrophe – a catastrophe that I shall remember in a minute or two. Perhaps it is this that gives my face its habitually anxious expression.'

The prevailing sense of impending doom was alleviated next day by the arrival of the first copies of *Picasso*. His first reaction was one of pleasure and satisfaction, and that night they dined regally at Les Antiquaires on the biggest lobster Patrick had ever seen, washed down with a bottle of champagne. Next day he slept late, and on waking 'looked at Pic: so familiar/unfamiliar'. However, even if there was no real diminution in his natural vigour, at the end of May Patrick suffered one of those terrifying mishaps to which he and my mother were oddly prone.

On 24 May the couple drove over the Pyrenees into Spain, exploring and observing birds and plants. After two days of satisfactory discoveries,

we took the car almost to the rock barrier & walked perhaps ½m. Seeing a bright blue flower on the inward side of the road I climbed up the unsafe, blasted-rock side – found it (a gentian), crept along for an easier way down, passing some perhaps lilies of the valley, made my way to a series of rock steps: the penultimate yielded & we fell curiously mingled to the road, where I found I had broken my left leg a little above the ankle. This was at about 5.30 M[ary] went down to Saldes & came back in 2 hrs with the excellent woman & blankets – v welcome, as the cloud was coming down.

An ambulance followed surprisingly quickly, together with a helpful man from Saldes with his Land Rover and a Spanish Guardia Civil whom Patrick described as 'both civil and kind'. They carried him painfully down the steep slope and into the ambulance. At Berga a solicitous French-speaking surgeon set his leg, but for the next forty-eight hours the pain remained unremittingly acute. Patrick was X-rayed twice, and while being trundled about on a trolley his foot became caught and bent backwards: 'the night was horrible'. The X-rays showed jagged ends to the fractured bones, and an attendant nun stressed that an operation was unavoidable.

It being impossible to return in the *deux chevaux*, a driver was summoned from Collioure. The journey home proved unexpectedly comfortable, and Patrick found it a great relief to be in his own bed at last. However, the pain continued extreme, and there was the 'added horror of the quite forgotten bed-pan'. After three exceedingly unpleasant nights he was taken to hospital, where under local anaesthetic his leg was straightened and reset with screws. The operation was long and intricate, and recovery proved slow. A fortnight later he was released, during which time he had slept little and read much. 'Watching television,' he found on the other hand, 'is, upon the whole, a melancholy/dreary pastime.'

His recovery was accompanied by constant bouts of pain and sleeplessness. Unable to write or work in the garden, Patrick chafed at his confinement. 'Collioure already sadly crowded, & more squalid than one could wish,' he lamented after venturing into the town. Even at home annoyances plagued him: 'Huns in the lotissement howled until 3 am, jigging up & down to a sardana [the Catalan dance]. O for a rifle.' 'Tempers grow short in this weather,' he acknowledged ruefully.

Not until the end of June did he contemplate resuming work,

and then only to find he could do little more than stare at the manuscript. Inspiration seemed to have evaporated:

> I re-read VII & VIII, not much impressed with VII, & assembling my ideas tried to work: but my mind seems to have weakened – flabby, sponge-like, with no grip, no resistance. It is really frightening. Superficially bright enough, but incapable of tackling anything without distress.

As ever, he concealed his mental and physical troubles from the outside world. To me, he blithely wrote that:

> I saw fit to fall off a 9000 foot mountain. I did not fall quite to the bottom, but far enough to break a leg in two or three places. And if you or Georgina ever feel the need to do the same, I do beg you to choose a place nearer than eight hours from any hospital, and to avoid, at all costs, the attentions of a drunken Spanish surgeon.

Patrick's stoical courage was such, that I fear I did not always take his setbacks as seriously as they deserved, and I am relieved to find that I wrote him a 'sweet letter'. Ever concerned for my welfare, he was delighted to learn that after a long delay Hodder wanted no more than extensive cuts in my grotesquely overlong manuscript of *Victims of Yalta*, and promised publication in the spring. He noted in his diary that he urged me 'to attempt a biography (Custine or Camelford) rather than an historical novel. He could probably do it quite well.'

Patrick had come across the aberrant Lord Camelford during his researches for *The Mauritius Command*.* A cousin of Prime Minister William Pitt, he pursued an extraordinarily picaresque

---

* On 25 November 1975 Patrick recorded in his diary: 'read some court-martials (Ld Camelford, particularly)'.

and melodramatic life, ranging from shooting dead a fellow naval officer in Antigua to attempting the life of Napoleon with a repeating pistol, before being killed in a duel in 1804. The suggestion proved apt, and two years later my book was published under the title *The Half-Mad Lord*. Not only did Patrick provide me with the idea, but at every stage he proffered invaluable advice, ranging from details of naval life and practice to effective prose style. He was always a perfect mentor, and until I read his diaries after his death I had little idea of the problems he repeatedly encountered with his own writing. Readers may share my astonishment at the extent to which he triumphed over obstacles, so that it is rarely possible to distinguish passages written in the full flow of happy inspiration, from those composed under extreme mental or physical distress.

Friends called regularly, generally to Patrick's pleasure. However, the Collioure painter Willy Mucha was unfortunate to arrive just as Patrick was getting back into his stride with chapter 9. 'Whitish-haired, fat, sweating, loquacious, ill-at-ease. His flow of talk is kept up by the repetition of the same words several times & the use of phrases such as vous comprenez ce que je veux dire.'

Whether the ebullient Willy was really uneasy I do not know: if so, it is not impossible that Patrick's evident irritation made him so.

Throughout this painful time work on *The Mauritius Command* proceeded fitfully, with constant expressions of self-doubt. Finally, on 22 July:

> I finished Ch X & with it the book in a strong burst of work (3/4000). I doubt the value of some parts (SM's wanhope*) & the credibility of others (Cl[onfert]'s death), & the attempted bang at the end – indeed the knowing cynicism of these last 20 pp or so. But at least I have time to put it by & read it again objectively in a month.

* Hopelessness, despair.

A week later Patrick explained some of his misgivings to his agent Richard Scott Simon:

> I do not want to be definitively labelled as a writer of sea-tales, because apart from anything else the scope and the material are limited, and I doubt whether I could produce above two or three more without repeating myself. Then again, the characters are likely to grow threadbare with use: and I do not know whether new people could take their place. I have just finished the present tale, <u>The Mauritius Command</u>, and I think I will keep it by me to re-read it with a fairly fresh eye before sending it to you in September.

Fortunately, these gloomy misgivings were not shared by those who approached the book from a fresh standpoint. On receipt of the finished typescript Richard Scott Simon responded enthusiastically:

> Many more thanks for The Mauritius Command, which arrived extraordinarily promptly one day before your letter. I have enjoyed myself very much with it and I'm sure the other Richard [Ollard – Patrick's editor at Collins] will feel the same. I shall get it round to him by hand tomorrow. I must say, I do find Stephen a delightful character. However, I must admit I had to skip the details of the operations as I am afraid I am not strong enough for that sort of reading unless I have a glass of gin or brandy by me.

A few days later Richard Ollard confirmed Simon's encouraging judgement: 'I have just finished THE MAURITIUS COMMAND and must congratulate you on a really splendid performance . . .'

The novel is unusual, in that it is the only one in the series whose central plot closely follows significant historical events. Relying principally upon William James, it adheres with a few changes to the remarkable succession of combined operations which enabled Britain in 1810 to seize France's chief island strongholds in the Indian Ocean. Four powerful French frigates had escaped the British blockade, and used Mauritius as a base from which to conduct a series of damaging raids on convoys of East Indiamen rounding the Cape. An inferior British squadron sailed from the Cape, and in combination with troops transported from the neighbouring British island of Rodriguez managed to retake the islands, and reduce the French squadron after a succession of hard-fought actions at sea and on land.[2]

As Patrick explains in his Introductory Note, he adhered closely to contemporary accounts throughout the main part of his narrative. He substituted Jack Aubrey for the historical Commodore Josias Rowley on the *Boadicea*, and introduced his fictional Irish peer Lord Clonfert as commander of the 18-gun sloop *Otter*, together with his drink-prone Scotch surgeon McAdam. The handful of fictional characters is merged with consummate skill with historical figures such as the able Colonel Keating, commander of land forces on Rodriguez, Governor Farquhar, and the brutal Captain Corbett of the *Africaine*. Patrick's initial misgiving on discovering that the Commodore's labours were to some extent eclipsed by the arrival of Admiral Bertie's fleet from the Cape was countered by converting him into an acquisitive old rogue with an eye to prize money. Stephen Maturin's intelligence role is happily slotted into the real-life suborning of the French militia through Captain Willoughby's distribution of inflammatory proclamations.

Since he was writing fiction and not history, Patrick happily created characters for his protagonists loosely or even unrelated to those of their real-life prototypes. The incisive Keating behaves as might be inferred from his gallant actions. Although imaginatively concocted, Admiral Bertie's genial greed is such as not seldom presented a frustrating obstacle to a deserving subordinate. Occasionally Patrick transferred a trait or incident from one character to another. Thus, Corbett's possible suicide (mentioned by James) is ascribed to the fictional Lord Clonfert. Overall, the marriage of fact and fancy is so skilfully interwoven as to make the distinction imperceptible throughout, historical and fictional characters freely intermingling in a memorable panorama.

While much of *The Mauritius Command* adheres faithfully to historical events, like its predecessors it includes themes and incidents reflecting Patrick's own life at the time of writing. Readers have been concerned to identify Jack's home, where he is visited by Stephen at the opening of the novel. Dean King suggests that: 'The house's name was inspired perhaps by the Ashgrove Cottage belonging to Susanna Thrale, the sister of the real-life Queeney Thrale, later Lady Keith.'³ While this possibility cannot be discounted, another also seems feasible. In the 1930s some cousins of Patrick lived in a pretty cottage in the village of Ashgrove, by Peasedown St John near Bath. While there is no evidence that he maintained contact with them, the fact that he visited Somerset at the time of writing may have brought the name to mind.

However this may be, the description of Jack's cottage reflects a combination of Patrick's and my mother's cramped quarters in their tiny home in North Wales, and the modest former vicarage where my grandparents were living at Barton St David in Somerset. From the latter Patrick appropriated their handsome satinwood furniture, as well as the unkind caricature of my grandmother intended by Jack's tiresome mother-in-law Mrs Williams.*

The year 1977 began with Patrick subjected to constant extremes of mood. In January: 'Black depression all day: no work apart from reading. This may or might be my door into madness.' Fortunately, by 1 February: 'These are good days. Mild steady work, more light, spring coming, wealth, 2 books in my head.' In April he further contemplated an ocean voyage of his own: 'I thought much about an advertisement by a man who offers to sail one across the Atlantic from Martinique to Port-Vendres by way of the Azores btween April 28 & June 6. With leg & book & hand, alas, it will not do.'

---

* I do not mean that Patrick envisaged Mrs Williams as a lively representation of my grandmother, but that his resentment on my mother's behalf appears to have led him to assign her an unpleasant character.

Not only this, but sufficient perils lay closer by. Patrick and his car invited danger at almost every turn. Thus on 28 April, on the road to Perpignan, 'we were v nearly killed by a car that rushed out of an obscure turning on our left without looking, but the good brakes held.' A few days later in Port-Vendres, 'a disagreeable old man backed into the car – I had thought he was leaving, but apparently he was only parking pretty. The inevitable & oh so useless fury and flood of blame [Patrick's own, I take it] depressed me . . .' There were two consistent factors in Patrick's driving mishaps: they recurred with alarming regularity, and were almost invariably the fault of the other driver.

On 10 June Georgina and I arrived for a fortnight's holiday, bringing with us (at my mother's warm insistence) our little daughters Alexandra and Anastasia. Next day Patrick noted ominously: 'play (M's store of toys a v great success) shrill piping of enormous volume. M however states that these are remarkably well brought-up little girls.'

The next day began well, however, with Patrick amused on learning that 'Anastasia, on being shown the sea, asked "Where is the tap?"'

Sadly, however, this equanimity did not last. That I suffered throughout our stay from severe backache probably did not help, and 'a tedious wrangle' about the implications of the Official Secrets Act developed at supper. Next morning Patrick's ill-humour continued, and I regret to say worsened as the days passed by. Unfounded complaints about the children abounded, to be recorded nightly in his diary. Inevitably my mother came to side with Patrick, and we gloomily realized that bringing the children had proved the direst of errors. I continued in pain, while Patrick's irritation made it hard for him to work, even in the inviolate privacy of his gallery below. On successive days he recorded 'A single page' and 'No work today'. However, he was not entirely without self-awareness, noting at one point: 'My conscience reproaches me.'

I am afraid neither my mother nor Patrick was attuned by nature to the carefree insouciance of little children. My sparse memories of my mother before she left me and my sister include almost nothing that was warm or affectionate. My wife suggests that this might explain why my mother and Patrick apparently decided to have no children of their own. (Equally, they may well have decided that they could not afford it.) It was generally only when infants had attained years of discretion in their teens that they gradually became tolerable: indeed, as occurred in the case of both Patrick's son Richard and me, subjects of genuine affection and interest.

It also occurs to me that a major factor in Patrick's mounting ill-temper lay in the fact that having very small children living in the very small house was a unique experience in his life – at least, since those distant days before the War, when as a young man he was married to his first wife Elizabeth. And my mother, doubtless with the best of intentions, had persuaded us to stay for nearly three weeks! The distraction made it impossible for him to work, and without work his life swiftly appeared meaningless.

As a fellow writer, I feel that much may be excused him on the grounds of an author's overriding need for peace of mind – a factor perhaps difficult for others to comprehend fully. Besides, there can be little point in resenting a trait that was clearly so deeply entrenched as to be ineradicable.

Nonetheless, never again did we repeat the experience of coming to stay *en famille*, and when eventually our son Dmitri and youngest daughter Xenia were invited to Collioure as adolescents, they were treated handsomely – if at times eccentrically. This applied also to my sister Natasha's sons when they in turn came to visit the house.

Two days after our departure Patrick received a welcome fillip:

Such a gratifying review in T[imes]L[iterary]S[upplement], surveying the naval tales from the G. Ocean on – brilliant achievement – astonishing erudition – & (which gave me a good deal of ignoble pleasure) saying that my rivals were punk (which I thoroughly believe).

As in many a writer's life, the uplift deriving from a flattering review tends to be short-lived: 'Alas, I am afraid that my natural state is one of disapproving gloom, if not of positive crossness. And I have almost forgotten how to do anything but work: slow, day-long bodging.'

Precautions had to be adopted against interruption, sometimes of an irregular nature. 'Manuel came, with presents alas . . . I did not see him, having concealed myself in the bath.'

A welcome visitor was Matisse's daughter Marguerite Duthuit, who came to stay for the month of August, when she regaled Patrick with many anecdotes of her father. Regrettably, the biography of the painter which Patrick contemplated writing never materialized.

In October he and my mother came once again within an ace of ending their lives. At the end of the month they drove to England to attend the wedding of Philippe Jonquères d'Oriola, son of close friends whose family château lies beside the road to Perpignan. The ceremony took place in the beautiful old Romanesque church of Tickencote in Rutland.

On their return journey, Patrick and my mother spent a night with their old friends Charles and Mary de Salis at Appledore in Kent, whence they set off next morning to catch the ferry at Southampton. What prevented this was recalled by Patrick on his initial recovery a week or so later:

At about 11 or 11.30 we were quite near Lewes – too early – & seeing a sign to Alfriston I said let's go & see the church. And I think I also said let's change [seats] – indeed I am sure I said it, but whether we did change or not I do not know. Vague recollections of the ambulance – M & I holding hands across the aisle – a policeman asking me what I remembered of the accident – nothing – casualty department – nurses hurting M – words about a catheter – a nurse begging me to be reasonable – men sewing up my scalp and eyebrow.

Patrick's condition was not good, but my mother's much worse: 'Left femur; left tib[ia] & fib[ula] just above the ankle; 3 ribs; ominous blood from right ear.'

The de Salises were notified, who visited them in Eastbourne General Hospital shortly afterwards. They in turn telephoned me, when I travelled at once to visit the hospital. I found them in bed, Patrick weak but cheerful, but my mother barely conscious. It was by chance that I was there when a policeman called, who politely questioned Patrick. As I left with him, I took the opportunity of asking what had happened. It became clear that my mother was driving, since the worst injuries were all on her left side. On emerging from a side road onto the main road without pausing, the vulnerable little *deux chevaux* was struck by a car coming from the left. The policeman tactfully intimated that my mother was clearly at fault. However, given that the other driver had not suffered any personal injury, combined with my mother's horrifying brush with death, I gathered that it had been compassionately decided not to initiate a prosecution for dangerous driving. To my knowledge my parents rarely if ever admitted to being at fault over their driving, and I am amused to see that in the following year my mother's Christmas card to my uncle Ivan referred firmly to 'The wicked car whose fault it was hit my side . . .'!*

I remember feeling at the time a little hurt that my mother had not alerted us to their coming to England, and am relieved to find in Patrick's diary for 13 November that 'in the evening she was so much happier: remembers Nikolai as one of the few solid realities in all the vile period of hallucination'.

Her condition made it clear that she would have to remain in hospital for some considerable time, while Patrick was sufficiently

---

* Patrick more candidly explained to his editor Stuart Proffitt in a letter of 13 November 1989 that 'we came to a crossroads, looked the wrong way, & woke up in an ambulance'. My mother typed the letter evidently without comment!

recovered to shift his quarters to the Heatherleigh Hotel in Eastbourne. My heart sinks, when I find that on 6 November he 'hired a mini: drove it v badly to Beachey Head, jerking and stalling'. A couple of days later: 'I went to Brighton, escaping another accident (at a roundabout this time) by very little.' Fortunately, he evaded further danger, and took advantage of his enforced stay to pay nostalgic visits to spots in and around Lewes familiar from vividly recalled childhood days, where 'memories came flooding up'. Lunching at a pub near Herstmonceux he suddenly felt 'something like happiness'.

After successive difficult operations, my mother's birthday on 4 November saw the beginning of a protracted recovery: 'Less pain, but oh so much wandering – is persuaded that the place is an hotel or restaurant, sometimes with a brothel below,' Patrick recorded.

On 30 November Patrick hit on the plot of his next novel *The Fortune of War* pretty well in its entirety:

JA & SM returning (as passengers?) in small frigate from E Indies – perhaps a preliminary piece about some E Indian, Javan activity. In the S Atlantic they fight one of those US/UK actions – are beaten & taken prisoner PoW in US. JA will not give parole. Hospital. Escape (by means of a former shipmate?) to Herapath, Mrs Wogan, DV. Audubon or A's friend. Painted black, perhaps. Might Johnson & US Intelligence play SM false? Further escape anyhow. SM taking DV aboard Shannon (says state of the war with France such that you can settle in Paris within months – just what was it anyhow? Then JA still passenger, but a v active one, action with Chesapeake. This leaves the possibility of the Cochrane stuff / ? & some war for another book. Alternatively it could start with the Cochrane disgrace ? & clear him after the action.

By 15 December 1977 the long-drawn-out ordeal was over. Patrick paid 'A last, rather sad, look at Lewes, Southover & the deathly [i.e. sluggish] Ouse', before retiring to bed for an early rise next morning. In the early hours they were taken in an ambulance to Gatwick, whence they flew to Montpellier, my mother being hoisted and carried with difficulty in a sort of canvas hammock. Driven to Collioure, they found the bridegroom's mother Claude and others of the Jonquères d'Oriola family awaiting them at the little bridge by the turning up to their house. Heroically, Claude and her assistants bore my mother home up the rough track. That her body was very light added to the poignancy of the occasion.

She and Patrick, although much wearied by the journey, were relieved beyond measure at being back in their snug home. Next day a huge backlog of mail was delivered, which included a parcel containing an eagerly awaited first edition: 'Persuasion & N[orthanger] Abbey are bright & beautiful, but I cannot take much pleasure in them yet.'

Patrick was by now becoming preoccupied with his forthcoming novel in the Aubrey–Maturin series. Already, in the previous November:

> I began to draw a rough plan of a sea-tale – Botany Bay, she-convict, iceberg, wreck – but I doubt there is enough in it for a book. (And anyhow there is the glamorous woman at sea aspect). In bed I thought of another entirely [*The Fortune of War*]: American war: JA defeated by heavy US frigate – POW – sees D[iana]V[illiers] – exchanged – serves as volunteer in Shannon.

However, current work translating Pierre Schoendorffer's *The Paths of the Sea* meant that it had not been until May 1977 that he made 'a tentative start on the naval tale'. The structure of the tale is provided by an amusing account of Jack Aubrey's elephantine blunderings on land, prior to his taking the ageing fourth-rater *Leopard* to Australia; its exciting chase and sinking of the Dutch 74-gun *Waakzaamheid*; and Jack's skilful extraction of his own vessel from a perilous encounter with an iceberg in the South Seas. The latter was based on the real-life adventure of HMS *Guardian* in 1790, commanded by Captain Edward Riou. Also on board was Midshipman Thomas Pitt, afterwards Lord Camelford, whose biography at Patrick's suggestion I was compiling at this time.[4]

Additional colour and intrigue were lent by the presence of the beautiful American spy Louisa Wogan and her lover Herepath. As ever, doubts assailed Patrick as he conceived and at times restructured the story. 'Is the story I have in mind (parallel between S[tephen]M[aturin] + D[iana]V[illiers] & Herapath & Wogan) dismally flat?' – 'Qu. Is Mrs Wogan straight out of a novelette?' – 'The book will end in anticlimax if not bathos' – 'I live much in the book, & altho I know it is pretty trifling I shall be sorry when it is done – shall miss it.' He abandoned a pleasing living for the chaplain Fisher: 'Rector of Little Zeal. Perhaps too corny.' For a while he cast about for alternative settings, obtaining local topographical information from Mary Renault at Cape Town, which in the event the *Leopard* never visits. As ever, he conquered such trying misgivings and alterations to produce a work containing some of his most dramatic encounters.

On 18 September he and my mother hit on the successful title *Desolation Island* (Patrick's original title had been 'A Voyage towards Botany Bay'). Finally, on 7 October: 'I added some little pieces to Desolation Island & packed it up. We both feel rather lost without it.' Three weeks later, Richard Ollard's response from his home in Dorset served to clear any lingering doubts Patrick might have nurtured:

I have just this moment finished reading Desolation Island & must congratulate you on a real tour de force. What a cracking good book in every way, so different from all the others & yet so perfectly in tune & in character. Certainly you have done nothing better & with the psychological insight, the mastery of narrative & above all the sheer visual power of your descriptive writing puts the book in a rare and select company.

The book was published to great acclaim in the following summer. Patrick sent me a copy for my birthday, accompanied by amusing advice on dealing with publishers:

> I am very glad you have changed to Cape [for Lord Camelford] . . . It is so very, very much better to be with a publisher one likes: and yet as far as my experience goes, even with very amiable, deserving publishers, it is as well not to see too much of them, but to remain rather distant. Otherwise they tend to become familiar and even overbearing, which is not to be tolerated and which always ends in tears – they are, after all, only greasy tradesmen, often half knave, half fool, but they often have remarkable pretensions.

This was the last in the series that he published with what he had increasingly found to be the unsatisfactory US publishing house of Stein and Day. While the change may have weighed with him, his advice to me was, I know, largely tongue-in-cheek.

The New Year of 1978 had brought a flurry of sympathetic good wishes, together with a visit culminating with an unusual experience on Patrick's part: 'Then in the afternoon Jacques [Dr Théodor], his mother, & [his wife] Caroline. the perfectly delightful child. A good tea party (though M rather worn) & on leaving the child insisted on kissing me on the nose.'

The first half of the year was devoted by Patrick to writing *The Fortune of War*. Encouraged by the additional support of his enthusiastic new US publisher, he had wasted no time in returning to the series. As ever, a primary concern was to reconcile his dramatic overview to historical events. Both factors were essential to his conception, but neither could be permitted entirely to over-rule the other. In March Patrick queried:

> How can I get JA on to Java & preserve historical accuracy? Blow him up in the S. Atlantic? He & SM looking for a boat. But in that case how preserve his followers? I did find to my distress that Javas

prisoners were all sent home from Brazil in a cartel: so where is my historical accuracy. (Get round it by having JA too badly wounded? SM will not leave him?

Persistent application ensured that the obstacles were ingeniously overcome, to the extent that readers are left with no inkling of knots that had been unravelled and seams skilfully concealed. On 26 July:

I finished the book after tea – quite a strong bout of work: 8 pp – with Broke's victory & the colours going up, not without a certain doubt that this is the end, at least of my story – perhaps an end irrelevant to the tale. Still, it is done (4 months & 3 days & I shall type it, leave it by, & consider.

This he did, and at the beginning of September: 'I finished my reading, not v pleased in the end (but I cannot see it clear – too close) & wrote a little introductory piece, boasting under the cover of false modesty.'

The latter allusion was to his exaggerated acknowledgement of extensive dependence on the considerable historical record.

Although Patrick freely availed himself of the novelist's prerogative of adapting historical events to dramatic requirements, he justly prided himself on meticulous accuracy with regard to those trifling details which convey to the readers so vivid a sense of participating in events of the distant past. I recall his indignation when a pedantic 'learned Dutchman' wrote claiming to have spotted an anachronism, where Captain Broke orders the forepeak to be made decent for Diana Villiers with a lavish sprinkling of Eau de Cologne.* This was on the unsatisfactory basis of the *Oxford English Dictionary*'s providing a first allusion to the scent in 1823 – ten years after the event. Obviously this cannot establish an

---

* *The Fortune of War*, pp. 264–65.

irrefragable *terminus ante quem,* and two years later a loyal lady fan in Somerset sent Patrick a reference to a Royal Navy captain's purchase of the commodity at Gibraltar in 1806. Patrick was delighted at having his intuitive perception borne out in this gratifying manner.

As ever, I derive additional pleasure from detecting hidden personal allusions in this fine tale. On page 10 Killick declines to obey Captain Aubrey's injunction to remove Maturin's wombat from his cabin, stubbornly declaring 'I duresn't sir.' The response is taken from that of a Devonian sentry in India during the Great War, whom my grandfather vainly ordered to kill a dangerous-looking serpent. Again, the name Jaggers borne by an elderly seaman aboard Aubrey's *Leopard* is that of the Appledore ferryman who used to row my mother across the Torridge in her youthful pre-war days. 'An exact list of the kings of Israel' (p. 61) was what my grandfather supplied as a hopeful substitute answer to an unprepared scripture paper while up at Oxford before the Great War, while Herepath's translation of a Chinese poem echoes Patrick's own unpublished ventures in the same field.

Particularly pleasing to me is the catalogue of the scholarly Captain Yorke's library in his cabin aboard *La Flèche.* On inspection Jack Aubrey 'could make out some of the nearer titles: Woodes Rogers, Shelvocke, Anson, the immense *Histoire Générale des Voyages,* Churchill, Harris, Bougainville, Cook, all natural enough in a sailor; then Gibbon, Johnson . . .'

In the story all these hefty tomes are dispersed to the elements with the destruction of *La Flèche* by fire. In reality, however, the greater part lived on to become part of Patrick's library, now in turn gazing reassuringly down at me from my own bookshelves.

For the book itself, I suspect most readers would share Richard Ollard's enthusiasm, conveyed in a letter of 19 October:

I finished THE FORTUNE OF WAR last night, and I must write to congratulate you on an absolutely splendid book. The inventiveness and originality are the equal of anything that you have done and the whole series deepens in richness and brilliance with each succeeding book. There is so much to admire that one hardly knows where to start. The description of the burning of <u>La Flèche</u>, dinner at the Herepaths, the thrilling sequences in Boston and the final climax of the action between the <u>Chesapeake</u> and the <u>Shannon</u>. All are memorable. The plotting and characterization seem to me marvellously accomplished.

Next spring Ollard forwarded this gratifying endorsement from John Bayley and his wife Iris Murdoch:

We have long been devotees of C.S. Forester and thought that nothing could fill the gap left by the creator of Hornblower. Then we discovered Patrick O'Brian. His series about the British Navy during the Napoleonic Wars are beautifully assembled. In some ways they are more sensitive and scholarly than Forester's tales and every bit as exciting. Captain Aubrey and his surgeon, Stephen Maturin, compose one of those complex and fascinating pairs of characters which have inspired thrilling stories of all kinds since the *Iliad*.

Meanwhile life at Collioure pursued its usual placid course. In September Patrick and my mother entertained an English judge and his wife at their home. A chance mention of my name led to the discovery that years before he had been the magistrate who fined me, as a youthful protester against the arrival in London of the Soviet leaders Bulganin and Khrushchev in 1956: 'Judge had been the beak who fined Nikolai for demonstrating against Bulganin – fined him too much – it had weighed on his conscience ever since & he reimbursed £5. A very agreeable pair indeed & a most successful evening.'

In the following month Patrick's improved financial position enabled them to buy a vineyard in the mountains behind Collioure:

'In Mlle de Maigret's window M saw a 40[hect]are vineyard f[rancs] 2M . . . If say Pierrot [Camps] or one of his boys would work it & merely give us our year's wine & some muscats that would be fine, particularly if the casot could be made a refuge.'

The property at Manay was purchased on 6 October. Pierrot and Hélène's son Michel took over tending the vineyard as planned, while Patrick henceforth conducted much of his writing in the isolated little *casot*, at times when excessive heat and swarming *estivants* in and around Collioure disturbed his writing at home.

In December Patrick received the customary birthday card from his brother Bun, and a few days later a copy of my latest book, which owed much to his original suggestion and subsequent detailed advice. 'Nikolai's Camelford, a handsomely produced book: he does not dedicate it to me, as I had more than half expected, but he does make all proper acknowledgements – until I saw them I was much wounded.'

This was not the first occasion that I had unwittingly given hurt. In September our son Dmitri was born, upon whom we had bestowed my father's name: 'At lunchtime a telegram to say that Georgina has a boy, Dimitri. No comment needed . . . I wrote to Nikolai, not without difficulty. The hurt cannot be expressed, yet it is impossible to write as though it had not been inflicted so v deliberately.'

In fact, it had never occurred to me that they should feel so strongly about the choice of a family name borne not only by my father, but also by his uncle, a young naval officer killed fighting the Japanese at Tsushima in 1905.

In the high summer of 1979 my mother underwent another of her persistent close brushes with mortality, from which once again she experienced a further near-miraculous escape. On 1 August she and Patrick drove up into the Pyrenees beyond the Tour Massane to retrace a walk familiar from an earlier expedition. There they entered the deep forest, 'wonderfully devoid of life'.

After a picnic:

we walked a little way up, towards the place of the strange cep, above the descent to the girolles. It all seemed rather unfamiliar, & at one point I saw M turn uphill, left-handed. This was about 1 o'clock or perhaps 1.30 & it was the last I saw of her until 7, she having contrived to scramble across country as far as the Coulomates, breaking a tooth on the way. In the meantime I had ranged to & fro, always in the wrong direction until at 5 I lost hope and drove fast down to Le Perthus, puncturing on the way, to the gendarmes. They were very, very good, grasped the point quite quickly, changed into bush clothing, laid on dogs & reinforcements in case of need, & drove up, 8 strong I think, with me following. M was there, pretty battered but virtually intact, having been led back by a powerful Pole. Her legs, if not her sense of direction, had behaved wonderfully. Farewells to the kind gendarmes – & they totally unresentful – & so home to whiskey, scrambled eggs, & a wonderful bath.

Next day, Patrick reflected: 'How quickly the true anguish fades – a thin recollection of a memory. But it was atrocious, never-ending at the time. Uncontrolled imagination – efforts little more than formal gestures. And indeed it could have ended horribly.'

These days Patrick was troubled by apprehensions of mortality, accompanied by vague feelings of guilt and starts of nostalgia for the vanished past. 'A vile dream of missing a boat-train again – missed it twice this time, or to be more exact the dream ended when I was torn between catching the boat & so abandoning a little girl who had been with me, & returning for her & so missing it.'

Could the little girl have been his small daughter Jane, whose funeral he missed attending in 1942?*

Some weeks later he suffered a bout of 'Ill temper, gloom, a kind of undefined resentment, easily (though no doubt falsely) rationalized. A looking at life & saying "Is this all?" The edge of something like despair . . .'

* See Appendix B.

On 1 December: 'By the afternoon we were both exhausted & I for one deeply unhappy – the edge of despair as I said in a perhaps whining poem a little while ago. If most men mind the decline of their powers as much as I do, <u>no wonder there are so many grim grey faces</u>.'

Even recourse to his beloved Samuel Johnson conjured up a troubling comparison with his own talent: 'An hour or so with [Boswell's] Johnson at 64 filled me with melancholy.' On the other hand, not all was bad in the contemporary world. In August, Patrick had observed a pleasing novelty on the plage St Vincent: 'some few bare-breasted women'. Johnson, too, would probably have approved, as his back-stage admiration of actresses in varied states of undress suggests.

Passages of his early life, when as a child Patrick had experienced periods of unreflecting joy, were brought to mind by an affectionate letter from his youngest sister: 'Joan wrote to me, having been given Pic[asso]: an echo of [step]Mother's voice over 40 years & more. She spoke of Kempsey, too.' This was the location of their early home in Worcestershire, where the two children had become close companions, while their kindly stepmother Zoe exerted a benign influence over the household.

Despite these personal worries and passages of self-doubt, Patrick toiled hard at his latest novel. One increasing concern was the little historical time which seemed left to him. Not having anticipated the enduring success of his Aubrey–Maturin creation, Patrick had set its initiator, *Master and Commander*, in 1801. Its most recent successor, *The Fortune of War*, had already reached 1812 – leaving a bare three years until Waterloo, climax of the epic struggle between Britain and Napoleonic France. Sensing the underlying problem, a loyal fan wrote to suggest that Patrick follow the example of C.S. Forester, who in a later novel turned to Hornblower's early life. However, this approach did not appeal to Patrick – not least, one presumes, in view of the fact that Stephen Maturin could not feature in any story antedating his memorable first meeting with Jack Aubrey at Port Mahon.

Initially, Patrick had intended to base his new novel on the trial of Lord Cochrane for his alleged involvement in the notorious Stock Exchange swindle of 1814 – when, with the substitution of Aubrey for Cochrane, the date of course becomes immaterial. On 20 October 1978, Patrick sent his literary agent Richard Scott Simon 'A sketch of the next Aubrey book':

> But although these tales have now reached the end of the war, or very nearly, and although I do like to keep to the historical sequence as much as I can, Richard Ollard observed (very rightly I think) that there was no real objection to my moving sideways in time. So before coming to the stock-exchange catastrophe it seems to me that I might very well intercalate some minor actions, fictitious but based on fact: one that occurs to me is the Royal Navy's bloodless removal of a small Catalan army serving Buonaparte on the shores of the Baltic . . . I am not quite sure that I can make this fit historically, but if I can it will present a perfect field for Maturin: at all events this is the sort of thing that I should like to use to delay Aubrey's temporary downfall and disgrace, which would probably end this volume, and end it in a way that the reader would see that more was to come.

By the New Year of 1979, Patrick had decided that the Stock Exchange scandal should be reserved for a future novel, which in the event proved to be *The Reverse of the Medal*. By June the current work was completed, at least in draft. He had for the present abandoned Cochrane's career as a model, its tense and vivid climax being the capture and ultimate imprisonment of Aubrey and Maturin in the notorious Temple Prison in Paris. The historical sources on which he drew for the climax of his tale, together with many of its colourful details, were the imprisonment and escape of the irrepressible Captain Sydney Smith from the same prison in 1796, Lord Camelford's subsequent incarceration there in 1803, and events leading up to the escape of Lieutenant George Jackson from the equally formidable gaol at Bitche.[5]

Patrick at first contemplated entitling his novel *The Temple*. Next, he toyed with the idea of *Blue Peter*, the name of Diana Villiers's magnificent Indian diamond. Wholly out of touch as he was with British popular culture, he went in October 1979 'To Collins, where I showed it to Sarah Wynn Evans: she called in the woman (Watt?) of Fontana who stated very strongly that BP would not do, it being the title of a famous children's TV programme.' On 3 December Richard Ollard suggested *The Surgeon's Mate*, to which Patrick immediately agreed. The book was published in May of the following year. On receipt of his complimentary copies, Patrick expressed himself as 'moderately pleased, but the jacket is rather tawdry & they have made a sad mess of the Author's note'. The latter contained perceptive comments on the role of the historical novelist. It is a measure of Patrick's overriding perfectionism that his original version of the 'Author's Note' differs (so far as I can see) not in the minutest punctuation mark from the published version!

As ever, personal touches are to be found in the novel. Jack's distress at his wife Sophie's failure to correspond with him surely echoes Patrick's dismay at my mother's failure to write when he was absent in Vienna for a few weeks in 1970. Readers familiar with my prolonged battle with Lord Aldington (Toby Low) over his responsibility for the betrayal of thousands of Cossack men, women, and children in Austria in 1945 will not need any reminder of the model for the unpleasant Colonel Aldington encountered in Halifax at the outset of the story, whom Jack shrewdly perceives to be 'not a well-bred man'.

As regards Patrick himself, we may note Jack Aubrey's eccentric father's embarrassingly outré political activities, which surely owe something to Dr Russ's perverse espousal of Liberal views in predominantly Conservative Sussex, when they were living at Lewes before the War. Again, Dr Maturin had 'performed three dissections of the calcified palmar aponeurosis with Dupuytren'. Patrick himself had undergone successive operations for the same ailment, which bears the name of the great French surgeon. Again, Maturin undergoes an acute attack of nerves when called upon to address the French *Institut* – a terror of public speaking which afflicted Patrick for the greater part of his life.

Reviews of the novel were, as ever, laudatory. Particularly apposite, given Patrick's introductory words concerning the specialized function of the historical novelist, was T.J. Binyon's perceptive praise in the *Times Literary Supplement*:

Here there is nothing of your ordinary historical novel, in which plausibility is vainly sought through a promiscuous top-dressing of obvious contemporary references and slang, which then stand out against the rest as glaringly as the fruit in a naval plum duff. Instead each incident or description is saturated by a mass of complex and convincing detail.

XI

Muddied Waters

> Repeatedly dwell on the swiftness of the passage and departure of
> things that are and of things that come to be. For substance is like
> a river in perpetual flux, its activities are in continuous changes,
> and its causes in myriad varieties, and there is scarce anything which
> stands still, even what is near at hand; dwell, too, on the infinite
> gulf of the past and future, in which all things vanish away.
>
> Emperor Marcus Aurelius, *Meditations*, v, 23

The New Year of 1980 began badly: a premonition of what was
to prove a strangely unsatisfactory year. 'Slow bodging at the
book [*The Ionian Mission*]: a couple of pp.'; 'Frustration, gloom. I
wake unhappy' run typical entries in Patrick's diary. A self-taught
course in Italian was proceeding well, as was his prowess at darts,
but these diversions afforded less consolation than did a sprightly
gecko who had taken up quarters beneath the Georgian tea-caddy in
the sitting room and subsequently shifted to the coal-scuttle, whence
it was rescued by Patrick, half-choked with black dust. Two months
later, he reproached himself further: 'How I wish I were not filled
with angry (or ready to be angry at the least excuse) gloom from
morning till night. Little joy, little admiration, much fault-finding.'

In May he recorded one of those bizarre dreams to which he was
prone, which tended to fascinate and alarm him in equal measure:
'In the night such a painful dream of M being a mad wolf perhaps

& of my beating her on the head as though to kill her (some glancing blows, some direct) & she saying meekly that she was born in Shrewsbury – that was all she could offer. Piercing distress.'

When his editor Richard Ollard wrote enquiring about the possibility of his being interviewed on television, the response illustrates his deep-rooted unease at the prospect:

As to my appearing on radio or television. I can imagine nothing more calculated to discourage people from buying what I write. I am a wretched, reluctant, inefficient, mumbling public speaker: I refused the French television with the Picasso book; only the other day I declined an invitation from Sandhurst to address the RMA in May on writing war-novels; and I would beg to be excused as far as the BBC is concerned, were it not for the fact that if your colleagues are right my indulgence may cause your firm to suffer as much or more than myself, which is hardly fair. So in the unlikely event of any really remarkable invitation, an invitation qui vaut le voyage, please tell them that they may count on me.

It can only have been fortunate that nothing came of this at the time, as will become apparent from the consequences eighteen years later when he reluctantly acceded to the BBC's request for an interview.

Patrick's depression at this time appears to have been largely visceral, as nothing particular appears to have occurred to dampen his spirits. *The Surgeon's Mate* had been completed in the previous year, and by that September: 'Another naval book, a parenthesis before JA's catastrophe, is beginning to take shape in my mind. Might I plot it out chapter by chapter, or would that be too rigid?' Next: 'I begin to see Collingwood quite clearly, & shall certainly use him',* and by November: 'I abandon the history of Franco-Turkish relations,

---

* The historical Cuthbert Collingwood features as Admiral Sir John Thornton in the novel. It seems curious to me that Patrick did not identify Collingwood by name.

hoping my readers' ignorance may exceed my own: in any case I can always be vague.' Next he despatched to Richard Ollard an outline of the projected work, and on New Year's Day of 1980: 'Today I began the <u>Parenthesis</u> & wrote about 1000 words. And now comes the time when all the floating ideas have to be penned, the choices made. This will not be an important book, but I am glad to be back at work.'

Three days later Collins signed the contract.

Patrick's difficulties in sustaining flow and balance in the opening chapters of *The Ionian Mission* were briefly interrupted by the next translation proposal from Collins. Unfortunately, this proved no more satisfactory, and on 20 February 1980 he noted: 'I began Beauvoir & read 20 pp: undergraduate stuff so far, & it would be difficult to translate. How I have to force myself to read a book I am going to work on – force really hard, although the subject might interest me. Why?'

A fortnight later: 'I did finish Beauvoir a dreary book.'[1] However, in mid-May he learned that 'Collins are not going on with the S de B. In a way I am relieved, but I regret not so much the money as the paid rest. Perhaps Weidenfeld may do it.'

Before this reprieve Patrick and my mother experienced yet another of their perennial brushes with death, which might so easily have brought his career to a premature end. On 11 March:

Perpignan in the afternoon, through strong cold tramontane. Just beyond Argelès, on the straight, a car in front braked violently (no light I think). It may be that my eye was off the road at that moment – a hitch-hiker? – but anyway I thought it impossible to avoid running into it – swerved, skidded & came to rest right across the road on the left-hand side in the path of a large van. It nearly stopped in time but not quite & crushed our front wing breaking its own headlight. No other harm, & surprisingly no fright either in M or me.

At the end of March Patrick and my mother travelled by boat to Gibraltar, after which they crossed to Tangiers and toured Agadir, Tetuan and nearby places. None of this itinerary appears relevant to the plot of his current novel, and as Patrick's notes are focused almost entirely on the rich birdlife of the region I can only suppose an ornithological break from what had temporarily become literary drudgery was the prime purpose of the expedition.

Regrettably, however, the enjoyable trip achieved little in the way of improving his continuing difficulty with writing. On 20 June: 'Looking back at diaries of only a year & 2 years ago I am grieved to see how my energy has declined – Imagination inventiveness too. In those days I wrote 'only 3 pp' (& 6 or even 8 were not unknown) whereas 3 is now quite a feat.'

Minor travails became major irritants: 'Some sod stole the hammock rope this afternoon: how it angered me. Youths crossing the drain & coming along our wall angered me – rude & defiant – I took one by the neck & v nearly cast him down – so at last I put barbed wire, I hope enough.'

Nevertheless, there were consolations: 'There is a young woman over the way who takes the sun stark naked: this pleases me, but tends to delay my work.'

As the year moved on, Patrick toyed with alternatives to fiction, including a biography of the naval hero Lord St Vincent, a cultural history of Spain, or a guide to the Roussillon. Returned to *The Ionian Mission*, his gloom momentarily led him to 'kill Pullings – doubt the soundness of his death'. Fortunately, a few days later he issued a reprieve: 'I resuscitated Pullings (how convincingly?).' It is a measure of his disciplined determination that he nevertheless persisted with what had largely been a Sisyphean task, beating the close of the year by despatching the final typescript on 3 December.*

---

* On 18 December Patrick recorded the impressive fact that 'M. having checked her figures, states that this is the 51st book of ours that she has typed. Strangely enough we had never counted them, or at least not for many, many years. Fifty books! I am amazed.' I cannot but compare this to the invaluable services rendered by Sophia Tolstoy to her husband.

As ever, Richard Ollard proved delighted with the outcome, notwithstanding a minor misgiving. On 16 December he wrote:

I have just finished reading THE IONIAN MISSION with the immense pleasure that your books always give me. Among the many felicities that struck me was one that you were kind enough to commend in my biography of Pepys, namely that you have made your central character age convincingly; that is he becomes different yet remains the same. Not easily done but here brilliantly achieved and the more effective by the reprise of his earliest exploits, amatory and naval, involving Admiral Harte and Port Mahon. The portrait of Collingwood – for such I take Admiral Thornton to be – is again admirable. And you have drenched your imagination in that thankless, cold, sodden, miserable Toulon blockade. And how well you have brought out the combination of tension and frustration which is the real experience of war, for most of its participants anyway.*

There are one or two places where I think the exuberance of your period sense has too-far out-distanced the lagging comprehension of your mere readers and I, shopkeeper that I am by nation and by nature, recommend a silent sacrifice on the altar of commerce. But you must be the arbiter of this, as of everything else.

Patrick returned a cheerful reply, promising to look into Ollard's suggestion. Nevertheless, despite this high praise from the critic whose judgement he probably valued most after that of my mother, on 31 December 1980 he recorded: 'Rather a sad end to an often sad & anxious year.'

Family affairs also obtruded into the normally placid course of his existence. Given Dean King's unchallenged assertion that: 'After Zoe's death [in 1964], O'Brian reached almost complete emotional

---

* It will be recalled that Ollard had served in the Royal Navy during the War.

detachment from his Russ family',* I feel it necessary to describe the situation as it really stood at the time. At the end of the previous May (1980), Patrick had received a letter (one of a longstanding, if at times intermittent, transatlantic correspondence) from his brother Bernard (Bun), informing him of their sister Olive's death. Although Olive had long become distanced from the family, Bun clearly assumed that Patrick would be concerned by the news. In December he and Patrick exchanged their customary Christmas cards.

About this time he received the first unexpected letter from his younger sister Joan, the sibling to whom he had perhaps been closest. Explaining that she had been living in Birmingham for the past thirty-five years, she expressed admiration for his recent biography of Picasso, and went on to enquire whether Patrick remembered their shared childhood in the spacious house at Kempsey, which she had glimpsed recently when driving past the village. Patrick was so touched by the letter that he retained it until his death – it was, so far as I am aware, the only Russ family letter he preserved. (It will be seen in due course that a brief rupture led him to destroy his voluminous correspondence from Bun.)

He promptly replied in affectionate terms. After explaining that he retained a few vivid memories of Kempsey, he eagerly enquired: 'if you should ever pass that way again, please would you photograph it for me?' He told her of his visit to Crowborough in 1967, where they had lived subsequent to Kempsey, concluding: 'I was strangely grieved, and I drove away without ever walking along the farther lane to the forest, which seemed quite unchanged.'

On 20 March 1981 he responded to a further communication

---

* King, *Patrick O'Brian: A Life Revealed* (London, 2000), p. 198. Later, in November 2003, the hitherto accurate Ben Fenton accepted this version of events, asserting that Patrick 'quarrelled with his siblings, rejecting them to the point where he sloughed off the name Russ, by deed poll, in 1945. The new O'Brian stayed in vague contact with his son, Richard, then cut him off for good.'

from Joan, concluding with another melancholy reference to his nostalgic Crowborough visit. Again, he explained poignantly:

> It fairly went to my heart, and I did not go down the leafy lane into Ashdown Forest as I had intended but turned the car and drove away into the present as fast as ever I could.
>
> And so there, my dear, I leave you
> With much love and many thanks
> Pat

Joan retained this letter, which is the last to have survived of their correspondence. According to Dean King: 'When Joan tried to initiate a correspondence with him, he wrote back saying he would rather not be reminded of his youth. Joan's pride was injured, and they never communicated with each other again.' Apparently, King never saw Joan's letter initiating the correspondence, while Patrick's responses over a period of months were, as has been seen, warm and welcoming. Neither of his extant letters expresses the slightest hint that 'he would rather not be reminded of his youth': on the contrary, in the second he confirms his overwhelming nostalgia for their shared childhood.*

Subsequent Russ family correspondence and memories indicate that Patrick felt obliged to explain to Joan (as he did likewise to their brother Bun) his inability to conduct too frequent exchanges, citing Nabokov's dictum that it is hard for an author to sustain any sort of regular private correspondence. The hypersensitive Joan took grievous offence at what she mistook for a snub, to which she made no reply.

It seems that Patrick remained ignorant of his sister's resentment, since he wrote to her again. Later, on learning of her husband's

---

* Although Patrick's boyhood and adolescence had been largely unhappy, he retained fond memories of brighter interludes and associations. In February 1982, walking up to Manay he lost one of a pair of light gloves he had taken off. 'Right vexed,' he noted – 'those gloves being a remnant of my youth.'

death in 1987, Patrick wrote to convey his condolences. Joan has been described to me by close relatives as intensely moody and liable to take offence where none was intended – characteristics doubtless springing from the harsh conditions of her largely loveless upbringing. Thus it can be seen that it was Joan who, acting on an irrational pique, decided to break off relations with Patrick, and not the other way round.

Patrick's unintended rebuff no doubt in part reflected the fact that 1980 and 1981 had proved on the whole troublesome years for his writing. Despite advancing years and a more and more satisfactory income, he also continued strenuous manual tasks about the house and vineyard. In January 1981, despite a painful attack of tennis elbow, he 'finished [painting] the bathroom ceiling . . . extreme agony between shoulder-blades – bath infinitely welcome. The thought of the sitting-room, which needs doing even more, indeed v much more, makes me blench.' A few days later he was subjected to a painful operation on his leg in the hospital in Perpignan. Four days after his return home he promptly began translating Simone de Beauvoir's first novel *Quand prime le spirituel*. Following Collins's abandonment of the project, a fresh contract had now been signed with Weidenfeld, working in collaboration with André Deutsch.

This translation proved generally uninspiring work. It was completed on 30 March 1981, after which he and my mother visited Paris, spending over a week largely viewing paintings in some of the principal galleries. The primary aim of the trip, however, was to consult with the author over tricky passages of the translation. 'Then I went to see Beauvoir, found her quite easily this time, smaller, older, but cheerful & v friendly – said really kind things about the Picasso book. Corrections all satisfactory . . .'

Sad news greeted them on their return home. Their beloved tortoise Caroline, a faithful companion for the past quarter of a century, had quietly died. Their relationship had always been close, with Patrick proudly recording in 1967 'Caroline 14" round waist'.

It took another fortnight to incorporate corrections and clarifications arising from his discussion with the author in Paris: 'I finished Beauvoir: a great relief – sadly squalid in parts . . . For its size the Beauvoir book has taken me far longer than any other: we have both spent more pains: & I suspect that it may be the most stilted of all my translations.'

Nevertheless, it was well received (under the title *When Things of the Spirit Come First*) both in Britain and in the USA, where it and its successor were published by Pantheon.* Despite his general dislike of Beauvoir's book, he completed its translation at the end of March 1981, and next day returned gratefully to his own fiction: in this case, *Treason's Harbour*:

> A v good night for once in the morning, not only made a Right-handed round [of darts] in 65 but began to arrange my thoughts for the next naval tales, particularly with regard to the villain Wray, a French agent (this prompted by the present wave of KGB agents discovered in MI5 etc).

By 10 February 1981: 'I had a pleasant idea for a piece of another JA book – SM overboard by night into the Pacific, JA after him – They are picked up by Polynesian Amazons. It was lively in my mind . . .'

Such was the sudden genesis of *The Far Side of the World*, which Patrick had initially accorded the unpromising title *The Pursuit of Happiness*. At first the project moved little further, Patrick lamenting ten days later that: 'My long S Seas tale will not do at present: it must take up a year / or thereabouts, & I have no year to spare.'

At home the world was changing, even in Collioure. On learning of a violent robbery suffered by a cloth merchant in the avenue

---

* For some reason of which I am ignorant, my parents' estimate of Pantheon was, initially at least, unfavourable. Beside the contract's heading 'PANTHEON BOOKS' my mother has written 'I HATE'!

de la Gare, my mother made enquiries of a Perpignan gunsmith for purchase of a pistol. When it became clear that there was likely to be difficulty in obtaining a licence, Patrick continued to rely for defence on my mother's old .410 shotgun, which he kept close to hand beside their bedroom. The next day Patrick 'read Othello in short burst: perhaps tragedy is for the young – the old feel it too much'. Even the hardships of earlier days evoked feelings of nostalgia: 'I dreamt of our familiar old extreme poverty & the triumph of getting through a day – mere living its own full justi-fication.'

On their return from Paris, Patrick sent Richard Scott Simon his 'Thoughts for further naval tales'. These were the preliminary schemes for his next novels, *Treason's Harbour*, *The Far Side of the World*, and *The Reverse of the Medal*. Simon responded enthu-siastically: 'What a wonderful letter to receive on Easter Saturday . . . I had expected one mouthwatering outline, but not three. Poor old Aubrey in the stocks! If it were not a cruel hope I would like you to write all three non-stop.'

The prospect of a single contract for the three proposed novels was briefly raised, with Patrick hesitant: 'For it there is the idea of 3 or 4 years security: against it the fear of block (it affects me rather badly at present) & the fact that it postpones my Gothic novel to a time when perhaps I shall no longer be able to write it.'

The 'Gothic novel' was a project which ran intermittently in Patrick's mind over the years, but in the event never attained frui-tion. It owed nothing to Horace Walpole's *The Castle of Otranto*, as might perhaps be expected, but was rather, as he had described it earlier, 'a v small-scale provincial Proust, observed by the narrator'. As the sole major literary project conceived by Patrick that never saw the light, it is intriguing to read the fullest outline of which I am aware. On 23 December 1976, he wrote to Richard Ollard:

Very roughly it would be a privileged narrator's report on a thumping great château & its inhabitants, a numerous family of 3 generations with a large number of friends & cousins in the neighbourhood, a sub-Pyrenean region sprinkled with remaining Protestants: the main story would turn on the relationship between the youngish middle-aged woman of the house and her undergraduate son's somewhat older Protestant friend, & upon her husband's view of this; but perhaps more important would be the view of this tight, Catholic, archaic rather timeless landowning class that I know well – it is much the same in Ireland, Austria & France, & it forms a remarkably lively element in the pattern of country life, altho it is now so little seen or spoken about.

In his reply, Ollard recalled the putative tale's 'inspiration I remember your telling me of after your visit to Austria', when he stayed at Princess Auersperg's splendid Schloss Goldegg. For the present, however, Ollard recommended sticking to the next naval tale.

The idea of a three-volume contract was scotched by Patrick's insistence on provision for inflation to be included for the subsequent advances. This was rejected by Collins, 'so we will carry on book by book. Just as well.' On 27 June:

RS sent a contract for The Dey of Mascara (a name that I had given, rather at haphazard, with the 1st tale of the 3 I proposed) 'in case it seems acceptable' – an advance of £5000 . . . & a 12½% royalty would have stunned me with joy even 10 years ago, let alone when we were up at Fron [after the War in North Wales]. Not that I am displeased: far from it indeed, & the contrary – a refusal – would have plunged me into despair.

On 11 June work began on building the long-deferred cloister on the southern side of the house. The project aroused not only great excitement in my parents, but eager curiosity on the part of their neighbours. 'People peer & even come most shamelessly into

'Huguette & dear Bennie (quite grown up) & a friend came after dinner & we all sat in the little cloister, which really does look v well' (Patrick's diary, 29 July 1981)

our court.' As the work progressed excitement became general, with my mother reporting that: 'At Joffre's a female neighbour told her that the cloister was "historique," and when lit "féerique".' This dramatic conception was little exaggerated, and the structure thereafter afforded the O'Brians undiluted pleasure. Even before it was complete: 'We ate then in the evening sitting out (how I love the cloister & the cloistered peace).' Not only did it provide a perfect setting for eating under the sky, entertainment, and relaxation, but for Patrick in particular it provided a secluded refuge from the outside world: 'the 1st aim is privacy'.

Altogether, 1981 had proved a generally unsatisfactory year. Patrick constantly doubted his ability to sustain the high standard of the preceding Jack Aubrey tales, and appears to have been generally plagued by misgivings with regard to his literary talent. In November he and my mother came to stay at our home in Berkshire. On the evening of their departure, I noted:

Mummy and Patrick left. Children very good, & visit I think a success. But I was surprised how Patrick had dwindled as a personality: even his moments of humour & interest seemed much slighter than I recalled, & I felt altogether he needed permanent humouring. Altogether all he did was predictable & v. restricted . . . We are mystified by Mummy & Patrick's unprecedented weekend visit.*

However, whatever the source of his disquiet, Patrick's achievements that year would have satisfied most writers. In the first half he had translated Simone de Beauvoir's novel, the most troublesome of all his translations, and in the second he had completed half of *Treason's Harbour* (ninth in the series). What left him dissatisfied was worrying concern over the quality of his work. In October he lamented 'A v poor day's work – declining powers?', and in mid-December he recorded: 'I am tired of this book. The tale runs quite well in my head – scenes, conversation – but when it comes to putting it down the happiness vanishes.' As in previous years, he compared his state of mind with that of his literary hero at the same age: 'Johnson at 66: an active man, though not a v happy one.'

In January 1982 he received a letter from me congratulating him on the brilliance of *The Surgeon's Mate*, in which I incidentally unburdened myself of a comparable attack of writer's block. I had no idea that he was passing through a similar period of distress – indeed, I do not recall that it ever occurred to me that he was subject to such setbacks.

As evidence of Patrick's generosity and kindness, I feel impelled to quote passages from his response's admirable *vade mecum* – which indeed might provide an invaluable guide for any writer temporarily stranded in the doldrums:

---

* My mother in particular appeared markedly ill at ease during her rare visits to our successive homes, which Patrick normally was not. I suspect it arose from an uneasy consciousness that she had been unable to provide a home for me and my sister during our childhood, and found our unconscious but palpable sense of independence troubling.

You wrote them [my words of praise for his novel] however at a time of sadness – of a particular sadness common (I imagine) to all writers, when their work does not advance, when they cannot bring their mind to a fine focus, and when poverty and loss of reputation seem only a week away. It is an eminently understandable sadness, for ours is a lonely, dangerous trade: a man writes a book wholly by himself; no one can help him essentially; & once he is committed to writing he has a long and perilous career in front of him, not unlike that of a tight-rope walker with no safety-net.

In your letter you spoke of the desperate measure of moving house again [we had only arrived in the previous year!], and the tag about voyages changing skies not minds at once occurred to me. It has probably occurred to you well before this, but writer's depression, like housemaid's knee, can be very severe & long-lasting, & in case it should still be upon you, blinding you to the obvious, allow me to observe that moving consumes as much spiritual energy as the writing of a book, that no London flat allows one to get very far away from one's children (a necessary condition for parental love in a writer), and that for their physical, mental & spiritual development London cannot compete with the country.

May I make a suggestion? It is that you should divide your day in two, giving the first part to your book & the second to perfecting your Russian, so that you could translate. Here industry is everything, and without the least original inspiration one can sit down and slog away: much the same applies to reviewing, and I think you would find the two of them a great help. Of course they would never make you rich, but they would tide you over bad times, they would keep you busy when your own writing will not come, thus preventing you from feeding on yourself (think of Burton* on that point), & they would perpetually exercise you in your medium.

---

* Patrick possessed a much-thumbed copy of *The Anatomy of Melancholy: What it is. With all the Kindes, Cavses, Symptomes, Prognosticks, and Severall Cvres of it* (Oxford, 1624).

Although in the event I did not pursue Patrick's advice regarding translations and reviews, his broader perspective was persuasive: no move to town occurred, and my book was eventually completed.

On 23 February Patrick experienced yet another of those disturbing dreams which so regularly troubled him:

> The saddest dream I have ever had: in it, not believing what had happened, I went up to Manay* in the rain – something to do with the water-butt – & there I realized (among other less selfish things) that no one would ever care again whether I was wet or dry & I bowed in a perfect agony, still ludicrously holding my umbrella & said 'Christ have mercy upon me, Jesus have mercy upon me' and I think that in my dream I said it to an empty sky.

In April 'The next book, perhaps called The Pursuit of Happiness, begins to take more detailed shape', and by June 'I wrote notes for Ch I of The Pursuit of Happiness (will that do, or is it too arch?). It might do with it being a code-name used by Blaine.' Happily, the more euphonious title of *The Far Side of the World* was suggested by Richard Scott Simon, and incorporated into the contract signed that month. The writing moved relatively smoothly for the rest of the year, punctuated only by occasional moments of self-doubt.

It was, as I recall, that summer that I found my neighbour at an al fresco luncheon in our neighbourhood to be a publisher from Collins. When I mentioned Patrick, he told me that the firm valued the quality of his work highly. At the same time, they felt that, while his books enjoyed a 'cult' following that the firm could rely upon for respectable sales, it had long been understood that they would never become bestsellers. Patrick probably shared this estimate at the time, but never permitted any adverse circumstance to deter his labours for long.

---

* Their vineyard in the mountains, where Patrick frequently withdrew to write in peace.

Some work. How different dialogue is from plain narrative: much harder unless you are in form, when it fairly flies along.

My eyes quite give up in the evenings; they have been getting steadily worse & I shall have to have spectacles.

I think I must turn from translation to my own work: we are both growing sadly jaded.

After dinner I tend to grow malignant, though well fed, warm, well-lit, & full of wine.

All in all, however, the year ended on a promising note.

M also did the quite encouraging (though at the same time terrifying) accounts, from which it appears that we end the year £3000 richer than we began it, that of the £7000 we need (or at least use) for ordinary living we have 3 in unearned income, but that writing (which implies health & a reasonably fertile invention) must provide the rest.

With the New Year of 1983 Patrick alternated work on the novel with pursuing his aim of completing a difficult translation by March. This was another work by Simone de Beauvoir, *La cérémonie des adieux*, which appeared in Britain and the USA under the title *Adieux: A Farewell to Sartre*. Social occasions interrupted progress, as well as a less congenial familiar disturbance: 'Cats howl & walk about in sex-mad bands.' Alas, there was no longer fearless Buddug to disperse their nocturnal ranging.* A persistently symbolic dream recurred: 'Early bed: not much of a night for either of us – too tired – but having missed still another train in my dream I caught it when all seemed lost – it pulled out, of course, but then stopped 50 yards along the platform.'

In the event, Patrick missed his train with the translation, but as in the dream not by much. In March he found 'Sartre is being

---

* The lair of the feline prowlers was situated among drystone walls around the foot of the road up to the house, where it gave off a memorably foul acrid stench of urine.

v difficult (& I think v foolish or at least airy) on the subject of freedom'; in April 'We are growing heartily tired of Beauvoir' which is 'in places quite incomprehensible'; and on the 14th 'I finished Beauvoir: hard labour & the end as unpleasant as anything I have done.'

Pretentious French intellectuals being not altogether Patrick's cup of tea, it took him a little while to get back into the flow of his novel. Nevertheless, it was duly finished on 14 September: 'There: I did finish the book, with real pleasure in the doing of it, in a burst of 7 or 8 pp.'

It has given real pleasure to its readers, too. On perusing it anew, I am pleased to note that Jack and Stephen's Amazonian captors are possessed of clubs 'topped with mother-of-pearl eyes on either side of an obsidian beak'. Such a formidable weapon, presented by the King of Fiji to my great-grandfather Francis Wicksteed during his voyaging in the South Seas, hung beside the front door of our home at Appledore. In my childish perception it would have provided the perfect instrument for greeting a burglar, and my mother will also have remembered it well.

There were disappointments to be borne at what should have been a propitious time. As Patrick reported to his editor Richard Ollard:

The vendanges, by the way, will be but a dismal ceremony: and the flowering vines having been blasted by a furious long-continued tramontane a few days after I last wrote to you – the carignan held up moderately well, but the grenache have barely a fertilized grape between them.

Worse still, his literary agent Richard Scott Simon gloomily reported: 'Stein & Day finally decided against taking any more of your books. We have now bombarded other American publishers with copies and will let you know as soon as there is good news.'

Although Stein and Day were proving thoroughly unsatisfactory publishers, the news was not cheering.* Ollard proposed a biography of the eighteenth-century naturalist and explorer Sir Joseph Banks, but Patrick felt daunted by the vast amount of research this would require. Nor did a translation of Sartre's *La Nausée* appeal, for reasons that may be surmised.

A consolation amid much surrounding gloom was his first meeting with two of his increasing body of influential admirers, the married writers John Bayley and Iris Murdoch. As Patrick possessed few friends in the literary world, the meeting provided him with enduring pleasure. After a visit to the London Library:

> Back [at the Challoner Club] in a hurry & indeed a cab which was just as well, since they arrived promptly. We have rarely met people we liked more – friendly, kind, full of talk. They were most flattering about my tales: but then on the other hand IM condemned Stendhal, Flaubert & really almost everyone except Proust & the Sartre of Les Chemins [de la liberté]. We should like to see v much more of them – he was of my opinion entirely about all the writing we spoke of.

As ever, Patrick continued supportive of my work, even to the extent of confessing to a mild competitiveness. 'An affectionate, happy letter from Nikolai: his Tolstoy book [a history of my family] is somewhat delayed, but already TV & journalists come. (This makes me repine a little, though indeed he does work v hard).'

Patrick's own writing so vividly affected his imagination as at times to interweave with reality: 'Only 2 pp – a discontented day. This may have been caused, at least to some degree, by my writing of S[tephen] M[aturin] in a fury at being carried past the Galapagos.'[2]

As 1983 slipped away, Patrick was troubled by renewed

---

* Terry Zobeck tells me: 'I have a letter from Sol Stein to Ollard telling him that Stein & Day were turning down *Treason's Harbour* – allegedly Patrick's kind of book didn't appeal to women and the major US chain stores wouldn't sell it.'

disturbing reveries. 'Ill dreams – crumbling cliffs high over the beautiful sea – fear of missing boat – & another in which I bullied small children quite disgracefully.'

In November, when driving to dine with friends in Perpignan, 'at a corner of the street going down from the cathedral a car, driven fast from our right, ran into us. M had a rib cracked or broken . . . car badly damaged.' Patrick, who was driving, was unhurt. I long ago lost count of the number of near-fatal traffic accidents in which they were involved: it seems indeed miraculous that they neither killed anyone, nor were themselves killed. Patrick was distressed about my mother's injury, but with her recovery became almost as emotional about their much-loved machine:

> It quite hurt my heart not to see our old car in the garage, nor in the market-place at Argelès. M brought herself to get into it [a replacement Renault] in the afternoon, but I doubt she will ever like it, the 2CVs having such symbolic value: it is after all 30 years that we have had them, & some wonderful journeys.

Two days later, Patrick journeyed to Perpignan, 'where with great difficulty I found the garage & the dead 2 CV'. Later he was troubled by a fear lest the injured car was being 'ostentatiously ignored'.

The New Year of 1984 opened with Patrick 'thinking, not exactly worrying, about this tale. Will solid uninterrupted gloom & disaster – ending in the pillory answer? And how can I set the scene & sum up for the next, if there is one?' The tale was to become *The Reverse of the Medal*, which among other novel factors is a rarity (along with *Post Captain*) in that the greater part of it is set entirely on land. As it turns out, however, Jack's 'gloom and disaster' are in fact punctuated with a great deal of humour and adventure.

That night it may have been Patrick's perturbed state of mind that provoked another of his recurrent eccentric fantasies:

Dreams: a dog in a gaunt almost deserted Russian factory most pathetically eager to be adopted – the adopter a cynical brute. Another dog, in an hotel, v carefully carrying book on its head – book dropped, dog dreadfully worried – I tried putting it on its head again – no go – but the book did balance on its withers, & it walked carefully off.

Two nights later Patrick's anxious condition assumed a graver tinge: 'A long, long, v long night, waking at 3 persuaded it was 7; wretched hours too, with the usual going-over of slights, humiliations, misdeeds, crimes, failures, rather than the pleasant dozing of the last few somewhat wakeful nights.'

On 9 January came melancholy news: 'James wrote to say that Barbara died just before Christmas.' This was their old friend Barbara Puckridge, whom they had first come to know during their heady days driving ambulances in Chelsea at the height of the Blitz. She had been in hospital for some time undergoing successive operations, but the blow when it came was still a grievous one. Participants in the romantically adventurous days of their youth were slipping from the stage. Patrick wrote no more in his diary that day.

Three days later he encountered another jarring intimation of mortality. His brother Bernard had arrived from Canada in London, where they arranged to meet. Patrick booked a table at Simpson's in the Strand. Arrived early, he:

was sitting in the bar when I saw an aged man coming down the stairs: it was Bun, strangely aged & changed & bent & deaf – he recognized me however. Then Fifi [Bun's wife], amiable & proper. We had a pretty good traditional lunch, with rice-pudding, & then she went off to shop while Bun & I looked at George St & Marylebone Lane – Rothe's [coffee-house] was still there, almost exactly the same.

Patrick and Bernard had attended Marylebone Grammar School together during the academic year 1925–26, for which they clearly shared nostalgic memories. Given the extent to which critics have taken up Dean King's influential though entirely imaginary picture of Patrick's callous rejection of his Russ siblings in 1964, it is instructive to note the extent to which they continued close long after, corresponding and meeting whenever circumstances permitted,* and on occasions like this sharing cherished recollections of what were clearly common happy experiences.

During 1984 Patrick continued work on *The Reverse of the Medal*, which by March found our two heroes firmly established ashore in England. As ever, he underwent periods of gloom, I suspect imperceptible in their effects to readers of the finished work. 'I am much depressed by feeling unable to talk about the tale with M. Extorted praise however is worse than worthless & disapproval would stop me dead.'

Even the most derogatory press review was as nothing in its effect on Patrick when compared with my mother's occasional unexplained lack of enthusiasm. Although I do not recall being present at such discussions, the overriding impression remains that my mother's views of Patrick's writing were broadly conveyed by a form of osmosis, rather than overtly specific criticism. Fortunately, a month later her enthusiasm had revived: 'I finished & typed Ch VI – rather short (9000 -) – M liked it. But now I am at a stand for details of imprisonment etc – can fake of course but should prefer correctness. M phoned L[ondon]L[ibrary], who will send a biog[raphy of Lord Cochrane].'

On 26 April Patrick and my mother decided to undertake a bird-watching expedition in the Camargue. Next morning they drove away in good time, on arrival spending a couple of hours

---

* Over a year later, Bernard mentioned in a letter to their younger sister Joan that Patrick's correspondence had become intermittent since their meeting in London, while correctly ascribing this to preoccupation with my mother's persistent ill-health.

viewing a heronry. After that they booked in at an hotel, where they observed a stork and two flamingoes flying overhead. Unfortunately, the expedition was unexpectedly cut short:

Then I said let us find the other heronry & look at the Rhone. We took the road to Le Sambuc & peering ahead at an intersection I did not see a car coming from the right – the collision sent us into a canal, the car on its side, water coming in fast – found the door (no safety belts D[eo] G[ratia]) – kind young man pulled M out & on to the bank – a long pause while a mad youth looked for M's bag & papers & flung other things into the water & I rescued books & some Questar (carried set up, alas) – then v kind gendarmes, ambulance, Arles. M's leg & hip extremely painful but no bones broken – hospital said 'you can go.' M consulted with them – human – I happened to have 300 francs in my wet pocket – taxi to Salin de G[rand] hotel – took us in, fed & clothed us with great kindness. Indeed kindness almost everywhere, even from the poor young Swiss people whose borrowed car I had spoilt, & their holiday.

My mother was in great pain, and the doctor declared that they should remain in the hotel for the weekend. Fortunately, the food and service were excellent, but my mother continued suffering, having to be carried up and downstairs on a chair. The car was wrecked, but miraculously the insurance company in due course decided to pay up. However, my mother remained weak and suffering for the remainder of May.

Meanwhile Patrick gradually recovered the flow of his writing, though the occasional crisis of confidence manifested itself as ever in a disturbing dream:

. . . I slept pill-less & dreamed wonders: a great English castle & then an unknown much-more-than-Dugommier* with a platform

---

* The ruined fortress on the ridge above their house.

– a sheer drop of perhaps 1000' to an estuary – the sea sparkling
away on the L – a voice telling me about it in the silence – the
horror of the void – creeping back from the edge.

Apart from fear of literary failure, Patrick had throughout his
adult life been assailed by dread of death. That December he
would attain the biblical climacteric. He and my mother were
constantly afflicted by differing ailments over the years, and
how they attained the ages they eventually did appears to me
near-miraculous.

Much of the year was spent completing *The Reverse of the
Medal*, while simultaneously conducting research into the life of
Sir Joseph Banks – some of which found its way also into the
novel. The latter required much more research than usual, moving
as it did into largely new territory. The climax of the story is
provided by poor Jack Aubrey's innocent involvement in a major
Stock Exchange swindle – the real culprits being his scapegrace
father General Aubrey and his dubious associates. The model for
this scandal was the historical trial in 1814 of the great frigate
captain Lord Cochrane, whose guilt or innocence has been much
canvassed by historians. It is unlikely that the truth will ever be
established beyond cavil, but a cautious verdict would suggest that
he was indeed duped by his co-defendants. What is beyond doubt
is the shamefully prejudiced conduct of the trial judge, Lord
Ellenborough.[3]

Patrick read through voluminous printed works in the London
Library, and conducted extensive research among original documents at the Public Record Office in Chancery Lane. In June he
lamented: '2 pp: I struggle with the law. How I wish I could have
used C[ochrane]'s own trial straight.' In the event, he provides a
colourful panorama of London life, ranging from a royal levee to
Newgate Gaol and a thief-taker's searches on the mudflats of the
Thames. An elegant setting for several episodes is provided by
Black's Club, of which Aubrey and Maturin are members. There

can be little doubt that by this is intended Brooks's in St James's Street,* to which club Patrick was in the process of being elected. On 13 June he attended a 'vetting' dinner arranged by his friend Admiral Sir Michael Culme-Seymour, and was duly elected in December. Henceforth he stayed regularly at the club during his visits to London, its elegant eighteenth-century architecture and gentlemanly atmosphere providing him with much valuable inspiration for his work.

In August Patrick informed Richard Scott Simon that:

The present novel, which I call <u>The Reverse of the Medal</u> (it deals with Aubrey's downfall) is finished. There are a few changes to make, & Stuart Proffitt, who really is very helpful, is having my account of the trial vetted by someone at Oxford, and then, when Mary has bashed out a fair copy, you shall have it, probably some time in September.

It was about this time that Richard Ollard retired as Patrick's editor at Collins. Having turned sixty in the previous year, he now decided to withdraw with his wife Mary to Dorset, where he could concentrate on writing his own historical works. Over the years he had proved an invaluable adviser to Patrick, admiring his novels hugely, and continued as a friend whose literary and historical advice Patrick respected as he did that of few others. (Richard had recently arranged for Patrick to be sent the magnificent Latham and Matthews edition of Samuel Pepys's diary, which afforded Patrick enormous pleasure for the rest of his life.) For a while there was some confusion at the publishers, with Christopher MacLehose and Stuart Proffitt overlapping in handling Patrick's work, until the latter succeeded permanently as his editor. Proffitt

---

* On the other hand, 'Black's' was earlier employed by Hogarth as a humorous alternative name for White's, the rival Tory club across St James's Street (John Timbs, *Club Life of London* (London, 1866), i, p. 109).

was as assiduously committed to Patrick's work as had been Richard. Since his texts tended to require little editing beyond correction of minor narrative inconsistencies and the like, it soon became apparent that the change would make little difference to his relationship with his publisher.

The finished version of *The Reverse of the Medal* was received with more than usual enthusiasm at Collins. MacLehose, with whom Patrick enjoyed an uneven relationship, wrote warmly:

> . . . first, let me thank you for another enchanted journey with Maturin and Aubrey. One lives on a different plane while reading your books, but this one transported me further than any before so far as I remember. It is a beautifully made, beautifully told story and it will not surprise you that it moved me to tears on four occasions – I have a mind to have Maturin's walk to Ashgrove Cottage hand-set in Monotype Garamond and framed.

Although much of the framework of the latter part of the book is skilfully adapted from Cochrane's unhappy experience, one senses the presence to an unusual extent of Patrick's own erratic life story. First, of course, is the heartless damage inflicted on his guileless son by General Aubrey, 'a really dangerous parent' whose 'tall bony figure' and hopeless irresponsibility recall the harsh and feckless Dr Charles Russ – that terrifying bane of Patrick's formative early days.

Not all the real-life elements are unpleasant, however. The shop of the 'French pastry-cook in Marylebone', whose coffee Maturin recommends to the French agent Duhamel, must be Rothe's coffee-house, patronized by Patrick and his brother Bun during their schooldays, which they had nostalgically revisited in January. Again, Stephen's anguish at his discovery of the unexpected destruction of his familiar refuge at The Grapes in the liberties of the Savoy recalls the comparable wartime destruction of the house in Redcliffe Road where I believe Patrick spent rapturous months on first encountering his first wife Elizabeth.* I suspect, too, that the intensity of Stephen's distress on learning of his wife Diana's desertion may have its origins in Patrick's acute fear, real or apprehended, lest my mother desert him for another about the time of their first coming together in 1940.†

The 'sperm-whale's tooth' presented to Jack by his long-lost African son Sam Panda was that treasured by Patrick from early years.‡ The original of the apiarist's guide 'Huber on Bees', brought by Stephen in error for Gibbon's philippic on the iniquity of lawyers, rested beside the table at which Patrick wrote in his little gallery at Collioure.§

Much more remarkable in this respect is the almost magical extent to which he appears to have anticipated a future event, with which he was to become emotionally deeply involved – my trial for libel in 1989. While Jack Aubrey is blithely confident in the near-perfection of the English judicial system, Stephen Maturin's estimate is grimly sceptical. Citing Gibbon's scathing indictment of lawyers in a passage the historian reluctantly omitted from *The Decline and Fall of the Roman Empire*, he tries in vain to warn Jack of the dark complexity of legal procedures. That Patrick did not regard all lawyers as Machiavellian deceivers is illustrated by Jack's counsel Mr Lawrence, an honourable and capable barrister. Both he and Stephen in vain warn Jack of the dangers facing him. Although English judicial procedure might indeed be preferable to

---

* Cf. my reconstruction of the event in *Patrick O'Brian: The Making of the Novelist* (London, 2004), pp. 152–6.

† This fear is most clearly evoked in Patrick's autobiographical novel *Richard Temple*, wherein my mother's fictional counterpart Philippa Brett abandons him for a glamorous wartime army officer. It will also be recalled how irrationally distressed Patrick became during a visit to Austria when my mother failed to write as often as he hoped.

‡ It had already featured in *Master and Commander*.

§ Patrick's working copy of Francis Huber, *Observations on the Natural History of Bees: A New Edition, with a Memoir of the Author* (London, 1841). Dr Maturin will have possessed one of the earlier editions, published in 1792 and 1796.

that of many other countries, those inexperienced in the ways of the courts could have little awareness of its pitfalls – especially in a case like this, where the government of the day possessed a strong interest in securing a verdict:

'I do not think the ministry set this matter on foot,' said Lawrence. 'That would be too gross even for [the Home Secretary] Sidmouth's myrmidons; but I am quite sure they mean to take every advantage of the situation now it has arisen . . . although the English bar shines in comparison with all others, it has some members who are perfectly unscrupulous, able and unscrupulous: they go for the verdict, and be damned to the means. Pearce, who leads for the prosecution, is just such a man.'

Above all:

'. . . pray let him [Jack] know that Pearce will rake up anything and everything that may be to his disadvantage, anything that may lower him and through him his friends and connexions, and that the prosecution will have all the resources at the ministry's command to help in the raking.'

The event confirms Lawrence's worst fears. The judge, Lord Quinborough, is:

a heavy, glum, dissatisfied man whose thick insensitive face had a wart on its left cheek; the judge had a loud, droning voice and he very often raised it, interrupting one counsel or another; Stephen had rarely seen so much self-complacency, hardness, and want of common feeling together under a single wig.

Pearce, the prosecuting counsel, a 'would-be handsome young man, smirking at the judge', employs every specious slur to black-guard Jack's character and career, while clearly enjoying a private understanding with His Lordship, who makes scant attempt to conceal his partiality.

Court procedure appears designed to assist the prosecution, with Pearce's lengthy concluding speech followed immediately by the judge's three-hour hostile summing-up. When Maturin questions the judge's intelligence, Lawrence explains that:

> He *was* an intelligent man. You rarely come to be a judge without having been reasonably intelligent at one time. But like many others he has grown stupid on the bench, stupid and froward and over-bearing and inordinately self-important . . . he is, as you know, a roaring High Tory and the present chance of destroying Radicals was nectar to him – and although he was intolerably prosy and repetitious he did do all he wanted to do.

Patrick himself had no personal quarrel with the English judicial system. His only direct experience arose from brief attendance at custody proceedings some forty years earlier. Although the judgment of the court was adverse to his application, he accepted that it had been fairly arrived at. A close friend, Nigel Curtis-Raleigh, was a judge, and again I never heard Patrick consider him other than conscientious and fair-minded in his office. His remarkable understanding of how prejudicial proceedings may become when powerful government interests are at stake arose in part from meticulous research, but above all from his remarkably keen perception of human affairs.

When I reread *The Reverse of the Medal* some years after its publication, I assumed for a time that he must have drawn extensively on proceedings during my own trial in the High Court for libel during the latter part of 1989. For that event notoriously included all – and more – of the machinations, judicial and extra-judicial, which characterized Jack Aubrey's ordeal so vividly depicted by Patrick five years earlier. There was the same element of a Tory government's covert interference in the judicial process, with evidence vital to the defence case suppressed on ministerial instructions, and deceptive last-minute submissions of false evidence by the prosecution – all presided over by a blatantly biased little judge who insulted defence witnesses and throughout openly espoused the case for the prosecution, while taking care to conceal the fact that he and the plaintiff (Lord Aldington) were close neighbours in Kent, where they belonged to the same small private Rye Golf Club. After the verdict sought by Judge Michael Davies on Aldington's behalf had been obligingly delivered by the jury, my highly experienced counsel Richard Rampton QC (whose character markedly parallels that of Lawrence in the novel) passed me a note stating simply: 'You have been the victim of a corrupt system.'

Or, as the Reverend Nathaniel Martin put it to Stephen Maturin at the outset of Patrick's next novel *The Letter of Marque*: 'It was a very gross miscarriage of justice.'

Like Jack Aubrey, I had been blithely confident that overwhelming evidence in particular of Lord Aldington's perjury in order to escape personal responsibility for the worst war crime in British military history would be bound to secure victory in court. Patrick followed the case and its protracted aftermath with close attention and profound sympathy, but like Stephen Maturin avoided attendance at the hearing. As Stephen explains: 'There are cases, I believe, when friends should be present only in the near-certainty of victory . . . onlookers are strangely out of place.'

Ironically, Patrick had appended to his great novel an historical note, which concluded with the reflection that: 'The reader may therefore accept the sequence of events [in the story], almost unbelievable to a modern ear, as quite authentic.'

Unfortunately for me, the sequence of events was unexpectedly to become all too believable to a modern ear. Nor was the irony lost on Patrick when the event transpired.

In the middle of August 1984 he received from his publishers a 'pamphlet of praise from various reviews, which pleased me. (M finished the book [*The Reverse of the Medal*] & praised it too, which pleased me even more).'

Meanwhile in Collioure terrible fires ravaged the region, as Patrick reported to Richard Scott Simon:

We have had two. The first came sweeping over the maquis driven by a strong north wind, and as we saw the clouds of smoke we thought it must overwhelm our mountain vineyard [Manay]: but no – when we went up we found that the firemen & the planes had stopped it on the very edge. Not a leaf was hurt. But then the second burst out some days later, when an even stronger wind was blowing from the south, and this time everything went including the cork-oak forest & all our high stretches of cistas and genista, and of course the entire vineyard. The green silence where I work in the summer is now quite flat, a uniform black.

As the year drew to its close, Patrick found himself dwelling on his long-lost past. He began reading 'N's book on Oxford, which has some fine things in it & which makes me v sad'. This melancholy reflection almost certainly arose from wistful memory of his youthful ambition to enter the University, a longed-for project aborted by his irresponsible father's failure to provide him with adequate educational qualifications.* Although his unaided talents had enabled him to equal (or even outstrip) the erudition of many academic scholars, his lack of formal qualification bestowed an ingrained insecurity which never entirely ceased to trouble him.

Now encouraging news arrived out of the blue of a lucrative Japanese contract for the first nine novels in the Aubrey–Maturin series. This amounted to a gift for which no labour was required: one, moreover, which arrived at a juncture when their income

---

* In Patrick's partially autobiographical novel *Three Bear Witness*, the protagonist is an Oxford don engaged in research on medieval bestiaries – a literary project with which Patrick himself had been engaged.

required a substantial boost. But money was rarely the prevalent issue with Patrick. Like most authors, he found it a gratifying material measure of success, but otherwise so far as there was sufficient for daily needs he was content if required with a modest reward for his work.

Finally, on 7 December came an anniversary which had for some time caused him increasing anticipatory disquiet. During the summer he had received affectionate letters from his brothers Bun and Victor, commiserating over my mother's continuing ill-health, and now he heard again from them and his sister:

> Bun & Nora sent me congratulations on my 70th birthday, & Vic on Xmas card . . . Going to bed I reflected 'It has happened at last: I am 70' but with an odd mixture of belief & disbelief.

XII

Travails of Existence

Having up to that time lived but very little among men, having known hitherto nothing of clubs, having even as a boy been banished from social gatherings, I enjoyed infinitely at first the gaiety of the Garrick. It was a festival for me to dine there . . . I think that I became popular among those with whom I associated. I have long been aware of a certain weakness in my own character, which I may call a craving for love. I have ever had a wish to be liked by those around me, – a wish that during the first half of my life was never gratified . . . The Garrick Club was the first assemblage of men at which I felt myself to be popular.

Anthony Trollope, *An Autobiography* (London, 1883), pp. 157–9

O n 2 January 1985 Patrick received a formal letter from the Secretary of Brooks's Club informing him that he had been elected a member. This was to afford him continuing pleasure during the ensuing years. His accruing wealth enabled him to entertain there in style, without exorbitant expense. Membership of the historic Whig club also provided him with insights into the late Georgian period, for like the other old London clubs it provided evocative embodiments of earlier more elegant and colourful eras. In due course Patrick became a familiar figure among members, and in May 1990 he was invited to contribute to a handsome history of the Club published by Constable.[1]

Meanwhile he was immersed in his fresh commission: the biography of Sir Joseph Banks. By 8 January: 'I finished Ch III moderately well I thought & showed it to M, but I am afraid she did not think much of it – polite, of course.' At the time I remember wondering what induced Patrick to undertake the task. Happening upon a recent bibliography of works relating to Banks in the London Library, it seemed to me that to write a fresh book likely to supersede its predecessors would require long years of toil which Patrick could scarcely wish to set aside. That he lived far from convenient access to libraries and other archival repositories represented another material disadvantage. However, what I ignored then was the fact that Patrick's novels had yet to attain their deserved extent of acclaim, particularly in the United States, leaving him with involuntary time on his hands. In consequence he was occasionally diverted into attempting some other genre, which about this time ranged from a history of the Merchant Adventurers to a biography of Sir John Barrow.* At Collins, Stuart Proffitt suggested his writing a Companion to Catalonia, another project long nurtured by Patrick, but in the event never achieved. What I also did not then appreciate was Patrick's hope, nurtured since his youth, of establishing a reputation as a scholarly historian.

Nevertheless, despite the daunting nature of the task the completed account was to prove a polished and well received piece of work. Besides, the research required (which his voluminous working notes show was indeed considerable) added substantially to his already profound knowledge of late Georgian history in its broadest aspects. Finally, Banks is clearly the primary model for

---

* On 4 April 1985 Patrick noted that: 'Dr T Lodge, the laborious translator of Josephus, wd make a fine subject for a biography.' He possessed a copy in his library, whose title alone afforded him pleasure: *The Famovs and Memorable Workes of Iosephus, A Man of Mvch Honovr and Learning among The Ievves. Faithfully translated out of the Latin, and French, by Tho. Lodge, Doctor in Physicke* (London, 1632).

Patrick's Sir Joseph Blaine, Stephen Maturin's intelligence mentor and fellow enthusiast for natural history.*

Patrick's daily round was almost invariably busy, his deep-rooted desire for self-sufficiency drawing him into recondite tasks other successful authors might well have eschewed: 'The upstairs lavatory v thoroughly blocked, & my countless buckets ooze into the cave [below, beside his little study]. Carrying them (or perhaps something else) started my wretched back again.'

At a more aesthetic level, while he might readily have bought tapes of musical works he enjoyed, he gained arcane pleasure by painstakingly recording them from the admirable French classical music programme France Musique.

Despite his determination to work steadily on Banks, Patrick could not prevent his thoughts from wandering back to his naval tales: 'my head full of book & indeed of Aubrey to some extent – SM & D[iana] V[illiers] floating away in a balloon, away & away – higher & higher over cloud – eagle passes, with wren on wing – told myth, sound of trumpets.'

It is perhaps a pity that this extravaganza features only in much muted (albeit more plausible) form in the finished version of *The Letter of Marque*. However, he had at present no contract for the next tale, which in the event proved unforthcoming for well over a year, while he had to wait a further three for an American publisher.

As ever, Patrick maintained contacts with his family. In March 1985 he received a request from his brother Bun in Canada, asking

---

* On 21 November 1985 Patrick noted: 'MEM In the appendix to Warren Dawson, under Pitt, the strong hint that J[oseph]B[anks] had at least something to do with intelligence.' Blaine's surname probably originated in that of Dr Gilbert Blane, whose *Observations on the Diseases of Seamen* was first published in 1785. Patrick possessed Blane's account of seamen's health during the Napoleonic wars included in Christopher Lloyd (ed.), *The Health of Seamen: Selections from the Works of Dr. James Lind, Sir Gilbert Blane and Dr. Thomas Trotter* (London, 1965), pp. 136–211.

whether his daughter and her husband, who were honeymooning in Europe, might pay him a visit. Alarmed, Patrick 'wrote at once saying that it was impossible, & later sent him a book'. The impossibility arose from my mother's continuing poor health – a contingency at once appreciated by his brother, and Patrick was relieved to receive 'A pleasant letter from Bun, not resenting mine – no invasion [i.e. by Bun's daughter].' Bun reported the reason for Patrick's diminished communicability to their sister Joan, whose shared concern Bun clearly took for granted.

In May came further family news. Patrick learned shortly after the event that his brother Victor had died, aged eighty. This was particularly distressing, as the brothers had been close in their boyhood. Victor's schoolboy diaries, now in my possession, record the extent to which he had as a child cared for his vulnerable little brother. It took some time for Patrick to come to terms with the unhappy news. On 28 June: 'At last I wrote to Bun about Vic's death: strangely painful.'

Despite frenzied accusations levelled against him following his death, it is indisputable that Patrick nurtured a strong sense of family connection. Geographical dispersion meant that the Russ siblings could meet but rarely, their correspondence being probably no more sporadic than that of most families in their situation. Nevertheless, throughout his life Patrick considered himself very much a member of the Russ family. Three weeks after Victor's death he happened to be in Oxford, where: 'On the war-memorial in the cloister of New College I was strangely moved to see my cousin Rupert's name.' This was his first cousin Charles Rupert Russ, son of Patrick's uncle Sidney, who died in 1944 at the age of twenty-four while serving with the Royal Navy in the Far East.

As the summer drew on, Patrick was alarmed by my mother's increasing debilitation, frequent inability to eat, and subjection to occasional fainting. She was diagnosed with a polyp, which to their immense relief was found not to be cancerous. On 2 August she was admitted to hospital in Perpignan to have it removed, but another was discovered which required a further operation. Their good friends Pierre* and Rirette de Bordas provided him with a room at their home in town, enabling Patrick to visit the hospital daily. A little later, however, driving outside the town, his attention was momentarily distracted by a crashed car at the wayside, in consequence of which he ran his own into another oncoming vehicle. Fortunately the driver (a German girl) proved understanding, and drove him to the de Bordases' house.

Returned to the hospital, he saw the surgeon, 'who spoke of no cancer but low tension, fragility, great shock of v long operation. He said the tension was so low that at times the operation had to be interrupted – no blood flowed – & that I think is why it was so v prolonged'. In her delirium my poor mother was proving an unconsciously difficult patient, managing to tear off her bandages and pluck out a needle, which left a pool of blood on the floor. Next day there was some improvement, but she was plagued by hallucinatory dreams. The hospital arranged for Patrick to be brought a bed beside her for the night.

During the days that followed my mother veered between momentary recovery, severe loss of appetite, and bouts of sleeping 'sometimes so deeply that I was alarmed'. At the beginning of the next week Patrick went to recover another less significant but nonetheless cherished patient: '2 CV being ready, the slow, noisy old creature with v poor brakes after the others, but homely.'

Now, however, my mother's release from hospital was postponed in consequence of a partial heart attack. Fortunately, the cardiologist reassured Patrick that the failure 'concerned only a small, unimportant part of her heart but she must follow the treatment – she may smoke her 4 cigarettes a day – kind, talkative man'. At the end of August he learned that 'M's heart will not bear an operation before 3 months: from his grave expression I had been afraid of hearing something v much worse, so this seemed acceptable.' Next day,

* Pierre de Bordas was my parents' dentist as well as friend.

despite suffering from 'colic, nausea and general discomfort', she managed to read the proof of *The Reverse of the Medal*. Patrick was impressed by the fact that, despite her sorry state, she 'had picked up a wonderful number of literals, missed by me in 2 readings'.

On her release from hospital, my mother returned home under strict instructions as to diet and the necessity for constant rest. In October she was told that she must continue lying on her back for a hundred days. Although she insisted on helping Patrick with proofs and other editorial tasks, she found herself frustratingly unable to type, still less lend him any material assistance with daily work in the garden and vineyard.

At the beginning of November my mother's condition continued little if at all improved: 'Still v hard beating of her heart nearly all the time now, with tension at 14. [Dr] Manya spoke (much more vaguely than could have been wished) of the need for rest – nothing but the gentlest movement . . .'

All this was necessary to regain strength for continuation of the operation. Meanwhile Patrick cooked all their meals, shopped, tended the garden single-handed, entertained sympathetic visitors, and struggled manfully to keep his work on Joseph Banks moving forward. With the coming of winter, he found himself prey to sickness: 'My cold, which has been hanging about for a day or so, suddenly came on at the same time [when my mother was "obviously feeling v ill"]: for about ½ hour I could scarcely breathe, a most surprising onset.'

Not long after, a momentary memory lapse left Patrick worried that he might have suffered a slight stroke. Their only (invaluable) assistance came from the faithful Ana, who came regularly to clean the house.

On the 14th: 'Manya came, bringing good news: Mailly [the surgeon] had telephoned about M & after talking it over they decided she could be operated upon under local anaesthetic in January. M apt to tremble, almost speechless with amazement.'

Attempts to lighten the gloom were not helped by their tiny television (Patrick was convinced that a small room required a minuscule set), on which, to his continuing mystification, 'much of the action was, as usual, filmed in darkness, so we gave up fairly soon'. As though this were not enough, a cassette player ordered from Harrods, when switched on, produced only 'a dull flat moaning'. Although electronic machinery regularly delighted in outwitting Patrick's best efforts, he never abandoned the struggle. Shortly before Christmas he 'arranged (more or less) the wilderness of flexes behind my chair' (part of Patrick's wiring system for the house). His seventy-first birthday on 12 December was cheered by 'a lovely card' from his brother Victor's widow Saidie, together with a letter from the faithful Bun. Nor was he displeased when my mother rallied sufficiently to beat him at backgammon, 'although I had borne off 9 men'.

Christmas Day raised their spirits considerably. Patrick relaxed with 'dear Chaucer, an even more considerable high poet than I had remembered'.

Dinner was hard labour for M, but it was quite remarkably good – a successful great bird & a 2 year old pudding, perhaps the best we have ever eaten – a pudding saved from a v nearly disastrous fall. Washing up was heavy going alas particularly the huge lèche-frite [dripping-pan], deep in grease, but after it we sat peacefully & contented till late for us, perhaps 11 o'c.

The New Year of 1986 began promisingly:

A pleasant beginning to the year, with a calm blue sky (at least in the afternoon) & quite a warm sun. Writing went well too: only 2 pp apart from some typing but they knit things together just as I had hoped & bring me handsomely towards the end of the chapter.

Next day they received a telephone call from the clinic in Perpignan, explaining that my mother was to report there on

Sunday, while the operation would take place the next day. Patrick was 'moved, excited, happy, but (& I imagine it is the case with M too) silently & at some depth terrified'. However, my mother telephoned next morning with dismaying news that the anaesthetist had declared that the operation could not take place for another six months without a cardiologist's assurance. Patrick drove her to the cardiologist, who after close examination under an advanced ultrasound machine pronounced that there was no reason not to proceed. 'Lord, the relief of my heart!' wrote Patrick that evening. 'M quite transformed.' On Wednesday a temporary breakdown of the car prevented his arrival in time for the operation, and he found her back in bed, 'Weak, dozey, perfectly lucid.'

My mother's recovery was inevitably slow but nonetheless fitfully evident. The strain on Patrick was throughout acute, and he recorded grimly 'a clear perception of myself as old. This has scarcely happened before on anything but an intellectual plane.' On 16 January he was relieved by my mother's return home, though continuing pain from the wound inflicted by the surgeon and acute stomach problems caused him deep concern.

Work on Joseph Banks proceeded slowly. However, one night Patrick unusually had 'A dream in which I <u>did</u> catch a train, though it had already moved. Adsit omen.' The omen did indeed appear propitious, when my mother at long last found herself up to resuming typing Patrick's completed chapters. On the same day she ventured down into the garden – her first visit since the previous July. By St Patrick's Day she had managed to weed the entire cabbage patch, and that evening at their customary annual feast she presented Patrick with a fine bottle of Hennessy brandy and 'a noble cake'.

Four days later Patrick experienced yet another of his myriad miraculous escapes from death:

A cold tramontany day in which, going to Argelès, I did perhaps the most foolish & dangerous thing I have ever done – supposed

the turning were clear 2 or 3 ahead passed a tanker – came face
to face with a heavy truck – just but only just squeezed through
– angry horns in my ears – feeling of intense guilt rather than relief.

That evening, however, saw cause for celebration. Dining out
at the Albatros in Collioure, 'M stood this – her first sortie for 8
months, admirably.' This material improvement continued slowly
but satisfactorily, and in April she proved up to entertaining my
sister and her two sons for a couple of days. A few days later:
'With a surprising shock & with real regret we heard of S[imone]
de B[eauvoir]'s death: I had never thought of it in connection with
her.'

With justifiable satisfaction Patrick reflected on his completion
of the Banks biography:

> I spent some of the morning trying to establish the history of the
> Banks book, but I did not record it accurately & another time (if
> it really has any importance) I will write dates on the MS. Anyhow
> the writing took from 26 Nov 84 until 22 March 86: 16 months
> with 3 months off from illness, travelling, guests & more reading
> or even 4, which would give a year.

Considering the extent of research required, this represents an
impressive feat.

It was at this time that Patrick received a letter from Arthur
Cunningham of the British Library, who explained that he was
compiling a bibliography of his published works. Patrick obliged
with corrections and additions, but jibbed at a suggestion that his
early works published under his natal name of Russ (to which the
bibliographer Cunningham had become alerted) might be included.
Justly (as it turned out) apprehensive of danger posed by the envy
of a small but shrill claque of English critics, Patrick courteously
declined: 'As for my earlier books, fortunately published under
another name. I must ask you to excuse me – I had much rather

they remained unread, and I wish all follies of youth could be dealt with in the same way.'*

At the same time, Patrick's strong sense of nostalgia for his early days and continuing attachment to his family were never far from mind. In June he spent a contented afternoon waxing some of his precious leather-bound books, while listening to Mozart. He achieved 'extraordinary success with Burn's justice,² which I have had man & boy these 55 perhaps 60 years'; i.e. in his adolescence. Two days later he was gratified to receive a letter 'from Bun with an oddly touching photocopied page from Vic's diary of January 1919 showing me in bed'.

Patrick and my mother had attained that decade when mortality begins to impinge with unwelcome regularity. In August Patrick 'went to see W[illy]M[ucha], pale – i.e. suntanned – & somewhat thinner but better than I had expected & though not v brilliant perfectly compos mentis'. In the following month I telephoned with the news that their old friend Nigel Curtis-Raleigh had died. A contemporary of my father at Wellington, his stays at Collioure in the 1960s had occasionally overlapped with mine. He was a jovial soul, witty and youthful in his outlook. He became a judge and married late, and unfortunately my parents found his wife tiresome. Whether she rashly contradicted Patrick, or they simply preferred their old friend to continue a bachelor, I do not know. Patrick's reactions to the news of his death were conflicting: 'It was a strange wound: I had regretted him much before this, but I wish the last time we met had been less painful.' In December

---

* In 1992, in a response to an admirer's polite enquiry into the origins of his literary career, Patrick explained: 'You are quite right in assuming that I do not like giving my personal history on the dust-jackets of my books. Jane Austen went farther, omitting her very name from the title-page itself; and I think she was quite right. These things seem to me not only distasteful but essentially irrelevant: the Altamira cave-paintings would be no more moving if the painters' names were known, and Anon's huge musical and poetic outpouring would gain nothing if the poor soul were split up into individuals.'

Patrick recorded my informing him of 'Nigel's memorial service: mixed feelings, regret predominating'. When my parents occasionally fell out with their friends, it is generally impossible for me to assess the cause unless I had been present. That they could be contrary at times in their social relations is undeniable, but on the other hand in my own case I found that patient tact normally achieved wonders. Then again, my relationship was naturally different from that of a friend, however close.

On 5 August 1986 I arrived for a ten-days' stay. Patrick met me at the station, after which: 'Dinner out & then prolonged sitting in the cloister – we drank a whole bottle of Banyuls (72, quite good).'

On the 6th, my mother proving somewhat exhausted by this excess, Patrick took me up to view their new property at Manay. On the following day he and I walked up to the Madeloc ridge, talking cheerfully all the way. 'My walk,' Patrick noted, 'was about 6 miles & did not tire me at all, a tiny triumph.'

Next day he and I drove and then walked up to the Massane forest. Unlike my own father, Patrick always took a paternal and perceptive interest in my personal affairs. As it happened, they had at this time reached a particularly dire point of crisis, and for reasons which now largely escape me, we faced a financial impasse. Our bank had issued peremptory notice that we could cash no more cheques, and we entertained a lively fear of the imminent arrival of bailiffs. My literary work had succumbed to a temporary blockage. My recent book *The Minister and the Massacres*, which indicted Harold Macmillan of prime responsibility for the otherwise unauthorized betrayal to their Communist foes of 70,000 Cossacks and 50,000 Yugoslavs in Austria in 1945, had come up against the determined hostility of the British Establishment. The Conservative government covertly commissioned a purportedly independent 'committee' to pronounce my book fallacious in successive publications; a Sunday newspaper adroitly blocked the customary press serialization by securing rights to publication of an extract and then cancelling the project the night before; while the BBC issued a secret directive (revealed to me by producers indignant at the censorship) that neither I nor my book was to be mentioned in any broadcast.

My supportive publisher Century Hutchinson had nevertheless commissioned a further book, which, however, not only required at least a year's work, but was for the first time in my literary career not a project which particularly inspired me. Dampened by these setbacks, I had rashly abandoned all other labours in order to plunge into an historical novel about Merlin – a long-standing favourite project, several times attempted and as often abandoned. Realizing that I had no practical means of sustaining an uncommissioned work which would take at least two years to achieve, I had in desperation sent my literary agent (the late Giles Gordon) what was to prove only the first third of the typescript.

More than understandably, my publisher indignantly rejected it – as did another, who roundly pronounced it unpublishable. Such was our deplorable state of affairs when I walked with Patrick in the shady stillness of the forest of Coulamates. He as ever was profoundly sympathetic, but what could be done? We had an overdraft (now stopped) against our home of £80,000, and unsettled school fees amounting to some £14,000: 'disaster immediately ahead', as Patrick recorded in his diary.

Having heard that our return path had been blocked, Patrick recommended our pursuing a rough track trampled down by boars. Unfortunately we went astray, having at one point to scramble up a precipitous slope, and arrived home late sadly mutilated by thorns. There we found my mother awaiting us in the doorway in a high state of excitement. Scarcely able to formulate the words, she explained that Georgina had telephoned with amazing news. Giles Gordon had rung to say that Bantam Press was delighted with my uncompleted text, and had agreed to pay £250,000 for the completed work and its two projected sequels. Furthermore, there remained the strong likelihood (subsequently materialized) of a comparable advance by a US publisher! My parents were overjoyed, and Patrick gravely advised me: 'Nikolai, if you have any more trouble over the overdraft, tell the manager *you're going to buy the bank!*' Next day, he confided to his diary: 'General, more temperate contentment, & I find to my satisfaction that the little spasms of ignoble jealousy that assaulted me have died quite away.'

He had in fact signed a fresh contract with Collins the day after my arrival for 'THE TWELFTH AUBREY/MATURIN TALE', which I do not recall his even mentioning to me at the time. This was *The Letter of Marque*, which in the event was to prove as successful as its predecessors. I find it ironical that Patrick, who was surely among the least envious of authors, was to arouse such embittered rancour among a marginal coterie of reviewers. During the last decade or so of his life, he was himself much in demand as a reviewer. His judgements were almost invariably as constructive as they were charitable. It was only to his immediate family, diary or publisher that he would express an occasionally acerbic verdict. He once told me that he found it hard to be overly critical of an author's work, knowing as he did just how much effort and concern go into the writing of serious books.

Next morning, with Patrick's strong approval, I gave thanks for our good fortune in the lovely baroque church beside the plage St Vincent. After lunch he and I set off for another round walk beneath the ridge crowned by the Madeloc tower. That evening we were rewarded with a capital dinner below at La Chréa in the Port d'Avall.

I left on 15 August, when Patrick drove me to Collioure railway station. I am happy to see from his diary that he and my mother had enjoyed my visit as much as I. As Patrick wrote on the evening of my departure: 'He took most affectionate leave & now it can be said that his being here was an unalloyed pleasure: & he gave every sign of enjoying it too.'

In September Patrick heard from Richard Ollard, who had sent him a book by a leading historian of the Royal Navy. 'I'm glad,' wrote Richard, 'you enjoyed what you read of Nicholas Rodger's book. It seemed to me a tremendous vindication of your own presentation of the C18 navy – as against the fashionable view of a floating Belsen, wh. never made any sense.' Rodger's brilliant study[3] does indeed show up the absurdities of the 'rum, sodomy, and the lash' school of popular historians and novelists.*

In the same month they received exciting news that land adjacent to their property at Manay had become expropriated by a bank – presumably as security for a loan – and was now for sale. Two days later they attended a Dutch auction in Perpignan and, at the extinction of three candles limiting the bidding, the 3.26 acres became theirs for a total (including tax and legal expenses) of 4,906,000 francs. Two days later they drove up to survey the extension to their land, which comprised two vineyards and a stretch of mountainside. The land had not been well tended, but Patrick reckoned that the path and spring 'could be restored without enormous labour'.

In October 1986 Patrick and my mother were visited by Stuart Bennett, an American antiquarian bookseller who had recently settled with his wife Kate in Bath. Patrick had bought from him a succession of Jane Austen's novels, in either first or second editions. He frequently emphasized to me the pleasure of reading classic works, if not necessarily in first editions, at least in those published during the author's lifetime. Elegant binding, distinctive print, the thought that the work had been read by the author's contemporaries, and the idiosyncratic smell of early editions add materially to the pleasure of reading.

---

* When an American reader bearing a name of Italian origin expressed incredulity that Jack Aubrey could have crossed the Atlantic without ordering a single flogging, Patrick began his draft response with the dampening words: 'I see that English is not your first language.'

Patrick assisted by Stuart Bennett at Manay

In July Bennett had written to my parents, asking if he and his wife might visit Collioure for a few days to assist with the vendange, which that year began in the plains on 19 September. They arrived at the beginning of October for a five days' stay. Stuart did indeed provide sterling assistance with the harvest, and the visit passed for the most part very pleasantly.

A major highlight was provided by a mutually satisfying exchange. In return for a recently acquired first edition of Jane Austen's *Emma*, Patrick gave him the original manuscript of *Master and Commander*:

Having said that I had no MSS & having then felt doubts I looked & found the 3 1st [manuscripts of the novels in the series], rather dirty but sound (S. Maturin was called Martin Joyce for the 1st few chapters). Told SB, who at once said that his Emma was worth more than 1 MS. This, & some other rather mercantile words displeased & grieved me & I turned the whole thing aside.*

---

* That June Bennett had bought his copy of *Emma* at auction for £900.

Next day, however, dining together at La Chréa:

> A truly magnificent bouillabaisse appeared, guided by SB, who a little before this had made a v handsome apology, so handsome that although I had become attached to the MS of M & C I let him have it. A v pleasant dinner indeed: certainly the best bouillabaisse we have ever eaten.

A week after the Bennetts' departure the three-volume set of *Emma* arrived through the post, to Patrick's high pleasure. He rationed himself to reading his new treasure of an evening in the cloister. His collection of early Jane Austen editions was now complete, and his eye frequently rested on the attractive set lined up on his bookshelf. The exchange was probably a fair bargain, although I suspect that today the total absence on the market of manuscripts of the Aubrey–Maturin series would make their value (above all, that of *Master and Commander*) very considerable indeed. On the other hand, the fact that the set of *Emma* had become Patrick's own has probably increased its already considerable intrinsic value.

On 29 September page proofs of the Joseph Banks biography arrived. For Patrick, this was always the most pleasant stage in a book's progress: finally it could be read as a polished whole, while tiresome errors could still be corrected. Three days later, 'I reached ⅔, reasonably pleased with the book, & liking JB.'

Here I cannot resist recapitulating yet another of Patrick's idiosyncratic dreams, occurring at this time:

> Last night I dreamt that M & I were lying on the couch [upstairs, in the sitting-room]. I said 'Look', pointing cautiously at a little bittern that was peering in through the window with intense curiosity. But the bird (brown, with paler frill, seen from beneath, like a grebe's) was not easily frightened. We entered into conversation & she said her name was Pataska (or something like that) & her

age 4 months. I said if ever she would like a bath she had but to come: but begged her to beware of cats, which made her look grave. She admitted that her feet (which were v odd) were not suited for digging a hole in which to bathe.

I fancy that the talkative animals and birds he regularly encountered in dreamland originated in his lonely childhood, becoming confirmed by a lifelong absorption in natural history. Also intriguing is the extent to which his absurdist sense of humour permeated his dreams. It is probable that this proclivity likewise arose in his infancy: as I have suggested, as an internalized counter to the grim power of those exercising repressive authority over him.

In December Patrick underwent a pang of nostalgia, when he was carried back in imagination to the dawn of their great adventure, when they arrived, penniless but excited, at their tiny cottage Fron Wen in North Wales: 'My diary of 1945 caught my eye – Fron, of course, in our first days. How it takes one back: but where was Cwmorthin & the house with a fireplace each end of the single room?'

As ever, an even earlier past resurfaced at Christmas: 'A birthday & Xmas card from Bun, rather curt – did he ever get TROTM [*The Reverse of the Medal*]? Says [their sister] Nora has seen a book of mine, presumably recently.'

A couple of days later a further card arrived from Victor's widow Saidie. It was pleasurable to contemplate those distant days, although at times also exquisitely painful.

As for their current state of affairs, yet another of Patrick's dreams is decidedly indicative:

Dream of circus horses dressed as camels pulling waggon: one (speaking from a gap in the camel's neck) told me that it had written a piece, but (laughing heartily) it was badly reviewed. The man of the waggon said yes, it was v badly reviewed. I told the horse that the man had shown it only the bad reviews, concealing the others, for fear the horse should ask for a rise. This was all in Fr., because I said augmentation.

Although 1986 ended on a happier note than it had begun, much of it had been a time of worry and frustration. While my mother had at last recovered from her dangerous heart operation, her health continued poor. She remained weak, and much subject to flux and other internal pains. Although the purchase of additional land at Manay had brought rejoicing, during one of their visits she had slipped and badly injured her shin. The ill effect of such unpleasant accidents was greatly exacerbated by her continuing constitutional infirmity, which caused Patrick constant distress.

He himself found his current work at times a tedious struggle. No further commission being forthcoming for another naval tale, he had been contracted in the previous November to translate the first of a massive two-volume biography of de Gaulle by Jean Lacouture.[4] He found the book in large part pretentious and even silly, and it is hard to tell whether he disliked the author or his subject more: 'I lowered my spirits still farther by looking into Lecouture, who is v French & who would be (perhaps only until I got into him) v difficult to make English. Vol I is 500000 [words].'

Although the work broadly proved little more than mere drudgery, as ever Patrick maintained the struggle every day.

XIII

Family Travails

In seeking to discourage, or at any rate to control, any overlapping of his London world and his Dorset world – especially the world of his own family – he can scarcely have been motivated by mere snobbishness or social vanity . . . although few . . . can have realised just how humble and isolated his childhood had been. It was simply that he felt his family affairs were his own business and no one else's: as he had told [his publisher] Kegan Paul in 1881, 'I have an opinion that the less people know of a writer's antecedents (till he is dead) the better'.

> Michael Millgate, *Thomas Hardy: A Biography*
> (Oxford, 1982), pp. 267–8

The 1st of January 1987:

was as beautiful a New Year's day as can be imagined, probably as good as our first. It was warm (67°) but there was a little breeze, & M was much smoked by her bonfire in the kitchen garden & then by another at Manay, where we spent the afternoon . . . I also began the twelfth naval tale (? A Return to Grace) & wrote 1000 words, starting perhaps mistakenly with SM (Blue Breeches & bustard), perhaps out of proportion). Again poor M's inwards were troublesome (though not very as it turned out) & she slept upstairs.

It was not until September, after completing her typing of chapter IV, that my mother thought of an alternative title *The Letter of Marque*, which Patrick promptly approved.

At first the writing went slowly, with his experiencing customary doubts about the approach to the new novel. A reviewer had recently (unfairly, in Patrick's opinion) objected to what he regarded as the excessive length of his recapitulation of the situation at the conclusion of the preceding novel in the series. This of course was a problem intrinsic to compilation of the huge *roman fleuve* which the novels represent: one which nevertheless required resolution.

Reading, as ever, was a joy – although it too could on occasion provoke personal misgivings: 'I read [Chekhov's] Oncle Vania [in French] with immense pleasure (perhaps "keenest attention" is the better expression), & admiration. My own work is painfully thin & trifling in comparison – lacks the overflowing life, too.'

Nostalgic immersion in their own past, when they were still young and vigorous, afforded occasional consolation:

I read the diary of our [1953] Iberian journey (lost, found, lost & found again) with great pleasure: how some things have stayed in my memory, thoroughly embedded, others only just present when stirred (e.g. my only cranes), & others quite gone (Lisbon cathedral). What a journey it was, & how the powers protected us, thanks be.

Continuing contact with his family brought added comfort. On 10 February his brother Bun wrote to their sister Joan: 'I had lately had a pleasant letter from Pat including a photo which I shall send on showing his vintage in its barrels. He says nothing about his poor wife who was sadly injured again a year or so ago. I am afraid she is going to be a permanent invalid.'

My mother's continuing attacks of ill-health would indeed provide a melancholy leitmotif to the remainder of their life together. 'How terribly vulnerable we are: misere nobis.'

Lesser irritations included the by now familiar but still unaccountable difficulties presented by their perverse little television set. A troublesome day was capped by 'a pretentious, artistic, invisible & inaudible film only redeemed in part by J. Fonda . . .' Nevertheless, persistence being one of his great virtues, a few days later Patrick patiently watched another 'largely invisible' programme: this time a rugby match between France and Wales.

The novel continued to fret Patrick: '1000 words + but I am filled with anxiety about the 80000 odd to come. Can I make a coherent tale out of the 2 naval incidents I have in mind + SM & DV? Has not my once overflowing imagination chilled?'

Shortly afterwards he became convinced that 'This is <u>not</u> an inspired book.' In fact the expedition of the *Surprise* covered by the first hundred pages is surely as vivid and brilliant as anything Patrick wrote. This gradually dawned on him, and he wrote a couple of days later: 'Almost my only work was correcting yesterday's & adding to it. I feel a little happier about the book: yesterday it seemed to me that I had wasted the tail-end of my life in translations & the like, & that I no longer had the lively imagination of these tales.'

In early March the first copies of *Joseph Banks* arrived, a book which had required exceptional labours of research. Unfortunately the initial impression was disappointing:

Banks came in the morning. This is the 1st book in 50 & more that we really could not rejoice about. The red of the jacket is hopelessly poor, the illustrations thin, mean & badly even mistakenly captioned, the type-face thin too & cold, the blurb has the piece about Collioure that I particularly asked to have left out, & the whole thing looks high-shouldered & meagre. It was only when I was in bed, gasping with much congested tubes [asthma], that I remembered that I had called most vehemently for a map on the end-papers, that it had been promised, & that it was not there.

Later in the month their old friend Jacques Théodor, an experienced underseas explorer, called for lunch. Patrick, as was liable to occur when his writing was proceeding unsatisfactorily, found him somewhat didactic and contrary, but was touched by the gift of a Roman amphora, brought up from the seabed off Campania by Théodor's colleague Jacques Cousteau.

In June Georgina and I came to stay for a week. Ominously, 'N told me of an alarming libel suit brought by Ld Aldington.' The stay was a successful one for all, with much walking, talking, and swimming. Patrick believed he had 'never seen him [me] look fitter or calmer in mind'; but, being considerably more perceptive than I in such matters, he concluded on the evening of our departure: 'I fear for him in this Aldington business. Win or lose he cannot but be distracted from Merlin, and if he loses it must be something like ruin . . . I think it could be called a successful visit, but it left M quite exhausted & cost her a kilo.'

Two days later Patrick received a further letter from Bun, announcing that he would be in London during the latter part of June, and suggesting a meeting. Having been over as recently as May, Patrick had to explain that his work did not permit a return at this time.

Joan's illusion, cited earlier, that writers enjoy unfettered time and facility for engaging in regular correspondence may also account for her equally erroneous assumption about this time that Patrick had deliberately rebuffed her.* Nevertheless, his diary shows that he and Bun continued their correspondence throughout the remainder of the year. Sadly, however, it transpired that Patrick

---

* In September 1995 Patrick wrote to Edwin Moore at Collins with a suggestion for inclusion in any future edition of their recently published *Dictionary of Quotations*. It was this apt admonition '(& it is a beginning that I use shamefully often)' by Dr Johnson: 'You are not to think yourself forgotten, or criminally neglected, that you have had yet no letter from me. I love to see my friends, to hear from them, to talk to them; but it is not without a considerable effort of resolution that I prevail upon myself to write.'

had unwittingly missed his last opportunity of seeing the brother to whom he had been closest. In later years time flits by at fearful speed.

In September Stuart and Kate Bennett again visited Collioure, returning to Richard Scott Simon in England with the typescript of *The Letter of Marque* – a novel which cost him more worry and misgivings than most. Despite this, I imagine I speak for many readers in finding its quality in no way inferior to others in the series. Fortunately he resisted his earlier idea that 'SM & DV (or at least DV) should have floated away in the balloon'.

His editor, Stuart Proffitt, was delighted with the book, writing on 22 October:

> I have never felt a storm in print as yours here; or so intense an action as the capture of the <u>Diane</u> (and in so short a space – I could not believe, on first reading, that all the actual fighting was compressed into no more than two and a half pages); or so desperate a delirium as Stephen's at the close; or quite so much delight as with his recovery and reconciliation with Diana. Its colours, lighter and more playful than those of <u>The Reverse of the Medal</u>, are quite wonderful; and throughout there is that sense that somehow it is telling you more than it is ostensibly telling you. I do not know what they will be comparing it to in a hundred years' time, or what they will be saying about it, but assuredly they will be saying something. And to think that I am probably only the third or fourth person to read it.

Meanwhile, Patrick had begun pondering the book's sequel: 'Some days ago I noted a possible beginning to XIII [*The Thirteen-Gun Salute*] & today I rather idly added to it, feeling the pleasant old atmosphere – raison d'être, after all. I think of summarizing the rest before going back to Lacouture.'

Translating the biography of Lacouture's *De Gaulle* appeared as much drudgery as ever, but true to form Patrick persisted: 'I think I can do 2000 words a day without pressing, & I do need time for garden, hedge & Manay [their mountain vineyard]'. It was perhaps in part the deprivation caused by his temporary separation from the novels that lay behind gloomy reflections on 'death, loneliness, heartbreak & the remark in Braudel about the poor walking about like the dead in the land of the living & grew v low indeed' – a reflection in turn provoked by his encountering a middle-aged man, 'usually accompanied by young woman & dog, now alone'. A few weeks earlier, my mother's Aunt Joan, to whom she and all the family were devoted, had died – a sad event that undoubtedly added to Patrick's troubled state of mind.

In February 1988 Stuart Proffitt sent Patrick detailed discussion of a new dustjacket design for the series:

> Fifteen years is a long time for such a large number of books to continue with the same cover style; and additionally we thought it about time to distinguish your books from those of your supposed rivals. The aim, of course, (which I do not think the old covers do) is to convey the quality of what is inside the covers and so to sell more . . .
>
> As The Letter of Marque has been read and talked about within the house, a number of experienced sales and marketing people have said to me that they do not think the Barbosa jackets on the hardbacks have particularly helped our sales on that side either.

In reply, Patrick concurred that a dramatic change was necessary, going on, however, to make the jocular suggestion of avoiding depiction of ships almost entirely. In a burst of enthusiasm, he instead envisaged 'vast orchids, flame-trees, scarlet spoonbills, huge colonies of penguins on the ice with sea-elephants, the Georgian houses and – why not? – a levee at St James's . . .'

Fortunately, Collins had fixed upon the perfect illustrator, whose magnificent maritime scenes would grace all forthcoming volumes in the series, as well as reprints of the earlier tales. This was Geoff

Hunt, a brilliant marine artist, who combined exhaustive technical understanding of sailing vessels of the period with evocative depiction of their splendours. On 29 February Hunt wrote to Patrick, expressing his enthusiasm for the project, which would result in a collaborative achievement comparable in some degree to the creation of Jack Aubrey and Stephen Maturin. His meticulous approach to the work meant that preliminary sketches were only submitted to Collins two months later. While Patrick's initial reaction was that 'They are so very sketchy that I can make little of them as they stand', he sensed that 'Mr Hunt's use of light and space may very well, as you say, lift them out of the commonplace ruck.' By June the artist submitted transparencies of paintings for the covers of the first four novels, which evoked the enthusiastic delight of editor and author alike.

Throughout this time my mother's ill-health continued a constant trial. That spring, Patrick found that:

What pleases me less is M's great weariness. She is quite bent [i.e. debilitated] with it & she is v weak. As we were coming home I saw a villager & said 'surely we know that man.' He was the Banyuls lotissements concierge, changed within perhaps 3 months into an old tottering man, by cancer of liver & pancréas.

While his translation proceeded haltingly and without enthusiasm, he as ever gained great consolation from his favourite authors: 'I read Lizzy Bennet's words to Darcy with even greater admiration. JA must have been in a splendid flow for those pages.'

Again: 'much bent by the end of the day. Still, I did read the Nuns' Priest's tale with great pleasure – greater than ever, I believe . . . what a dear man Chaucer must have been.'*

On the other hand, during a visit to London he experienced in

* As Terry Zobek points out to me, this contradicts Patrick's oft-repeated dictum that the character of an author can bear no connection to his creation!

Harrods an upset familiar to many authors: 'Depression began when I passed through the book dept & saw not a single one of my own – a whole row of [Dudley] Pope, no O'B.'

Back home he pushed on doggedly with the Lacouture translation, occasional consolation being provided by memories it aroused of his wartime service with Political Warfare Executive, which had involved close contact with the Free French in London: 'I have returned to Churchill & although to be sure he had immense faults & sometimes wrote horrid English, the de Gaulle seen by Lacouture is a little silly yapping dog in comparison with him. Roosevelt was obviously a wrong un.'

Odd dreams continued to trouble or amuse him. On St Patrick's Day:

> By night one of those not uncommon dreams of nakedness, but the circumstances were unusual: we were at Monique's party – beforehand I had asked what to wear – Monique [de Saint-Prix] had said, no doubt facetiously, 'Nothing' – I alone took her literally – we sat down, & when Rirette & 2 more women (said to be her sisters) came in I felt unable to stand up & greet them.

A month later found his routine labour if anything more depressing. 'The change of pill did not answer: it was not enough to begin with – there were dreams, to be sure, but precious little sleep (& such gloom).'

Next morning (18 April) brought one of those miraculous shifts in fortune which occasionally transform an author's laborious task:

> However, the post brought v good news from R[ichard]S[imon]. Harvill [the UK publisher] says they have to have Lacouture by Feb 89 – if I cannot do it, will I release them from their contract?* And

---

* Patrick's contract provided for him to translate both weighty volumes of Lacouture's book.

not only that, but Collins want to contract for 2 more naval tales
in order to relaunch the new-jacketed paperbacks (ready in about
Oct) on a large scale: they will pay a total advance of £20,000
(though book 1 must be ready by end March 89). Then there were
royalties of about £3,000. R[ichard]S[imon] advised dropping the
translation & writing the tales, if I felt capable of delivering them.
I telephoned to agree . . .

At one fell swoop the dispiriting prospect of struggling with
uninspired translation work for another year was dismissed, while
he could now revert exclusively to uninterrupted concentration
on the 'naval tales' which inspired and delighted him above all
things. He replied by return, enthusiastically accepting the enticing
terms. At the time volume 1 of Lacouture was nearing completion:
two days later: 'The rest of the day was spent struggling with
Lacouture, sometimes with absurd little difficulties such as the
right rendering of en principe & on verra bien'; a week later:
'Today I just looked at Lacouture & then turned away'; by the
beginning of June: 'If ever I do a translation again, which God
forbid (at least of this kind) . . .' Finally, on 5 June: 'We finished
de Gaulle & packed him up . . .' In the event, the dreaded volume
2 was translated by another, and in this satisfactory way Patrick's
impressive twenty-eight years' translation work came to a close.
It was only latterly, with a particularly long, difficult and often
uninspiring work, that what had hitherto proved a lucrative and
in large part constructive task had evolved into a more and more
insupportable burden.

The day after his literary agent's cheering announcement, Patrick
found that: 'Simon's good news sinks in (though I must admit I
am afraid of book 14 [of the naval tales]: conceivably I might cut
13 in 2). Yesterday & the day before I failed in the last stage of
my [Rubik's] cube – could not tell why . . . Qu. a connection?'
Even the good news bore yet another unwelcome admonition of
mortality, with the contract on its arrival including 'disagreeable

clauses' providing that: 'Within 180 days of the incapacity or the death of the Owner ... the Publishers and the Owner or his executor will select jointly a writer to complete the Work ...' Nevertheless, even while he struggled to finish Lacouture, Patrick permitted himself to direct his mind towards the forthcoming adventures of Captain Aubrey and Dr Maturin. 'In the Sc[ientific]. American I read about the platypus, astonished at her poisonous spine – should like to use it in a tale. SM to NSW to see (? rescue) Padeen.'

Used in a tale it was – as the memorable conclusion to *The Nutmeg of Consolation*.

As in the previous year, Georgina and I came to stay for a week, in June 1988. Patrick found me 'very jolly, affectionate & in excellent form, though his trial with Aldington comes up next June – he has some most impressive people on his side, but I wish it were over. Morally A[ldington] has not a leg to stand on, but that is neither here nor there.'

As may be seen from *The Reverse of the Medal*, Patrick possessed an instinctive appreciation of less savoury niceties of the English legal system of which I at this stage continued happily ignorant.

On the 23rd we celebrated my birthday, at which we were regaled with 'Exceptionally good grapefruit [from the garden] ... the 1st fresh ones G had eaten'. Next morning Patrick and I bottled thirty litres of wine from 1986 and a sixty-litre barrel of 1987. I felt an unanticipated pang, as he calmly intimated that I needed to understand the process in case of their sudden demise. 'I am so glad he knows about these necessary details,' he wrote matter-of-factly that evening.

We shared in the excitement next day on the beach, when Patrick produced a copy of a letter received that morning from Charlton Heston: 'a film star who likes my tales and who would like to talk about making them into films – the young [i.e. Georgina and I] say he is v well known'. Our stay passed pleasantly, with the customary animated conversations, swimming and walking.

Patrick participated in the latter, although much afflicted by a severe cold.

Not the least melancholy aspect of my protracted battle with the British Establishment, which continued until the close of the century, was that this unexpectedly proved to be the last of my family holidays with my parents, after so many long and happy years, in the homely familiar Correch d'en Baus which I had helped to build more than thirty years previously.

Throughout the summer my mother continued painfully weak, while Patrick suffered constant attacks of what at times he suspected to be a recurrence of the asthma that afflicted his early childhood. Unfortunately his dauntless stoicism led him to underplay or omit this factor in correspondence, which may have affected an unfortunate family misunderstanding which arose at this time. Although it has been seen that Patrick had over the years maintained regular correspondence with several of his Russ relations (in particular his brother Bun and sister Joan), his overriding commitments remained his writing, constant attendance on my invalid mother, extensive correspondence with publishers, literary agent and innumerable admirers of his books, gardening, viticulture, and ornithology – to say nothing of entertaining local friends and occasional visitors from abroad. When Bun and Joan at times sought to increase their correspondence, Patrick was obliged to explain that his commitments did not permit any great expansion of their existing exchanges.

In his privately printed memoir, Bun asserts that 'We had not been a very close family, emotionally, perhaps because of my mother's early death and the subsequent preponderance of housekeepers coupled with my father's active mind but failing physical health which necessitated cutting short some of our schooling.'[1]

This is largely pious fiction, suppressing as its does the fact that the children's inadequate education was largely due to their father's selfish or foolish improvidence. Moreover, as I have explained earlier, when in differing degree lack of contact occurred it arose primarily in consequence of geographical distance or other happenstance concerns. The fact is that their relationships differed little from those of thousands of their contemporaries, above all those whose youth or early middle age had been thrown into turmoil by five years of universal war.

It would be superfluous to emphasize this factor, but for speculative assumptions indulged by Dean King in his biography of Patrick.[2] These in turn would by now have become long forgotten, were it not that they became in turn seized upon by critics, whose effusions in some more meretricious cases became misguidedly perpetuated on the internet. In fact King's fancies may readily be shown to be without substance.

'Patrick's reasons for detaching himself from his family were complex,' pronounces King. The obvious objection to this gratuitous assertion is that Patrick did *not* detach himself from any of his brothers and sisters, save Bun – and even then only briefly. The ironical fact is that in two cases alone did permanent rifts arise among Dr Russ's offspring, in both of which it was close family members who elected to detach themselves from Patrick! The first was his son Richard, who, by his own confession and for reasons which remain in part mysterious, summarily broke off relations with his father from 1963 – to Patrick's enduring distress. The other was his notoriously testy and eccentric sister Joan, who in 1981 took offence at an imagined slight – one so trivial that Patrick appears to have continued unaware that it even occurred.

In June 1988 Bun wrote to Joan, complaining *inter alia* about Patrick's decision to change his name, together with what he took to be his disinclination to maintain links with his family. However, in the following month Bun wrote to Patrick himself, explaining that his daughter Elizabeth, who had expressed fondness for her uncle after their meeting in Paris, would like if convenient to pay a visit to Collioure. Patrick's eventual reply, sent on 12 July, in a letter bearing clear indications of haste and distress, explained his current difficulties:

I should have answered earlier, but my recent life has been very much disturbed, ill-health of course being the primary cause.* I have had to deal as best I can with a series of crises, and although for the moment the worst seems to be growing less acute there is still a most shocking decline in physical & spiritual strength that fills me with anxiety. It threatens to be of long, indeed of indeterminable duration, & <u>obviously in the circumstances no visit is remotely possible</u>.

Unhappily, at the very beginning of the trouble, when the difficulties seemed merely transient, I contracted to write two books in the near future: the contracts have heavy penalty clauses attached, & this, as you may imagine, complicates the situation.

However, whining will do no good, and I will only ask you not to take it amiss if I neglect correspondence – I should have added, by the way, that in case of extreme emergency I can rely on the support of [my mother's] affectionate, intelligent family.

Bun took what was surely needless offence on receipt of this mildly worded and entirely reasonable explanation. To Joan, he snorted: 'Well, I can't cope with non-communication and I shall not write further unless I receive a sensible answer.' In fact Patrick had made no suggestion of ceasing their correspondence, but merely explained why it could not be maintained as frequently as might be desired so long as current conditions prevailed. The touchy Joan, who was likewise angered by Patrick's apologetic inability to conduct regular correspondence, responded to Bun that 'the best thing to do in the face of such persistent rudeness is to maintain an unequivocal silence. He has been consistently blocking all communication with one and all, so why bother?'

Although he assured Joan that 'I don't intend to write to him', Bun shortly afterwards wrote an injured letter to Patrick, together

---

* Patrick's distress was such that his flurried explanation left Bun a little perplexed as to whose ill-health was under discussion. It was of course primarily my mother's.

with another to Elizabeth, warning her not to call on the household at Collioure. She, however, ignored the advice, and arrived there on 18 August:

> . . . M came diffidently in & said Canadian niece was on the phone. I coped as well as I could – gave her a drink chez Pous [the Café des Sports] – asked her to lunch there tomorrow – explained impossibility of invitation [into their home]. She had left her consort & 3 children on faubourg plage, so I necessarily saw them – man pleasant. She seemed affectionate, pretty good at not asking questions v anxious for family connexion (why?), properly shocked at what she had done.

Next day, however: 'Lunch was less successful than I had hoped: a spate of questions – what did my mother die of so young? Was I afraid that my wife might die any minute . . .'

For her part, Elizabeth found him charming and attentive. A few years later, she described her visit to me:

> During the summer, my 2nd (and current) husband Bill, his son and my two children ferried, drove, camped, trekked and generally made our way from S. England to N. Spain, down along the west side of the Spanish/French border until we reached Andorra (gawd awful), and then drove to Collioure. The month would have been August. There were 5 of us – including 3 lively pre-teenaged kids – so we camped in a campsite a mile or so away from the port. Against my Dad's wishes (I believe Dad was irked by but wanted to respect Pat's wish for isolation – if that's the correct word), I phoned Pat. Your Mum answered, was very cheery and pleasant, and said he was out and it was agreed I should call back again later. I did so, Pat answered and we arranged to meet at the harbour and he would take me out for lunch. He expressed the wish that it be only myself with him for lunch.
>
> We met at the agreed place and time. I introduced my husband

and children who then went swimming and Pat and I went for lunch in a really amazing restaurant [the Café des Sports]. Perhaps you know of it. The walls were covered with paintings, some originals. It had quite a character to it, the food was good and we spent about an hour or so. Again he was polite and friendly without being overly warm. He brought two bottles of wine for me, one from each vineyard. He bemoaned the changes in Collioure since he and your Mum had settled there. We chatted about many topics, his vineyards, your Mum's delicate health (on the phone she sounded hearty and cheerful, as she had done on another occasion when I called when I was in Montpelier in 1995. Pat was on a trip and so I didn't speak with him), how Pelican was changing the look of his book covers and re-issuing some, he asked me about my work in London, my Spanish (not Catalan!) my mother, my stepmother – when he asked about them, I took the liberty of asking about his own children. He denied Richard's existence!* I mentioned Connie [one of Patrick's elder sisters] and Joan and members of the family I would have been seeing in England. He talked about Picasso, another manuscript he was working on for the series . . .

Yes, my father often spoke about Pat and frequently shared his letters with me (to and from). In my mind's eye I can still see Pat's handwriting and the wonderful way he expressed himself. I know Dad was very proud of Pat's accomplishments, even though there was slight sibling rivalry.

It seems that, relying on that restricted part of these exchanges between Bun and Patrick to which he managed to obtain access, Dean King misunderstood Bun's largely unjustified complaints, pronouncing confidently that 'O'Brian's reasons for detaching himself from his family were complex . . . A few well-placed words from Patrick could have gone a long way in smoothing

---

* I suspect this reflects no more than Patrick's concern not to discuss so painful an issue.

over familial relationships. But O'Brian was not predisposed to reconciliation . . .'[3]

How King believed himself privileged to interpret the inner workings of Patrick's mind is left unexplained. In fact, Patrick had on successive occasions explained to both Joan and Bun the very real obstacles to his maintaining any *regular* correspondence.* Besides, so far from being 'not predisposed to reconciliation', save for one interlude arising from mutual misunderstanding Patrick maintained contact with Bun pretty much as before. At his birthday in December he received his brother's customary congratulatory letter, in which Bun made it clear that he was 'much confused at his daughter's conduct – a handsome letter'. Patrick described his own prompt reply as 'rather odiously magnanimous' (i.e. affectionately generous). Their contacts in the following year will be described shortly.

On 29 July Patrick received his first copies of *The Letter of Marque* without much immediate enthusiasm: 'The lettering has spoilt the picture [on the dustjacket] & in any case I was not moved – too long a wait – ? too old – but I liked seeing Bayley's kind though mistaken words again.'

The picture in question was the first of Geoff Hunt's, whose maritime masterpieces adorned this and all subsequent volumes, to the unabated delight of Patrick and his readers alike.

John Bayley's conclusion was as generous as it was justified:

O'Brian is particularly successful at conjuring the whole life of a ship, the camaraderie, the formality, the talk of the officers in the ward room and the men on the gun decks. He makes brilliant use of the speech patterns of the time, but escapes any suggestion of quaintness . . . O'Brian is a master of rapid and unobtrusive aperçus; and all of the characters . . . live in their own right and on their

---

* King himself notes Patrick's daunting workload from 1988 onwards (*Patrick O'Brian: A Life Revealed*, p. 304).

own terms. Like Farrell, O'Brian has solved in his own individual way the intractable problem of getting history – in terms of habits, assumptions and ideas – into the texture of the novel . . . [Jack Aubrey] is a Lord Jim without the author's philosophic pretension, and in his context far more convincingly contrived. [In him] O'Brian's combination of sagacity and magic is at its best.*

As ever, I am intrigued to observe personal touches in the tale. The 'Blue Breeches' episode at the outset recalls the hero's regular encounters with wayside eccentrics in the rollicking Regency realm of Jeffrey Farnol, an immensely popular historical novelist living in Lewes at the time of Patrick's schoolboy days in that picturesque town. Sir Joseph Blaine's elegant house in Shepherd Market reminds me of Patrick's pointing it out as we strolled by one day. Regrettably, I did not note the number – just as I can no longer identify Stephen Maturin's Catalan castle, which Patrick once indicated far below us in Spain during a walk in the high Pyrenees long years ago. The 'poor Senhouse', borne off in a balloon never to be seen again, was Patrick's much-disliked editor at Secker & Warburg in the 1950s. Cullis, the dentist whose huge fee so impresses poor Padeen, is Michael Cullis, a Foreign Office friend from early days. More welcoming is the tender portrait of Jack's matured and beautiful Sophie, in whom I recognize my own Georgina, whose calm courage during our time of trial so impressed Patrick at the time he was writing the novel.

Stephen Maturin's seaside exultation, when 'he felt rising in his heart that happiness he had quite often known as a boy', recalls Patrick's enchanted explorations of the beach at Seaford in his childhood. Likewise, the Miss O'Mara whom Jack employs as his children's governess is named after one of the few beloved by Patrick in his infancy.

---

* I imagine that Patrick's allusion to Bayley's 'mistaken words' reflects his dislike of being compared to another author. In this case I do not believe that he regarded J.G. Farrell as in any way inferior, but simply different.

With the autumn of 1988, Patrick found himself diverted from work on the next novel in the series, *The Thirteen-Gun Salute*, into momentary reassessment of the early novels in the series for the forthcoming paperback reissue by Collins:

> I spent the day with M[aster] & C[ommander], correcting some & making alterations mistakes [for the new paperback series]. Some of the book's liveliness comes from the fact that this was my 1st adult encounter with the RN – I could describe many things that could scarcely be described again, or not often, in later books – but although I like what I have read (only 100 pp) I may have over-rated it. The last 2 have perhaps more weight & depth.

Next day Patrick was excited to learn that Stuart Bennett had managed to secure for him at auction a magnificent set of the 1810 edition of the *Encyclopaedia Britannica*.[4] This would place at his fingertips the surest guide to the state of knowledge at the precise period of his historical writing, removing all possibility of his perpetrating needless anachronisms.

News of an old friend's grave illness brought from Patrick the poignant adjuration: 'God help all loving couples at the end. Amen, amen.' Five days later Hugh Forster, a cherished visitor at Collioure in earlier years, was dead.

In October Stuart Bennett came again to stay for a couple of nights. Unfortunately Patrick was suffering under great strain, recording that on the day before his departure:

> I felt curst snappish however & said some rude things about US [Bennett being American] – flag-worship & so on – that I regretted later. Still the atmosphere improved much in the course of the v pretty day & we had a most agreeable dinner with cassoulet & Manay 79 & quantities of Banyuls, M bearing up perfectly well.

That evening Patrick candidly observed that his problem arose from the fact that: 'I have an unhappy way of being v glad to see guests on the 1st day & hating them the next, or at least being dreadfully bored & put out.'

Over the years I had frequent occasion to observe this characteristic at first hand. Only latterly have I come to appreciate that it arose from the difficulty he encountered when there was an outside presence (however intrinsically congenial) within the house. He tended to become overridingly tense, and unable to proceed with his work. This in turn made him temporarily doubt his capacity. Had I appreciated this in early years it might have prevented much bewilderment and occasional resentment. Not a few guests departed understandably dismayed, or even angered, at this inexplicable change that unexpectedly overshadowed what had promised to prove a convivial stay.

Returned to *The Thirteen-Gun Salute*, Patrick detected another of his literary troubles – one shared, I imagine, by many authors:

The other day, looking for a reference to Clonfert's fabulations in M[auritius] Command. I read quite a lot of the book: it seemed to me much better, more full of life & of living people in a highly-populated world, than what I am doing now – in short that I was declining. But on recollection I find that I have thought this with every book.

In November Ian Chapman, chairman of Collins, circulated their authors with the unwelcome warning that 'News International plc has announced a predatory bid for William Collins', while declaring the company's intention of vigorously opposing the attack. In common with most of their other prominent authors, Patrick at once rallied to the publisher's defence, 'expressing full support as author and shareholder'. However, the takeover materialized, and in the following February a newly appointed chairman sought to reassure the company's generally sceptical authors.

Nevertheless, with Stuart Proffitt continuing as his editor, Patrick himself did not record any difficulties experienced under the new regime.

On his birthday at the year's ending Patrick noted with quaint precision that he had now achieved '74 years: 27,010 days & odd 29th of February'. This quirky calculation unconsciously echoes the entry he had inscribed in his brother Victor's schoolboy diary more than sixty years earlier: 'Patrick Russ 10 on December 12th on which they say he was born 1914'.

It was in April 1989 that my mother suffered a grievous tragedy. At ninety-nine, her mother Frieda Wicksteed had finally begun failing fast, and she and Patrick flew to England to visit her at her nursing home in Burnham-on-Sea. A week earlier she had suffered a stroke, and when my mother arrived 'she was scarcely present'. All my mother could do was sit sadly beside her, the only consolation being (as she reported to Patrick) that 'the nurses are very, very kind, thank God'. There being nothing more that could be done, she and Patrick returned home. Next morning I telephoned with the sad but not unexpected news that her mother had died. Since her elopement with Patrick fifty years earlier, relations between mother and daughter had been awkward, which in a way made the present loss the more unhappy. Now the link with carefree childhood days at Appledore and on Lundy had passed for ever.

Although my grandmother had lived to a great age, retaining her intelligence, beauty, and charm to the end, the loss inevitably aggravated my parents' accruing concern with mortality. Shortly after their return from England to Collioure, Patrick noted: 'We spoke of our deaths. We should both like to be buried in the village with nothing but local friends (but proper notice to them – Indépendent – Lafitte to cope) & children told later. I shall write Bun a letter to be posted long after.'

My mother's constitutional fragility, which so exercised Patrick, is exemplified by a painful accident occurring at this time: 'Poor

M cracked a floating rib as she started up from a dream about my black hat being left out in the dirty rain.'

Troubles were brewing also in Patrick's family. In the New Year he had received 'a letter from Bun with a present of about £500, v

My mother in North Devon in the 1920s

kind but embarrassing'. For Bun's birthday in March, Patrick sent him a copy of his newly published *The Letter of Marque*, and in the following month Bun mentioned to Joan that he and Patrick were now engaged in regular correspondence, from which he had belatedly come to appreciate the grave and unrelenting nature of my mother's illnesses. Again, in July Bun mentioned in passing to Joan that: 'I hear occasionally from Pat, quite pleasantly. Evidently his wife is very frail indeed and this must limit his ability to travel, but apparently he keeps pretty busy and he speaks of having to write two books.' Unfortunately the prosperous Bun, who privately expressed disparagement of Patrick's writing, patronizingly insisted throughout on assuming that his younger brother was teetering permanently on the edge of bankruptcy.* He had compounded the offence by sending Patrick the £500, while tactlessly reminding him of money he had lent him thirty-five years earlier. As he complained to Joan: 'He seems to resent the fact that in thirty or so years since he and I joined forces in having his house built, I have referred to the fact from time to time . . . he seems to have felt that I was competition.'

An element of farce entered these exchanges, as a cheque for £500 which the irritated Patrick sent 'to shut him up' crossed and recrossed the Atlantic, he having forgotten to enter the date on the cheque.

However, a much more serious difference arose out of a wholly novel contingency. In March 1989 Bun proudly informed Joan that: 'You will be amazed and perhaps amused to know that I have ventured to write an autobiography, complete with photographs, illustrations and so forth, combining the verses I have written in the last sixty years and the prose I have lately put together.'

When the news reached Patrick, he was much perturbed, and promptly issued a strongly worded request to his brother to make no reference to him, fearing (presciently, as it turned out) that revelation of the fact that his original surname was Russ would be seized upon to his disadvantage by envious critics. Bun's response reassured Patrick that 'he makes virtually no mention of me'. However, Patrick, having somehow become aware that the assertion was in fact untrue, issued a further eloquent request for reticence. Unfortunately he received a flat refusal to comply, in

---

* On 7 May 1989 Patrick recorded that: 'We worked out tax papers, from which it appears that the UK unearned income was £5762 gross, unearned, & £17638 for writing & expenses £9225.' In August of the following year 'M showed me her account books – she has been working hard these last days bringing them up to date – & I see to my astonishment that we possess £90000+ in ready money. Shares of course have dropped abt 20%, but even so we can call Croesus cousin.'

what he described as 'a rude, typically domineering letter from Bun', while the latter at the same time declared to Joan that: 'I do not pretend to be an author with a capital "A". For all I know, Pat resents my competition, but he does not need to do so.' Bun's son Charles told me that their father had long grown more and more envious of Patrick's fame. However absurd, this appears to be true, being confirmed by his claim to Joan that Patrick had taken exception to 'a footnote in reference to his prowess as a translator and author and he may, if he sees a copy of the book, which I doubt, become enraged at the idea that I am borrowing a little lustre from his own fame'. Although I am unaware whether Patrick ever obtained a copy of the offending work, he somehow discovered what he considered a damaging betrayal, in consequence of which Bun received what he described to Joan as 'the most fearful letter from Patrick'.

Clearly, the coldness which followed Patrick's outraged response was largely brought about by Bun's tactless bravado. On 16 January 1990 the latter wrote to Joan: 'as far as I am concerned, Patrick has exiled himself from my list. I did not send him any form of greeting for his birthday or Christmas and I have heard nothing from him since the letter which offended me so much.'

This temporary distancing became mutual, with Patrick noting shortly afterwards that: 'I have tossed out all the tedious correspondence with Bun.'*

Bun's magnum opus, privately published in Canada in October 1989 under the odd title *Lady Day Prodigal*, confirmed Patrick's worst fears. Bun included in the text a photograph of the adult Patrick at their meeting in Paris in 1974, and worse still inserted

---

* Bun's unsympathetic refusal to comply with Patrick's modest request appears a trifle hypocritical, in view of the fact that his autobiography withholds all reference to his own first wife (whom he had abandoned at the outbreak of war) and his two sons by that marriage, whom he appears to have treated with marked indifference. I am grateful to his son Charles for a detailed account of this sensitive matter.

a gratuitously tactless note recounting Patrick's marriage 'into the Tolstoy family' and describing him as 'a keen amateur ornithologist and an excellent writer'.

In reality, of course, the likelihood of anyone outside the Russ family's reading the book (half of which is given over to doggerel verses composed by its enthusiastic author) was very small indeed.*

Despite all this, the rift was eventually healed in the following spring of 1991, when Patrick received a letter from Bun belatedly explaining that he had been in hospital for months, having suffered a stroke and becoming afflicted by a dangerous bone cancer. On 3 May 1991 Bun's secretary reported that 'he has received a very pleasant letter and 2 books from Patrick! Mr Russ is very pleased.' Thenceforward cordial correspondence was resumed between the brothers, together with Bun's wife Fifi and daughter Elizabeth. At the end of the year Patrick received 'A letter from Bun, speaking of his cancer with great fortitude – moving.' Patrick responded by return, 'kindly to Bun'. This affectionate relationship continued up to Bun's death in the following summer. On 5 February 1992 Patrick noted: 'I should have said yesterday that there was a rambling letter from poor Bun, wanting me to come out, together with a note from his secretary.'

If blame is to be apportioned at all in the dispute which for a brief year interrupted the brothers' friendship, it surely lies primarily with Bun's perverse refusal to accept Patrick's fully justified (if indignantly expressed) request to be omitted in any readily identifiable form from the published memoir. Overall, however, it is clear that the difference owed much to long-term misunderstandings between two brothers of very different temperaments, who had been able to meet on only two or three occasions over the past half-century. Nevertheless, even the temporary coldness that did occur would have been greatly curtailed had Patrick become

---

* When Dean King's lucubrations were first launched in the press, Patrick was for a while persuaded (wrongly) that they originated in Bun's tactless work.

earlier aware of Bun's tragic final sickness. This sad chapter closed when his widow Fifi telephoned on 27 July with the melancholy but long-anticipated news that Patrick's cherished childhood companion was no more. From the biographer's point of view, the loss of the letter of condolence Patrick wrote to Fifi four days later is much to be regretted.

Thus the evidence is wholly at variance with Dean King's groundless allegation that Patrick arbitrarily severed relations with his family. Overall, his relationship with the brother who was closest to him is well summarized by Bun's daughter Elizabeth, who remained close to her father throughout this time:

Because my Dad and Pat kept up a steady correspondence, Dad would always give me Pat's letters to read. I felt very kindly towards him – he was the only real uncle with whom I had the feeling of any familial connection. (My mother's only sibling, a brother died when I was quite young but because of living in Canada, I had never met him.) Dad didn't seem to keep in regular contact with any of his other brothers – however, he did correspond with all his sisters and perhaps you know that he assisted with Nora's move to Victoria. He acquired a house – a pretty cottage style – close by his and they visited often after that.) Some years later – it was December 1967 – when I married, Pat sent the wedding gift of a Wedgewood teapot which, as I mentioned, I still have.

In June Patrick was gratified to learn that our daughter Anastasia found *The Golden Ocean* listed among set books for her examination, and on the 23rd 'It was Nikolai's birthday, & when we drank his health we wished him a fortunate year to come with even more than usual fervour.' The emphasis reflected the forthcoming trial hearing for Lord Aldington's libel action, which had now been postponed to the autumn. Patrick followed the complex succession of events throughout with deep interest and concern. While impressed by the extent of public sympathy for our cause, as well as the impressive list of public figures (including his fellow authors Graham Greene and Alexander Solzhenitsyn) who had declared themselves in my favour, he remained presciently apprehensive of the outcome.

In Collioure there were further signs of change in the air – not all unpleasant to Patrick:

> After lunch . . . I swam Au Racou: crowds, but clean fresh sea, people having fun, quietly upon the whole. Many Dutch. Bare bosoms a matter of course, pleasant in the girls who have grown up with it & are utterly unselfconscious. I swam my 100 strokes, sunned for ½ hour & came back.

Two days later he returned to the beach to swim, 'in the hope of natural sleep. Many Dutch: many bosoms, showing extraordinary variation even in the young. They are less attractive than I thought.' With August crowds arrived, less appealing than the Dutch bosoms:

> Evening acerbity went rather far & I walked through the crowds in the night – had not been there for a great while – getting my espadrilled feet wet, seeing many changes, among others a proliferation of 'art galleries' all brightly lit, all obviously derivative – people gaze into them with a look of earnest stupidity.

Happier considerations were, however, in the offing. On 27 September Patrick was gratified to receive 'a v agreeable letter' from an editor at the major American publishing house of Norton. It began promisingly:

> Dear Mr. O'Brian,
> I do not think you can imagine, even with my help, the pleasure it gives me to write this letter, or the even greater pleasure I have had from reading the few O'Brian titles I have allowed myself thus far.

Although I look forward to publishing the entire Aubrey/Maturin series, nothing will compare to the almost guilty delight I take in simply reading. The publishing will be a satisfaction, and a good deal of serious work.

There followed an outline of the Norton proposal, which was 'to publish THE THIRTEEN GUN SALUTE in hardcover at the same time that we launch the first two titles of the series in a trade paperback format'.* Their ultimate intention was to publish all of the series, both those already in print and those to come.

The editor's attention had been drawn to the series in London, during a visit to the literary agency Sheil Land, with which Richard Scott Simon's agency had recently amalgamated. During his flight home he read *The Reverse of the Medal* with mounting delight, and swiftly realized that Patrick had mastered to a wonderfully effective degree an almost entirely original means of withdrawing the curtain that divides us from our past.

The day after his receipt of this letter, Patrick responded with enthusiasm:

Many thanks for your very kind letter of September 21st. I am delighted that you should be publishing my naval tales and more delighted still that you personally should like them – it does make such a difference in the sometimes difficult relations between author and publisher. (Have you, in parenthesis, seen the recent Proust-Gallimard correspondence? It throws fascinating light on a connexion of this kind).

His only minor reservation lay in a suggestion for promoting the series as 'better than Hornblower'. In his draft response, he explained that 'I am after all aiming higher than Forester did and it may [P's own deletion] be that John Bayley's kind words on the

---

* In the event it was *The Letter of Marque* that they published in August 1990.

blurb of *The Letter of Marque* and Binyon's on that of *The Far Side of the World*' might be preferable. The editor willingly conceded the reservation, declaring 'I take your point about"different from Hornblower," and it will be part of our job to suggest to the reader that there are pleasures awaiting him of which he, or at least Forester, had no conception.'

Ten years had passed since the series had last found an American publisher,* and Patrick could now look forward on a permanent basis to the transatlantic success that had so often appeared secure, only to elude him.

Meanwhile, *The Thirteen-Gun Salute* was published in the UK in October. Richard Ollard was delighted, on receiving a copy of the typescript, to find the book dedicated to himself. Reviews were overwhelmingly favourable, with the Oxford academic T.J. Binyon writing in the *Sunday Times* what Stuart Proffitt considered 'the most extensive and appreciative notice, I think, any of the novels has had for some years':

> Considered as a whole, the sequence is an immense achievement. That O'Brian is not as well known as he undoubtedly deserves to be stems from the fact that he has chosen to write in a genre at present devalued (that of the historical novel) and has, moreover, taken as his subject the navy of the Napoleonic wars, thus inviting a comparison with CS Forester's Hornblower series.
>
> But other than that subject matter, the authors have little in common. Forester writes essentially straightforward adventure stories, whereas O'Brian's novels are adult, subtle and complex . . . His heroes – the reckless extrovert Aubrey, and Maturin, introverted and suspicious, a perfect intelligence agent – are not static, but change and mature with time.

---

* *Desolation Island* had been published by the unsatisfactory firm of Stein and Day in 1978. On 13 August 1979 a contract was signed with Berkley Publishing Corporation for *The Fortune of War* (providing for a $5,000 advance), but nothing came of this.

Patrick replied that he regarded the review as 'one of the most percipient and valuable that I have had, and wonderfully encouraging. On the other hand it does mean that I have to go on writing at my very highest pitch.'

Throughout this time Patrick continued concerned by my forthcoming legal action, undertaken by Lord Aldington to rebut my accusations arising from his primary role in major war crimes perpetrated in Austria in 1945. 'M telephoned Nikolai, cheerful & confident, busy answering the opponent's case. Trial starts tomorrow & is likely to go on till Xmas, God help him.'

Patrick's gloomy reservation was to prove more than justified by the event. The trial and its protracted ramifications represent another story which can only be touched upon here.

My mother remained an invalid throughout this time, her condition not helped by tensions aroused by the trial: 'No English papers, & M is low about N.' Three days later Patrick noted: 'This was the day the Berlin Wall came down.' None of us anticipated that this would eventually result in President Yeltsin's personal intervention, granting me access to documentary evidence confirming that I was correct in all my principal conclusions condemned by successive judges on the English bench. As the trial drew to its close, so damaging were the indications of Aldington's guilt and consequent perjury, that even Patrick began to entertain a momentary expectation that Judge Davies might, against every indication, prove honest after all. 'The telephone rang in the evening – I had a sudden wild hope that it would be N with news of his success: M answered: a wrong number, & rude.'

On 1 December: 'Then in the evening M telephoned Natasha: her news was so shocking that we could not take anything like full possession of it.' The proceedings had concluded with the judge's summing-up. He adopted the precaution of denying the jury access to the 41-day trial transcript and the hundreds of official documents on which the case depended.* This meant that the jury effectively had to reach its verdict on the basis of three days' inevitably tendentious summing-up by Aldington's counsel, followed by the weekend break, and then what amounted to a further three-day plea on Aldington's behalf by the judge. In consequence, he contrived to persuade the jury to find me guilty, and above all (as he emphasized) 'not to award Mickey Mouse damages'. To this they obediently responded with the record award of £1,500,000 (subsequently condemned by the European Court of Justice as a gross infringement of my right to free speech). Patrick wrote to me on 6 December with burning indignation:

> My dear Nikolai,
>
> Many a time have I tried to speak to you on the telephone, but always in vain, so I shall write the few words that I had so wished to say as early as possible: first that the case was heard before a slow, foolish, malignant fumbling old man, so prejudiced from beginning to end, from 'self-styled' to 'wet'† and beyond that he made the earlier Dreyfus tribunals look impartial. And secondly that your reputation has not suffered – far from it – in the minds of any people whose good opinion is worth having.
>
> With much love to you both and to the children
>
> Yours ever
>
> Patrick

---

* One juryman's inability to read the oath at the outset of the trial revealed him to be illiterate. The judge pronounced the consideration irrelevant. He further declared, unprecedentedly, that he had personally investigated each juror's background.

† Judge Michael Davies had instructed the jury that I was to be regarded as a 'self-styled historian'. Patrick commented in his diary: 'No more so than Gibbon, who did not even have a degree.' Davies further suggested to the jury that they regard Nigel Nicolson, a leading witness for the defence who had fought with the Grenadier Guards from North Africa across Italy to Austria, as 'a wet'. No record of Judge Davies's military service during the War has yet been discovered, although he was eighteen in 1939.

Having learned that the governors of Wellington College had unanimously agreed to waive Alexandra's fees for as long as she remained there, he and my mother promptly offered to meet our second daughter Anastasia's school fees.

New Year's Day of 1990 brought heartening news that the fiery spirit of the *Colliourencques* had not been altogether extinguished by encroachments of modernity. In his diary Patrick noted:

> More gossip: Odette, having run into a sinless car at Argelès [the next village north of Collioure] calmed her trembling nerves with whiskey & Coca C. Then leapt into her car again, drove to Pierre's love-nest & tried to kick the door in. Later Pierre came & said he was sorry: might he return?

The petite Odette's dauntless spirit is exemplified by the fact that her faithless husband had in younger days been judo instructor to French paratroops garrisoned in the Fort du Miradou above the town.

Meanwhile, Patrick was experiencing one of his periodic bouts of self-doubt. By the beginning of March he had completed *The Nutmeg of Consolation*, and confided to his diary: 'I wish I could think of another naval tale – just the bones. Writing them has become a way of life.' In April his publishers forwarded a request for passages from his books to be included in a forthcoming *Faber Book of Tales of the Sea*. To this he replied that: 'so long as I am not in the company of [Dudley] Pope or [Alexander] Kent, I do not mind appearing in the anthology.' This might appear a little churlish, but for the fact that a certain class of reviewer persisted in assuming that all novels set in the time of Nelson's navy were much of a muchness – which apparently did not amount to much. The editor, a retired naval officer, took grave offence at what he considered Patrick's excessive fastidiousness. He did not appreciate that the latter's concern arose from a real apprehension that readers of the anthology might assume from the association that his were no more than semi-juvenile seafaring adventure stories.

More constructively, an editor at Norton came up with a suggestion that the naval tales should be accompanied by an illustration of a contemporary man-of-war's rigging, etc. As others have advanced the same idea, Patrick's response is interesting:

> I think it would be a mistake to have a diagram of a ship. It cannot be done well in a small space, and anything else would throw the whole thing badly out of balance – would make it look technical, complex, boring. Ignorance of the smiting-line fairlead is immaterial; a painstaking search for it would be fatal to the narrative.*

However, this was not an issue momentous enough to fight over, and the diagram appeared in the US edition of *The Letter of Marque*.

In April Proffitt reported that Charlton Heston, one of Patrick's prominent admirers, had bought Geoff Hunt's original painting for the cover of *The Thirteen-Gun Salute*. A few weeks later Patrick received a friendly invitation from Heston to attend the London première of his film of *Treasure Island*. In view of the actor's enthusiasm over the possibility of making a film of one of his novels, Stuart Proffitt urged the benefit of accepting the invitation. In the event my mother's ill-health prevented her travelling, and Patrick journeyed by train and ferry to London, where on the evening before the première he gave a dinner at Brooks's for Heston and his son Fraser, which proved to be a success. 'A better party than I had expected – nothing brilliant,

---

* Patrick had evidently changed his mind since he wrote *The Golden Ocean* more than thirty years earlier. As my mother's diary records, on that occasion he himself provided both the diagram of HMS *Centurion* and an accompanying list of sea terms. However, I assume these were requested by the publisher, with whose requirements he could scarcely quibble at this delicate opening of his momentous series of maritime tales.

but general amiability, unusual appreciation, & no personal questions at any time.'

On the following day he attended the film, on which, however, he was less enthusiastic: 'Hestons welcoming, kind about yesterday. Film indifferent – much overacting, rolling of eyes, violence – but with some pretty good pieces of ship at sea. Hestons kinder still afterwards – many colleagues who like my books, much praise . . .'

Later that year Proffitt reported on a publishers' meeting with the actor in New York, at which he had discussed publication of his memoirs. On his return Proffitt reported to Patrick that:

Naturally he did not want to talk about himself at all, but about you, which I must say made an impression on my boss, who was with me . . . When I asked him what he wanted from his publishers he said, 'To be in distinguished company, and of course there is no company more distinguished than that of Patrick O'Brian'.

My mother's persistently poor condition constantly troubled Patrick while in London. The day after his return: 'Coming down [from Manay] we looked at the cemetery. The site indeed is v fine, but I had misunderstood Ms account (she had been there with Hélène [Camps]) & the shining granite vaults & artificial flowers distressed me.'

The old cemetery in the town had long been full, and while Patrick was away my mother began enquiring about graves. Today, the new cemetery on the hill above the town has become a place of pilgrimage for Patrick's many admirers from around the globe.

On 10 September my mother arrived at the hospital in Perpignan, where she underwent examination by a cardiologist. He recommended a pacemaker, but not as a matter of urgency. On her return home, gravely confused by the effect of powerful anaesthetics, she slipped and tore skin off her leg while descending the iron ladder to their bedroom below. Her stay in the hospital 'was all horribly familiar from Eastbourne & the last operation', reflected Patrick – no human contact, constant prattling, and frenetic activity. Next day, fortunately, she was greatly improved and acceptant of kind Dr Manya's recommendation that the pacemaker be fitted as a matter of urgency by a specialist from Toulouse. On learning that its installation should greatly improve walking, gardening, and even travel, Patrick felt an exultation hard to contain.

A few days later, however, my mother awoke in the night suffering from cruel spasmodic pains in her bowels. Together they were rushed to the hospital in an ambulance. By the time she was settled with a tube passing from her nose to her stomach the hospital cafeteria had closed, and Patrick was obliged to walk to Perpignan station for a meal. Passing through a tunnel along the way, his attention was attracted to graffiti, among which he found worthy of record that 'someone had written FUCK OFF & someone else had added EVERYONE'.

That night Patrick joined my mother in the hospital, where both slept exceedingly badly: 'at one time M was in such a bad way as to forget French & feel she was dying'. Despite much suffering, the operation was pronounced a success. It is unclear to me what precisely was wrong at this stage, but my mother's fearfully debilitated condition meant that she underwent several days of suffering, attended throughout by an anguished Patrick. It was not until the end of the month that she was able to return home, with the prospect of insertion of the pacemaker in three weeks' time. Patrick was briefly consoled 'with vivid dreams (topless nurse in bed with me, though with disappointingly pure motives)'. But on waking he was plagued by 'Sombre, sombre thoughts. And the old, damned back-ache.'

Throughout the coming weeks my mother's condition continued to distress Patrick, with inevitably ill effect on his work:

M's heart is worrying. Sometimes, for no evident reason & when she is sitting down, it takes to beating at 110 or even more; & sometimes the pulse is v fast . . . I hope all this has not divorced me from the book again.

. . . I typed, but with only moderate satisfaction (I shall lose my way in this book if I do not get well back into it quite soon).

The year 1990 – pivotal in many respects, troubled in others, ended on a melancholy note. Walking up the ridge to the point assigned as his milestone turning-point, Patrick found even that remote spot sadly altered. Vegetation and rocks looked oddly different, and the white stones with which he had marked note-worthy days had mysteriously disappeared.

XIV

The Sunlit Uplands

Words move, music moves
Only in time; but that which is only living
Can only die. Words, after speech, reach
Into the silence. Only by the form, the pattern,
Can words or music reach
The stillness, as a Chinese jar still
Moves perpetually in its stillness.

T.S. Eliot, *Burnt Norton*

The New Year of 1991 saw no amelioration in my mother's pitiful state of health: '17° & 6°: an even more beautiful day. But M was poorly throughout it – heart 112, aorta beating violently, general malaise – to such a degree that she wisely retired before the Helmuts came.'

Helmut Vakily, a painter of Persian origin, had hitherto been a welcome visitor over the years – but she was no longer up to receiving visitors. So wretched indeed was my mother's condition, that Patrick took the unprecedented step of asking his literary agent for information about a professional typist. Fortunately, however, for the present she continued capable of summoning up her strength for the task when occasion demanded.

What Patrick could not have foreseen was that a bare week was to pass before he encountered one of the greatest transformations in his literary career. On 7 January 1991: 'We had just been picking grapefruit when Christopher MacL[ehose, at HarperCollins] telephoned: said there was Snow's piece on the front of NY Times – he was touchingly pleased . . .'

Towards the end of 1990 a devoted American fan, Richard T. Stearns, 'snarling and raging', had sent Patrick a forthright denunciation of an ill-natured review of *The Letter of Marque* by a pseudonymous writer in the *New York Times Book Review*. Patrick responded appreciatively, noting sadly that:

> I am sorry that the New York Times man did not like <u>The Letter of Marque</u>, and I particularly regret that his review should have arrived on the very morning that I intended to work again on my fifteenth naval tale after an enforced interruption of two months: praise from such a source would have had little effect, but quite illogically disparagement, when I am in the act of writing, angers and depresses me to a disproportionate extent. In this case it has stopped the flow.

He was not exaggerating. His childhood unhappiness had instilled in him an instinctive fear and resentment of adverse reflection on him or his work, above all when it appeared (as in this case) aggressively malignant.

On this occasion, however, the historian and novelist Richard Snow unexpectedly pulled out all the stops to laud Patrick's creation, in one of America's most influential literary journals. A few days after MacLehose's telephone call, a copy of the *New York Times Book Review* arrived at Collioure, a New Year's gift whose effect on the little household may be imagined. Snow had persuaded the editor to allow him nearly three densely packed pages, in which he exalted to the skies 'AN AUTHOR I'D WALK THE PLANK FOR'.

After recounting his earlier bafflement on prematurely encountering *Master and Commander* – which threw him back into the arms of the seafaring novels of Alexander Kent and the like – Snow subsequently happened on a second-hand copy of the novel at a street fair. Whether it was because he was older, or on account of a growing fascination with history, he now found himself gripped by an unexpected passion:

. . . this time I understood what I was reading. For one thing – and I had managed to miss this completely on my first go-around – it was funny; every page shone with humor, sometimes mordant, sometimes wise, and always growing naturally out of the situations it illuminated.

But behind the humor, behind the storms and the broadside duels that I *had* understood on my first encounter, loomed something larger: the shape and texture of a whole era. Without ever seeming antiquarian or pedantic or showy, O'Brian summoned up with casual omniscience the workaday magic of a vanished time. The furniture of life was all unobtrusively here: clothes, curtains, the sauce on the fish, the absent-minded politeness of daily intercourse with grocers and friends, everything whose inconsequence insures its almost immediate oblivion, and which is so hard to retrieve without an ostentatious show of 'research.' In fact, the story was told with such scrupulous respect for every nuance of the world in which it unfolded that I might have been reading the prose of Jane Austen's seafaring brothers (two served in the Royal Navy), had they shared her gifts. Before I finished the book, I was convinced it was the best historical novel I'd ever read.

Today the piece remains one of the most effective introductions to Patrick's masterpiece that one could wish. On receiving a copy from Stuart Proffitt, Patrick gratefully recorded: 'He also enclosed a piece about the series by Snow, perhaps not v wise but full of earnest praise, & fulsome though it was it had a most encouraging effect on bringing XV [his current work *Clarissa Oakes*] to life.'

The 'perhaps not v wise' reflects no more than self-mocking modesty, and Snow's review more than sufficed to restore Patrick's equanimity. He wrote to the writer, praising his 'long, deeply perceptive and encouraging article', which 'gave me great pleasure', and enclosing a copy of his *Joseph Banks*.

Despite this fillip, during the early part of the year Patrick suffered renewed bouts of depression, arising from a combination of concern for my mother's persistent worrying weakness,* and his own consequent difficulty in moving his novel forward. Seeking to divert himself during a gloomy February:

These evenings I read Le Faye's monumental JA,[1] trying to remember the relationships. Qu. is this digging into private affairs, particularly money (privatissimo), decent? JA's own background is said to give one a greater understanding of her books: I doubt it. Of the books as an accurate mirror of her time, yes: as novels, no.[†]

It is not difficult to detect personal considerations in Patrick's dismissal of literary biography, with its 'digging into private affairs'. His publishers found this frustrating when seeking to stimulate publicity for his writing. Their attitude is understandable. For a start, knowledge of Jane Austen's 'own background' must clearly assist in establishing whether her novels do in fact represent 'an accurate mirror of her time'. Furthermore, Patrick's view is scarcely consistent with his unalloyed admiration for Boswell's magnificent *Life of Johnson*, in which the smallest detail is included to flesh out the subject's life.

Unfortunately, my own continuingly precarious legal plight ensuing on the disastrous Aldington trial in 1989 added much to

---

* A typical diary entry at this time reads: 'Poor M's asthenia grows worse: she was v kind about Ch V in the morning, but by the evening quite worn out – inspissitated gloom with both, so catching it is.'

† Terry Zobeck reminds me that Patrick discusses Jane Austen's earnings at some length in his introduction to the HarperCollins edition of *Mansfield Park* (*The Complete Novels of Jane Austen* (London, 1993). Indeed, slipped into Patrick's copy of *Jane Austen's Letters* is his three-page analysis of her finances!

my parents' worries throughout this time. On the other hand, compensation lay in the fact that reassurances of the justice of our cause continued to appear. In January, Patrick visited an Englishman living at nearby Sorède: 'He spoke, not knowing of the relationship, of N's trial & how it discredited Eng. justice.'

At the beginning of March 'M wrote to Georgie as we had agreed, promising help in emergency to [£]10–15000'. Later in the month: 'Nikolai telephoned in the evening, v handsome about our offer of contingent 10,000 +, & delighted by Nutmeg's reception. Position worrying and uncertain, depending it seems on Aldington's whim – possibility of European court.'

Throughout this worrying time (my mother's pacemaker afforded her constant trouble, before it was discovered that it required readjustment) consolation was afforded by a regular visitor, whose presence much comforted them: 'Robin came down & flitted about the garden with us, gently singing from every branch . . .' There was also a 'hedgepig', who devoured bread and milk each evening but was rarely to be seen. Nevertheless: 'Book was v heavy going: what <u>has</u> flowed in my mind, even weeks ago, no longer flows; but by flogging I did 2 pp.'

As ever, Patrick's dreams tended to reflect their troubling circumstances: 'I lost my way, friends, belongings & having wasted time looking at a false narwhal horn (in fact twisted goat) I ended on a desolate railway line far out in an unknown countryside.'

A few nights later: 'Such a vile, everlasting dream: I was looking for Peugeot's HQ in some vast, shabby town with confusing streets – could not find it – lost myself & the car – on & on, hope dying – all grey.'

Collectors of first editions of Patrick's novels will wish they had been by when Patrick put out his dustbins in the second week of July:

We culled the shameful stores of my books & discarded another 3 sacks – another small one to come. I had been stupid in my 1st attack, throwing away all but 1 Surgeon's M.* The plan is now for me to have a set of paperbacks, M the same with her hardbacks, & a store of 1 H[ardback] + 2 P[aperbacks].

He was shortly to regret this precipitate action, when in November John Saumarez-Smith of the Heywood Hill bookshop told him that first editions of the earlier hardback naval tales were beginning to fetch about £40 a volume.

Further in July Patrick received gratifying news that he had been elected a Fellow of the Royal Society of Literature, founded in 1820 by King George IV to 'reward literary merit and excite literary talent'. The honour would have been particularly gratifying to Patrick, as George IV was the aesthetic (if dissolute and neurotic) Regent to whom his favourite author Jane Austen dedicated her *Emma*. From his literary agent he learned further that a copy of *The Nutmeg of Consolation* had been added to the Queen's bookshelves at Balmoral. (Patrick replied to his editor Stuart Proffitt that: 'I was charmed to learn that the Queen should have (among other things) Nutmeg. I think only Queen Anne had closer naval connexions.') In November HarperCollins provided total sales figures for the fourteen novels in the maritime series already published. In Britain alone it amounted to the satisfying totals of 73,353 hardback and 757,291 paperback![†]

As though all this were not encouragement enough, he received confirmation that the British Library proposed to publish (for the first time in the case of such an undertaking) a bibliography and literary appreciation of his published works, under the skilled editorship of Arthur Cunningham, the Library's Head of Publications. Patrick was requested to provide an autobiographical sketch, an

---

* Terry Zobek comments ruefully: 'The rarest of them all – I paid $1,500 for mine!'

† On 2 December 1991 Norton in the USA reported sales figures of 20,300 for the three hardcovers published, and 89,247 for eight hardbacks. This was of course only the beginning of Patrick's astonishing transatlantic success.

invitation he guardedly approved. An underlying worry accompanied this signal honour, however. In the first place, what was he to do about his juvenile works published under the name Patrick Russ, a name he had spent so long concealing; and, as a corollary, how was he to continue sustaining the privacy to which he so firmly consigned that earlier existence he had long ago put behind him?*

This belated recognition of his achievement was gratifying, but remorselessly advancing years continued to provide nagging reminders of human frailty. Meeting in the streets of Perpignan one day, his old friend Pierre de Bordas showed Patrick his right hand racked with arthritis, explaining that he was retiring from his dental practice. 'How pleasant he was, but how we shall miss him,' he reflected. Pierre and his wife Rirette were among their little circle of close friends, with whom Patrick and my mother could share their deepest concerns.

Such concerns included Patrick's longstanding confrontation with the invention of the automobile. Driving home down the mountains from a shopping expedition in Le Perthus 'in a shocking head wind', 'something fell from the back seat – stopped to put it right – the open door flew out of M's hand, wrecking the hinge. After she had held it for some miles I tied it more or less shut' – after which they just about made it home.

Following another particularly bad asthma attack, Patrick asked himself: 'Qu. How much is state of mind?' Despite the constant assault of such painful bouts of illness, he finally completed his book on 19 May 'with quite a powerful burst of work'. Provisionally entitling it *The Truelove* (the title retained by the American publisher), he was in due course induced by my mother to rename it *Clarissa Oakes* – the title it bore for the British market.† By 10

---

* It was about this time that he even raised objection with Proffitt to the revelation of the year in which he was born!

† Stuart Proffitt reported back that: 'Both Richard [Ollard] and I greatly prefer <u>Clarissa Oakes</u> as the title. It has a nicely Jane Austenish ring to it, and may encourage critics to make those pleasing comparisons with Austen again.'

June my mother had recovered sufficiently from what had long appeared an endless succession of wearisome ailments, and 'began typing <u>Truelove</u> & became calmer, happier, better'. Despite her physical weakness and constant pain, on 3 July she 'finished the book – such a feat!' exclaimed Patrick gratefully.

When he received what he described as 'a pleasant letter' from Norton with 'proposals for a photograph of me on the next jacket', he commented bluntly: 'No, sir.' His intense dislike of being photographed seems at first glance odd, as he was in fact to the end of his life a good-looking man. It aroused in him an oddly visceral fear, and in addition he was adversely affected by those photographers who misguidedly require a fixed pose, which he like many found stressful. The few good pictures taken throughout his life tend to be snapshots, particularly those rare ones catching him unawares. It is possible that the irrational malignity evinced by some of his critics was in part intensified by the strained – almost menacing – appearance posed photographs tended to give him.

On the other hand, he continued enthusiastic over Geoff Hunt's masterly dustjacket designs. As the latter's annotated plan for the cover of *Clarissa Oakes* exemplifies, the pains he took to accommodate them to textual detail are surely unparalleled since George Cruikshank's collaboration with Dickens and Ainsworth. Despite expressing a minor reservation over the narrative passage selected for illustration, Stuart Proffitt expressed his confidence that 'it will make a fine jacket'.

Apart from constant attacks of ill-health, my parents continued absorbed in my unremitting battle with the British government and courts. In September Patrick received a 'long letter from N, who is really ill-used by the Establishment with all its dirty ramifications'. On 16 October:

The post seemed ordinary enough, but it contained not another history of N's trial but an explosive series of letters from Sir

B[ernard] Braine, an MP & P[rivy] Councillor, to Min of State
FO laying out FO's complete & possibly criminal duplicity –
concealment & even destruction of documents, all in favour of
Ld A & his friends.

The voluminous correspondence was indeed explosive. The
Foreign Secretary Douglas Hurd was familiar with Lord Aldington,
both socially and in the latter's capacity as Deputy Conservative
Party Chairman and a former junior minister. Well before my trial
opened in 1989, the Foreign Office and Ministry of Defence had
secretly authorized the withdrawal from the Public Record Office
of numerous files vital to the defence case. Many of these with
equal secrecy were passed to the covertly government-commis-
sioned 'Cowgill Committee', which in close collaboration with
Aldington published a succession of professedly independent
'reports' before and after the trial, alleging that I had misrepre-
sented evidence and engaged in other gratuitous chicanery in my
book *The Minister and the Massacres*.

On discovering that a file essential to the conduct of my case
was among those removed from public access during the trial, I
had applied to the Public Record Office for its restoration. After
a protracted delay, which conveniently lasted for the duration of
the trial, I eventually made further application – to be informed
that the file had become unfortunately 'lost'. I reported this to my
friend Sir Bernard Braine MP, then Father of the House of
Commons. As a fellow Privy Councillor he took the matter up
with Hurd, who responded that the file in question had just been
discovered by a cleaner in a Foreign Office broom-cupboard!

After conducting his own investigation, Sir Bernard concluded:

This disgraceful activity . . . was designed to pervert the course of
justice in a case concerned with one of the most shameful episodes
in British history. I have been in parliament for 42 years, and have
held office under two prime ministers. I cannot recollect a previous

instance of officials conniving at the suppression of records in order to prevent justice being done in the courts.

While I continued my fruitless battle against the British Establishment, being represented in successive hearings without payment by eminent lawyers outraged by this and other evidence of covert official interference by Aldington's colleagues and friends in government and the judiciary, Patrick and my mother remained frustrated and depressed by their inability to do much more than sympathize with my plight. It was in a way worse for them, being unable to assist in what was plainly becoming a battle that could not be won. In contrast, I was buoyed up by a combination of belief in the rectitude of our case, support pouring in from around the globe, and a rash conviction that we would nevertheless triumph in the end. In view of the undisguised antagonism of every judge before whom I appeared, my misguided optimism can with hindsight only be regarded as quixotic.

Towards the end of October I met Patrick during a visit to London (my mother was too weak to accompany him), when he was concerned to learn everything about our progress: 'Pretty good dinner, much talk, he looks v well but thinner,' as Patrick noted afterwards. He generously offered to pay our son Dmitri's school fees for his first year at Eton. Beyond that, he could not be sufficiently confident of his financial position or health, but if we were prepared to take that risk he would continue paying for as long as was required. In the event the popularity of his books continued to accrue dramatically, and Dmitri eventually passed into Oxford, with Patrick throughout continuing his generous support.

Although Patrick's (and my mother's, naturally) assistance to their grandson was motivated by familial affection, it seems likely that he also derived vicarious gratification from seeing Dmitri enjoy the education he himself had been denied by his own father's improvidence. Equally, it will be recalled how much he and my mother had sacrificed in their earlier, impoverished, days for the education of his son Richard.

Patrick crowned his kindnesses to us in 1991 by sending me for Christmas a magnificent copy of John Selden's *Titles of Honor* (London, 1631). He had obtained this wonderfully erudite work in June from Stuart Bennett, and might justifiably have been a little reluctant to part with what he described in his accompanying letter as 'a bulky great Christmas card'. Patrick's letters to all his correspondents were invariably perceptive, funny and lively, and it comes as something of a shock when I find him complaining at about this time 'how bad I am at writing letters – slow, laborious & I am afraid affected'.

Finally came the festival itself, a picture of domesticity:

Christmas Day, & as beautiful a Nativity as I can remember, pure sun, never a cloud, clean air, cold in the shadow: I picked an opening standard rose-bud this morning & a full-blown rambler in the afternoon. Now, after dinner (smoked salmon from Galway, saddle of lamb, Christmas pud) I sit with a glass of brandy at hand . . .

In January 1992 Collioure was visited by heavy snow. At the end of the month Patrick wrote to his literary agent:

Did the papers tell you about our snow-storm? I think your gardening heart would have bled for me when the vile stuff retreated enough for me to go down & see what damage it had done. Flattened gardenias, cistuses, rosemary & the like I had expected, but not a broad-topped ancient arbutus, 25 feet high, snapped off with its trunk broken right through 2 or 3 feet from the ground, nor branches torn off the grapefruit-tree. Still, the broad beans, deep under snow, survived perfectly well . . .

Just before Christmas they had treated themselves to 'an exceedingly powerful but silent motor-car, the idea being to drive Mary to England in it . . . I brought it home safely enough, but then it ran powerfully and silently into the garage wall.' Shortly before travelling to London for a week Patrick undertook a trial run to Narbonne, to see how my mother would fare in so long a drive. Fortunately she found it comfortable, and on 27 February 1992 Patrick, wisely preferring a shorter journey by road, drove to Toulouse airport, whence they flew to Gatwick. Arrived in London, my mother found herself quite done up by the journey, and 'the fuss at the end (finding keys, room etc) destroyed her and she went to bed'.

Next day Patrick was interviewed by the author Francis Spufford ('Such an agreeable young man'), after which he was reluctantly driven to Kensington to be photographed. A couple of days later he signed three hundred copies of *The Nutmeg of Consolation* at Hatchard's bookshop in Piccadilly. That evening his publishers held a dinner in his honour. The guests included T.J. Binyon, A.S. Byatt, Iris Murdoch, John Bayley, Penelope Fitzgerald, Richard Snow (who had written the recent enthusiastic review article which caused so potent a stir in the United States), A.N. Wilson, and other well-known figures in the literary world. Patrick was troubled to find 'poor Alan [Judd] with no black tie, sad'. Patrick himself had been worried about tying his black tie correctly, having brought a made-up spare in case of emergency. His concern arose from a perennial fear (at times entering his dreams) of finding himself incorrectly dressed for a formal occasion. Richard Ollard made a 'kind speech', to which Patrick responded with what he modestly feared was a 'feeble reply'.

Next morning Richard Ollard called, 'bringing a man who wanted to shake my hand'. After this, Patrick was interviewed by Judd for BBC radio: this proved an intelligent exchange, which to his relief he felt went well. On the last day of his visit to London the dreaded event was all but anticipated, when he 'was v nearly killed by a large van racing up towards Piccadilly as I crossed from Brooks's to Boodles, thinking myself safe ½ way over'.

The visit, which had pleased Patrick and his publisher alike, had proved a great success. Back at home, he took time to overcome an anticlimactic restlessness ('We both feel a general anxiety: it is not directed at any particular cause, though causes can always be found'). Wrestling with tax returns continued a perennial headache, and he requested me to confirm if required that he was domiciled at our home in Berkshire. I naturally agreed, but have never discovered whether this proved advantageous or not. I rather doubt that Patrick really knew either.*

On 28 May they were greatly encouraged by yet another startling new development in my ongoing legal battle:

> M could not finish dinner – lay down – early bed. I was following her about 1030 when N rang – such news! Guardian article prompted reply from a (I hope highly-placed & retired) Min of Defence official who told Guardian journalist that he was sick of the whole thing – the way the trial had been managed – all M of D resources open to Ld A – his counsel† briefed by Govt every evening – concealed documents – the lot. Journalist says this will be front-page news & an unholy stink.

In fact the official in question was still *en poste*, and proved to have been appointed to head the covert government operation to pervert the course of justice. The journalist in question was Richard Norton-Taylor, a fearless investigator in the high tradition of the old *Manchester Guardian*. The yet braver official met him to explain the whole undercover operation, insisting only that their discussion should be held in the open on the Embankment, to obviate any risk of eavesdropping by the authorities. Subsequently my lawyers obtained copies of sensational documents, including obliging

---

* 'M is much harrassed by this tax qu. – spent much time typing the figures – I disappointed her by not sending them off today – a reluctance to part with £10000 odd – is peace of mind worth it? Data is so slight – vague memories of municipal control in 92.' In 1997 Patrick privately confessed to forty years' perplexity over his tax status.

† Charles Gray QC, subsequently appointed a High Court judge.

exchanges between government ministers and Lord Aldington, as well as with the purportedly independent 'Cowgill Committee' (Brigadier Cowgill, its 'Chairman', was discovered by a friend working at the international detective agency Kroll's London office to be a former officer of MI6, with no scholarly qualifications anyone could discover). In addition, a list of the chief state papers withheld from the defence was revealed, including the crucial one that had been discovered in the broom cupboard, which eventually guided us to the official signal establishing the true date of Aldington's departure from Austria in 1945. This was an issue vital to the defence case, on which it was now clear he had perjured himself throughout the trial in order to establish his alibi.

Meanwhile Patrick's own work continued highly satisfactorily, with Norton announcing that they were spending $45,000 on advertising, and requesting his approval for a Patrick O'Brian newsletter.

At the beginning of June he flew again to London, primarily to attend a ceremony at the Royal Naval College, at which Richard Ollard was awarded the prestigious Caird Medal. That evening Patrick entertained Richard and his wife Mary to a lavish dinner at Brooks's. Later Richard told me he felt strongly that Patrick should also have received the medal, but that he was in no way jealous and indeed extraordinarily complimentary to Richard.

In August Patrick received a letter passed on by Alan Judd from the Chancellor of the Duchy of Lancaster, containing warm praise for *Master and Commander*. This was William Waldegrave (subsequently Provost of Eton College), who became one of Patrick's most enthusiastic admirers and friends, as well as a contributor to the British Library's tribute to his achievement.

In October Patrick and my mother returned from another busy visit to London, to find the long-awaited *permis de construire* from the *Mairie* for final completion of the cloister. 'We should have been furious if it had been refused but we do not quite know how we like it now that it is granted.' Perhaps his agitation accounts for a more than ordinarily bad dream a couple of nights later:

'indifferent sleep – waking mind imagining traps about tax & insurance, dreaming mind having M about to be hanged (for murder I think, clearly proved) & the embarrassed judge tying the knot in a fine new white noose.'

That autumn Patrick volunteered for his American publisher a picture of his sylvan refuge about the time of the vendange, in response to clamorous requests for information from admirers concerning their favourite author:

Here is the promised photograph of myself picking grapes. If you like to add any observations you may say that the vineyard is about 1000 feet up in the foothills of the Pyrenees; at its lower edge a cork-oak forest runs down to a distant stream; the Spanish frontier can be seen a few miles to the south, & on a peak to the W stands a 13C watch-tower [Madeloc] that guarded the coast from Moorish raiders. The vineyard itself is small, producing a full-bodied red wine drawn mostly from black & grey grenache with a fair amount of carignan & a little muscat, excellent as a vin nouveau, indifferent for the next four or five years but then improving steadily. There is a little stone house [*casot*] among the vines & here O'Brian sits writing in the high summer, when there are too many people on the coast: for although it is only twenty minutes drive away it is wonderfully quiet, peaceful, & rarely too hot. This remoteness however has its disadvantages, since wild boars live in the dense maquis above & the forest below: they grub up the stone-pine kernels sown in hope of a future grove, & although they do not eat the grapes their playful young skip about the terraces knocking them off when they are ripe & damaging the dry-stone walls, while the aged boars root in the earthworks designed to protect the little house and road from the equinoctial storms. But the boar is little to pay for the other creatures that live up here – golden orioles, bee-eaters, three kinds of eagle, ocellated lizards, badgers and the occasional genet, to say nothing of the honey-buzzards standing northwards by the thousand on their spring migration under a pale blue sky.

Patrick at Manay

In the New Year of 1993 Patrick began looking through the manuscripts of his published novels, some of which were 'in horrid disorder & most inefficiently numbered'. His interest had been piqued by a recent enquiry from Boston University as to whether he would accept $3,000 for the entire collection to date. As the event would show, the sum offered was indeed 'absurd' (it was subsequently raised, but insufficiently to meet Patrick's expectations), but the offer alerted him to the fact that the manuscripts clearly enjoyed considerable financial value.

A couple of days later Patrick experienced the next of a long-standing series of contretemps between him and their smart new motorcar: 'on my return from below I ran the car into the coal-hole wall, spoiling the off door'. A fortnight later: 'On the way [to Manay] I hit the protruding kerb by the Chiberton a frightful blow, losing the enjoliveur & denting the wheel. I am afraid it also dented M's confidence in the driver, never v strong, perhaps irreparably.' My mother's misgiving was further justified, when next day, 'looking forward to see whether any car were coming down, I ran straight on to an elevated iron & concrete drain-cover, stranding the car with an awful bang & grind . . .'

All this was par for the course, and Patrick swiftly recovered his equipoise:

> Looking for the [Chicago] Sun remark (PO'B best in the world) I glanced through scores of reviews, many astonishingly good; & this together with those letters & a v curious realization that came to me walking that we probably h*ad no more than 10 years if as much of real life put my spirits into an equally curious hurry.

It may have been this consciousness that led shortly afterwards to his return with my mother to:

> the graveyard, where we found our own, small, low, quiet, utterly unpretentious, well made, 3 fine llosas covering it. Helène's [Camps] family vault is just the other side of the path, we are between Pous & Serre, & we know most of the names all round. It is all I could wish, & I think in sight of the house, or nearly.

On 9 January 1993 Patrick received warm congratulations from Richard Ollard on receipt of the typescript of *The Wine-Dark Sea*, a title suggested by my mother. At its conclusion Patrick wrote of the exceptional labour involved in producing the novel:

> Writing quite hard most of the day [6] pp I finished the book, not without a moderate satisfaction. It is true I forgot JA's promised command & my early note of his v last words, but it don't signify. When did I begin? Last year, for sure, & I should think that this is the longest-lasting, most interrupted book I have ever written. I began on 11 VI 91, which makes 18 months + It will be about 110000 [words] I think.

The novel received as high praise as any of its predecessors, with Christopher Lehman-Haupt concluding a laudatory review in the *New York Times*: 'Even without a dictionary or a nautical guide, the feel of M. O'Brian's prose is so convincing that when you finally look up from his pages you are surprised to find that the room is not rocking. You could even get seasick from the stillness.'

Regrettably, Patrick's satisfied mood was not permitted to last for long. Since the end of the previous year discussions had been in progress with Norton and Sheil Land regarding a proposed interview by Mark Horowitz, an American writer who was a particular admirer of the Aubrey–Maturin series. Patrick was at first a little reluctant, but given that Horowitz had been commissioned to write a lengthy piece for the influential *New York Times*, he agreed.

He booked Horowitz into a Collioure hotel, and drove to meet his aeroplane at Perpignan on 5 February. After dropping him at his hotel, Patrick encountered flooding at the foot of their hill, which obliged him to desert the car and ascend on foot. The dinner which had been arranged at home had in consequence to be abandoned, and Patrick booked the Chréa restaurant in the Port d'Avall for their visitor to dine alone. Although he had consented to the interview, he felt uneasy throughout much of the protracted five-night visit. As I have described Horowitz's visit in some detail in the first volume of this biography, I will not repeat what I have written – save for one or two details omitted there.[2]

Despite fleeting moments of irritation, after dining together on the last night of the visit, Patrick described it as a 'Pleasant meal . . . & we talked in an ordinary communicative manner: he said pretty things on parting. I am glad it ended so well.' Writing a week later to Arthur Cunningham at the British Library, he cheerfully volunteered that 'I hope he will write a good article: he certainly wrote a good review.' It had boded well, when Horowitz reassured him before his arrival:

I know I'm supposed to probe my subject thoroughly on all things private and professional, but frankly, in this case, I'd be content with a brief tour of the vineyard, a glass of Collioure and a few moments of browsing in your library.

This was not entirely candid, since during his stay he made several not very subtle attempts to uncover something of Patrick's origins and upbringing. That was natural enough, of course, given that any professional interviewer is likely to be concerned to discover more than his subject may be prepared to concede. At one point he pressed Patrick with the leading question: 'Can I say you were born in Ireland?' Patrick was plainly irritated by this, but does not record his response. I suspect that he avoided any direct answer. The proof version of his interview which Horowitz submitted to him for comment states that Patrick 'was born in 1914 into a family of some distinction', and it was only in the published version that Horowitz altered this to 'was born in 1914 into an *Irish* [italics inserted] family of some distinction'. The omission in the proof can scarcely have been accidental, and since Patrick makes no claim to Irish birth in his contribution to the British Library Festschrift (a copy of which he showed Horowitz), it seems likely that the latter inferred the assumption on the basis of Patrick's surname.*

The point would be trivial, but for the belated melodramatic public 'discovery' that Patrick was not in fact Irish. As I showed in my earlier volume, he selected the unusual spelling O'Brian when changing his name by deed poll in 1945 for a chance reason, which had nothing to do with any assertion of Irish origin.[3] At the same time, he had become deeply enamoured of Ireland during his lengthy

---

* Had Patrick's correspondence with Horowitz not survived, it would have been natural to assume that it was he who advanced the claim to be Irish. The American writer subsequently suggested to Dean King that Patrick had intimated as much to him during their discussions, but that was several years later, by which time his change of name had become widely known and discussed.

stays in Belfast and Dublin in 1933 and 1937. Overall, he was generally careful to avoid any claim to Irish origin. There can be little doubt that the motive for his change of name was to establish a total break with his generally unhappy and unsatisfactory early life, which he sought to repudiate with a mixture of shame and disgust. His marriage to my mother in 1945, which coincided with his change of name, marked the great watershed of his life.

Thus he strongly wished to consign his life prior to 1945 to oblivion. Unfortunately, however, as a successful author his personal life became more and more subjected to scrutiny. When from time to time a publisher or reviewer assumed him to be of Irish origin, he could not easily correct them without revealing his original name, and in turn his earlier life – which he was desperately concerned to suppress. If (as sometimes happened) he was tempted into claiming an Irish connection, he did so only with evident reluctance – followed, more often than not, by considerable regret. Over the years, as has been seen, he had developed a romantic dreamlike affinity with Ireland and the Irish, which seems at times to have attained an illusion of imaginative reality.

Returning to Horowitz's lengthy article, Patrick was angered that the writer (who had after all been his guest) appeared to accuse him of being 'a liar, a snob (both intellectual & social) & one who flaunts his learning'. Although his indignation did eventually dissipate, he was persuaded not to react directly, but to ensure for the future that 'stringent conditions' be imposed in advance of further interviews – as though that could ensure compliance!

Before receiving the final version, Patrick acknowledged to Horowitz that 'I agree the imprecision that I imposed upon you does give some degree of uncertainty here and there: but if you like to pin France by stating that I was at the Sorbonne, please feel free to do so.'

At one time I would frankly have questioned this assertion, but since my belated discovery that I was wholly wrong in the first volume of this biography in doubting his claim to have attended a Devonshire preparatory school, I have become increasingly wary of rejecting out-of-hand assertions relating to that early period of Patrick's life where evidence is markedly sparse. As a young man before the War he certainly travelled to Italy and Ireland,* and it can only be said that it is not impossible that at some point he undertook researches at the great Paris university (note the cautious 'I was at the Sorbonne') for his projected book on medieval bestiaries.†

Horowitz's interview did not appear in the *New York Times* until May, following which he sent Patrick a copy, accompanied by what the latter described as 'a letter from which it appears that he is absolutely unaware of having given the least offence. Q. difference of usage between US and UK?' In his secluded refuge at Collioure, Patrick remained wholly unaware of the pressures under which journalists operate. However, he was sharply reminded that opening the door on his early life even a little could invite the attention of prying eyes. Shortly afterwards his agent at Sheil Land irritated him by pertly confessing that: 'I actually know so little about you that what's in this article is interesting . . .'

Meanwhile Patrick himself privately conceded something to public interest, when his editor at Norton advanced 'thoughts on the legitimacy of personal interest, citing me on Pic[asso], which is a point'.‡ A point it undoubtedly is, for when we read Patrick's own words in his biography of the artist, we find that:

---

* His early visits to Ireland were doubted by Dean King (*Patrick O'Brian: A Life Revealed* (London, 2000), p. 75).

† It may be noted that in order to have joined the French section of PWE (Political Warfare Executive) in 1941, Patrick must surely have been fluent in French to an extent far in advance of that required for his matriculation seven years earlier.

‡ On 30 June the editor wrote suggesting that: 'When an artist's work – I do not mean a single naval painting or symphony – becomes important enough to us, we long to know how it has happened, where it comes from; and satisfying this curiosity about the artist's life may lead to important perceptions about our own lives. Think of the book, the quite wonderful book, you have written about Picasso.'

The relationship between father and son is obviously of the first importance for an understanding of Picasso's character; but like everything else to do with him it is immensely complex and full of apparent contradictions . . . Picasso dropped his father's name, a most unusual step in Spain . . .[4]

My overriding impression is that Patrick's banishment of his past was fundamentally instinctive rather than measured. Throughout his voluminous diaries his formative early years are accorded sparse mention (it should be remembered that he did not expect the diaries to survive his death, let alone be made public), and in the few instances that occur it is interestingly the happier interludes that receive glancing allusion.* Furthermore, I think it likely that, having decided to suppress and, as an inevitable consequence, to some extent doctor his past, in later years he found himself saddled with a burden which, like Pilgrim's, could not readily be shed.

In April Patrick and my mother repaired to London to conduct another significant interview, this time for the *Daily Telegraph*. The interviewer was the Cambridge polymath and Pepys Librarian Dr Richard Luckett, and the occasion was altogether more satisfactory. Their conversation was conducted in Patrick's bedroom at Brooks's, business transactions being forbidden in the public rooms of the principal London clubs. Patrick was delighted with the gentlemanly and erudite Luckett, who confined the discussion entirely to his writing, for which he expressed huge admiration. (As Richard Ollard remarked to Patrick: 'What a thoroughly nice man he is as well as a very learned & sensitive one.') Afterwards they resorted to Wheeler's celebrated fish restaurant, where the Cambridge

---

* During a subsequent visit to London at the end of June, Patrick found 'Baker St almost unrecognizable; George St wholly so'. His exploration of the area was once again clearly undertaken in order to evoke poignant memories of the generally happy year he spent with his brother Bun at Marylebone Grammar School in 1925–26.

scholar entertained Patrick to 'fish & chips (glorious cod) & bread & butter pud'.

Although Luckett was a little dismayed by inevitable editorial cuts to the published version of his interview, they fortunately did not include this amusing anecdote:

> I met O'Brian when he was in Ireland earlier this year, correcting proofs. He had just been accommodating an editorial objection to one passage, in which a motley group of seamen is being treated by Maturin in the sickbay of HMS *Surprise*, at sea off the coast of Peru in 1814. The chief ailments of seamen at the time were occupational (hernia) or nearly so (the pox), and Maturin was treating a seaman called Douglas Hurd for the latter.
>
> One should remember that O'Brian's stepson is Nikolai Tolstoy, and that the present Foreign Secretary [Douglas Hurd] was indirectly involved in the Aldington affair, which left Tolstoy with immense damages and costs. O'Brian, on reflection, agreed with his editor and changed the sailor's name to 'Douglas Murd'.*

Further pleasure was afforded Patrick by Norton's republication of his early novel *Three Bear Witness* in the United States. Objection had been raised to the British title, which it was feared might suggest a forensic disquisition, and it had been with Patrick's approval that it was renamed *Testimonies* for the American market when originally published by Harcourt Brace in 1952. He was delighted with Norton's move, as the semi-autobiographical work conjured up memories of the adventurous (if impoverished) time my mother and he enjoyed in North Wales after the War.

Furthermore, Patrick gained immense pleasure from the fresh dustjacket that adorned the HarperCollins publication. Geoff Hunt had been commissioned to paint the tiny house in the wild valley of Cwm Croesor where Patrick and my mother had struggled to

---

* The quick-witted Patrick had of course fastened on the French *merde*.

eke out a rural idyll. My mother conceived of the scene, suggesting that it might be copied from a photograph. However, with his customary painstaking attitude towards his work, Geoff travelled to the spot to recreate the setting from nature. His painting depicts their cottage Fron Wen beneath the towering peak of the Cnicht mountain. Five years later, he sent the original to Patrick, explaining that:

> I'm not sure that I have captured the sense of place at all, but I hope something will come through to you. I was lucky to be there on a wonderful day – it had been raining for about a day and a half, but this cleared in the early afternoon as I arrived, and the mountains were spouting water-streams, jewelled and bright in the sunshine. The other thing I remember was the fascination of the sheep-flocks, the way they made endlessly-changing patterns as they moved.

At this time Patrick was gratified to learn that his registration for Public Lending Right (PLR) in Britain resulted in the information that 236,000 copies of his books had been borrowed from public libraries. One happy consequence of his spectacularly burgeoning income was its enabling him to achieve an ambition nurtured over the past quarter-century. This was completion of the cloister on the south side of their property, which would provide them with an enclosed space in which to dine, read, and relax, as well as shielding them from the gaze of passers-by mounting the public track that ran past their front door – to say nothing, too, of what Patrick termed 'the furious tramontane'.

A year before, Patrick wrote longingly: 'How I hope the estimate of the full cloister will be within reach. I look at the maquette & its space & privacy with longing.' The maquette was a plywood model he had carefully constructed some years earlier, on which he was wont to gaze with imaginative anticipation. The section screening the road had already been erected, but now that the *permission de construire* had finally been obtained, and sufficient funds accumulated, work began in the spring of 1993. As the walls and internal pillars supporting the ambulatory roof began to rise, my mother became fearful that they would lose their view of the Château St Elme on the ridge above, and the distant perspective of the mountains and Madeloc tower to the west. Fortunately, it emerged that the fortress could still be seen above the curved tiles of the ambulatory, while Patrick's original plan of walling off the entirety of the western side was modified in favour of an open entrance to the iron staircase descending to the *casot* and vineyard below, through which the mountain view remains prominent.

A further benefit lay in the extension of its tiled floor beyond the rocky outcrop on the western side, which not only increased the size of the cloister, but provided space beneath the overhang for construction of a dark room paralleling the gallery below the northern wing where Patrick conducted his writing. This new 'undercroft' (as Patrick termed it) was used to store books for which room had run out in the drawing room and gallery (they included his precious volumes of the Navy Records Society), a laundrette, and the treacherous television set that so frequently bedevilled his recreational hours.

On 15 June the triumphant couple 'went up to the General's [above the railway tunnel] to look & the new brilliantly white piece was quite charming: undercroft too, though I cannot but regret the stupidity all round in the matter of floor & headroom.' A month later their pleasure remained undimmed: 'How we enjoy sitting in the cloister! But M has just discovered that in the turmoil we forgot our wedding day.'

Patrick had briefly contemplated creating a fountain at the heart of the terrace, but more practically contented himself with his original plan of an orange tree, from which my mother made her delicious marmalade.

Early in the year Patrick had received a telephone call from his editor at Norton, inviting him to visit the United States in order to promote his books. He was apprehensive, since his previous visit in 1973 had been conducted for the purpose of researching his biography of Picasso, which did not involve any lectures or interviews:

> . . . I demurred – no good at public speaking, hate QQ. [questioning] personalities – he said lunches, book-signing might do . . . I said I should send him tape (BBC)* to show the limit of my powers and would brood over the letter he was sending – everything depended on book [*The Wine-Dark Sea*] anyhow. He agreed. Most happily M had listened to most of this (at least ½ hour) on the upstairs phone – knew all – was firm for acceptance.

Although my mother's support for the project was fortunately decisive, Patrick remained apprehensive – particularly in view of what he (although I rather fancy nobody else!) regarded as the disastrous Horowitz article. It was personal questioning that he dreaded, and he pondered such possibilities as 'an alternative address beginning with answer to "how did you come to write about sea?"'

At home climatic conditions were grim. Dreadful rains lashed the Côte Vermeille, at one stage subjecting Collioure to a fortnight's unceasing deluge, and Patrick feared the grape harvest had been obliterated by vines being utterly soaked and beaten down. Not only this, but their embanked road had been rendered virtually impassable. This made their forthcoming departure the more acceptable.

Buoyed by my mother's consistent advocacy of the expedition, Patrick eventually agreed to go, and on 16 October they flew to London. There they spent a busy fortnight's preparation for their journey, during which Patrick completed purchase of a suit and hire of a dinner-jacket, looked in on a state occasion at the House

---

* His wireless interview with Alan Judd.

of Lords (where he found 'peers, & above all peeresses dowdy, dusty'). After that he made another brief excursion to Ireland, from which my mother excused herself. There he was taken on a visit to County Cork by the Irish journalist Kevin Myers, his wife Rachel, and their dog. Patrick was probably in a tense state, since at one point he sharply rebuffed what he perceived as offensively personal questions posed by Myers. However, Rachel managed to calm things down, and when they flew back from Cork next day, Patrick found them 'Perfectly civil & pleasant – no personal QQ – but I think they had quarreled & it seemed that my yarns were not cordially received.'

Encouraging news on the eve of their departure for the States was that Patrick's book sales in the US were now 560,184, which amounted to total proceeds of $3,391,000. As the weeks passed by, the figures continued to mount spectacularly.

It was probably with some relief, therefore, that Patrick and my mother flew to New York on 31 October, where it had been arranged for them to stay at the celebrated Knickerbocker Club. There followed the next day a swift succession of interviews, and the day after that Patrick was invited to a dinner at the New York Yacht Club hosted by John Lehman Jr, formerly President Reagan's Secretary of the Navy. The next day Patrick gave his long-dreaded first formal address at the Princeton Club. For this it might be said that he slightly cheated, delivering instead of an extempore talk a reading from *The Wine-Dark Sea*.

After some adjustments to microphone I began with at least an appearance of confidence. In fact I did not mind v much & carried on quite brassily. SM[aturin] to me rather slow, JA[ubrey] rather BOP [*Boys' Own Paper*] but on the whole it was well enough – no strong emotion – & I dealt with questions. When it was over we had dinner & although I had little appetite I was pleased with myself enough to feel disappointed at lack of praise.

His editor had suggested omitting Maturin's role, possibly reflecting the fact that Patrick was ill-equipped for imitating accents, including Irish.

At a press interview the next day, Patrick tried to secure a draft copy of the Horowitz article before printing, which was naturally refused. His editor managed to allay Patrick's apprehension somewhat by 'agreeing that if the article were still obnoxious I should not be asked to give any more'. Each day Patrick signed quantities of his new novel at Barnes and Noble and other major bookshops, occasions from which my mother's constant ill-health generally barred her attendance. On 6 November the party set off by train to Philadelphia and then Washington, where Patrick was compensated for conducting further huge book-signing gatherings by visits to the splendid museums and art galleries. Particularly impressive, he told me afterwards, were visits to a debate in the Senate and attendance at a judgment in the Supreme Court – appropriate, as it happened, since the judges were hearing a case of infringement of copyright.

One unfortunate evening occurred when he was entertained to dinner by his enthusiastic admirer Ken Ringle, whose name Patrick bestowed upon a Baltimore clipper in his novels. Eleven sat down to dine, but he found 'the noise might have been for 50. Poor R & Roberta his companion had worked v hard & did work v hard, but it was a dreadful party & I grieve to say the loudest, most domineering man was probably my interviewer [not Ringle].'

It would be in poor taste to record this, but for the fact that Ringle himself subsequently lamented the unanticipated brouhaha:

. . . as O'Brian fans know, his knowledge and appreciation of cuisine is one of the hallmarks of the books. I fed him venison, which he liked ('A white-tailed deer, you say? Very good.') as he did two of the four wines, including – to both my surprise and his – a midnight cuvee pink champagne from California.

But the party cannot, in retrospect, be called a success. He was stooped and frail, straining to be polite in a noisy dining room. His silver head was bowed and his hooded eyes looked weary. He only came to life the next day in an appearance at the National Archives, where he seemed staggered by the size and enthusiasm of the crowd and their intimate knowledge of, and passion for, each of his books.

Asked why he had never before come to the United States, he replied testily: 'Penury'.[5]

Patrick was indeed not only weary, but suffering from an incipient cough. However, cheering news arrived next morning that MGM had offered $35,000 for a film option on *Master and Commander*. After that he visited the museum and ship USS *Constitution*, where he was formally presented with a handsome copper bolt mounted on an oak plank from the vessel. Although the mount is not large, it is impressively heavy, indicating exceptionally well-seasoned oak – as Royal Navy frigates of inferior construction found to their cost in the war of 1812. After their return home, Patrick received the bolt by post and learned that he had been appointed an Honorary Trustee of the USS *Constitution* Museum.

Exhausted by what had been a heady mixture of pleasure and strain, acclaimed as a great success by their hosts in the USA and colleagues in London on their return, the ailing elderly couple returned gratefully to their cosy home beneath the Château St Elme. 'Undercroft sadly damp & mouldy, all else well, the kitchen a delight, but still to be explained [how it worked!].'

The enthusiastic reception Patrick received during his visit to the United States was exhilarating, but it was a relief to be home, checking the vines at Manay, watching birds on the salt lakes beyond Perpignan, and conducting his familiar evening walk up the ridge and past the Dugommier fort.

This year of continually accruing success was crowned by the news in November that the Samuel Goldwyn Company had finally agreed on a contract for an option on rights to *Master and*

Commander. New Year's Eve of 1993 was marked by a reminder of their shared wartime days, so full of excitement and hope, from my Uncle Ivan in Denmark, together with a prayer reflecting an uncertain future: 'Cards: one from Ivan, remembering Chelsea . . . having wished Nikolai a happy new year [*re* legal problems] we went to bed.'

XV

Epinician Acclaims

I find it does a man good to be talked to by his sovereign. In the
first place, a man cannot be in a passion.

James Boswell, *The Life of Samuel Johnson,*
LL.D. (London, 1793), i, p. 502

Patrick regulated his life by many curious little habits, some
amounting almost to superstitions. Above his armchair in
Correch d'en Baus perched the fine sixteenth-century chamber
clock he had owned since Chelsea days. An accomplished amateur
horologist, he regularly attended to its welfare, his trusty guide
being William Derham's slim octavo volume *The Artificial Clock-
maker. A Treatise of Watch and Clock-work* (London, 1732). On
occasion he would remind me that its sonorous strike provided
the heartbeat of the house, or what he once termed in his diary
'a comforting, necessary presence'. His distress was accordingly
acute when, one day in January 1994: 'Clock stopped & my heart
died within me.' His marginally superstitious cast of mind was
further provoked on 25 April of that year: 'My little silly omens
for this book (times of [Rubik's] cube) were all disastrous.' Looking
ahead, that autumn: 'I saw fit to begin XVIII [*The Yellow Admiral*],
though the cube gave a bad omen.'

At the end of the month he spent a fortnight in and out of
hospital at Perpignan, undergoing unpleasant operations for

bladder infection and gallstones. As ever, television provided an unsatisfactory diversion. At the end of March Patrick found himself disappointed with the film of *Cyrano de Bergerac*: '. . . the v well-spoken of Depardieu's Cyrano turned out to be costume piece with hero rushing to & from bullying, slashing with sword – all the old crap – shouting too.'

Patrick will have been accustomed to more classical renditions of Rostand's play staged in the apt setting of the Château Royal.

Shortly afterwards a reminder of their distinguished American actor friend proved even less rewarding. Patrick's television set disappointed him with tiresome regularity, obdurately declining to improve with the years. 'We tried Chuck [Heston]'s Ben Hur, but could not bear more than 10 wordy minutes. Their clothes are always made of v thin cloth.'

Patrick regarded the apparatus as something of a complex living entity, possessed of a malevolent will of its own. One such struggle may stand for many more:

> . . . in arranging magnetoscope for the Henry V film [Laurence Olivier] I found that the Ivan the T[errible] part II had in fact been recorded, which is something of a satisfaction. For Henry I put on the dreary Fellini tape – itself superimposed on World Cup football, since the Shakespeare (poor soul) was to last longer than anything I possessed otherwise. Everything turned on properly, but alas it was the most primitive ham acting, much of it of course in darkness, and M could not stand ½ hr. I lasted somewhat longer in the hope of Agincourt, said to be remarkable, but then I too crept off leaving the machine running. Qu. will it record the rest of the film? No, it went back to Fellini.

Undeterred, Patrick continued his Homeric struggle to make the wretched machine *work*, however entrenched its perverse resistance to reform. Some time previously, for example, 'we watched Deneuve & Depardieu in a film . . . in the dark of course & largely inaudible.

After an hour we could take no more but retired full of admiration for both' – possibly on account of their skill at acting under such tenebrous conditions.

Persisting ill-health hampering work on his current novel *The Commodore* doubtless accounts for a troubling dream: 'A disappointing night, however. M cramped dreadfully & I had a foul dream: bill for breakfast in Venice £5 – I only had 30/- left her there & hurried back to hotel – COULD not find it – never did.'

It was at this time that Patrick received his first intimation of Dean King's unwelcome biographical project. Norton passed on a detailed outline of his proposal via HarperCollins, which included a request for Patrick to write the foreword to King's proposed 'Patrick O'Brian Companion'. Patrick's response was stern:

I have always been luke-warm about the idea of a companion . . . Yet clearly there are readers who think it important to know the difference between a smiting-line and a twiddling-line, and those who very naturally long for maps . . . yet on the other hand, what are his [King's] own technical qualifications and literary powers? . . . he speaks of a contribution by me with rather surprising assurance; and I have the impression, perhaps mistaken, of a confident, somewhat journalistic taking-over of what is after all my domain.

If Norton or Collins feel inclined to encourage the project, I should raise no objection: but I should certainly have to know very much more about Mr King's abilities as a writer before I associated myself with it in any way.

King's proposed academic collaborators appear to have faded away on learning of Patrick's reluctance to co-operate, but he himself remained undeterred, and published his unauthorized companion single-handed in 1996. Fortunately, an authoritative and beautifully illustrated companion has since been published by the leading naval historian Brian Lavery.[1]

On 12 April the post brought a copy of the Collins edition of

Testimonies, bearing Geoff Hunt's magnificent dustjacket illustration of their tiny cottage in North Wales. It was accompanied by the HarperCollins publication of Patrick's *Collected Short Stories*, but Patrick unfortunately found 'the tales utterly ruined by Byatt's cruel (intended?) comparison with [Georgette] Heyer' on the rear of the dustjacket. This pained comment illustrates Patrick's extreme sensitivity to what he considered inappropriate comparisons. The citation from A.S. Byatt runs as follows:

> Narrative addicts all have writers to whom they return regularly to cheer or console themselves. Mine are Georgette Heyer, C.S. Forester, Margery Allingham and Dick Francis. I have just discovered another, Patrick O'Brian, and he is in many ways better and more satisfying than any of them.

Byatt's comparison was surely intended to evoke authors whose impact on readers at a susceptible time of life leads them to return in later life to their work with undiminished pleasure, regardless of their literary quality. In fact, the characteristic remarked by Byatt is one shared by many admirers of Patrick's great *roman-fleuve*, who proclaim the pleasure they derive from regular immersion in its vividly depicted world.

Despite this aggravation, on 25 April Patrick completed writing his current novel 'in quite a flurry of excitement, &, for the very end, delight . . .' Originally entitled 'The Middle Passage', he was obliged to abandon the title when advised by Norton that a book by this name concerning the Atlantic slave trade had recently gained a National Award in the United States. After some discussion, it was decided to call it *The Commodore*, despite that being the title of one of Forester's Hornblower series.

After being checked and typed by my mother, the text was sent to the British publishers in May. As ever, Richard Ollard was delighted, writing in haste: 'what a delight and what a triumph The Commodore is. The aging & development of the characters, the newness of the background and the deepening of the constants in it – I write hurriedly & no doubt like St Paul foolishly.'

The story begins off the coast of West Africa, where Jack Aubrey is despatched in command of a small squadron to engage in suppression of the slave trade, whose brutal nature is vividly exposed, together with Britain's exemplary record in suppressing the cruel institution. The expedition, although successful, proves to be partially intended as cover for assembling a force to frustrate a renewed French attempt to land on the coast of Ireland.

As ever, the novel contains personal touches which could not be known to the reader. It is not difficult to detect Patrick's indignation at continuing revelations of the underhand practices of the British government and judiciary in securing Lord Aldington's victory in the courts, when Sir Joseph Blaine explains to Maturin underlying factors of the innocent Jack Aubrey's condemnation in *The Reverse of the Medal*:

> You might think it a far cry from the Solicitor-General and a long-established eminently respectable firm of lawyers to a band of criminals; but the eminently respectable know the less respectable and so down to the very dregs; and where raison d'état or what can be disguised as raison d'état is concerned I believe that even you would be astonished at what can happen.[2]

Less significant allusions may be touched on briefly. There can be little doubt that the continuing expansion of Jack's originally modest Ashgrove Cottage with successive injections of wealth from prize money corresponds to Patrick's pride in the upstairs room, northern wing, and cloister his earnings had enabled him to add over the years to their original one-room *casot*. Sophie's heartfelt lament to Stephen that 'we were so much happier when we were poor' echoes a recurring refrain in Patrick's diaries, as well as what my mother occasionally lamented to me. Stephen's bestowal of a Munster farm on his servant Padeen recalls Patrick's bequest of their Manay vineyard on Michel, son of their close friends Pierre and Hélène Camps. Similarly, the she-potto which Maturin's colleague Whewell presents to a delighted Stephen is a precursor of my mother's beloved dachshund Miss Pätz, also known as 'Miss Potts', who helped her drive ambulances during the Blitz, when she became also known as 'Potto'.[3] Again, the precious volume 'Elzevier Pomponius Mela *De Situ Orbis*', brought by Whewell on board the *Bellona*, eventually descended down the centuries into the possession of Patrick himself – having by then sadly lost its title-page.[4]

Finally, we may note Diana Villiers hunting 'with Ned Taaffe's hounds' in Ireland. Edward Taaffe was Patrick's close Irish friend (of whom tantalizingly little is known) in 1930s Chelsea, with whom Patrick recalled voyaging under sail in the Atlantic.

The 19th of May saw the arrival of the British Library's Festschrift in Patrick's honour, which understandably caused some stir at Correch d'en Baus: 'Then post brought . . . copy of the Telegraph's reproduction of Chuck's B[ritish]L[ibrary] article &, from Cunningham, the elegant little book itself. These things put me & I think M into quite a flurry of spirits, scarcely calmed by driving to the Madeloch . . .'

The 'elegant little book' is indeed a worthy testimonial to Patrick's literary prowess – the first for a living author to be produced by the august institution, under whose great Panizzi dome he had toiled more than half a century earlier on his abortive scheme to compile a scholarly book on medieval bestiaries. Entitled *Patrick O'Brian: Critical Appreciations and a Bibliography*, contributors included the erudite naval historians Brian Lavery and Nicholas Rodger, the American neuropsychiatrist Professor Louis Jolyon West (discussing Maturin's medical skills), William Waldegrave, and Charlton ('Chuck') Heston, together with literary appreciations by John Bayley and Richard Ollard. Patrick himself contributed a brief and characteristically evasive autobiographical essay, together with two of his short stories and a collection of poems. Finally, the editor Arthur Cunningham contributed an authoritative bibliography, while Stuart Bennett provided a sample collection of reviews over the decades.

Patrick very properly insisted that the reviews included should be broadly laudatory (indeed, they were not hard to find). However, as Cunningham pointed out to him, 'I have omitted any mention of your early pseudonymous novels.' This suggests that he had inferred the name 'Patrick Russ' to be a nom-de-plume, although it may be that the scholarly Cunningham was more aware of the actual circumstances than he vouchsafed.

Patrick made many suggestions for the work, not all of which were adopted. 'I think we should have out the photograph of Bennett & me carrying grapes half naked,' he remarked – advice which Cunningham wisely ignored. Despite this, Patrick was delighted with the finished product, a special edition of which, signed by all the contributors, was presented to him during a visit to London shortly afterwards.

Patrick had since childhood been intrigued by the narwhal, with its impressive rapier-like horn (actually, a canine tooth), and had long desired to possess such a 'horn'. A serious obstacle lay in the fact that narwhals are among internationally protected species, which means that their horns, regardless of age, are forbidden to cross national frontiers. Eventually, he was informed of a Canadian dealer, who could arrange for the purchase to be collected in Switzerland. There remained the problem of transporting it back to France. The dealer suggested use of a motorcar, which was unlikely to be searched: 'Apparently this is the preferred method in Europe.'

On 18 June Patrick and my mother drove to Geneva, where they met a dealer who handed over the horn in a cardboard tube. This they inserted into a fishing-rod bag, and set off for the French frontier. Their apprehension was extreme when faced by French *douaniers*, but all passed smoothly, and the horn was installed at Collioure. In due course it made its appearance in *The Hundred Days*, where it is broken in consequence of Killick's foolish antics, being subsequently mended with great skill. This course of events closely followed reality, Patrick's precious horn being likewise damaged and repaired.

On 30 June Patrick suffered one of his intermittent low moments, lamenting that 'We are dreadfully dismal: joy in life is all gone', but was cheered shortly afterwards when John Saumarez Smith reported that:

> I hear from one of our old friends/customers, Sam Goldwyn Jr, that he has bought the film rights to the Aubrey series. He says that the last time Heywood Hill [bookshop] recommended his taking up film rights was in about 1960 when we told him to buy rights to James Bond – it was a pity he didn't!

Sadly, Patrick did not live to see Peter Weir's magnificent film of *Master and Commander*, with Russell Crowe as a convincing Jack Aubrey.*

Increasing financial security enabled Patrick to put into effect projects close to his heart. During their early years at Collioure he and my mother had contributed as generously as they could from their sparse resources to fund his son Richard's educational expenses. Now he could afford to be lavish in supporting our children. In August he 'wrote to Eton bursar about putting a year's fees aside in case of sudden death'. This was for our son Dmitri's education, whose progress he followed attentively. As well as being delighted with his successes, he and my mother were tolerant of any setbacks occasioned by his youthful years. When I broke news to them of the boy's being rusticated for having been found in a Windsor pub, my mother made an urgent plea for me 'not to be angry with him'.

It is refreshing to observe how relatively little Patrick was affected

---

* In April 1995 Goldwyn had considered starring Mel Gibson as the film's protagonist.

by material success. On 10 October he learned from Barclay's Bank that their combined accounts totalled no less than £535,836. Next day, however, he set the news in proportion: 'One pleasant thing (& it is astonishing how the huge sum left us indifferent, even obscurely resentful) was that I tried recording a piece of TV on the magnétoscope, & it worked.'

The year concluded on a generally high note, marred only by increasing intimations of mortality. Just before Christmas he gazed disconsolately upon 'photographs of Admiralty speech – I had no idea I looked so v old, pale with age'. Happiness was restored, however, by completion of their second garage extending beside the lane.

By the beginning of 1995 Patrick's international success seemed secure, even in his eyes. In January he wrote to Stuart Proffitt at Collins:

Thank you very much for your note about the million mark [paperback sales in the UK and Commonwealth alone], which if my calculations are right, means rather more than fifteen miles of books standing side by side.

It tickles my vanity, but at the same time it makes me uneasy: is not such a vast figure obscurely discreditable? If so, I shall have to put up with it.

The new book [*The Yellow Admiral*] advances, but very very slowly. Workmen are in the house painting doors & shutters, making a path for Mary to go down to the garden, providing the garage with the kind of door that turns on its horizontal axis. Thieves took away my fine powerful Citroën BX in the night, drove it to the outskirts of Perpignan and then destroyed it entirely by fire. And I have lost all the notes on inclosure of commons that I made last time I was in London – a matter of real importance to me for the present tale. These things would slow down any writer short of an evangelist.

Patrick suddenly 'felt old, really old, & discouraged' (he had attained his eighty-first birthday in the previous month), becoming increasingly prone to fatigue and loss of memory. He wrote asking me to provide him with accounts of boxing matches contemporary with the setting of his novels, which I was able to do, but he then found he had mislaid his copies of the Hammonds' books on eighteenth-century rural economy.* Eventually both notes and books were run to ground, but his recurrent back ailment began playing up again, and the following month found him momentarily contemplating bringing the series to a finish, though 'The idea of parting with Aubrey & Maturin grieves me.' Fortunately this did not happen, but various mishaps of mind and body meant that he would not complete the current novel until the beginning of the following year.

After the success of his visit to the United States two years previously, Patrick's publishers had arranged another more extensive tour for the spring of 1995 to promote publication of *The Commodore*. On 6 April he and my mother flew to Washington, arriving at dead of night. As ever confused on journeys, they missed their onward flight to Charleston, and were obliged to take a taxi. After some time Patrick began to suspect that they were travelling in the wrong direction. Their destination being the South, he tentatively enquired whether the driver was aware that Charleston lay in South Carolina. Their driver, who proved to be an all but monoglot Turk, enquired cheerfully: 'South Carolina: where him?' 'It is below North Carolina,' responded Patrick. That being the sum total of his knowledge, he suggested that they enquire at the next garage, where they obtained an exact itinerary.

At dawn they arrived at the house of Patrick's editor, where they spent a couple of days recovering. Patrick admired a distant

---

* Patrick had apparently forgotten that he possessed a source much more apt to his need than the Hammonds' dated works. Beside the desk where he wrote, on the floor beneath the bottom bookshelf, lay a handsome green vellum-bound ledger he had picked up in the 1930s. This contains a contemporary register of depositions concerning Essex enclosure acts in the reign of King George III.

view of 'Charleston the charming town', and waxed still more enthusiastic over the rich range of birdlife in the vicinity, including many species new to him. Also pleasing was 'a huge alligator'. All this, however, proved a severe strain for my poor mother, who spent much of the time in bed. Fortunately, she had recovered by the time they departed for the next stage in their journey. This was the great naval base at Norfolk, Virginia, where they were greeted enthusiastically by Vice Admiral George Emery, who commanded 'not only the American nuclear submarine flotilla but also that of NATO (surely the most powerful sailor known to man)'. Emery proved to be a devoted admirer of Patrick's naval tales, confiding that it was his practice at the end of a major Atlantic exercise to take his submarine to the ocean bottom, where he would regale himself with a volume of Jack Aubrey's adventures.

The Admiral escorted them on board the USS *Hampton*, the newest and most powerful warship under his command. Patrick was fascinated by the workings of this remarkable vessel, and gratified by my mother's being formally accorded the status of Honorary Submariner of the US Navy. After this they were driven in 'immense VIP limousine' to the Newport Mariners' Museum. There Patrick conducted an interview with John B. Hightower, President of the Museum, before an audience of some 450 sailing enthusiasts.* Patrick enjoyed the question-and-answer format, and spoke with confidence about his writings and their inspiration. The courtesy and sympathetic interest evinced by the audience reconciled him to public appearances in the United States, although his instinctive reaction remained one of extreme apprehension.†

---

* Among them were Terry Zobeck, compiler of the forthcoming authoritative bibliography of Patrick's works, and his wife Sandy.

† Dr Maturin was likewise ill at ease before making a public speech (*The Surgeon's Mate*, pp. 125, 127–30). Similarly Pugh, another alter ego of Patrick, confessed he 'was unsuited for my teaching duties [at Oxford]; I performed them badly and with a great deal of pain, and to the end I could never stand up to lecture without dying a little private agony' (*Three Bear Witness*, p. 33).

Note Patrick's marked resemblance to a wary
Stephen Maturin boarding the *Surprise*

My mother once told me in earlier years that he found public speaking so distressing as to bring him near to fainting. On this occasion the only setback was a night spent at the 'vile Radisson Hotel overlooking Hampton road – pretentious, rude, & nothing worked. Poor night & wretched breakfast.'

After lunch next day at the Pentagon 'with a most hospitable and even more knowing group of admirals', they flew to New York, where Patrick engaged again in a question-and-answer session, this time with Richard Snow. It was Snow's enthusiastic article 'An Author I'd Walk the Plank For' in the *New York Times Book Review* of 6 January 1991 that had done so much to launch Patrick as a bestselling author in the USA. Again Patrick enjoyed the occasion, which was followed by a congenial dinner.

This, however, my mother was again unable to attend, as her health continued to deteriorate. Next day a doctor pronounced her to be recovering, but she remained weak. Patrick was obliged to leave her behind while he attended a reception on board HMS *Rose*, replica of an eighteenth-century 22-gun frigate, later used in the film *Master and Commander*. The occasion was employed to launch publication of *The Commodore*. Surrounded by photographers and admirers, Patrick pleased his hosts by noting the similarity of the ship to the *Surprise* of his novels, enjoyed sharing a bottle of Veuve Clicquot with the celebrated US television journalist Walter Cronkite, and formally fired the evening gun.

Privately, however, he was mildly disparaging about the vessel's reconstruction, describing it as a 'Pleasant foolish ship, accurate in parts'. On the other hand, he was unreservedly delighted with the orchestra, which played music appropriate to the frigate's historical era. The director, Richard Kapp, wrote afterwards to Patrick, reminding him that 'when I told you we had just recorded three suites of Johannes Fasch . . . you replied that you cherished his lovely Sicilienne! I can't imagine receiving that response from anyone else.' Patrick happily acceded to Kapp's request to assist in selecting compositions likely to have been enjoyed by Aubrey and Maturin.*

On Easter Day Patrick and my mother attended mass in St Patrick's Cathedral, where they were impressed by the immense congregation and atmosphere of 'general unaffected piety'. Although he was never a Roman Catholic, he was strongly sympathetic to the Church's ethos. After a packed programme in New York, they

---

* Subsequently Kapp produced an excellent CD of music familiar to Jack Aubrey and Stephen Maturin, entitled 'Musical Evenings with the Captain: Music from the Aubrey/Maturin Novels of Patrick O'Brian'.

Patrick fires the evening gun aboard HMS *Rose*

flew to San Francisco, where Patrick conducted a television interview, followed by the now familiar question-and-answer session:
this time conducted in Herbst Hall by the US poet laureate Robert
Hass.

Among the audience was Thomas Perkins, a wealthy businessman, who was at once charmed and alarmed by Patrick's
'lightning quick wit and rather acerbic manner'. A keen yachtsman,
Perkins had been introduced to Patrick's work in the previous

autumn by an academic friend. After reading all sixteen volumes of the naval saga then published, he became so enthralled that he read them over again. By now his enthusiasm knew no bounds, and he asked his close friend the bestselling novelist Danielle Steel if she thought O'Brian would be offended were he to make him a liberal offer. To which she sensibly responded: 'I get about 20,000 letters per year from readers and I have yet to receive a single one offering to do anything for me – he will be delighted even if age and circumstances prevent him from accepting.'

Perkins, who had no idea where in the world Patrick lived, accordingly wrote to him via his publisher on 26 September 1994:

> You have enriched my life through the Aubrey/Maturin series and I would like to offer you a 'thank you' which I hope you will be able to accept.
>
> I have a large modern sailing yacht, the Andromeda la Dea, 154 ft in length which combines great luxury with remarkable sailing ability . . . This winter she will be in the Caribbean and next summer in the Mediterranean.
>
> My 'thank you' is to offer her to you exclusively and at my full expense complete with her regular crew of seven (including an excellent chef) for any 14 day period you would like (after March 1st) in either of the two seas.

Patrick's response was swift: 'My wife and I accept it [the kind offer] with an almost indecent haste and eagerness.'

In due course Perkins was informed of Patrick's forthcoming American lecture tour, and invited him to dinner at his Belvedere residence. The evening after the Hass interview, Patrick and my mother arrived at the impressive home of his generous well-wisher. The occasion proved a great success. In Perkins's own words:

> Mr. O'Brian was utterly charming, if perhaps a little aloof. He took tremendous interest in an Admiralty Board (dockyard) model I have

Andromeda la Dea

of an English First Rater of 1702. He understood everything about that ship and greatly augmented my own knowledge. After the other guests departed, we settled into a series of brandies by the fire and I discovered: 1) his capacity for serious drinking greatly exceeded my own; 2) his reserve only eased very slightly in the presence of this unknown American (me) and; 3) his knowledge of the practical aspects of sailing seemed, amazingly, almost nil.

After a half liter of cognac had vanished (and we were still calling each other Mr. O'Brian and Mr. Perkins), I produced a chart of the Mediterranean and we began to discuss the agenda for his cruise.

I had learned that the O'Brians' home was in Collioure, a village on the Mediterranean coast of France just north of the Spanish border . . . The harbor of Port Vendres lies nearby, where *Andromeda* could pick all of them up. O'Brian then suggested a cruise circumnavigating Sicily, a stop in Greece, dropping by Beirut and winding up with a comprehensive tour of the Balearic islands. I was stunned! How, I wondered, could this old salt possibly comprehend a tour of over 3,000 nautical miles with numerous port calls, in only 14 days in a yacht capable of only about 12 knots?

As I began to explain the physical limitations of time and space he added a desire to drop the hook in Naples, Capri and Tangiers as well.* While I could not reconcile this plan with reality, I assumed it was the wine in control and then I was both startled and pleased when he added at the evening's end that he had a major non-negotiable condition to accepting my offer; namely that I personally would join him, Mary and their guests aboard my yacht.[5]

Polished American manners and uninhibited enthusiasm for his writing afforded Patrick increasing confidence in interviews conducted before an audience – a medium with which he had hitherto been so profoundly uneasy.[6]

After enjoying a wide range of marine birdlife viewed from vantage points overlooking Alcatraz and the Golden Gate, they flew on to Portland, Oregon. There Patrick was introduced to his interviewer for the evening. This was Knute Berger, a Seattle-based journalist, who has likewise described his amusing encounter. He

---

* I feel sure this fantastic odyssey represents a specimen of Patrick's sardonic sense of humour. He was after all more familiar than most with sailing times and distances in the Mediterranean.

had been warned that Patrick disliked meeting his interviewer beforehand. Berger enquired why:

> I was baffled – I had hoped to get to know my subject a little bit, perhaps establish a bit of rapport. But Starling Lawrence said that they had done just that in the Bay Area. O'Brian had drinks with Robert Hass, then America's poet laureate, right before the event. They'd hit it off, and had a great conversation. So, what was the problem?
>
> The problem was, when they got on stage, O'Brian became very annoyed that Hass asked him some of the same questions he'd already answered over cocktails. Why was this man hounding me, he thought? We've already discussed this. Why is he being repetitive? I've already answered these questions. O'Brian became prickly and stopped answering, the interview became awkward and O'Brian was not happy. If O'Brian was going to suffer through an 'uncivilized Q&A' with a man, he certainly wasn't going to do it twice. So it was decided that I wouldn't meet O'Brian until we walked to the theater at showtime . . . Our walk to the Arts & Lectures venue was friendly and I carefully avoided any discussion of a topic that might come up.

Berger's tact paid off, and they corresponded afterwards. He observed that: 'O'Brian seemed like a figure from another time – polite and mannerly, unused to the modern world, except as a literary stylist.' Unlike some media types, Berger was content to know little about Patrick's personal life, save insofar as it might illumine his literary creation: 'O'Brian was very loath to have his private life examined – and it was a controversial life with a tragic upbringing and first marriage – but more than simply protecting a past, he seemed determined to protect the zone he'd created that allowed him to create.'

The perception is shrewd, and I wonder how Berger became acquainted with these details of Patrick's early life. After all, some years were yet to pass before Dean King published his revelations of Patrick's youthful misery and unfortunate first marriage. However, more significant than this minor mystery is Berger's blithe lack of concern with Patrick's early travails, save to the extent they might have affected his subsequent literary achievement. It is regrettable that others have not shared his gentlemanly restraint.

Next morning Samuel Goldwyn arranged for Patrick and my mother to be flown to Los Angeles, and that evening they were hospitably received at his splendid ranch-style home in the hills outside Hollywood. Patrick found Goldwyn, a massive figure well over six foot tall, charming, and his wife delightful. The dozen guests included Charlton Heston and his wife Lydia. It has been seen that, like Goldwyn, Heston was an enthusiastic admirer of Patrick's work, and they remained in contact thereafter. Patrick's American literary agent, who was also present, recalled that: 'O'Brian was charming in his cryptic, Old World way. Sam asked him his impressions of Los Angeles, and Patrick said he found it "fresh" – which a little mystified the company.' Patrick himself noted that evening:

> v. kind welcome – fierce great Pic[asso] of [his mistress Françoise] Gilot in the hall. Then Hestons came, as friendly as could be – in to dinner, 10 or 12 of us. M sat next to Sam G (who proposed a toast to us, most civilly) . . . then to modest but respectable library for coffee & cognac.

Next day Patrick was enraptured by a visit to the Mojave Desert, where he glimpsed much wildlife, including 'A prairie dog beside the road, straight as a meerkat'. On the following day they met Goldwyn again over lunch at the Hestons' 'decently splendid' home. Afterwards Patrick was taken to the university (UCLA), where his interview was conducted by Heston – 'Chuck v good – kind reception.' Sadly, however, my mother's health had deteriorated considerably, and she was rushed to the UCLA hospital. It transpired that she was undergoing a severe bout of pneumonia, but excellent medical treatment enabled them to fly to England on 29 April.

After a week in London, the O'Brians were as ever glad to return to their peaceful home at Collioure, always invigorating in the spring. A few weeks later they set out on their long-planned fresh adventure. Following Tom Perkins's generous invitation to invite half a dozen guests aboard his yacht *Andromeda*, Patrick approached the Waldegraves. Unfortunately ministerial duties prevented William's taking advantage of the offer, but Richard Ollard and Stuart Proffitt were glad to accept. Also attending was a representative from Patrick's literary agency, and the little party assembled at Collioure on 1 June. Next day Perkins telephoned to announce that *Andromeda* had docked at Port-Vendres, and the party gathered on the quay, where Patrick was enthralled by the 'glorious great black yacht – happy meeting with Tom P'. Patrick and my mother showed Perkins around Collioure, who was particularly delighted with 'their modest and charming home', in which Patrick proudly displayed their home-grown wine.

Next day they set sail for the Balearic Islands, which Patrick had last visited in 1968, when gathering material for his immortal depiction of the opening encounter of Jack Aubrey and Stephen Maturin in Minorca, at the outset of *Master and Commander*. Tom Perkins was wholly enthralled, recalling afterwards:

Underway to Menorca beneath a sunny sky with a twenty knot following wind, the sailing was marvelous and O'Brian was delighted. I introduced him to the helm, but he seemed to have no feeling for the wind and the course, and frequently I had to intervene to prevent a full standing gybe. I began to suspect that his autobiographical references to his months at sea as a youth were fanciful. He had no idea of the limitations of even a big yacht like *Andromeda* in terms of the handling and actual distance we could cover in a day. However, he and Mary adapted quickly

Patrick at the helm alongside Tom Perkins

to the yacht with no trace of seasickness. Mary, quiet, kind, interesting and interested, was wonderful to have aboard. However, she was very frail. They were both nearly 80 and I constantly feared she would take a tumble with the ship's motion, but thankfully this never occurred.

At Patrick's suggestion, Perkins skilfully guided his yacht through the narrows to Port Mahon, where Stuart Proffitt boldly descended into the water and swam ashore. There Patrick guided them around sites familiar to readers of *Master and Commander*, and drew the party's attention to the rich birdlife of the island. After this, at his suggestion they circumnavigated the great natural harbour in the ship's tender.

That evening an unfortunate dispute broke out among the guests (in Patrick's words) 'about biography, vulgar curiosity & the like'. Ollard, as a biographer of Samuel Pepys, held opposed views on the topic as strong as Patrick's, and the latter (as he privately acknowledged) became somewhat testy. Fortunately, the good-natured Perkins appreciated Patrick's personal concern with the issue, which was apparent from his display of anger at what he described as the prospect of 'some post-doctoral American fool' probing into his private life. Ollard was well able to hold his own in the argument, but my mother became distressed by the altercation. Afterwards Patrick himself regretted extremely 'the confusion & hostility'. However, a good night's sleep restored the company's equanimity.

As the cruise continued, Patrick retired each afternoon to his cabin to continue work on *The Yellow Admiral*. To my mother's great surprise, each day he showed Tom Perkins the result of his work, which to her knowledge was the first time he had ever done such a thing for anyone save herself. Later, he presented his valued new friend with the galley proof of the completed novel, with corrections in his own hand. To this he subsequently added the original manuscript.

Privately, Patrick confessed to his customary feeling of strain at being in company for longer than he found comfortable. At one point he lost patience with his earnest but ill-informed literary agent, who became 'loud, positive, contradictory, & bossy much of the day . . . more so at dinner – spoke with ignorant disrespect of the Q[ueen]'. Afterwards Richard Ollard reproached him for uttering what he regarded as an overly cantankerous reproof, but Patrick remained unrepentant. At the voyage's conclusion he 'parted on the coolest of terms' with the by now thoroughly tiresome agent. Nevertheless, once they had disembarked at Port-Vendres, he looked back on the cruise as a pleasurable highlight of his literary career.

Tom Perkins, whose departure a few days earlier had contributed to Patrick's accruing disquiet, in any case possessed good sense and amiability sufficient to ride out minor awkwardnesses, and continued a warm friend and admirer of Patrick to the end:

My friendship with Patrick continued until his death in January of this year [2000]. We corresponded. He and Mary stayed in my home. They were aboard my schooner *Mariette*. We met at his club,

Brooks [*sic*], in London. He was a genius and his books remain a towering, towering achievement. I miss him greatly.*

Shortly before embarking on the *Andromeda*, Patrick had received news of yet another tribute to his achievement:

JSS telephoned just as I was walking in upstairs – I have won the HH prize (£10000): it is to be presented at Chatsworth on 23rd June. We were not much elated: M is v low these days; & as far as I am concerned money has largely lost its meaning.

John Saumarez Smith was the erudite manager of the Heywood Hill bookshop in Mayfair belonging to the Duke of Devonshire, and it was he who had devised the newly established Heywood Hill book prize. The other judges were Mark Amory (literary editor of the *Spectator*) and Roy Jenkins, a former Foreign Secretary.

Shortly after their return to Collioure, Patrick flew to England. Sadly, my mother's continuing poor health did not permit her accompanying him. From London he travelled with Stuart Proffitt by train to the Duke's seat at Chatsworth in Derbyshire, grandiose setting for the prize's award. They were accompanied by other friends, including Saumarez Smith himself and Alan Judd, whose novel *A Breed of Heroes* Patrick particularly admired.[7]

The occasion was one of what were perhaps the two most splendid celebrations of Patrick's lifetime achievement, both of which occurred in 1995. On arrival at Chatsworth, a slightly dazed Patrick found

---

* The contrast between the enthusiastic attitude of his generous American host and an unfortunate specimen of British philistinism is illustrated by the BBC's circulation (16 August 2004) of a belated commentary by James Landale on Perkins's article. For Landale its sole significance lay in his claim that 'fresh evidence suggests the legendary writer couldn't even sail'. No more, it may safely be asserted, had Shakespeare fought at Agincourt or Homer accompanied the wooden horse within the windy walls of Troy. With regard to Perkins's reflection, it must be recalled that any sailing experienced by Patrick would have occurred over sixty years earlier!

an assembled crowd of admirers before the magnificent façade of the palatial home of the Devonshires. A huge marquee had been erected, a band played, and Patrick was greeted by a 'welcoming though rather distraught Duke & Duchess'. After the Duke's introductory address, the microphone was handed to the playwright Tom Stoppard, who declaimed a brief eulogy and presented Patrick with his cheque, to happy applause from the audience.

A grateful but profoundly uneasy Patrick then returned thanks. Uncertain how best to respond, he introduced what was I believe a unique public reference to his early life: 'I launched into my ¼ prepared anecdote, which went quite well (though I left out the main or only point) & was v kindly received.'

As Alan Judd reported afterwards: 'It was, O'Brian told us, his first literary award; in fact, his first prize of any sort since he was given a pen-knife by the headmaster of his prep school in Paignton for keeping on running when everyone else was way ahead and out of sight.'

Back to that sunny June day at Chatsworth: 'The food, a most astonishing great spread . . . People ate v heartily. They wandered about. D[uke] v kindly showed me house, library, growing steadily friendlier. Then, all those I knew having disappeared I walked about the splendid grounds until it was time to go.'

On his return to London a private dinner in Patrick's honour, arranged by John Saumarez Smith, was held at Brooks's.

The year 1995 represents what may perhaps be regarded as the apogee of Patrick's public recognition. In May he learned that he was to be awarded the CBE (Companion of the British Empire), which led to an initial minor embarrassment. Confirming the appointment, the Secretary of State for National Heritage went on to explain that 'honorary awards are given to non-UK nationals, such as yourself, and do not form part of the twice-yearly honours round'. It seems that the minister assumed Patrick to be an Irish citizen, to which the latter responded with this wonderfully baroque explanation – first:

that a childless cousin meant to leave me his land in the Co. Galway, the second that after a particularly acrimonious divorce my new wife did not choose to bear the same name as the first. Then there was the question of birth: although I was begotten in Ballinasloe I was born prematurely in Buckinghamshire.

This is the sole occasion known to me that Patrick ascribed his change of name to my mother's wish – which in itself is not impossible. For the rest, it is impossible to believe that Patrick did not have his tongue firmly in cheek: the passage reads as though borrowed from *Tristram Shandy*, or one of those Gothic novels that made pretty Catherine Morland's spine tingle in *Northanger Abbey*.

The Secretary having evidently accepted Patrick's picaresque birth tale, the ceremony took place at Buckingham Palace on 25 October:

The car was there & waiting after breakfast so we got into it & reached the Palace in good time – just as well since there were crowds outside & in. M[ary] & N[atasha] soon led off & the recipients in another direction through rather grand rooms with Life Guards & Blues motionless gleaming – to picture gallery with van D[yck] . . . Poussin. Rubens sadly ill-hung & dirty where a gold-laced person showed us what to do & how to address HM. Then we filed off & singly entered the ball-room (I think) where HM sat on a low dais. with officials behind her – my time came, [?] called out – 5 steps forward, left turn, bow, 5 steps forward. HM, holding the badge of the order 'I am so glad to be giving you this.' Me: 'How v kind of you to say so.' She then hung the cross of the order round my neck & said I had written many books ? mostly about the RN – I agreed but could not fit a majesty in, which I regretted. As I went out they took off the X & gave it me back in a case. Long pause while others were decorated – v. splendid scene, mostly red & gold. Anthem. Then a herd-like swarming out – M & N found, & car.

Patrick receiving a CBE

I believe the award meant more to Patrick, as a lifelong monarchist, absorbed in history and tradition, than any other honour he received. Privately, however, he confessed he would have preferred a knighthood, which would have included my mother in the honour.* Still, Her Majesty's congratulatory words on the success of his naval novels were doubtless sincere, since I am told that the Duke of Edinburgh keeps a set in each of the royal residences. True to absent-minded form, Patrick subsequently lost the insignia of his decoration during a taxi journey, when he had to request a replacement from the Palace. Once back home, he preserved it in his especially hollowed-out copy of *The Golden Ocean*, originally designed to conceal small sums of money.

---

* The amiable singer Cliff Richard was knighted on the occasion Patrick received the inferior award.

Even the grape harvest that year seemed set to celebrate Patrick's *annus mirabilis*. Writing to his editor at Norton on 25 September, he rhapsodized:

> Yesterday we finished picking the grapes – very beautiful grapes in spite of recent heavy rain – in our little mountain vineyard. There were three times as many as last year: indeed they overflow the vat which holds only 400 bottles, and we shall have to have a little separate brewing.

Pressure of advancing years meant that Patrick was obliged to reduce the extent of his previously arduous physical labours at Correch d'en Baus. The vineyard had now to be abandoned, being given over to trees and shrubs. At the bottom of the slope two grassy areas, sheltered by hedges from prying eyes, continued to provide a delightful refuge. There, too, Patrick kept his orchid house. Once there had been vegetable patches and beehives, but those cosy days of self-sufficiency were fast slipping away into poignant memory.

At the beginning of December John Saumarez Smith reported his negotiation of the sale of manuscripts of the first thirteen Aubrey–Maturin novels for the relatively modest sum of £60,000 to the Lilly Library at Indiana University. The Library continued thereafter to add related material to their Patrick O'Brian collection, which now houses the fullest collection of his papers not in private hands. Since then few if any manuscript materials have appeared on the market, while first editions of Patrick's works continue to rise in value by the year.

Three months later Patrick wrote to Edwin Moore at Collins, ruefully acknowledging:

> Yes, I did know about the ludicrous price of my early edition: I belong to the same club as John Saumarez Smith, who runs a bookshop in Curzon Street and one day when we were lunching

side by side he told me, thereby ruining my meal. Not long before, Mary & I had grown tired of chests & cupboards crammed with those copies that come by terms of the contract from publishers and that I very rarely give away (forced praise is a bore to both sides): so we carried two massive loads down for the incinerator.

As the New Year of 1996 opened, it might have appeared that Patrick had attained a career summit achieved by but a handful of authors. Despite this, his introspective character left him continuingly vulnerable to misgivings and bouts of depression. 'Discontent much of the day, however – we frip or subfrip but what we should do without one another the Dear knows – wither away?' he noted. A few days later, and 'I am bereft of book & purpose.'

Perennial frustration lay in the ever-increasing technical complexity of the contemporary world, from which that of Jack Aubrey provided a refuge. 'I found a small vacuum-cleaner' – but next day Patrick lamented:

I tried putting up the vacuum-cleaner – a frightful struggle – holes mismeasured – instructions misunderstood – but at last I got it into place, with the machine charging . . . A rotten day, but at night I dreamt a JA & SM piece with great pleasure – visual images, SM being smaller & older than I had thought, in an old black coat.

Despite his accruing wealth, Patrick continued determined to repair everything possible within the house through exercise of his own ingenuity:

I proved [read proofs] most of the day, when I was not trying to fix a hook into the bathroom wall to hold a dangling cable: from utter simplicity it turned into a great blundering task with machinery brought in & a most indifferent result at the end – frayed temper of course.

The 'dangling cable' comprised part of Patrick's haphazard installation of much of the house's erratic wiring system. Nothing
daunted, he spent the remainder of the day wrestling inconclusively
with his Rubik's Cube, which today continues to baffle our grandchildren.

In March Patrick underwent yet another painful operation on
his left hand at the hospital in Perpignan. He felt his age continually, a complaint not consoled by the cheery acknowledgement
of a beggar he tipped in the street outside: '*Merci, l'ancien!*'

The modest size of Correch d'en Baus precluded much addition
to its contents, collected in earlier years, which imparted cherished
memories of his shared past with my mother. Now that they
possessed two garages, however, Patrick toyed with the idea of
converting that adjacent to the living room into a library (its
construction was completed in May 1995). Some bookshelves were
eventually installed, but in the event housed only rows of unwanted
translations of his books. In consequence only a trickle of new
books could be managed within the house, among Patrick's favourites being the splendid five-volume Oxford edition of Dr Johnson's
correspondence, which he was fortunately invited to review. At the
same time, he had for some years possessed easy access to whatever
books he required beyond his own highly personal collection in
the invaluable London Library, founded by Carlyle and Thackeray,
and constituting what must surely be the best private-subscription
library in the world.

In addition, he had amassed a quirky collection of artefacts, not
a few of which found their way into the texts of his novels. In
this way, as in others, his own life became in a sense physically
infused into that Georgian realm of the mind he inhabited with
such facility. These, as I look around me, include the harpoon that
gashed the side of Skogula the sperm whale in *Beasts Royal*;[8] the
copy of William Winstanley's *The New Help to Discourse. Or Wit
& Mirth, Intermix'd With more serious Matters* (London, 1716)
given by Commodore Anson to Peter Palafox in *The Golden*

Ocean;[9] the whale's tooth mentioned in *Master and Commander* and *The Reverse of the Medal;*[10] a set of pincers for extracting musket balls or splinters, once presumably the property of Stephen Maturin MD; the handsome 'black scrutoire', in which Jack preserved his correspondence in *The Nutmeg of Consolation;*[11] and the folio copy of Sir Richard Baker's *A Chronicle of the Kings of England From the Time of yᵉ Romans Government unto the Death of King James* (London, 1696), prominent among books in Jack Aubrey's library noticed in *The Yellow Admiral.*[12]

By the autumn of 1996 honours continued to accrue thick and fast, to Patrick's mingled gratification and bewilderment. Early in the year he had received a letter from Max Hastings, editor of the *Evening Standard*, who proposed celebrating his literary achievement with a formal banquet at Greenwich. That guests were required to pay handsomely for their attendance confirms the enthusiasm the occasion aroused, not a few having flown in for the occasion from the United States. It was hard to conceive of a more appropriate venue for the author of so many books extolling the record of the Royal Navy, and Patrick gladly accepted. The dinner was held on 11 October, and he was reassured on learning that he might select as many guests as he liked.

Patrick and my mother flew to England, she unfortunately feeling far from well. The occasion was one of great splendour, being held in the magnificent Painted Hall. At the same time, as was generally the case with Patrick, the expedition was accompanied by a succession of minor mishaps. On the day of the event, our son Dmitri, whom Patrick had invited, arrived at tea-time. After changing into evening dress, they were joined by Patrick's editor Stuart Proffitt, and set off in a taxi. By the time they had crossed Lambeth Bridge, Patrick discovered that he had left their invitation behind. Fortunately, a lively fear that he might be denied entry proved illusory, and having with some difficulty discovered the entrance to the building, the four were ushered into an anteroom, where they found hundreds of guests assembled.

The noise made it difficult for Patrick to hear, but he was relieved to find many friends present. Next, the company moved on to the hall, where, once settled at their tables, Patrick and my mother were ushered in, accompanied by a naval commander and attendant bearing a halberd. Trumpeters of the Royal Marines played a fanfare, and the assemblage applauded enthusiastically. Patrick found himself seated next to Lady Layard, wife of Admiral Sir Michael Layard: both the Royal Navy and US Navy (Admiral William J. Crowe) were well represented at the occasion. On his right was William Waldegrave's wife Caroline, 'looking lovely'.

William Waldegrave, then Chief Secretary to the Treasury, delivered the address. After paying eloquent tribute to Patrick's great literary creation and the pleasure it had afforded millions, he noted that:

> He is a private man. He is not a man who has sought the limelight. There is therefore something utterly delightful about the way the tide of recognition for his achievement has come flooding silently but inexorably in from every quarter of the globe and every kind and condition of people.

Next, the actor Robert Hardy, whose recorded readings of his novels Patrick much admired, read a passage from one of the novels. Finally, following the Loyal Toast, a nervous Patrick arose to speak. At first the modest disclaimer of the orator's ability to speak effectively in public rang true, but among so unreservedly enthusiastic a following his confidence swiftly grew. He concluded by declaring 'on this occasion, when there are even more general officers and admirals present, I am sustained by my fervent, my very fervent wish to drink to the Royal Navy, that glorious service, and to the navies of our gallant allies.'

The Royal Marine band played the retreat and (in Patrick's own words) 'then (I believe) I was led away'. Friends and admirers rejoined him in the anteroom, surrounding him with plaudits which left the happy author a little dazed, 'after which I ill-advisedly looked at the chapel, thus losing M for some time'. Five years later, many of those attending would gather in the same chapel for Patrick's memorial service.

Among admirers present was his generous fan Thomas Perkins, on whose yacht he had sailed in the previous summer, together with Danielle Steel. Next morning, after being filmed for an interview by the BBC, Patrick and my mother were whisked in a Perkins limousine to his country house for the night. This was Plumpton Place, a magnificent Elizabethan pile on the Sussex Downs, not far from Patrick's beloved childhood home at Lewes. He enjoyed the intelligent conversation, admired 'the park-like garden – moat, pools & remarkable outbuildings (a fulling mill with such a gush of water)', and shared an enthusiasm for Perkins's collection of clocks, which included a particularly fine seventeenth-century Knibb.

Back in town, invitations continued to pour in. The Duke of Devonshire wrote from Chatsworth, inviting Patrick to become a special member of his private club, Pratt's. This Patrick was delighted to accept, but other requests he turned down. A month later he received 'Invitation to 10 Downing St. 6 30–8 on 5 XII', to which he sent 'reply to PM's office, civilly declining'. In the New Year 'Ambassador [to France] invites us . . . to dinner in honour of I think CIGS* – declined'. Not long after, Stuart Proffitt 'telephoned at tea-time. USN admiral invites me to Marblehead [Harbor, Connecticut] of <u>Constitution</u>'s cruise – begged him to decline for me.'

The year 1996 had proved a golden year for Patrick. As though the Greenwich banquet and its aftermath were not sufficient reward for any author, let alone one who had struggled for so long against poverty and disappointment, at the end of November his literary agent:

* Chief of the Imperial General Staff.

telephoned to say that there was a strong probability of a film (M[aster] & C[ommander]) & could director/man in charge come & see me? I said no, I must get on with book & we agreed that I should say when I was coming to London. Some exhilharation [*sic*], but not much.

Exciting as this was, unalloyed happiness lay elsewhere. Once again safely ensconced with my mother at their snug home in Collioure: 'Before bed I read some more P[ride]& P[rejudice] – some best pure J[ane]A[usten] (Collins – elegant females – Mr Bennet). How I hope that in 200 years people may laugh, reading me.'

A fortnight on, 'Quite late I finished P & P, the dear book.'

Television, on the other hand, persisted in presenting insuperable problems. Never dreaming that his might be a faulty set, or that he was remiss in handling it, Patrick was constantly angered by its inadequacy as a medium of communication. Thus, he enjoyed a crime film, despite the fact that 'little of the sound could I hear'.

Nor was this the only device with which he waged sporadic war. October found him wrestling with 'muddled instructions' for the washing machine. Many of his battles with the perversities of modern technology were recorded in dialogue form on slips of paper, which were soon mislaid. 'We lose so many things now & waste so much energy angrily looking [for] them'; 'Late in the day I found Froude under Freud.'

Another troublesome factor was provided by his tax status, which had by now become an increasingly pressing issue. Patrick confessed to having undergone forty years' perplexity over the matter. Until quite recently his income had been too small for the issue to matter. In fact, it was not resolved until several years after his death, and then only with difficulty. As I understand it, he paid little on his constantly accruing wealth. It seems that one difficulty lay in the fact that the French tax authorities believed he was paying his due in Britain, while in Britain the Inland Revenue understood that it was owing to the French. My impression is that in consequence he paid neither (at least, not in full), and his estate was not mulcted until some years after his death.

On 2 July Patrick was delighted to receive 'a more than civil letter from TCD and formal invitation to dinner. I replied, accepting, but on going up, I saw M returning from the town & coming so painfully up the hill that my heart smote me – could I leave her for 4 days like this?'

The invitation was to receive an honorary doctorate from Trinity College Dublin, the university where Stephen Maturin gained his degree, and where Patrick and my mother had visited me during my five years of study.

On Wednesday 9 July Patrick flew to Dublin. Next day he sought in vain his 'old den' in Stephen's Green – presumably a location familiar to him from his visit in 1937. On Wednesday degrees were awarded in the Examination Hall:

> . . . about 5, presented to Chancellor & made [response amid?] Mild to ecstatic applause. Then the 5 of us in turn, described (v well) by Orator, were also made & given our diplomas – back in procession to the Provost's house – welcome drink – back to pub – feet up – fetched again to banquet . . . I sat next to friendly Provost – speeches, all indifferent – food rather poor – hall and silver splendid . . .

His diploma described Patrick *inter alia* as a writer 'of Irish stock'. Since he had not been asked for personal details, this can only have been an assumption on the part of the University authorities. Sadly, this means that we learn no more of the colourful Gothic romance of his lost inheritance and mysterious conception in Ballinasloe.

On 12 July he flew home via Barcelona airport. The taxi driver lost his way for an hour en route, when Patrick realized that our younger children Dmitri and Xenia (who had a longstanding arrangement to stay at Collioure) were arriving any moment at Perpignan. Swift driving brought him there just in time to pick up the children, drop their luggage at their hotel in the rue de la Gare, and bring them up to the house.

I had warned the children of Patrick's occasional eccentricities when in the company of the young, but in the event he proved hospitality itself. They swam daily, but at the outset poor Xenia was handicapped by stepping on a treacherous *oursin*, which prevented her playing tennis on the courts which Patrick had booked. He carefully removed the sharp spines with a razor blade, just as he had done to me forty years earlier. The children were lavishly wined and dined each evening at the excellent La Chréa restaurant in the Faubourg and the celebrated fish restaurant La Côte Vermeille in Port-Vendres, and on the 14th witnessed from above the spectacular Bastille Day fireworks around the harbour at Collioure. However, they found their grandmother stooped and old, being more often than not obliged to leave during dinner, or absent herself altogether.

On the fourth day, leaving the injured Xenia at home, Patrick drove up to the further of the two mountain-top medieval watch-towers visible from their house:

I drove M[ary] & D[mitri] up to or nearly up to the Massane – far too many people alas, & the air rather thick – but ¾ of the way up M asked if she could be let out at once – the usual emergency, I thought: but no, she preferred to walk down. Having viewed the tower (horrible Germans) we turned. She had gone a long way, but on looking back she stumbled & v nearly fell – D pleased me by his real concern. She was not up to dining at La Chréa, but fortunately young appetites cleared the enormous dish.

Although I had warned the children (actually, teenagers) to be on their best behaviour, given Patrick's odd temperament they could not resist a minor sally. When after a prolonged silence Xenia ventured a tentative remark, Patrick threatened to break a water jug over her head 'should she interrupt again'. Despite this, being greatly tickled by his customary lapses into archaic diction, she had dared Dmitri to introduce one of his favourite terms 'prodigious' into the conversation that evening. When the apt moment arrived, Dmitri boldly thanked his grandfather for the 'prodigious fine dinner'. Patrick accepted the compliment with equanimity, and fortunately the impudent youngsters somehow managed to contain their mirth until they were safely back in the hotel.*

Although my mother was undoubtedly in poor health at this time, I cannot help wondering whether she was not also assailed by guilt, regret, sorrow, or a combination of all three. Dmitri and Xenia were after all separated by roughly the same age as me and my sister Natasha, and it could be that she continued racked by memories of the children she had abandoned at so very young an age.

Long ago, as a fearless teenager, she had galloped bareback along the Appledore strand at low tide, shot rabbits in her father's fields, and slept alone in the Victorian lighthouse on Lundy. Now everything was fading in a haze of tormentingly sad reflections.

For Patrick the situation was in many ways different. Although he had done all he could for his son Richard, their estrangement at the latter's wish had become total. Now, however, he loved his grandchildren, and was happy helping them in different ways. In January 1992 he wrote poignantly in his diary: 'Letters from g-chn (how I wish they wd not call me Uncle).'

Whether or not he mentioned this to me I do not recall, but before long they were to his intense pleasure addressing him as 'Grandpa'.

For all his occasional quirkiness with young people, he retained much of the humour and charm of his youth, which was greatly

---

* It is curious that Patrick must surely have known that his hero Dr Johnson expressed disapproval of the term 'prodigious'! (James Boswell, *The Life of Samuel Johnson, LL.D.* (London, 1793), iii, p. 89 – Patrick's own oft-perused copy).

appreciated by them. Nevertheless, he too suffered from punishments inflicted by old age. Walking in Perpignan that autumn, a harsh glimpse of fading mortality seized him – accompanied, as ever, by a flash of humour:

> Lord, how tiring city pavements are for an aged rustic . . . one of those disconcerting views in a shop window showed a stooped old man hobbling painfully, as Taid [half a century before in Cwm Croesor] had done – no ease or swing.

XVI

Triumph and Tragedy

As I now look back upon that tragic time, it is for him that my heart bleeds, – for them both, so singularly fitted as they were to support and cheer one another in an existence which their own innate and cultivated characteristics had made little hospitable to other sources of comfort. This is not to be dwelt on here. But what must be recorded was the extraordinary tranquillity, the serene and sensible resignation, with which at length my parents faced the awful hour. Language cannot utter what they suffered, but there was no rebellion, no repining; in their case even an atheist might admit that the overpowering miracle of grace was mightily efficient.

Edmund Gosse, *Father and Son* (London, 1907), pp. 79–80

As the year 1997 drew to its close, Patrick and my mother continued plagued by ill-health and mental travails. The latter's worsening condition led to her increasing inability to type Patrick's manuscripts to a professional standard. Like Leo Tolstoy's wife Sophia, since their first meeting she had typed every one of his books – often more than once – starting with *A Book of Voyages*, on which such high hopes had been pinned when with the arrival of peace in 1945 he resumed his literary career. However, Patrick was beginning to find her work increasingly erratic, giving him little choice but to consider an alternative recourse. On 18 September he noted unhappily: 'My idea of having I-V [of *The*

Hundred Days] typed professionally upsets M, who has typed everything I have written. What to do?'

A week later, matters were no better: 'Poor M paid heavily for her activity yesterday & her typing today & spoke much at random, & her strength quite left her at bed-time. How I wish I could think of some way round this immense task of copying a deeply obscure T/S without wounding.'

Equally, she could not bear the prospect of being no longer his indispensable helpmeet. Even her superlative cookery was becoming a trial: 'M began making marmalade from the casot tree: she cut everything up, put the pips to soak, weighed the sugar & I fear exhausted herself.'

This was the orange tree in the courtyard, which produced a gratifying crop each year. The recipe came from my mother's well-worn copy of Elizabeth Raffald, *The Experienced English Housekeeper, For the Use and Ease of Ladies, Housekeepers, Cooks, &c.* (London, 1776) – and delicious it was, too.

Patrick was not only more and more troubled by concern for my mother's health, but also by his own occasional mental perturbation. The 4th of November 1997 was to prove my mother's last birthday. Such occasions had always been marked by an intimate celebration over little culinary treats, but on this one melancholy prevailed:

A poor sad birthday, I am afraid . . . vile pâté en croute . . . & although the ordered cake was pretty good poor M was overcome by nausea quite easily – to some degree perhaps worry about grand-daughters. Alexandra in black NY doing a stage [internship] with Bantam [my publisher], Anastasia to go to Moscow apparently alone in the new year . . . Still, she [Mary] did eat a little something (egg) in the evening & I think she slept.

By a cruel irony of fate, just as Patrick's literary career attained ever greater success, his pleasure in his achievement began at times to diminish correspondingly. As I recorded Richard Ollard's telling me after Patrick's death:

> Effectively Patrick only came alive when writing. In material terms he was content with modest circumstances. After his success and huge influx of money he commented once to Stuart Proffitt that, though he was now in a position if he chose to take the whole population of Collioure to dine at the best fish restaurant in Port-Vendres, the treat was infinitely less pleasurable than when he and Mummy would take a fortnight planning the dinner as a treat, savouring the anticipation. Now the keen pleasure derived from anticipation was gone.

On 12 December Patrick attained his eighty-third birthday. He continued hard at work on *The Hundred Days*, with Stephen Maturin and the ship's surgeon Jacob en route to visit the Dey of Algiers. Progress was fair, but he found himself more than ever prone to muddle over his notes, wasting time in frustrating pursuit of mislaid references. These and other worries were, however, dwarfed by my mother's continuing ill-health. An arrangement had been made for their food to be brought up each day from the town, and the customary birthday treat which they had indulged annually since 1940 arrived: 'Kind Chréa [the restaurant in the Port d'Avall] brought up not only the salmon, chicken & apple tart that I had ordered, but also a civet de chevreuil & a tarte Tatin, remembering the day.'

However, it proved of scant avail, as my mother's body was failing and her mind wandering. 'Poor M had her iron injection this morning & it made her feel v, v poorly indeed; & curiously enough much deafer.'

Apart from the overriding worry of my mother's declining health, they were increasingly troubled by the inconsiderate purchasers of the site on the southern side of their house. The builders' labours were unavoidably cacophonous, and it became clear that, even after work ceased, their new neighbours were likely to pose an intrusion on their cherished privacy. I recall an anguished telephone call, in which my mother declared that they would have to leave their beloved home. The developers had taken advantage of a French law permitting building directly onto the structure of a neighbour's house. The tragedy was that Patrick had for some time become sufficiently wealthy to be in a position to pay any asking price for the land, but for some reason which was never made clear to me the sale had been kept secret.

Deeply pained by the prospect of being overlooked in their beloved garden, Patrick arranged for a high green plastic screen to be erected from top to bottom of their common boundary. Owing to the closely planted trees which now grew on their former vine terraces, this provided considerable protection, while being entirely unobtrusive.

However, this could not prevent the neighbours, should they choose, from peering down from their terrace into my parents' snug enclosed garden below, beside their little orchid-house. He decided his only recourse was to plant a fully grown magnolia tree at a strategic point. There being no means for it to be brought into the garden from the narrow riverbed lane below the house (the sole available point of access to the garden), he hired a helicopter to deposit the tree from the sky into a rocky cavity prepared for its reception:

About 9 the helicopter appeared: it circled, viewed the hole & returned to the place on the side of the road where the magnolia (unknown to us) had been laid, picked it up & delivered it (densely enveloped) in great style, & . . . mates guided it in the hole, almost upright & at just the perfect depth. They straightened & unwrapped it before lunch, & afterwards they came back & fixed 3 guys. It was wonderfully unharmed, & although its tapered form does not always give all the protection I had hoped for, a year or so may deal with that.

In the event, the poor tree lasted only a few years before it died. Fortunately, its demise occurred after Patrick's death, when it was left for me to arrange its removal.

With the opening of 1998 grim premonitions of mortality redoubled. On 4 January, Patrick noted: 'We were both strangely exhausted today – even my walk up to the General's* was a toil.' On the other hand, mingled excitement and apprehension in the household arose from the imminent arrival of a television crew. For some time exchanges had been passing between the BBC on the one hand, and Patrick and his literary agent on the other, with regard to a planned extensive interview. Naturally shy and reclusive, Patrick was ever reluctant to raise his head above the parapet.

Two months earlier he confessed in his diary to general feelings of 'Ill-temper, general gloom &, by night, remorse of conscience reaching back nearly 70 years'. Such a calculation being generally pretty accurate with Patrick, it is possible that the remorse included his childhood antagonism towards his frightening father. As readers of the first volume of this biography will be aware, the resentment appears largely justified, his father Charles Russ having been for the most part as oppressive as he was neglectful towards his small and timid son. Indeed, it was almost certainly his troubled formative years that made Patrick the shy and introspective character he continued to be for the rest of his life.

There can be little doubt that there was one issue that particularly troubled Patrick's conscience. This was his desertion of his first wife Elizabeth for my mother during the War. However, while this was unquestionably reprehensible, he was scarcely the only person to have been divorced: above all, during that troubled era when hundreds of thousands of married couples underwent prolonged enforced separation.† The gravest aspect of this rupture

---

* The house situated above the entrance to the railway tunnel emerging from the mountainside beyond their home.

† In fact the divorce rate in Britain doubled during the Second World War.

was his leaving Elizabeth with their two small children, the second of whom (Jane) was cruelly afflicted by spina bifida, of which she died in 1942 at the age of three. Although it was probably this that haunted Patrick the most, it is untrue that he abandoned the poor little girl in the callous manner alleged by hostile critics. In reality, he effectively maintained marital relations until Jane's sufferings were concluded by her death.*

Sadly, it would not be long before events found ill-informed – in some cases it is hard not to believe, gratuitously malicious – misinterpretations of the issue being levelled at Patrick on both counts. It is ironical that what might have appeared irrational fears were in his case to become realized to an extent that even his acutely sensitive nature could scarcely have anticipated.

With regard to the proposed BBC television interview, which had been under discussion for some time, Patrick's instinctive reaction was to decline. However, he was under strong pressure to comply. In the first place, his publishers and literary agent were naturally eager to grasp the opportunity to publicize him and his work. Still more potent an influence was exerted by my mother. Patrick had conducted a couple of lengthy interviews on French television, which proved highly successful. My mother had been delighted by his performance, and added her voice to those anxious to see him similarly brought before English viewers. Reluctantly, he agreed. Unfortunately, living as he did in France, he continued largely unaware of major cultural divides between the two countries. Whereas his French interviewers had proved polite, literate, and above all almost exclusively concerned with Patrick's literary work and inspiration, their British counterparts not infrequently tended towards titillating gossip and personality 'exposures'.

The interviewer flew in on 7 January – Patrick having confusedly driven on the previous day to Perpignan to meet the wrong

---

* In order to avoid interrupting the narrative, I examine this contentious issue in Appendix B.

aeroplane – when they conferred over a 'huge lunch' in his favourite restaurant at Port-Vendres. That evening he noted of the interviewer that 'his ideas on writing are primitive but he is quite agreeable'. Next morning he patiently underwent the tedium of a preliminary interview, and was photographed on a rock by the harbour with the castle in the background. A persistent factor in the interview was a succession of covertly probing questions about Patrick's private life. 'All rather long & wearisome, & the interviewer would insist on biographical material in my novels – would have none of it.'*

The filmed interview took place on the following day:

p.m. all of them + TV camera crammed into gallery [the tiny study below, where Patrick worked] – questions, verging upon 3d degree – v keen (fortunately) on authenticity [of the historical background to his novels], evidence of which I have in abundance . . . parted on good terms but at a time when they could not be offered a drink, which was a pity. Good fellows in their way, probably good craftsmen, but heavy and unread. It was extremely wearisome.

Thus the interview proved harmless enough. Nevertheless Patrick (rightly, as it turned out) remained apprehensive of being in some way besmirched by the programme. Unfortunately, he momentarily forwent his prior determination not to admit to any autobiographical element in his novels, when at one point he acknowledged that an aspect of Jack Aubrey originated in a brother who had died in the War. In 1927 Patrick's elder brother Mike had emigrated to Australia, when Patrick was eleven. His exciting letters home, describing thrilling adventures and the colourful wildlife of the

* I assume the interviewer had in mind the Aubrey–Maturin series, with which his interview was exclusively concerned. As I have shown, much fuller autobiographical material is to be found in his novels *Three Bear Witness*, *The Catalans*, and *Richard Temple*, as well some of the short stories, published and unpublished.

outback, stirred the lonely boy's enthusiastic imagination and served to inspire some of his early books. After war broke out, Mike joined the Royal Australian Air Force. Eventually his squadron was posted to Britain, where he resumed contact with his family. He visited Patrick and my mother at their house in Chelsea, when Patrick's youthful admiration was confirmed by the dashing figure of his genial giant of a brother. Tragically, Mike was shot down during a bombing raid over Germany on 4 May 1943. All this Patrick recounted freely to the interviewer. Unfortunately, after half a century's residence in France, Patrick was unaware of the degree of sensationalism and trivialization that had already begun to characterize much (although certainly not all) that was produced by the BBC.

For the present, however, all other concerns were subsumed beneath the tragedy which had now become imminent. My mother's fragile health declined swiftly. On 18 February she was taken to hospital in Perpignan, but her sadly debilitated constitution proved unable to survive further repeated probing. After three weeks of successive operations, the long-dreaded event arrived on 9 March 1998:

> At noon a nurse called to say that M did not seem to be doing well – Dr J would like to see me. She was in fact dead. They had disconnected the ventilating machine, & she died. Dr J saw me down by the theatre – humane, considerate, sad . . . there was one point (after Dr J I suppose) when I saw her 'laid out' quite beautiful & well.

On returning home Patrick telephoned me with the desolating news, and in a dazed state fulfilled a dinner engagement in Banyuls with good friends whom 'I did not like to refuse'. Afterwards, back in the empty house, he noted wanly: 'A very strange lost state indeed.'

Two days later I travelled to Collioure with Natasha for the funeral. The service was held in the church by the harbour, attended by a gathering of warm-hearted friends among the inhabitants, many of whom had known my mother and Patrick since their arrival here half a century before. Following the service, we accompanied Patrick and our mother to the new cemetery above the town, where they had acquired their plot. It was a clear, cold day.

Patrick was understandably distrait, and as I recall we spoke little about his bereavement, which pained him too deeply for discussion. After all, they had remained passionately in love since first they came together in 1939, throughout which time they had never been apart for more than the occasional week or two. Only to his diary did Patrick confide the extent of his misery and loss. Three days after our departure, he noted: 'Just now I looked at the front of this book – the photographed portrait [by Willy Mucha] – such a jet of love.'

Next day he found himself adjusting to partial acceptance of his bereaved state: 'At some time in the morning I think, I found (as an evident fact) that I did not believe in M's absence. This did not mean a presence: but the awful loneliness went quite away – it is extremely difficult to express: yet the contradiction is only apparent.'

At times it seemed that she had not really died at all, but remained protectively by his side. Preparing to leave their impossibly lonely house for London, he discovered characteristically that he had lost his passport. He hunted high and low to no avail, until he finally happened on it. 'In the end, the v end, I tried (why?) our coffee-pot, & there the dear, dear soul had put everything – I like to think she had moved my mind.'

Although Patrick's introspective character made it hard for him to discuss his loss with others, however close, he obtained much solace (more, perhaps, than they appreciated) from letters arriving from kindly sympathizers. Thus, to me he wrote:

Yesterday I had a dear little letter from Anastasia, dated 16 February, and another came today, dated the twenty-sixth, from which I understood that you had told her about her grandmother – a letter that did great credit to her heart and her power of expression. I was deeply moved.

Looking again I find that I had my dates confused: but in any case that was the sequence, and this evening I shall try telephoning her again – she is a dear child.

That my mother's growing frailty had for some considerable time prepared Patrick for the eventual tragedy did little to palliate the loss when it occurred. Many of his readers will have guessed that Stephen Maturin's beautiful wife Diana Villiers was in considerable part a reflection of Patrick's own Mary. Since his current novel in the Aubrey–Maturin series, *The Hundred Days*, was published in the autumn of 1998, it might naturally be assumed that Diana's death in the story followed on that of my mother.* In reality, the fictional conception had long anticipated the real-life event. As early as Christmas 1993 Patrick noted in passing: 'DV to drive 4-in-hand over a bridge.' However, Diana escaped her fate for another three books, and it was not until 5 June 1996 that Patrick queried: 'Is my killing of DV. (unaccompanied by lover) too offhand & done-on-purpose.' Two days later, he acknowledged that 'my disposal of DV does seem pretty crude'.

It can hardly be coincidental that my mother's fictional persona was made to die in a traffic accident – a fate my mother had narrowly escaped on innumerable occasions.

Many readers are likely to have found the account oddly cursory – even strangely unfeeling. Diana's fatal accident is not described, but merely alluded to at the outset of the tale in a placid conversation between two half-pay lieutenants. Indeed, his first draft did

---

* 'He had written the scene as Mary lay dying . . .' (Dean King, 'The secret life of Patrick O'Brian', *Daily Telegraph*, 1 March 2000).

not even make it clear that she *had* died. In a handwritten memorandum lying before me, Patrick notes: 'In proof I must make sure that DV was killed. Ch I – implication is not enough.'

Towards the end of that year, 'I showed M the beginning of XIX (about ½ ch I): she was kind of course – said it was dreadfully sad but made no comment on DV's disappearance.' Clearly, she recognized the implication, but accepted what Patrick wrote as driven by a reality of its own.

In dramatic terms, it is hard not to believe that the death of so striking and sympathetic a character, whose adventurous career readers had pursued since Jack Aubrey first clapped eyes on her when out hunting in *Post Captain*, might have been treated with considerably more drama and pathos. However, so real was Mary's alter ego Diana to Patrick, that I believe he could not bring himself to dwell on so distressing an event. When Stephen himself is depicted as reflecting on his loss, the reader might be excused for not recognizing its subject in the terse allusion: 'Stephen . . . gradually sank deeper and deeper into his own reflections, all necessarily of a kind as painful as could well be imagined.' Later, when the dead Diana is momentarily brought expressly to his mind, her name is again not mentioned, and we learn no more than that: 'he felt the familiar chill grip him, the sort of frigid indifference to virtually everything . . .'

One senses that the death of Diana (which, after all, need not have occurred at all) was introduced for a purgative purpose, and that Patrick found it impossible to face fully even an imaginary death of my mother. But face it he now had to, however briefly and obliquely. So closely was his fictional Diana bound up with his recently living Mary, that it was not long before he could forget whose death had come first. 'I think I had killed DV long before I was a widower, but I should need to check in diaries.'

Throughout his life Patrick had suffered from occasional spasms of *timor mortis*, which inevitably intensified now that he was a widower eighty-four years old. Intriguingly, in chapter 6 of *The Hundred Days* he makes Daniel, master's mate on board the

Surprise, reminisce affectionately about what is clearly the old building of Lewes Grammar School, which Patrick had attended from the ages of nine to twelve. The autobiographical detail continues, with Daniel's premature withdrawal from the school owing to his father's indigence, together with the consolation the boy finds in books – some of those named being from Patrick's own pre-war collection. It seems likely that this belated nostalgia reflected increasing consciousness that his earthly existence was remorselessly approaching dissolution.

From the moment of my mother's death, Patrick sought to dispel his distress by shifting restlessly between Collioure, London and Dublin. Immediately following her death, he came to stay at our home for a few days, where he was particularly charming to the children. Despite his innate wariness of young people, he had latterly come to take an increasingly paternal interest in his grand-children, as he regarded them.* Now he joined them in playing ping-pong (with remarkable skill), chatted about their lives and hopes, and charmed them with his ever-youthful exuberance. He accompanied Georgina and me on a visit to nearby Oxford, together with our son Dmitri, whose fees he was generously paying, where we visited Worcester College. There he conferred with Dmitri's tutor, Dr Harry Pitt, and presented the College library with a magnificent sixteenth-century edition of Montaigne. Afterwards he

---

* In 1988 Patrick explained to his brother Bernard that he was much sustained by my mother's 'affectionate, intelligent family'. In particular, he expressed pride in Alexandra's completion of a pilgrimage to Santiago, and concern for Anastasia's safety in Moscow. Subsequently, in February 1998 he recorded his delight in Dmitri's progress: 'Such an encouraging letter from Dmitri, labouring on (I think) a building-site near home & earning £5 an hour: an extraordinary change from a schoolboy to an articulate young man.' Our youngest, Xenia, who was still at school, he described as 'a poppet': 'A dear little Easter card from Xenia.' Such reflections might readily be multiplied, markedly contra-dicting ill-informed claims that Patrick was uniformly averse to children. He also followed with close interest the careers of my sister's sons Michael and Robert.

expressed disappointment at what he took for Dr Pitt's lack of enthusiasm for the gift – which I confess led me secretly to wish he had only bestowed it on a more appreciative recipient! Patrick's warm concern for Dmitri's progress surely aroused memories of his own burning desire to study at Oxford – an ambition frustrated by his father's parsimonious failure to provide him with any adequate educational opportunity.*

Clearly Patrick had come to acknowledge that *some* children could, after all, be delightful. Significantly, it is at the conclusion of *The Hundred Days* that he makes Stephen Maturin display affection for two pleasing children, whom he rescues from slavery in Algiers.

As Patrick parted from us at the entrance to Worcester, we watched him disappear on foot for Oxford railway station, a lonely figure in a well-worn mackintosh clutching a bag of his travelling possessions. As ever, he made little use of his now considerable wealth to indulge in small luxuries like taxis.

While he remained distraught under the weight of his loss, the BBC continued preparations for its documentary broadcast. After his stay with us, Patrick moved on to Dublin for a week. There he accepted a request for a further interview. Although not Irish, like many others (including me, following five unforgettable years at TCD) he had become deeply enamoured of the country, on occasion it may be to the extent of half believing himself an Irishman.† It was in Dublin in 1937 that he had completed his early novel *Hussein*. Now he enjoyed 'a walk right round the [Stephen's] Green looking

---

* By curious chance, my wealthy father similarly declined to pay for my university education, which I was only enabled to achieve through the generosity of my maternal grandfather Howard Wicksteed. At that time access to student grants was (surely unjustly) barred to candidates whose parents' income was adversely affected by a means test, but who at the same time declined to pay for their offspring's tuition.

† In February 1997 Patrick noted in his diary: 'A day memorable only for sadness & a profound depression, caused I think by . . . a flow, in an all too familiar voice, of false reminiscence.'

for my bench', possibly where he had penned the book's conclusion. Next day, 'I walked about, rediscovering a little of my youth but not v much, legs being not what they were 60 years ago.'

It was during this visit that he experienced a typically quaint mishap. Staying at the Shelbourne Hotel:

> About midnight I, putting my breakfast-list on the outer door, locked myself out with no clothes on at all – tried a descent in main lift, meaning to call porter through a crack – met by [?]. Up again to the service-lift – rang the alarm – in no time a man came up, gave me a coat, fetched a key, & let me in – no fuss.

Ever restless, Patrick abruptly upped sticks and flew back to Collioure: 'Home . . . A degree of sadness that I had not expected, & some refinements upon it.' Next day, driving up to visit his vineyard at Manay:

> . . . passing the cemetery I said. 'Why. It's the cemetery', adding in commonplace, almost facetious tone 'where we shall all end'. Then realizing what I had said, I was v deeply saddened: & reflecting on my not going to see the grave, bow over it, pray over it, or whatever. I drew what comfort I could from the reflection that it was wrong to sentimentalize, to make a fetish of a body. It was not then, but I think at home that I had a strong, infinitely comforting sense of presence.

In May the BBC crew returned to Collioure. The eager interviewer, who by now (under instruction?) evinced desperate concern to extract details of Patrick's private life, encountered a stone wall at every approach. When at one point he enquired in some exasperation how long Patrick had lived in his house, the indignant author riposted: 'I'm not going to answer that: the next thing you'll want to know is how much I paid for it!' Afterwards he feared the discussion had not gone as well as might be wished. He felt old and tired, and could no longer seek my mother's advice. 'Not a v good day . . . A good deal of pain, little sleep.'

Meanwhile a disturbing report reached him from Christopher Dowling at the Imperial War Museum. A colleague had informed him that the BBC was employing a researcher to uncover evidence of Patrick's wartime service with British Intelligence. He responded with some alarm that: 'They were tedious here [at Collioure], but I had no idea that they could possibly dig down into my Intelligence background. I do hope that your colleague was impenetrably discreet.' He himself had volunteered nothing on the topic, being bound by his oath under the Official Secrets Act.

Patrick continued to be assailed by increasing bouts of physical debility, poignant grief at the loss of my mother, disturbing dreams, and recurring consciousness of mortality: 'A night of asthmatic coughing – remedies no good – & it occurred to me that I might die. Today I began letter to Nikolai for Hélène [Camps] to send if I do . . . Strange weakness today – legs – & stupidity. Should I write my post-mortem letter to Nikolai.'

The letter, which he in due course conveyed to me by hand, contained among other requests 'when you come down destroy my diaries (if I have not already done it) and any private, intimate correspondence'.*

This I fully intended to do, and was only prevented by two wholly unexpected circumstances arising immediately after Patrick's death. In the first place, I discovered to my surprise and dismay that the diaries had vanished from our house at Collioure. Not long afterwards it transpired that it was about the very time that he handed me his letter that Patrick reluctantly acceded to a literary agent's urgent request to place his diaries temporarily in her keeping, with a view to possible publication of extracts. Having retained them until the distracted Patrick was dead, she then failed to return them to our home at Collioure where they belonged (the

---

* The letter is dated 27 May 1998.

house and all its contents having been bequeathed to my sister and myself). In this way I was prevented from destroying them, had I wished to do so.

Whether I would in fact have fulfilled his earlier injunction is hard to say,* since swiftly following this setback there occurred the publication of Dean King's unexpectedly hostile biography, which in turn provoked much equally ill-informed British press criticism of Patrick's personal character. I now found myself placed in a wholly unanticipated quandary. Should I implement Patrick's seemingly unequivocal request, or had this development radically altered the situation? Clearly, it had: his diaries having unexpectedly been abstracted, their destruction now lay beyond my power. More importantly, at least with hindsight, fulfilment of Patrick's instruction would leave his reputation unjustly besmirched by King's book to a degree that neither he nor I could have anticipated. In addition, I had to consider the significance of Patrick's failure to destroy such scattered records as lay to hand where he worked.†

Finally, there was the matter of the substantial archive of correspondence and other manuscript materials relating to him and my mother which I had accumulated during the long years of our close relationship. Possibly through inadvertence, Patrick never made any allusion to such personal records.

---

* His subsequent loan of the diaries to his literary agent shows that he continued in two minds about the issue of their disposal. I suppose, too, that I may be allowed greater familiarity with Patrick's state of mind than outsiders excluded from his private concerns.

† When Patrick died, his London lawyer hastened to Collioure accompanied by a young woman from his office, where in my presence they conducted a painstaking search of the house, having declined my invitation to stay in the house in order to lodge at the expense of the estate in a neighbouring hotel. Bemused by the suddenness of Patrick's death, I did not think to question their actions. This I should have done, since the lawyer was fully aware that the house and contents belonged exclusively to my mother's estate, which on her death passed into the possession of my sister and myself. Subsequent enquiries failed to elicit any satisfactory explanation of this unaccountable intrusion.

After much reflection, it seemed to me all but certain that Patrick would have changed his mind when faced with fresh and unpredictable circumstances – just as he had done a year before his death, when he discussed with me the question of his granting Dean King's request for an interview. He had been prepared to take my advice then, being diverted only by learning of King's unfortunate publication of an adverse piece in the press. Further to this, it struck me that I, both as a professional writer and as the only living person to have known Patrick intimately for so many long and eventful years, found myself unexpectedly placed in a situation where I felt duty bound to protect his reputation from what swiftly became widely accepted slanders, whose effective refutation rested on the substantial range of documents in my possession. Moreover, many of these papers were of a character that I was uniquely placed to explain. The diaries in particular are replete with allusions to people whom in most cases I am the only person left in a position to identify. But all this is to anticipate matters.

At the beginning of 1998 Patrick's literary fame had gained an enduring apogee. His novels were devoured by enthusiastic readers the world over, receiving consistently glowing reviews. In 1937 he had been gratified to receive a £50 advance for his novel *Hussein*. Sixty years later, he noted that: 'I was discreditably excited by accounts, which say we have 2 million +.' A week later his literary agent 'telephoned – she has bumped . . . [Norton] up to $800k + better terms of payment', and shortly afterwards recorded 'huge US contract for [volumes] XIX & XX ($1,600,000 in all, I think)'.

His early ambition had been achieved beyond any conceivable anticipation. In material terms he could indulge himself as he chose, contemplating leasing a flat in the Albany (where Lord Byron had once resided), and idiosyncratically buying himself a golden cup. The satisfaction was real . . . and yet had come too late. The companion of his life and literary endeavour was dead, his health was perceptibly declining, and death itself beckoned. But worse was yet to come. His own mother's premature death had not only deprived him of maternal protection in his infancy, but assisted in transforming his giant father into a frequently grim tyrant. A lasting damaging effect of his deprived childhood was a deep-rooted apprehension of what he feared to be the malicious character of many of his fellow humans.

His thin skin left him exposed to bouts of what at times almost amounted to persecution mania. In the early days I was occasionally assailed by his unexpectedly resentful moods, when it was only my mother's devotion and his considering me a son rather than stepson that removed the possibility of a permanent rift. It was ironic, therefore, that it was in his brilliantly successful old age that he experienced an increasing succession of unprovoked and unaccountable embittered attacks, which seemed to confirm with a vengeance his most fanciful fears of treachery, envy, and deceit.

Patrick had now become something of a Melmoth the Wanderer. It was at home at Collioure that his most cherished memories were rooted, yet he could not stay there long before the memories and solitude grew too much to bear, and he found himself compelled to depart. As he noted: 'I had not quite fully realized how much of one's life is lived with reference (or relatively) to one's other half (or probably a good deal more than half).'

On his next return home he experienced one of those eccentric accidents to which he was ludicrously prone:

Shopping at Mme Camps, with change & counting, I contrived to lose the outer door key. The Duffars have fenced the far side, the pyracantha denied entrance by Mme Dreuille [his neighbours on either side], so I climbed on to the roof, thence to the cloister tiles – dear postière [postwoman] urged me to desist – & so [I] dropped on to the marble table. For a moment all was well but then I lost my balance (on the sundial?) & fell – a grazed elbow & broken marble were all – found spare key. Postière gave me letters, but disapproved.

It appeared (so Patrick told me afterwards) that she believed he had rashly injured himself on purpose.

It was not only to his diary that Patrick confided his concerns. After his death I discovered a plethora of little notes distributed about the house, frequently worded in the form of internal dialogues. A typical example reads:

I MUST NEVER PUT IMPORTANT THINGS IN NEW, CLEVER PLACES: A LITTLE WHILE AGO THOUGHT IT UNWISE TO HAVE CARDS, PASSPORT & WALLET ALL TOGETHER, SO MOVED THE WALLET. I DID FIND IT AGAIN BUT ONLY WITH DIVINE HELP & AT THE COST OF EXTREME ANGUISH.

On 21 August Patrick received a telephone call from his oldest Collioure friend, Odette Boutet, whom he had first met during his exploratory visit to Collioure in 1949. 'Then Odette [telephoned], with more or less fictitious journalist who would [like] to write my biography.'

Patrick had received his first warning of this contingency over a year before, when Richard Ollard wrote to warn him: 'Stuart [Proffitt] tells me that you are being pursued by an unwished for biographer called Dean Smith or some such name. Rest assured that he'll get nothing out of me.'*

The biographer proved to be an American writer, Dean King, who had enterprisingly hit upon a potentially fascinating topic for a biography. However, he now learned for the first time that the

---

* Proffitt himself had assured Patrick in June of the previous year: 'Now, as to Dean King, we have neither seen nor heard anything from him; if he shows up here he will be turned away immediately and I will do my best to make sure he is run over on the Fulham Palace Road. But I am in one way not surprised that he is doing what he is: you may recall my feeling a year or more ago that at least one of these creatures would be bound before long to embark on such an enterprise. I only hope that he is not only first but also last.' Proffitt diffidently suggested the advantages of appointing an authorized biographer, hinting that William Waldegrave might be approached.

project would prove mired with difficulty. As the reader will by now appreciate, Patrick would not brook the least threat to his privacy. Unfortunately for his purpose, King had made his intent clear from the outset, when he conducted a lengthy interview with Odette, who, unwarned by Patrick, innocently described her close friendship with my mother and him during the early years of my parents' settling in Collioure.

Warned by this, the indignant Patrick firmly declined to receive King, and wrote at once to all his friends and publishing colleagues, strongly urging them to have nothing to do with his would-be biographer. A few weeks later I in my turn received a letter from King, in which he declared his interest in republishing my biography of Lord Camelford, written at Patrick's suggestion many years before, and requesting an interview. King also raised in passing the subject of his proposed biography of Patrick. I replied that I was happy to discuss my book and activities generally, but explained that I had undertaken at my stepfather's request not to speak about my parents' private life.

When King arrived at our Berkshire home, he spoke barely at all about Camelford, focusing instead on unearthing details of Patrick's life.* However, I firmly deflected these discreet probes. No further mention was made of the proposed republication of *The Half-Mad Lord*. The consequence of Patrick's ban was that King now found himself able to speak to few who possessed any intimate acquaintance with Patrick. Among prominent exceptions were Odette Boutet and Patrick's estranged son Richard, as well as a handful of people with whom Patrick had for the most part long lost touch, whose silence he had in consequence failed to request. For the present, however, King and his proposed biography were forgotten, as Patrick received his first unpleasant shock: one premonitory of much worse to come.

---

* When approaching John Saumarez Smith, director of the Heywood Hill bookshop, in search of information about Patrick, Dean King described himself as 'an American bookseller'.

On 30 September the BBC finally aired its hour-long documentary, under the title *Patrick O'Brian: Nothing Personal*. Since Patrick could not view it in Collioure, he asked me to report back by telephone. In the event, I felt largely able to still his apprehensions, since the programme appeared for the most part innocuous, and at points even laudatory. His closest friends were like me delighted by his flat refusals to answer what he regarded as personal questions. William Waldegrave spoke for many, castigating the fact that:

> the BBC (which nowadays behaves no better than the commercial companies, and sometimes worse) had put out ridiculous advance publicity making it clear that the <u>only</u> purpose of the programme was personal prying. So I switched on prepared to be furious; and ended up delighted. Not that it wasn't an absurd programme; I'm afraid it was: but it was an utter rout of the busybodies. There were you batting away impertinent questions like Len Hutton playing schoolboy bowling.

The actor Robert Hardy, with equal contempt, 'watched the BBC's attempt to invade your castle, with growing irritation at the present consuming desire to ferret out unnecessary details'. Richard Ollard's verdict was succinct: 'I thought you were <u>dazzling</u> – yourself, & no dam' nonsense.'

One point, however, had aroused alarm in Patrick. As has already been seen, the interviewer at his home in Collioure had managed to extract from him mention of the fact that the character and physique of Jack Aubrey owed much to his elder brother Mike, who had been killed in a wartime bombing raid over Germany. In the documentary this response was juxtaposed with a BBC reporter's visit to the archives, where he enquired after a pilot officer named O'Brian, who had been shot down as Patrick related. An assistant holding up an official list of the relevant deaths was duly filmed declaring that no such name was to be found in their records. This was of course correct, since Mike had enlisted under his baptismal name of Michael Russ – O'Brian being the name assumed in 1945 by Patrick alone of his family.

It seems the BBC was already apprised of the reality, since Patrick's literary agent had informed him five days earlier that the Corporation had discovered his change of name, a revelation it then leaked to the *Sunday Times*. On 29 September she reported further that the BBC interviewer David Kerr 'has found my early books [published under his original name Richard Russ]'. The BBC had also been careful not to inform Patrick of their 'discovery' of the absence of a 'Michael O'Brian' from the official records. So it seems that by the time of the interview they were in a position to know that, had they troubled to question him, he would have been able to explain the circumstances. But that of course would have removed the opportunity for implying that he had lied.*

All this conspiratorial activity reads oddly, when set beside BBC producer Mark Bell's assurance when negotiating Patrick's agreement to the interview, that 'the film would aim to be a thoughtful and measured appreciation of Mr O'Brian's achievement as a writer, and we would not want to intrude on any private part of his life'.

Had Patrick consulted me, I would have warned him of the likelihood of such skulduggery, of which I had considerable

---

* The slur proved effective. The *Daily Telegraph Television & Radio* reported that the interviewer 'finds no evidence for an elder brother on which O'Brian tells him Aubrey is based'. The point was ponderously emphasized by Andrew Alderson: 'O'Brian under fire for "fictional" life', *Sunday Times*, 27 September 1998. Patrick was mortified by the smear, noting the same day that '100 Days goes on sale, so malignance could hardly have been better timed, & sadness & depression returned in full force or even worse.' The BBC's justification provides a nice example of specious prevarication: 'Kerr said he had not gone back to the author with the results of the inquiries because O'Brian had made it clear that he did not want to answer "personal questions".'

personal experience.* As it was, I now sought to reassure him by saying that few viewers would have noted, let alone be likely to remember, the malicious slur. With this he was perforce obliged for the present to remain content. Patrick's legion of devoted readers across the world evinced little concern with irrelevant details of his personal life. Regrettably, however, the attitude of a vociferous ill-natured segment of the London press and would-be literati was very different. Envy of his astonishing literary success and accompanying wealth, combined with an insatiable requirement to provide dramatic personal 'revelations', continued to gather momentum in such quarters.

As Patrick himself wrote a week later:

Small rain in the evening spoilt my intended work, & I tended to brood on what I take to be the jealous ill-will excited in small journalists etc by what I may without gross immodesty call relative success . . . I grew more cheerful & had quite a good dinner; then in bed I listened to Tallis with real enjoyment – a longish pause for pain, pills & then sleep again, with a strange, v affectionate coming together.

Even in death, my mother was able to console him.

All these worries preyed upon Patrick to the extent that he decided to pass the winter between London and Dublin, where there would at least be much to distract him. He arranged for his post to be forwarded to me, which he gave me carte blanche to sift, passing on only what appeared of interest. On arrival in

---

* After Patrick's death, the Irish journalist Kevin Myers criticized him harshly on grounds that my mother, had she been alive, would have advised him against co-operation with the BBC. Not only was Myers in no position to know the facts, but in fact the opposite was the case. When the project was first broached, Patrick noted in his diary for 1 June 1994: 'Letter from BBC, who would like to do a 50' programme about my work – I recoiled, but M[ary], V[ivien]G[reen] & S[tuart]P[roffitt] were v much in favour . . .'

London he encountered the first of what was to become an increasing flow of more or less hostile press articles. Warned by me that the *Daily Telegraph* intended to publish on the Saturday what I feared might be an 'unpleasant' feature article about him, he apprehensively avoided the attention of members of Brooks's Club (where he was staying), by breakfasting around the corner in Jermyn Street.

The article, which occupied two entire pages of the newspaper, proved dismaying to Patrick: 'It had a large number of accurate details, some inaccurate (the first almost certainly from a family source), & above all a singular malignance. It did not worry me much at first, but uneasiness grew.'

His apprehension was understandable. Although he had taken the surname O'Brian at random in 1945, adopting it from that of a nineteenth-century sea captain upon whose record he had chanced, it inevitably led many who had not known him at the time into the supposition that he was Irish. He had spent some months in Belfast and southern Ireland in 1933, and again in Belfast and Dublin in 1937 when writing his early novel *Hussein*. These protracted visits instilled in him a lasting love of Ireland as a sort of Happy Otherworld, leading him on occasion to hint at, or (rarely) even silently accept, the presumption that he was Irish. Since the true reason for his change of name arose from an over-riding desire to banish his wretched childhood and tormented early adulthood, he was desperately concerned to suppress those early years – even to some extent from his own memory. The change of name occurred when he married my mother in 1945, an event which proffered opportunity for beginning his life anew.

Rereading the article today, I can however detect no trace of 'malignance'. As Patrick himself conceded, its content was almost entirely factually accurate, and (as he would *not* however have admitted) comprised what I would have thought matter of legitimate public interest. The author, Ben Fenton, had conducted considerable researches, his prime source evidently being surviving members of the Russ family.* The article's only serious error lies in its dramatic but fictitious account of Patrick's alleged first encounter with my mother during an air raid in 1941, when in fact their romance began long before the Blitz, before the outbreak of War. A few days later the *Telegraph* published a second major article by Fenton, containing a detailed rebuttal of the BBC's canard that the bomber-pilot brother on whom Patrick claimed Jack Aubrey was partially based never existed.

A handful of journalists and others professed pious outrage on learning that Patrick had changed his name. A well-educated mutual friend even telephoned me to say that he felt 'betrayed' by the 'deception'. It seems that he and others felt foolish for having accepted Patrick's adopted name as that of his birth. An extreme, but far from unique, example was the writer Jan Morris. At the end of 1999 she had published a glowing review of *Blue at the Mizzen*, which included a perceptive assessment of the Aubrey–Maturin œuvre in its entirety (*Observer*, 21 November 1999). Less than a year later, however, on reviewing Dean King's 'extremely thorough' biography, she pronounced that: 'In O'Brian . . . I am reading the work of an artificer, a contriver of genius and, well, a liar' (*Observer*, 3 September 2000).

I continue to find such startled reactions baffling. After all, having accepted the 'deception' at close quarters for the greater part of my life, I might be thought to have had reason to feel more aggrieved than most! Although I assume I was aware of his change of name even before my first visit to Collioure in 1955, I do not recollect its ever having aroused in me anything but the most fleeting interest, far less concern. I continued to find Patrick the

---

* There is no indication in the article of his having consulted Patrick's estranged son Richard, who had long distanced himself from all his family. On the other hand, the detail of my mother's being accompanied by her dachshund Miss Potts when driving her ambulance during the Blitz can, I imagine, only have derived from me. Today I have no recollection of being consulted at the time by Mr Fenton, although it seems I must have been.

same person writing the same books, whatever his original name. Nor have I found myself unable to enjoy *Candide*, *Middlemarch*, *Huckleberry Finn*, *Alice in Wonderland*, *Lord Jim*, *Animal Farm*, or the works of innumerable other authors who likewise elected to write under names other than those received at their birth.*

Still more pertinently, I have yet to hear of any critic's succumbing to a fit of the vapours on learning that C.S. Forester's baptismal name was in reality Cecil Smith. Further parallels with Patrick's career are striking. Acutely embarrassed by his modest social origin and erratic upbringing, Forester was deeply concerned to suppress or reinvent his early life. On a visit to the United States in 1939, he warned his wife that, on her arrival: 'If I'm not meeting you meet the reporters quite frankly: talk about Hollywood and lecture and so on . . . It'll be all right. I'm very much a public figure here by now. *But don't know anything about me before we got married* . . . [italics inserted].'[1]

Clearly, there must be a reason for this disparity of treatment of the two celebrated maritime authors, whose works have so often been compared. Being personally acquainted with one or two of Patrick's former admirers who turned bitterly against him, following the revelation of his change of name and occasional assumption of Irish origins, my interpretation (for what it be worth) is as follows. Although the reclusive Patrick tended to keep even those whose acquaintance he valued at discreet arm's length, there were some among them who liked to represent themselves to their readers or friends as bosom confidants of the famous author. When it was belatedly revealed that they were ignorant even of his real name, they felt foolish, and reacted accordingly. Of course, there may be another reason, although at present I cannot think of one.

As it turned out, Patrick's suppression of his early life proved

---

* Walter Scott and Jane Austen even had the impudence – *horribile dictu* – to publish novels anonymously!

to be a disastrous mistake. An Irish admirer admonished him about this time that 'you created what you thought was a fortress – but it proved to be a prison'. On the other hand, such morbidly irrational reactions may well have appeared to justify his secrecy. As a great Irishman wrote, objecting similarly to an overly personal newspaper article:

> It is full of anecdotes and particulars of my life. It therefore cuts deep. I am sure I have nothing in my family, my circumstances, or my conduct that an honest man ought to be ashamed of. But the more circumstances of all these which are brought out, the more materials are furnished for malice to work upon: and I assure you that it will manufacture them to the utmost.[2]

Reverting to Fenton's article, although initially troubled by his revelations, by the time Patrick arrived at our home that evening his equanimity appeared quite restored, and he was even preparing to take belated advantage of public awareness of his change of name. Alerted to the imminent publication of Fenton's piece two days earlier, Patrick wrote in his diary: 'I read most of <u>Caesar</u>, written 70 years ago & almost entirely forgotten: it is rather silly, childish & moderately dull, but not downright discreditable or embarrassing & I think I should like to protect copyright.'

Caesar was Patrick's first book, published when he was only fifteen, which appeared under his original name of Patrick Russ. For this reason all his books and short stories published before 1945 had been omitted from the British Library's lavish tribute.[3] Now he seized the opportunity to regain credit for his precocious early works, acknowledging privately that: 'There are, it seems to me, certain advantages [to public awareness of his change of name] – openness.' Would that he had grasped this much earlier!

If elements of the lesser literati chafed at Patrick's continuing immense popularity, this was emphatically not the case among another class of reader. On 26 October Patrick entertained the Second Sea Lord, Admiral Sir John Brigstocke, to dinner at Brooks's. Patrick found Sir John 'a very agreeable thorough sailor', while his guest wrote next day to thank him, enthusing that 'We really must make you an honorary Admiral! Not only have you brought reading pleasure to millions, you have also educated them in British naval history, and its significance. This has inspired many to join the Royal Navy, and to maintain its honour and record of success.'

Sir John's counterparts across the Atlantic were equally complimentary, prominent among his admirers being Admiral Jay L. Johnson, Chief of Naval Operations, and Vice Admiral George W. Emery, commanding the Submarine Force of the US Atlantic Fleet. President Reagan's Secretary for the Navy, John F. Lehman Jr, presented him with a copy of his memoir *Command of the Seas*, inscribed 'with admiration and appreciation'.*

At the beginning of November Patrick returned to Dublin, where he received as ever a warm welcome from the Provost and Fellows at Trinity. By now, however, news from his literary agent that King was definitely preparing his biography greatly distressed Patrick. A few days later I flew over to stay with him in his rooms provided by the College on the ground floor of Botany Bay, where I found him at first a little low, although seemingly cheered by my visit. He was further delighted by becoming further intimate with our youngest daughter Xenia, who had accompanied me to acquaint herself with Trinity College, which she hoped to attend in the following year. Patrick's mood was, however, volatile, and his lifelong fear of finding himself the butt of ill will manifested itself when one night during my visit he was turned away by a porter from the dining hall. In reality, as I learned, this was occasioned not by malice, but because there happened

---

* Lehman also wrote an encomiastic review of *The Wine-Dark Sea* in the *Wall Street Journal*.

to be a special dinner hosted by the College to which only faculty members were invited.

What surprised and pleased me on the occasion of my stay in his rooms was Patrick's unexpected and to me quite astonishing openness. My relationship with him had always been filial and affectionate, but I had long eschewed raising any topic of an overly personal nature. Now, however, he became for the first time both unusually confiding and (still more surprisingly) prone to discussing his inner feelings openly. I slept on the sofa in his sitting room, which provided opportunity for late-night cogitations over liberal libations of Power's excellent Irish whiskey. He now expressed considerable agitation at the news that Dean King intended to publish his unauthorized biography. He had consistently refused to be interviewed by him, a problematic issue which we discussed late into one night.

On his arrival at Trinity, Patrick had found awaiting him a further request from the aspiring biographer to grant him an interview for what he cautiously described as 'a literary article'. Now, as the evening drew on with much conviviality and intimacy, Patrick suddenly asked me to state frankly what I thought should be his response to King's request. While I myself possessed personal experience of misrepresentation by a small but vociferous coterie of the British media, for Patrick to seek my candid advice on so very personal an issue was all but unique in my experience.* My response was that, it being impossible to stifle hostile criticism, I had found that co-operation provided the simplest and safest course. While this risked (even at times occasioned) distortion, I believe the prime concern of most journalists is to secure a good story. Moreover, the likelihood on the whole is that an interviewer will naturally prefer a protagonist's first-hand account to that

---

* Although it did not occur to me at the time, Patrick was clearly feeling the loss of my mother, for whom I may have provided a natural substitute at this distressing time.

concocted by ill-informed outsiders. Besides, all press comment being inherently ephemeral,* there was little to be gained by any fruitless attempt to avert malicious distortion. Patrick listened attentively, and to my great surprise suddenly expressed agreement with this view.

Next day he telephoned his literary agent, asking her to inform King of his change of mind, and consenting to an interview. However, her response dramatically altered his decision. It transpired that King had just published a lengthy article in the influential US magazine *New York*, which provided a detailed account of Patrick's family background, while dwelling somewhat obsessively on the falsity of any pretension he might have to being Irish. That it included a number of speculative inaccuracies cannot have improved Patrick's indignant estimate of the writer.

His anger at this invasion of his privacy seemed to me understandable. He promptly informed his agent that in no circumstances would he have anything to do with King. Not long after, I learned more of this dramatic episode. That the world was beginning to grow acquainted with Patrick's 'secret life' had become all too evident. The BBC had opened the door on his past by a crack, and shortly afterwards Ben Fenton's well-researched articles let in the first flood of light. It was clear that King's desire for a scoop was becoming seriously endangered, and I was informed that his US publisher had urged him to move quickly to establish his prior claim to authority by publishing an outline of his discoveries through a reputable outlet. It was this that led him to rush out his article for *New York*. Now he belatedly discovered that he had inadvertently wrecked what was for him potentially the scoop of a lifetime. Anguished pleadings and apologies via Patrick's agent availed him nothing, with the result that he was prevented from

---

* Our discussion took place before the internet changed everything, with its unfortunate policy of indiscriminately perpetuating errors and falsehoods in what amounts to perpetuity. In addition, Wikipedia and similar sources are not seldom given to censoring rebuttals of factual error.

accessing not only Patrick himself, but the testimony of practically all those surviving family members, friends and literary colleagues who actually knew him.

Patrick's indignation was total, and it was further unfortunate for King that his wrath was exacerbated by occasional tactless remarks from people who had seen the *New York* article. When King sent me for comment a draft account of an event in which I had supposedly been involved, I prepared a reply pointing out one or two of his more blatant inaccuracies, together with a general warning against the dangers of groundless speculation. I first despatched a draft copy to Patrick, who was by then back in Collioure. He telephoned by return, angrily upbraiding me for entering into *any* contact with King, and declaring that he wished to have nothing more to do with me! It was only when I gently pointed out that what I had sent him was a draft, not to be despatched without his approval, that he relented with equal suddenness.

I cannot help wondering what would have been the outcome had King's unfortunate venture into print not occurred. While I feel certain that Patrick would have proved pretty much as reticent as was his wont, he might, I imagine, have corrected some of King's wilder misrepresentations. Above all, even had the latter gained nothing else, it would have provided a major fillip for his biography could he have cited his subject's co-operation. As Patrick wrote to Richard Scott Simon in the New Year of 1999: 'The wretch King is absolutely determined to be a nuisance, but at least we can cut him off from anything that gives the book an "authorised" air.'

Equally, given the combination of Patrick's reserve with King's lack of critical acumen and marked tendency towards speculative sensationalism, it is quite possible that readers would have benefited little from the exchange.

The knowledge that a biography likely to prove gravely damaging in effect, if not intent, was imminently to be published afflicted Patrick with bouts of depression, sleeplessness, and suspicion. Stuart

Proffitt at Collins was so concerned that he flew to Dublin on Patrick's return and took him on a tour of the Irish countryside. While he enjoyed this, his apprehension proved in no way diminished. When his former editor Richard Ollard inadvertently failed to send him a Christmas card, he worried lest he had been affected by the adverse publicity: 'Could it be on account of articles in press?' Occasionally he quaintly sought solace by viewing the video film of the Queen's bestowal of his CBE, which seems to have brought him greater consolation than Proffitt's assurance that press criticism exercised no perceptible effect on his continuingly soaring book sales.

Despite his own melancholy problems, Patrick followed my own travails with his customary sympathy and understanding. In one of his many letters to me at the time, he wrote with passion:

> How sorry I am about the horrid, <u>horrid</u> time you had in that vile law-court. I wish I could accurately recall the Old Testament's words about human justice, likening it to a woman's filthy rag. I had it from the Vulgate, and the Latin was particularly powerful. But there is this reflection: Aldington has to live with Aldington, & as Lady A said long ago 'There will be tears again tonight' – a fairly permanent state of affairs, no doubt.

XVII

Melmoth the Wanderer

... the most austere and bitter accidents that can happen to a man
in this life, in æternum valedicere, to part for ever, to forsake the
world and all our friends, 'tis vltimum terribilium, the last and the
greatest terror, and most irksome and troublesome vnto vs.

[Robert Burton], *The Anatomy of Melancholy: What it is.*
With all the Kindes, Cavses, Symptomes, Prognosticks,
and Severall Cvres of it (Oxford, 1624), p. 279

In 1998 much undeserved pain was inflicted on Patrick by the
BBC's insinuation that he was a liar (an accusation robustly
corrected a few weeks later by Ben Fenton in the *Daily Telegraph*),
and then – more damaging – by Dean King's would-be exposé in
New York magazine. Worst of all was the knowledge that the
hard-earned climacteric to his long and arduous literary life found
itself more and more threatened by publication of what he felt
certain (rightly, as it turned out) would be a profoundly damaging
biography by the same writer. Deeply troubled by this looming
threat, assailed by recurring insomnia, bouts of illness and lapses
of memory – above all, wretched in the poignant absence of my
mother – the pleasure that might have been expected from his
astonishing accession of fame and wealth persistently eluded him.
On a lowlier, but nonetheless troubling, level, deprivation of my
mother's management of their accounts (which she had handled

since at least 1945) left him regularly bewildered by the smallest bills.

For the present, however, he had benefited from his winter's stay in Dublin. Trinity College had afforded him a warm welcome, and the exclusive Kildare Street Club, which he had been able to use in consequence of a mutual arrangement with Brooks's, accorded him honorary membership. He had acquired some good friends in the city, and from his diary it is clear that he derived comfort from my visit and that of our youngest daughter Xenia. His tour of the Irish countryside with Stuart Proffitt likewise afforded him pleasure, as did his renewed familiarity with Dublin, above all with its evocative memories of his youthful stay in 1937, when he wrote his successful novel *Hussein*.

Perhaps most gratifying of all at this stage, despite constant misgivings he had at last completed *Blue at the Mizzen*. In February 1999 he reported to Richard Scott Simon: 'I have indeed had a pleasant time here in an agreeable little set of rooms, writing 60,000 words of a new book.'

When the book was published later in the year, it bore the inscription:

> I dedicate this book, *donum indignum*,
> to the Provost and to all those many people
> who were so kind to me while I was
> writing it in Trinity College, Dublin

The College, where I too had enjoyed exceptionally happy days forty years earlier, did indeed provide Patrick with a warm and much-appreciated refuge. As the Provost, Tom Mitchell, wrote to him on 9 December 1998: 'I hope you will long continue to enjoy life at Trinity and in Dublin. You will be welcome in the College at any time and for as long as you wish. Good luck with the arduous, anxious but exhilarating *ars scribendi*.'

It was about this time also that Patrick received an appreciative visitor at his rooms in Trinity. The Honourable Mr Justice Deeny was a graduate of Trinity, who subsequently became a High Court judge in Northern Ireland. A devotee of Patrick's novels, he had seized the opportunity, when on holiday in the Roussillon some years previously with his wife Alison, of requesting a visit to the reclusive author. The judge's Irish charm, tact and intelligence worked wonders, when Patrick, unusually, welcomed them into their home. That evening he insisted on taking the couple out to dinner at his favourite fish restaurant in Port-Vendres. While Patrick and the judge discussed naval practices in the time of Nelson, my mother described to his wife their initial years of poverty following their arrival in Collioure.

In 1996 Deeny and his wife attended the banquet held in Patrick's honour in the Painted Hall at Greenwich, where they again spoke briefly. Now, learning that Patrick was in Dublin, he obtained an invitation to visit him at his rooms in Botany Bay. Although such delicate matters were not raised, the Judge's keen forensic mind privately scouted the bizarre sensitivities of critics outraged by Patrick's change of name. As for his supposed claim to be Irish, Deeny commented:

> I can only say for my part that he never said anything to us to suggest either that he was in fact Irish or that he had been on active service in the war. As to the former he seemed one of those Englishmen who was proud of some connection with Ireland which in his case he did not elaborate on.

Aspects of their conversation reveal the surprising extent to which an intelligent and sympathetic interlocutor could extract fascinatingly candid personal information from Patrick. So little is known of his life between completion of his education in 1933 and his lengthy visit to Ireland in 1937, that it has even been questioned by Dean King whether he ever crossed the Irish Sea at that time. It is to Sir Donnell Deeny (as he subsequently became) that we owe this invaluable glimpse of his initial stay in the North: 'Indeed he said his first love was from Belfast. She was called Mona Fitzpatrick . . . I have to say that he also admitted to taking another girl up to MacArts Fort which she told him she was not meant to climb.'

It seems that it was not only the incomparable landscape and poetic imagination of the Irish that generated Patrick's love affair with the green isle. Possibly, too, the judge's introduction of Bushmills whiskey to Patrick's palate contributed to the relative candour of the conversation.[1]

A poem he composed at the time to which this memory relates has fortunately survived, poignantly commemorating his adolescent love affair:

> Dear Mona FitzPatrick '32 (or '3)
>
> A boy – a man – I loved in County Down:
> In the evenings, the sweet dusk of that summer
> I used to turn my face to the North
> writing writing and counting the days for a letter
> (I was a boy)
> longing the days long, my hands out to Ulster
> I stood in the secret dark of the evening.
> And now, on the evening path of a mountain, unthinking it
>   came fresh again:
> familiar, familiar the sadness pervading
> heart-worn the prayer for a wind from the north.[2]

The allusive expressions 'my face to the North . . . my hands out to Ulster' indicate that the poem was written in the Irish Free State following his encounter with Mona in Ulster. This chance reference shows that Patrick paid at least two substantial visits to Ireland before the War, which entrenched his profound love of the island of saints and scholars.

With the arrival of spring he returned home to Collioure. Hitherto I have been enabled to follow Patrick's activities not only from my own memories, but above all from the diaries he had kept since 1969 – that for the pivotal year 1968 having regrettably been purloined at the end of his life. Frustratingly, that which he kept for the last year of his life also vanished in suspicious – although entirely distinct – circumstances. On 31 December 1998 he purchased a diary for the coming year at Read's bookshop in Nassau Street, around the corner from Trinity. That he fulfilled his intention of continuing his daily entries is attested by an acquaintance who saw it on several occasions in the Westbury hotel where he was staying at the end of 1999. Since he was not in the habit of carrying sizeable diaries around with him, it is all but certain that it was in his room when he died there on 2 January 2000. About that time, however, it disappeared in circumstances which have never been explained. The London solicitors responsible for administering Patrick's estate refused to investigate the matter. For reasons which I am unable to specify here, I have reason to believe that it was abstracted from his hotel bedroom, and I fear destroyed in Dublin shortly after his death.

In April 1999 Patrick returned to Collioure, dismayed to find an enormous accumulation of post awaiting him. In September he had received an invitation from Annemarie Victory in New York, inviting him to participate in a Mediterranean cruise on board *Sea Cloud*, a magnificent four-masted barque with a fully manned crew to handle the vessel under sail. It had been constructed in 1931 at Hamburg for the Post Toasties heiress Marjorie Merriweather Post. The interior was luxuriously but tastefully furnished and decorated. Any doubts Patrick might have nurtured were stilled by Annemarie's assurance 'that you will not make any speeches nor respond to personal questions. I assure you that the other guests on board . . . will be more than happy simply to meet you and share conversations about Captain Aubrey and Dr. Maturin . . .'

The prospect was certainly exciting, with Patrick sailing in a vessel so closely recalling those whose handling he has described more vividly than any novelist since Stevenson or Conrad. (It still baffles me when Patrick's detractors assert that his extensive reliance on imagination and research rather than practical navigation represents a *blemish* on his literary achievement!)

Despite the very considerable cost of the cruise, Annemarie encountered no difficulty in filling the cabins with guests, many of whom had travelled from the United States to participate in this unique experience. Patrick was unsure how long his temperament would match up to days away from his writing, spent among potentially garrulous or inquisitive strangers. He agreed to board the vessel when it put in at neighbouring Port-Vendres, and to disembark two nights later at France's great naval base of Toulon.

As Patrick told me afterwards, his fears proved groundless, and he thoroughly enjoyed the voyage. His admirers were polite and discreet, and he found his fellow guests of honour cordial and interesting. They were Walter Cronkite, the veteran US journalist and broadcaster, the naval historian David Lyon, who was preparing a prosopography of Patrick's seafaring novels, and Lyon's wife Eleanor Sharpston (whom Patrick privately termed 'the Lyoness'), an international lawyer who first met her husband on a converted gaff-rigged Baltic trader in the North Sea. All three were experienced amateur sailors. Patrick's spirits rose among this congenial company. After he left the ship, Eleanor Sharpston wrote to him:

> It has been a delight for me to have opportunity to renew, on board Sea Cloud, our earlier slight acquaintance. I do hope that, as well as being duly lionised by your devoted American followers, you have had some time and space for yourself and for 'Blue at the Mizzen'; and that you have enjoyed being back at sea under square sail as much as I have relished my forays aloft.

In the event Patrick became sufficiently relaxed to deliver a short talk while on board. One particularly enthusiastic admirer was an

American bibliophile named David Mattie, who had longed for Patrick to sign his collection of first editions of the Aubrey–Maturin series, now handsomely rebound in leather. Although Patrick had of late succumbed to his US publishers' pressure to engage in occasional public signings of single volumes, he had never before agreed to such a collective signing. Now, however, he consented to fulfil Mattie's request to sign the entire set in the privacy of his cabin. Mattie having since died, the twenty volumes* were, I noted, recently offered for sale at £50,000.

Subsequently my wife Georgina and I came to know Annemarie Victory well, when we joined *Sea Cloud* in successive years on Mediterranean cruises, where I delivered lectures to admirers of Patrick's life and work. She told us of her emotion when she accompanied him at his final disembarkation. Tears were coursing down his face, as he recognized the taxi-driver bringing him home as the one who had taken my mother on her final journey to hospital.

Returning to Patrick's activities in 1999, in August he reported to Richard Scott Simon: 'I have lived alone, keeping a sharp eye on bread, milk and butter I have not indeed abandoned writing, but my filing has assumed that neolithic form of putting every day's post on the nearest flat surface. In some cases the depth is now quite surprising.'

He went on to express gratitude for:

your very <u>very</u> kind letter about my British Library juvenilia . . . The little books themselves are charming objects, and that dear man Arthur Cunningham took endless pains with their appearance. They were pretty well received, but in spite of your praises and William Waldegrave's I have, as yet, barely looked on them, for fear of being made to cringe.

---

* *Blue at the Mizzen* must have been signed on its publication later in the year.

The books in question were the British Library's handsome reprint (by arrangement with HarperCollins, who paid Patrick £50,000 advance) of his youthful tales *Caesar* and *Hussein*, issued in a single slipcase. The original titles had been published under the names of Patrick Russ and R.P. Russ respectively. For some time Patrick had resisted their republication for this reason,* but now that his change of name had become public knowledge there was no longer sufficient justification for concealing their existence – although the author's name now appeared as Patrick O'Brian.

HMS *Victory*, 30 September 1999†

Towards the end of September Patrick flew to England to attend the annual dinner aboard HMS *Victory* at Portsmouth, to which he had been invited by the Second Sea Lord, Admiral Sir John Brigstocke. The company was as ever small and select, many of

---

* On 24 August 1993 Patrick had responded to the editor's request: 'But as for the early novels, no: I am sorry to disappoint you, but I should much rather leave them in their decent oblivion.'
† Patrick is fourth from left in the back row.

the guests being accompanied by their wives. Patrick felt a sharp twinge of regret as he recalled that, had he been able to accept the invitation Sir John sent him in the previous year, my mother would have accompanied him.

On this occasion he was the guest of honour, and had been invited to provide a short address. As ever, this filled him with apprehension, and in London he sought Richard Ollard's advice as to whether on such an occasion notes were likely to prove advantageous. Richard's sage counsel was to compile them, if only as a source of confidence or reserve aid should he become momentarily stuck.

Patrick's scribbled note, covering a single side of A4 paper, makes for intriguing reading, representing as it does his final autobiographical résumé. After explaining that he 'began life as a child but a sickly child', who experienced 'little or no school but reading', he ventured onto a controversial aspect of his career. Cryptically he continued: '& then sea Phantome II first sailing Westminster?'

The allusion is to the magnificent barque *Belem*, which he had seen in the harbour at Port-Vendres eight years earlier. It had indeed belonged to the Duke of Westminster, who sold it in 1922 to Sir Arthur Guinness. Guinness renamed it *Fantôme II*, a detail not recorded by Patrick when, years before, he jotted down notes on the *Belem* (the name to which it had reverted some twenty years earlier), on the occasion of her visit to Port-Vendres. It was this yacht that Patrick claimed to have crewed by invitation of his 'particular friend', a young Irishman named Edward Taaffe, who bore a familial or other close connection to the owner.

There appear to be three alternative explanations of the account Patrick gave his fellow-diners aboard the *Victory*:

1. His claimed voyage or voyages aboard *Fantôme II* represent pure invention, inspired by the splendid sight of the vessel under sail rounding Cap Creus in 1991.

2. He mistakenly believed that the voyage had occurred, having become persuaded of its truth over time.

3. He had indeed engaged in such a cruise or cruises more than half a century earlier, memories of which influenced his subsequent literary inspiration.

I do not believe that in the present sparse state of evidence it is possible to be certain which of these alternatives is correct. My own inclination, for reasons set out in my Appendix C, is with some reservation to accept that the last may after all be true.* Frustratingly, I have been unable to discover anything about Edward Taaffe, beyond the fact that he and his wife Kathy undoubtedly existed as Patrick's close friends in the 1930s. This is a pity, as clearly confirmation could well lie there.

Be all this as it may, Patrick's speech was warmly received, for which he afterwards thanked Richard Ollard, saying he felt it had gone down well in consequence of his advice.

Earlier in the month Patrick had written to the Provost of Trinity to alert him that our daughter Xenia would shortly be arriving to begin her studies at the College. The Provost's secretary responded, reassuring him that 'I hope she will make contact and if not I will make some discreet enquiries and make sure she is finding her feet – I hope she will be able to take the rough and tumble of TCD as it is today – quite different from when her Father was a student!'

Concerned by the friendly warning, Patrick flew to Dublin for a few days at the beginning of October to ensure Xenia was safely settled in.

That done, he returned again to Collioure, where he stayed for a month working on the manuscript of his as yet untitled 'XXI'

---

* Terry Zobeck writes: 'I think you are correct. I would add that it is hard to credit that after all of the fuss created by the BBC program that Patrick would make a claim that might be proved false and raise more fuss and hurt.'

in the Aubrey–Maturin series. He was finding the work increasingly arduous, explaining to Edwin Moore at Collins that: 'For some time I have been somewhat indifferent, and what I facetiously call my memory has been worse by far.' A month later he responded to an invitation from the Constable, Field-Marshal Lord Inge, to dine at the Tower of London, with the lament that 'at the moment I am sadly perturbed by a difficult chapter and I can hardly see beyond the boundaries of an overcrowded desk'. On 9 November he agreed to sit for the moulding of a plaster bust by his old friend Rirette de Bordas. Her husband Pierre's photograph of the occasion is the last to be taken of Patrick in his beloved Correch d'en Baus – that dear cosy home which I would say was, second only to my mother, the great mainstay of his work and inspiration.

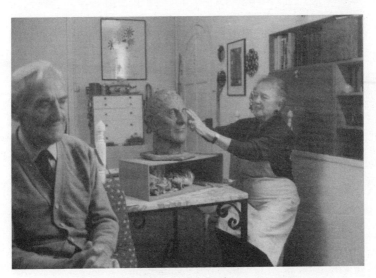

The last photo of Patrick in Correch d'en Baus

When in January I entered his deserted study, I found on his desk a copy of Horace, in which he had marked this passage:

'The years, as they pass, plunder us of all joys, one by one. They have stripped me of mirth, love, feasting, play; they are striving to wrest from me my poems. What would you have me do?'*

Immediately after this final visit, he flew at his US publishers' request to New York to publicize the newly published *Blue at the Mizzen*. There on 15 November he was interviewed by his genial admirer Walter Cronkite before an enthusiastic audience at the New York Public Library. Although he appeared his usual self at the gathering, he felt his strength waning fast and was obliged to cut his visit short.

After a brief stay in London, Patrick returned to Dublin for the last time. Exhausted by the hectic succession of flights between New York, London and Dublin, he was in a sorry state of mind. As the century drew towards its close he noted: 'TCD again: 26·XI·99 and I am sadly at a loss . . .' His Dublin acquaintance Helen Lucy Burke told me that Patrick returned much disturbed by what he described as excessive pressure from his literary agency to fulfil the stressful engagement.

In his Trinity rooms, Patrick resumed work on what was to be his final, incomplete and untitled novel. In it (as he told me), Jack Aubrey was to cross the Atlantic from South America, pay a visit to Napoleon on St Helena, and undergo adventures in the jungles of West Africa. The last part of the work would have drawn much on the intrepid late Victorian explorer Mary Kingsley's *Travels in West Africa*. At the close of 1998, Patrick recorded: 'I finished, with great applause, Mary Kingsley's <u>Travels in W Africa</u> – a jewel of a woman.'[3] Work on the text of the novel began in May 1999, but despite much preparatory labour only three chapters had been completed in preliminary form by the time of Patrick's death.

---

* *Singula de nobis anni praedantur euntes; / eripuere iocos, Venerem, convivia, ludum; / tendunt extorquere poemata: quid faciam vis?*

A scrap of paper he left behind suggests that he envisaged eventual happy endings for his two friends:

final (?) solution: SM marries Christine her brother having died & they live in the house near Woolcombe.

At some point soon JA may say 'I had so looked forward to peace [modest wealth, country delights, greenery, fishing, hunting (his own pack even).

That Jack's leisure is not entirely to be reduced to such innocent bucolic pursuits is suggested by a cryptic admonition – surely uttered by the cautionary Stephen: 'a snowy bosom shd be contemplated with an equally untroubled even frigid eye.'

Returned to Dublin, Patrick first stayed in his Trinity rooms, where he was much cheered by the presence of our youngest daughter Xenia, now enrolled at the University. She remembers wandering with him arm in arm through the streets of Dublin, where he laughed and joked, even skipping on occasion, and occasionally pausing to point out the scene of some incident from his stay in the city in 1937. Now he planned to settle there, and entered into negotiations for purchase of a flat, the principal stipulation being that it should have a room suitable for his granddaughter. I suspect that Xenia's departure for the Christmas vacation contributed towards reviving Patrick's loneliness and confusion, exacerbated as it was by the importunate pressure that persuaded him to undertake his stressful visit to New York.

Immediately on the term's ending, Patrick moved to the Westbury Hotel in Grafton Street. Sadly, annotations in the manuscript of his novel show that he was becoming more than ordinarily confused, even a touch paranoid. His apprehension, expressed to me during my stay in his College rooms, that Trinity no longer wanted him, began to pervade his thoughts. This delusion appeared confirmed when the Provost's secretary, Daphne Gill, arranged the move. In reality, it was far from the case: both Provost Thomas

Mitchell and Daphne Gill were very fond of their at times cranky but generally fascinating guest. The truth was entirely mundane: the Michaelmas term had ended, and the College servant ('skip') would no longer be available to care for his rooms.

For the remainder of the month Patrick toiled fitfully at his work, by this time more, I suspect, as refuge and consolation than inspiration. As December drew towards its close, he lamented: 'I am absurdly sleepy', while his book 'creeps on with petty pace'. Cruel old age and deep loneliness in the absence of my mother, and now that of his granddaughter Xenia, combined to enhance that latent paranoia which had bedevilled much of his existence. On what was probably the last day of his life, at the advent of the new millennium, he wrote sadly:

No: there is quite a lot of III – LdL's [Lord Leyton's] dinner or part of it – missing It is not in the MS binder: but I remember now that there was a table-plan in the lower L[eft] marge Alas, I cannot find it: lost pages, two lost MS chapters are the almost daily bane of my life: could there be a malignant hand?

On the evening of 2 January 2000 the telephone rang at our home in Berkshire. It was Helen Lucy Burke, the Irish journalist whom Patrick had befriended, who broke the news of his death. Seemingly bright and cheerful as ever, he was about to go out to dinner with a longstanding family friend, Youg Azzopard-Vinour, who owned a flat in Collioure overlooking the church and plage St Vincent. Patrick arose from his armchair, took three or four steps across the carpet towards the door, and suddenly collapsed unconscious on the floor. He was rushed to St James's Hospital, where he was pronounced dead.

At his prior request, his death was kept secret, while formal preparations were made for the transport of his body to Collioure. Georgina and I travelled by train with our four children to Collioure, where we were joined by Natasha and her two sons

Michael and Robert. Patrick had wished no one else to be present, save his friends among the inhabitants of Collioure, who crowded the church by the harbour. The service was quiet and moving, after which we all followed the cortège in cars up the hill, to the cemetery where Patrick was laid to rest beside our mother. They were together again, as they had been since that memorable summer of 1939.

On 27 April a memorial service was held at Greenwich Hospital, scene of Patrick's triumphal banquet in 1996. Georgina and I were present with our children, as were also Natasha and her sons. Lessons were read by Anastasia and Patrick's nephew Stephen Russ.* Charles Dibdin's lovely 'Tom Bowling' was sung by a solo tenor. Tributes were delivered by Lord Waldegrave (as he had become), Admiral Sir Michael Layard, Richard Ollard, and me.

I was moved to see that Richard Ollard was close to tears when delivering his encomium. He could be a stern critic of Patrick and his writing when occasion required, but proved a perceptive judge of his strange and at times unfathomable character. I feel it fitting to close with something of what I recorded of his subsequent estimate of Patrick's character, which I noted down after the latter's death:

Richard's underlying feeling towards Patrick was warm. He regarded him as fundamentally a kind, affectionate creature, but all kinds of laciniations formed. He constantly saw slights where they did not exist, which spoiled the flow of geniality. He was unusual in a man of letters in including no other authors amongst his friends – except conceivably Simone de Beauvoir. He was always extremely kind to Richard about his work, and consistently a generous reviewer. There was never anything laboured about

---

* Stephen is the son of Patrick's brother Victor. After Patrick's death I established contact with him and his mother Saidie, both of whom provided much helpful information for this biography.

Patrick's writing. Though he found William Golding's last book laboured in parts, he still reviewed it kindly. He was not jealous of other writers – not even C.S. Forester . . .

Richard last saw Patrick when dining in Brooks's about three months before his death. They dined *à deux*, when P. conveyed no hint of ill health. However Richard had latterly noticed a certain falling-off and loss of grip both in his writing and physical state. Patrick once said with feeling that he was only tolerably happy when writing: everything else was but dust and ashes.

Only the last sentence requires serious modification. It is unquestionable that he would have placed my mother at the forefront of his armoury of happiness. Again, only those fully intimate with him could appreciate the extent of his passionate commitment to their house and garden in Collioure – to say nothing of mountain walking, ornithology, astronomy, English, Irish and French literature, classical music (*before* Debussy!), and regular interchanges with a handful of intimate friends living locally. This fruitful existence was preserved almost entirely separate from that of the literary world – one which he in any case largely eschewed. As I have said, after my mother's death, writing provided only intermittent compensation from that irreparable loss. But now they are together again, safe where the arrows of posthumous envy cannot touch them.

Envoi

At the end of 1952 Patrick constructed this model of the *casot* they built three years later, which formed the core of the house where they lived for the remainder of their lives. After his death I found the little tin box reposing within, which proved to contain a tiny piece of paper with this message to his Mary:

for M
a spare heart of gold
with love from P

Appendix A

Collioure: History and Landscape

There is no sky more blue in France than in Collioure.

Henri Matisse

As Collioure played so influential a role throughout the latter half-century of my parents' lives, it is helpful to know something of its history, as ancient as it is colourful. Patrick in the early years of his residence there spoke to me of his intention to write a history of the town, a project for which in the event he never found time. Its early inhabitants may have watched Hannibal's army, when in 218BC he passed northward with his elephants on his march to the Alps and Italy, since he is recorded to have encamped at nearby Elne.* In Roman times Collioure was known as *Caucholiberi*, but the earliest recorded historical event in its history was its siege and capture by the Visigothic king Wamba in 673.[1] In the early Middle Ages, it was ruled for two centuries by the independent Counts of Roussillon, until in 1172 it came to be absorbed into the kingdom of Aragon. When Aragon was united with Castile after the marriage of Ferdinand and Isabella in 1469,

---

* He travelled 'either by the coast road or by the easy Col de Perthus a little way inland' (Dennis Proctor, *Hannibal's March in History* (Oxford, 1971), pp. 35–6).

Collioure became part of the kingdom of Spain, until in 1642 it was besieged and captured for King Louis XIII of France.[2] The transfer of the province of Roussillon to French rule was confirmed at the Treaty of the Pyrenees in 1659, when Collioure became permanently French. However, the inhabitants of the Roussillon continued proudly Catalan in speech and loyalty until very recent times.

It was a source of pleasure to Patrick that one of the royal commanders in the siege of 1642 was the original of Dumas's d'Artagnan. This is recalled in the novel, when the musketeers are depicted at the siege of La Rochelle as drinking the wine of Collioure. It was this detail that swayed my mother's father, Howard Wicksteed, into acceptance of their move. Like many Englishmen of his day, he regarded the volatile French with deep suspicion. However, as a lifelong devotee of *The Three Musketeers*, he was grudgingly persuaded to accept Collioure as a desirable asylum.

The town's chief claim to fame lies, however, in its outstanding beauty. In the autumn of 1904 Henri Matisse arrived for the first of several prolonged stays in Collioure, where he was joined by his friend André Derain.[3] Their paintings have made the town famous throughout the world, and the picturesque church on the rocks by the harbour, with its imposing clocktower, has been reproduced on countless postcards, travel posters and paintings – regrettably few of the latter approaching the standards set by Matisse and Derain. Baedeker in 1914 described the town as 'picturesquely situated', and for some years before that tourists, principally from England and Germany, had begun visiting.

The most impressive view of Collioure is that from the little lighthouse at the end of the pier, which affords the visitor a broad perspective of the whole town, with its rugged mountainous backdrop. (It is fortunately possible to avoid looking at the exceptionally hideous rash of housing to the south that disfigures the rocky promontory beyond the Port d'Avall.)* The most striking object is the great castle, whose towering frontage dominates the little harbour. Although of medieval origin, contrary to popular opinion it never had anything to do with the Templars, who merely owned a building nearby which was demolished centuries ago. Although occasionally occupied by the Counts of Roussillon and their successors the Kings of Aragon, the castle's primary purpose was to protect communications between the south and the frontier with France, which then lay to the north of Perpignan, beyond the great castle of Salses.

The Château Royal at Collioure from the Plage St Vincent

After passing into the hands of the king of France in 1659, the castle was considered an important defence against any

---

* During our early years at Collioure this outcrop was appropriately the Faubourg's rubbish tip, much frequented by local rats.

attempt by Spain to recover the province. From 1668 it was incorporated into the mighty chain of barrier fortresses erected by Louis XIV along the length of France's extended frontiers. No longer, however, did it play a key defensive role. In 1642 it had taken less than four weeks for Louis XIII's troops to batter their way through the town's largely medieval defences. Furthermore, Collioure's fortifications were primarily designed to resist an attack from the sea, whereas now they had to face the more likely prospect of a land assault. Accordingly Louvois, Minister for War, decided to upgrade the castle and its defences in accordance with current scientific military requirements. France's greatest military engineer, Vauban, added the great outworks, with their magnificent scarps and counterscarps, which survive almost unscathed to the present day.[4]

It was at this juncture that Collioure faced a brief crisis, which could have resulted in its disappearance from the map. Vauban, adjudging the town to be of scant value from a military point of view, urged that it be razed to the ground and its inhabitants moved to neighbouring Port-Vendres, which enjoys a much deeper harbour, and is more readily defensible on the landward side. Fortunately, Louvois overruled this draconian proposal, and the Château Royal and its surroundings were massively strengthened and extended. This in itself involved considerable destruction, since much of the old town and its church obstructed open space required to permit Vauban's cannon unrestricted fields of fire. Accordingly the church and many other contiguous buildings were levelled to the ground, when the town was reconstructed in much the form it enjoys today. Her walls were massively rebuilt, on the seaward side of which gun embrasures at ground level still gaze out across the water towards the harbour mouth.[5]

Paradoxically, it was this work of demolition which produced what is widely regarded as Collioure's most picturesque feature. From 1684 work commenced on building a new church on the rocks beside the bay, and it is the view it affords from the town that comprises one of the chief attractions for visitors from all over the world.

To protect the castle from domination by the hill to its north, Vauban constructed Fort Carré, a square fort above Fort Miradou with a deep dry moat, whose strength does not become apparent until one has ascended the hill. He also arranged construction of the lofty Fort Miradou itself, still occupied as a barracks by the French Army. (In my younger days, the quay proclaimed in large white-painted letters the defiant inscription 'ALGÉRIE FRANÇAISE'.) Collioure conceivably possesses more fortifications to the square mile than anywhere else in France. On a ridge to the south perches the Château Saint-Elme, an attractive little star-shaped fort erected under the direction of the Emperor Charles V, when he arrived to inspect the defences of the region in 1538. At the other end of the ridge is a ruined early nineteenth-century fort named after General Dugommier, who in 1794 skilfully recaptured Saint-Elme from an invading Spanish force, which had occupied it to direct destructive fire on the Faubourg.

Beyond the town the Pyrenees begin their grandiose ascent to the west, two mountains being dramatically crowned by thirteenth-century watchtowers, the Madeloc and Massane. A walk up the zigzag path through vineyards and above to the Madeloc reveals a succession of small forts on every other hilltop, together with an isolated roadside barracks, now roofless, which my parents at one point contemplated purchasing and converting into their home. Ironically, apart from the abortive Spanish assault of 1794, no enemy has in fact attempted any serious attack on France at this point since Vauban undertook his impressive labours.

Relics of a more recent invasion today remain largely unremarked. The southern skirt of the harbour is occupied by the Faubourg of Port d'Avall, whose frontage boasts a fine round tower, erected in the eighteenth century as a customs post. The quay itself was built by Wehrmacht engineers during the Second World War, and a German gun emplacement (whose setting is vividly described in Patrick's short story 'The Walker') also survives on the cliff edge beyond Fort Miradou.

Appendix B

Patrick and His First Wife Elizabeth

It often happens that those are the best people, whose characters have been most injured by slanderers, as we usually find that to be the sweetest fruit which the birds have been pecking at.

John Hawkesworth (ed.), *The Works of Jonathan Swift, D.D. Dean of St. Patrick's, Dublin* (London, 1755–68), ii, p. 179

The gravest charge levelled against Patrick relates to his desertion of his first wife Elizabeth, together with their two little children. Thus, in a review of Dean King's biography published in the *Observer* (3 September 2000), Jan Morris dismissed Patrick's alleged personal deceptions as trivial, while nevertheless condemning him as a man on grounds advanced by King:

The life of innocent deceit takes on a profounder meaning, though, when one remembers that in 1940, O'Brian abandoned his wife, their three-year-old son and a handicapped baby, and went off with Mary Tolstoy, already the mother of the future writer Nicholas Tolstoy. This act of betrayal is perhaps a more real reason for O'Brian's reluctance to talk about his early life. To judge by this book it was his only cause for shame, and his affair with Mary matured over the years into a long, happy and honourable marriage . . .

Nevertheless, Morris oddly concluded with this harsh endorsement of King's accusations: 'In O'Brian . . . I am reading the work of an artificer, a contriver of genius and, well, a liar.'

Morris's judgement was measured, at least to the extent that it did little more than uncritically echo the findings of the book under review. Less so was an embittered tirade by a food writer named Rachel Cooke, published four years later and perpetuated on the internet. After a lofty dismissal of Patrick's literary talent, she declared that, among other gross offences: 'In 1940, O'Brian walked out on this girl, his son and a baby daughter, who had spina bifida.' Overall: 'The truth of it is that O'Brian was a horrible – some might even say vile – man: a snob, a liar and an atrocious father.'[1]

I am grateful to Terry Zobeck for urging the necessity of responding to the prime accusation that he deserted his baby daughter on account of her terrible ailment. It is not my purpose to defend or condemn Patrick's morality or conduct, but to set out the evidence as fully as it is known to me. He never discussed his first marriage with me, nor I imagine with anyone else save my mother.

The charges relating to Patrick's abandonment of his wife and family are grave, and readily summarized. Dean King's biography provides the first and fullest version:

The winter of 1939/40 was bitterly cold, with a North Sea wind that ravaged the Suffolk countryside. The **duck-pond at Gadds Cottage froze solid**, and one day Elizabeth badly burned her hand when she gripped the freezing handle of the outdoor water pump too long. Because of the war, coal and coke were rationed, but at least in the country Patrick could find brush and cut wood for fuel, and **he could hunt for food. When snow covered the ground, he buckled on cross-country skis and went in search of hare and partridge** . . . *Whether Patrick walked out of Gadds Cottage after an argument or failed to return after a research trip to London is unknown. What exactly caused him to leave the family in that*

*summer of 1940 is also unclear. An urge to be involved somehow
in the war, not to be left out of history while helplessly caring for
a doomed child, may have overwhelmed his sense of responsibility
at home. He may have felt guilty about being the father of a crippled child, a stigma in that day since the malady was often
attributed to the infirmity or wickedness of the parents. He might
have been unable to stand the daily torment of watching and hearing
his infant daughter suffer. Elizabeth was emotionally stretched to
the limit . . . The tension exaggerated the personality differences
between husband and wife and provided many reasons for resenting
their current existence. Patrick's creative endeavours suffered.*[2]

The first point to note is the paucity of factual information on
which King based his harsh indictment. Not only is the greater
part of his charge (here italicized) self-evidently speculative, but
in fact not one of his conjectures is correct. In particular, the notion
that Patrick could have felt that 'being the father of a crippled
child, [was] a stigma in that day since the malady was often attributed to the infirmity or wickedness of the parents' is patently
absurd. Patrick's father was a doctor, while his uncle Sidney was
a distinguished Professor of Physics at the Middlesex Hospital
Medical School. To suggest that anyone possessed of such a background, or indeed any other educated person at that time, might
have subscribed to a superstition of so medieval a character beggars
belief. No evidence is provided by King to substantiate his melodramatic surmise.

The passages marked in bold in this Appendix, while accurate,
represent no more than King's unacknowledged inference from
family photographs reproduced between pages 236 and 237 of his
book. Although he omits to say so, apart from this such factual
elements as are to be found in his four-page account of the Russ
family's stay at Gadds Cottage derive exclusively from Richard
Russ, who was in 1940 aged three, and not yet five when he and
his mother in fact left the house. Given his age at the time, it is

534

unsurprising that Richard's recollections amount to no more than that his parents kept ducks and a goat, that he on one occasion dropped cutlery into their pond and on another broke a duck's egg, and that his uncle and aunt fed him hard-boiled eggs at their final departure on the eve of the little boy's fifth birthday. Interestingly, what he does not suggest is that his father was notably absent from the household during this time. When the journalist Ben Fenton spoke to him not long after his interview with Dean King, he found that Richard 'had little memory of the early part of his childhood when his parents were still married . . .'[3]

Nevertheless, at the time of publication of King's book, Richard repeated the charges in the press:

> O'Brian left, returned to London and lived alone in Chelsea where he drove ambulances during the war and continued with his writing . . . I was four years old when he just got up and left without any warning or reason. I think he did it on the spur of the moment. It was a selfish thing to do. One of my uncles had to drive over and take my mother, my sister and me to his house and look after us . . . I think he couldn't cope with the grief and shame of having a disabled child. There was a stigma attached to it in those days. He took it as a reflection on himself.[4]

That Richard was entitled to resent his father's desertion of his mother is unquestionable. However, I must again emphasize that my task is not to act as judge of my stepfather's morality, but insofar as is possible to ascertain the facts relating to the accusations.

The first point to note is the startling inaccuracy in King's chronology, when he asserts that Patrick deserted his family in 'that summer of 1940'. The date appears to have been arbitrarily introduced by King himself, who cites no evidence in its support. It is contradicted by both Elizabeth and Richard himself, who subsequently stated: 'I was five when he left us to pursue his affair with Mary, Countess

Tolstoy, back in London.'[5] Richard's fifth birthday was on 2 February 1942. The precise year of Patrick's ultimate departure might appear insignificant, until the circumstances be considered.

It is on Dean King's account of Patrick's abandonment of his family and their consequent evacuation of Gadds Cottage 'in that summer of 1940' that denunciations of his departure in consequence of his discovering Jane's incurable sickness rest in their entirety. From the *contemporary* testimony of her mother Elizabeth we learn that: 'From 1938 to 1942 he [Patrick] lived with me in Suffolk and was supported by me and his brother. In 1942 he left me and went to London . . .'[6]

Thus, we learn on impeccable authority that Patrick 'lived with' Elizabeth and their children throughout the whole of baby Jane's tragically brief life! Moreover, there are other factors to consider. Dean King was unaware that Patrick and my mother had in fact begun their affair in the summer of 1939, when he was twenty-four and my mother twenty-two. The year is established from evidence in my possession. As I now believe, the precise date of their first encounter was 4 July of that year. In her diary for that date in 1966, my mother wrote cryptically 'MP day' – that being their customary affectionate joint acronym. Given therefore that Patrick was conducting a passionate affair with her from the summer of 1939 onwards, how may this be reconciled with Elizabeth's assertion under oath that he lived with *her*, without her detecting any appearance of infidelity, until 1942 or 1943? Her divorce and custody proceedings provided Elizabeth with the strongest motive for representing Patrick as an unkind, unfaithful husband and cold-hearted parent. Her solicitors would naturally have pressed her to provide damaging evidence in support of her applications. What could be more dreadful than his having gratuitously abandoned his child on discovering that she suffered from an incurable illness?

On the other hand, the reader may well wonder how even the most confiding of wives could have described an absentee husband as 'living with her'. Clearly he was not, as King and his followers have assumed, absent so far as Elizabeth was concerned. Yet how is this to be reconciled with the fact that, from 1940 onwards, Patrick and my mother were conducting a secretive affair in Chelsea, of which Elizabeth remained ignorant until September 1943, when she was belatedly alerted by a neighbour?* Surely Patrick could not be in two places at once?

Paradoxically, there exists a sense in which he could. Elizabeth had accepted from the outset of their marriage that Patrick's struggle for their financial survival obliged him to be absent on frequent occasions for weeks or even months on end. Thus he spent the first half of 1937 in Ireland, writing his novel *Hussein* – the book he dedicated on its publication in the following spring to his 'dear wife and small son'. Immediately on his return to their home in London he departed for two or three months to Italy as a paid courier. At the beginning of 1939 he and Elizabeth were for some reason living at separate addresses in Chelsea when their daughter Jane was born.† Later that summer he spent time seriously ill in hospital, and afterwards disappeared for a while – allegedly to recuperate. In fact he had by this time met my mother, and may have seized the opportunity to spend time secretly with her.[7]

On the eve of their departure from London, Patrick addressed two affectionate letters to Elizabeth from his parents' house in

---

* In August 1945 Elizabeth attested that 'In 1942 he [Patrick] left me and went to London where he lived with the woman named in my Petition.' While not impossible, it seems likely that the date 1942 rests on hindsight, Elizabeth being unable to provide evidence of adultery occurring before the autumn of 1943.

† Jane's birth certificate attests that in March 1939 Patrick was still living in the family home at 24, Gertrude Street, while Elizabeth's address is given as 301, King's Road. Since they were at the time on affectionate terms, a likely explanation is that Elizabeth moved out temporarily (the two addresses are within walking distance) in order to permit her husband to continue writing in peace. They can have occupied no more than a couple of rooms in the four-storey Gertrude Street house, which was inhabited by three other unrelated individuals (*Register of Electors*, 1937).

Sussex, where he was still recuperating from his summer illness. The second was in verse, in which he dwelt romantically on their coming bucolic existence, when he would provide a living from fields and hedgerows, 'quite happy to be / Alone with Campaspe [baby Jane's second name] and Richard and thee'. Patrick's words are so fond as to indicate that he continued to love his wife and children, despite the sudden onset of his overwhelming passion for my mother. Such situations have been known, and there is in addition reason to believe that Patrick remained for a time apprehensive that my mother's implausible passion for her impecunious married writer might fade as swiftly as it had arisen.

After a year spent with his family in the Suffolk countryside, Patrick left Gadds Cottage for London in the autumn of 1940, where he joined my mother driving ambulances for the London Auxiliary Ambulance Service in Chelsea during the Blitz. Not only was this a gratifying patriotic duty, but in Patrick's case it provided him for the first time in his life with a regular income. The relief this afforded his impoverished little family cannot be exaggerated. Patrick's total income from his writing in 1939–40 amounted to £6 16s 6d for his short story 'No Pirates Nowadays' (on receipt of which he noted with palpable relief 'Hack's price, but very acceptable'), and 'The Mayfly Rise', which earned twelve guineas 'just when funds had completely run out'. It was their dire impecuniosity that compelled Patrick and Elizabeth to withdraw to rural Norfolk, where they led a near-subsistence existence in the rented cottage found by Patrick's brother Victor.

Now, in the late autumn of 1940, Patrick found himself in possession of a modest but nonetheless sufficient income of £3 a week! He forwarded the whole of this on a regular basis to Elizabeth, who conceded in custody proceedings a few years later that 'he provided me with three pounds a week to maintain myself, our daughter (now deceased) and Richard'.

Patrick's service with the ambulance unit required an eight-hour shift throughout a six-day week at all hours of day and night under exceptionally hazardous conditions, with Sunday providing scant time to recover for the next stint.[8] If Patrick's visits home were at times few and far between, there is no reason why his absence should have aroused untoward suspicion. Their situation was no different from that of millions of young couples in those fraught days. Again, wartime conditions made travel difficult at any time. The fact is that withdrawal into the countryside represented normal experience for more than two million children (including my sister and me) and a proportionate number of mothers during that perilous time.

A year later, in September 1941, Patrick obtained a post at the headquarters of Political Warfare Executive (PWE) at 2, Fitzmaurice Place (afterwards Bush House), where he and my mother worked until the end of the war. As he had a half-day free on Saturday and all of Sunday, while his income was increased to five pounds a week, there would have been little now to prevent his paying regular visits to his family in Norfolk. That he did so on a fairly constant basis surely provides the likeliest explanation of Elizabeth's otherwise baffling testimony that he continued living with her throughout that time. In addition, evidence attests to the fact that Patrick remained throughout this period deeply attached to his children, regardless of his relationship with their mother.

There exist further considerations why Patrick should have taken care to maintain a convincing semblance of marital relations with Elizabeth, until the time he and my mother first set up home together in (or conceivably before) September 1943. There are indications that they lived apart in Chelsea for much of the time before that.* This could have arisen from the contemporary propensity of landladies to disapprove of unmarried couples cohabiting in their premises.

---

* There is a hint (but no more) in one of my mother's notebooks that they moved into shared quarters in November 1941. If so, it appears that they nevertheless succeeded in covering their tracks for a further one or two years.

During their first two or three years together it seems Patrick continued at times apprehensive that my mother might drop him as suddenly as she had taken him up. Her family and friends strongly disapproved of their liaison, her background could scarcely have been more different, and those closest to her wondered what she could see in the penniless aspirational writer.*
Were she to desert him, where could he turn if not to his wife and children? This hypothesis is not entirely speculative. In his intensely autobiographical novel *Richard Temple*, the hero's upper-class inamorata Philippa Brett (who is unmistakably based on my mother) unexpectedly deserts him at the conclusion for 'a tall, thin soldier . . . this was the hour of the fighting man and now he seemed splendid – Sam Browne, decorations, gleaming buttons here and there'. London in the early Forties was filled with dashing young officers from British and Allied forces, who were only too anxious to make the most of their leave in town.

It is not necessary to assume that Patrick was being entirely hypocritical, were he to have been influenced by such a consideration. As I have suggested, it is likely that he continued to nurture a residue of guilty affection for his pretty and loyal young wife.†
Such things have happened, and in these precarious circumstances it is not inconceivable that he was concerned to keep his options

---

* It seems that many of Patrick's friends regarded his extramarital liaison with distaste. On 2 February 1970 he confided to his diary: 'This time 32 (?) years ago I was in Rachel's room & they looked at me wth wondering condemnation.'

† The protagonist of Patrick's unpublished autobiographical story 'George' is depicted as nurturing a mixture of shame and lingering affection towards his abandoned wife Margaret. 'He felt a deep movement, a revulsion, something uneasy about Margaret. They had never had any very close relationship; it had all been very immature; but was it not rather – ? If another man had done it, what would he have said? A solemn pompous bubble labelled Cad eddied about his unwilling thoughts . . .'

open.* However, once he and my mother had set up house together, such apprehension naturally dissipated.

As has been seen, the apparent discrepancy between Elizabeth's assertion that she and her husband lived together until 1942 and his actual absence in London is further accounted for by her having throughout their marriage become accustomed to lengthy absences on Patrick's part. This, she explained to the court in 1944, arose from his being obliged to earn a living by acting as a courier abroad. When Richard was too little to remember much, Patrick had lived initially for over a year in the family home at Gadds Cottage. That he was in fact leading a double life remained completely unknown to his betrayed wife.† This in turn suggests that he maintained sufficiently regular contact with his family during 1941 and 1942 to allay suspicion. Indeed, it seems reasonable to suppose that his weekly £3 postal order was generally accompanied by a letter. (One of the surviving letters he wrote to Elizabeth before they left London makes it clear that they had corresponded every week during his protracted absence at his parents' home in Sussex.)‡ Had he vanished altogether from 1940 onwards, it is plainly inconceivable that Elizabeth could have

---

* In his novel *Hussein*, written when he was married to Elizabeth and two years before he met my mother, Patrick included this reflection: 'Hussein was always faithful to Sashiya, for she was more important to him than anything else, and he always guarded her memory very close to his heart; but he was, like most men, faithful in his own way' (R.P. Russ, *Hussein: An Entertainment* (Oxford, 1938), p. 212).

† It is possible that Patrick saw little of my mother during the initial year he spent in Norfolk. All I have been able to discover of their relationship during 1939–40 is that they were together for his birthday in December 1939, and that she gave him some of her brother's winter clothes, her skis, and the little .410 shotgun with which he killed game for his family's daily subsistence. Given their impoverished near-subsistence circumstances during that year, Elizabeth could scarcely have survived any protracted absence on Patrick's part.

‡ A fragment of one such letter from Patrick to Elizabeth indicates that their son Richard also corresponded with him regularly. Given the boy's age, this can scarcely have occurred earlier than 1941, before his and his mother's return to London in the spring of 1942.

considered him as 'living with' her for another two or three years. Indeed, another versifying letter from Patrick describes in jocular vein one such visit. The date of his arrival is given as 14 June, and allusions suggest that the year in question was 1941 or 1942.

Fortunately, this reconstruction of the relationship between husband and wife at this time is not entirely dependent on informed reconstruction. In an affidavit drawn up in 1949, Elizabeth drew the court's attention:

to the piece of paper now produced to me marked 'C'. I cannot recollect the date when this was written but it is in my husband's handwriting and was written to me when he was concealing his whereabouts under a British monomark. At that time he had not begun to adopt the attitude of hostility he has since shown and he was proposing that I should take a job as a Matron at a Boys School: he regarded me as eminently suitable for such a position and pressed me to seek for such employment. This is corroborated by the portion of one of his letters exhibited. The other side of the same piece of paper gives some clue as to our relations at that time before these unhappy difficulties arose [in 1943, when she belatedly learned that Patrick and my mother were living together].[9]

Unfortunately the letter alluded to is missing from the file in the Public Record Office. Nevertheless, its tenor is clear from her reference. Elizabeth regarded their marital relations as continuing cordial throughout the time Patrick returned to London from the autumn of 1940 onwards.

There was no occasion in court proceedings for Elizabeth to explain why she departed Gadds Cottage after nearly three years. Although her existence was throughout penurious, it had undergone no material change by the time she sought refuge with Patrick's brother Godfrey in Norwich at the beginning of 1942. By far the most likely reason for the move is that Richard had now reached an age when it was time for him to begin his schooling. This would

not have been practical at their home in the remote Suffolk countryside, where Elizabeth was tied at home by the presence of her
sick infant daughter. At the same time, we know that Patrick
continued throughout Richard's childhood and youth profoundly
concerned that he should obtain a good education, where possible
at a private school. It seems likely, therefore, that his letter
suggesting that Elizabeth seek employment *at a boys' school* was
written about this time.

Her practical knowledge and maternal nature might be expected
to have afforded sufficient qualification for employment as a
preparatory school matron, which would in addition be likely to
enable her to have her son educated at the school free of charge.
Whatever the reason for her not adopting this course, it seems
probable that Patrick's letter (which Elizabeth regarded as attesting
to continuing affectionate relations between them) was written on
the eve of January 1942, when his wife adopted the alternative
measure of going to live with Patrick's brother Godfrey and wife
Connie outside Norwich.

This said, we are still left with Elizabeth's plaintive declaration
that her husband 'refused to see her [baby Jane] or offer any
sympathy' at the time of the child's tragic death. This is a distinct
but nonetheless grave charge, not to be lightly dismissed (although
it is not at all the same as the groundless accusation that it was
discovery of the little girl's spina bifida that caused Patrick to leave
home).

Ironically, Elizabeth's heartfelt complaint implies that Patrick,
prior to this tragic climax, *had* been seeing Jane and evincing
sympathy for her plight. Nevertheless, that he was absent at the
time of her death remains a serious charge. Given that he had
hitherto manifested effective concern to allay any suspicion on his
wife's part, it seems possible that a particular reason arose for his
absence at so poignant a moment.

What that reason might have been will probably never be known
for certain. However, the cause of a temporary absence on Patrick's

part on this tragic occasion may be illumined by an inscription 'for Mary, she being sick in the Hospital of St Bartholomew the Less. 30th March 1942', written by him in a fine folio volume[10] he gave my mother *the day before Jane's death*. How serious was my mother's ailment, and how long did it endure? Beyond this, we simply do not know what was the situation of the couple in London at that time.

Since no response by Patrick to Elizabeth's accusation survives, speculation on the issue must remain as tantalizing as it is unprofitable. Naturally, he could not have given his wife what was probably the true reason, which would have made it all the more reprehensible. Nevertheless, he and Elizabeth continued for some time after this date on sufficiently amicable terms to discuss questions relating to Richard's education in London.[11]

A further material consideration lies in the fact that Elizabeth, while undoubtedly a good woman and devoted mother, was capable of considerable confusion over aspects of her relationship with Patrick. A single instance may possibly stand for others. In a court affidavit dated 26 April 1949, she declared that Patrick 'treated me very repressively, not allowing me to have a newspaper, **to visit a cinema** or to listen to a wireless'.[12] Here her memory was undoubtedly at fault. Shortly before their departure for Gadds Cottage in 1939 (where the issue could no longer arise, there being no opportunity of visiting a cinema in their bucolic retreat), Patrick wrote to Elizabeth from his parents' house at Crowborough, declaring his love for her and enquiring solicitously about her and their daughter: 'Will Campaspe be at the crèche now? If she is you might go to the cinema as an escape from unhappiness.'*

It is unfortunate, too, that pages have been abstracted (stolen

---

* Lilly Library, Patrick O'Brian collection. Thirty years later Patrick recalled a visit to the cinema in Chelsea in 1938, the year before he met my mother, when he was still living happily with Elizabeth: 'Quai des Brumes. What simpletons we must have been in 38, to swallow such romantic crap, the tale so lame & inexpert. Good photography, no doubt, & the early Gabin was acceptable.'

by an unscrupulous reader?) from the official file of Patrick's court submissions relating to his divorce and custody proceedings. Since the missing pages comprised part of Patrick's testimony, much more would be known of his side of the dispute had they been preserved.

As I would again emphasize, it is not my purpose to espouse a partisan view of the dispute between Patrick and his wife, but to cite the evidence showing that the principal charge against him (that he deserted his family on discovering the nature of his daughter's illness) is demonstrably false, while other factors are at the least insufficiently clear to allow of glib judgements over half a century later.

Finally, one other element in this unhappy story may throw light on Patrick's feelings at the time. Dean King compounded his account of Patrick's supposed callousness by asserting that his abrupt departure from Gadds Cottage was unaccompanied by any provision for the family's welfare: 'Whatever the reason, one day he simply left, never to return, leaving his eldest brother Godfrey and his wife Connie, when they heard what had happened, to drive out and rescue the stranded family . . .'*

Since the whole account of Patrick's 'simply leaving' on the eve of Elizabeth's removal to Norwich is demonstrably fictitious, it seems probable that it was in fact he who appealed to his kindly brother Godfrey to provide the family with a temporary haven.

Three months later, immediately after Jane's death, Elizabeth departed for 'London with Richard to find employment'. What there was no occasion to mention in her subsequent affidavit was how, being possessed of such scanty resources, she managed with apparent facility to find somewhere to live in the distant metropolis. Her new

---

* *Daily Telegraph*, 28 February 2000. 'For nearly two years, they [Elizabeth and Richard] had lived in a state of limbo in the home of Patrick's oldest brother and his wife in Thorpe-by-Norwich' (King, *Patrick O'Brian*, p. 93). It has been seen that in reality they stayed at Godfrey's home for a mere few months in 1942, before departing for London.

home, where she was to spend the rest of her life, was a small upstairs flat in 237, King's Road, just around the corner from the house in Upper Cheyne Row where Patrick and my mother were to install themselves in the following year. The choice of Elizabeth's residence was not the result, as might appear, of pure chance. It cannot have been coincidence that close friends of Patrick occupied the ground-floor flat of number 237. They were Francis Cox, an artist whom Patrick had known since his bachelor days in Chelsea, and his wife. When his son Richard was christened in 1937, Patrick conferred on him the additional name Francis, from which it appears that Cox was godfather to the boy. When Patrick and my mother moved to Wales after the War, they invited Cox to stay. And when my mother visited London during that time, it was with him and his wife that she lodged at 237, King's Road. Thus the Coxes were friends of Patrick rather than Elizabeth, and in the circumstances it is surely likely that it was Patrick who arranged with them to provide accommodation for his wife and son.

Aspects of this unhappy story undoubtedly remain discreditable to Patrick. However, the question addressed here is whether the widely canvassed allegation be true that he deliberately abandoned his wife and children in 1940, simply because he was chillingly unprepared to associate with a grievously ailing infant daughter. The belief that this explains his departure from Gadds Cottage only appeared credible in consequence of Dean King's fanciful claim that Patrick and my mother first met, in what were in reality entirely imaginary circumstances, during the late summer of 1941. King's erroneous speculation that Patrick had left Gadds Cottage the year before of necessity implied that his departure could have had nothing to do with his love affair with my mother. In fact, with the correct dates restored, and Patrick's continuing support for and affectionate relationship with his wife attested on oath by Elizabeth herself, it can be seen that their final rift arose from a combination of exceptional circumstances obtaining from the onset of war, Patrick's desperate need to obtain an income sufficient to support his family, and last (but certainly not least), his and my mother's growing involvement in their passionate covert love affair.

Thus, there is not the slightest justification for asserting that baby Jane's cruel affliction provided the reason for his departure from Gadds Cottage. In fact, a likely contributory explanation of Patrick's sustaining the pretence of a continuing marriage so effectively as to deceive his wife for two and a half years, up to and after their daughter's death, is that he could not bring himself to sever relations so long as the infant Jane remained alive.

Appendix C

Patrick's Sailing

I must go down to the seas again, to the lonely sea and the sky,
And all I ask is a tall ship and a star to steer her by,
And the wheel's kick and the wind's song and the white sail's shaking,
And a grey mist on the sea's face in the grey dawn breaking.

John Masefield, Sea Fever

In the first volume of this biography I gave reasons for concluding that Patrick had not, as he claimed on several occasions, sailed as a young man on board 'an ocean-going yacht'.[1] Today, I feel my dismissal requires modification in the light of evidence of which I was then unaware. The issue would not of course invite particular concern were it not for the fact that, in the eyes of Patrick's small but persistent band of detractors, it provides a prime justification for damning him as 'a liar'.

My present reservation reflects the general consideration that absence of evidence does not constitute evidence. A striking example may suffice to illustrate this, while also enabling me to correct an error perpetrated in my previous volume.

On pages 63–65 I adduced reasons for discounting Patrick's recollection of having attended a preparatory school at Paignton, near Torbay in Devonshire. I have since found that Patrick was right, and I wrong. I had overlooked his brief diary entry for

8 November 1981, in which he describes a visit he made to Devonshire with my mother, which settles the matter decisively:

> . . . so to Paignton, where (in pretty bitter cold) we walked upon the faintly familiar sand, looking at the perfectly familiar Thatcher [a large rock at the tide line] – thro the unknown town to a naturally unknown pub where we ate a pasty & asked the way to Grosvenor Rd. – no boyhood there alas.

In view of the allusion to his 'boyhood' familiarity with the town, it would be perverse to doubt Patrick's assertion that he attended a school there.* The concluding reference incidentally also suggests that the school had ceased to exist.

I would further emphasize that the brevity of Patrick's allusive references to his early sailing is of a piece with his broader concern to preserve his life before he married my mother in 1945 as secret as possible. His concern to preserve his privacy is far from unique among authors.

What previously persuaded me that Patrick had not, as he declared, engaged in his youth in a voyage or voyages in a ship under sail was the following entry in his diary for 12 October 1991:

> In the afternoon we walked beyond Dugommier [the fort above Collioure], M[ary] going well . . . Then going down into P[ort-]V[endres] we saw a fine vessel on the further quay & went to look: the barque Belem, built at Nantes in 1898, 50m + long, 8,60 wide, 500 tons, drawing 3,8m. (These figures may be wrong: I did not note them at the time,† but she sails tomorrow at 11 & I hope to

---

* Patrick also alluded to his preparatory school in an interview with Peter Guttridge (*Independent*, 3 July 1993).

† But a note inserted in his diary indicates that he *did* 'note them at the time'! And why did he copy into his diary that evening both the deleted and corrected sets of measurements? I continue to find aspects of this episode puzzling.

check them before then.) . . . 58m long 8.80 wide 3.6 draught 750 tons crew 16(?) built 96 sold to D of W 1914 then to Sir A.E. Guinness ocean-going yacht until 52 then navire ecole à Venise 1979 Caisse d'Epargne (Ecureuil) 85 to NY (S of Liberty) 12 staysails & jibs 10 square sails can make 12k under sail.

Next day:

Early I went to PV, checked the Belem's measurements & contemplated her rigging. Then we went a little before 11 & she was making ready – people gathered but not too many – & almost on time she cast off & motored towards the jetty. We had scarcely hoped to see her set any sail, but a slight N breeze had sprung up & as she passed out of the port she did so with 3 fine staysails. We could not tell her direction but at all hazards hurried up the devilish Béar road: & there suddenly she was far below, heading SE under courses, topsails & most fore & aft sails, looking perfectly lovely, the staysails white interrupted curved Ds catching the sun between the square sails – lovely proportions – an entity. We moved farther up; she moved farther out, setting the topgallants & eventually remarkably broad & deep royals. Her course was erratic at 1st . . . but eventually she settled for I suppose Cap Creus & sailed gently (3 or 4k?) into the blue. Such joy. (& in such a horrible, horrible world).

From this I gained the impression that it was the first time he had encountered the vessel. If so, it would be incompatible with his claim to have sailed in her during his youth before the War. On reflection, I do not now feel that my reasoning was altogether decisive.

Closer consideration suggests the possibility that Patrick may not have realized that it was the same vessel as that in which he afterwards claimed to have sailed more than half a century before. Under the Hon. Arthur Ernest Guinness's ownership she had been rechristened *Fantôme II*, reverting to *Belem* some years after his death in 1949.[2] As was seen in the last chapter, a passing allusion

The *Belem* outside Port-Vendres in 1991

in 1999 indicates that it was aboard *Fantôme II* that Patrick believed himself to have sailed in his youth – a name he failed to mention when inspecting the ship at Port-Vendres in 1991. Could it be that after long years he did not appreciate that the *Belem* was in fact one and the same with *Fantôme II*, in which he claimed to have sailed in his youth?

Terry Zobeck has drawn my attention to an allusion I found in one of Patrick's notebooks, whose significance I had overlooked. In May 1972 he kept a journal of a visit he paid to Ireland, which includes this tantalizing passage: 'Dublin again, & I am strangely reminded of New York: but only by the old-fashioned mouldering squalor of many of the smaller shopping streets (so like upper 8th Avenue) . . .'

When could Patrick have visited New York before this time? His first recorded visit did not occur until the following summer of 1973, when the unprecedentedly substantial advance he received on being commissioned to write his biography of Picasso enabled him to travel to the States to view the artist's paintings held in art galleries there.

His life from 1939 onwards is too fully documented for there to be any possibility of his having visited the United States during or in the aftermath of the War, and in any case before 1973 he lacked financial means for undertaking so expensive a voyage. Nor do my mother's meticulously kept financial accounts record one, which must at that time have been conducted at their own expense. Yet the phraseology of his 1972 allusion unmistakably evokes personal memory, rather than a description based on hearsay or photographs. It seems that we must look to his pre-war years, presumably those following completion of his education in 1933.

A material objection to this suggestion is posed by the fact that he married at the beginning of 1936, after which he and his wife Elizabeth lived in considerable poverty. However, in 1945 she deposed that 'BEFORE the war the Respondent was a Courier and spent most of his time abroad on business'. This suggests more than his sole recorded visits to Ireland and Italy, and it is conceivable that Patrick employed his 'courier' activities as a pretext to cover other expeditions less justifiable in the eyes of an impoverished and at times lonely wife.*

Patrick himself was fairly reticent when questioned about his youthful sailing experience, and there are trifling variations in what he vouchsafed on different occasions. The fullest and most measured account is that which he provided for the British Library Festschrift:

> One of the compensations I have spoken about was the sea. The disease that racked my bosom every now and then did not much affect my strength and when it left me in peace (for there were long remissions) sea-air and sea-voyages were recommended. An uncle had a two-ton sloop and several friends had boats, which was fine;† but what was even better was that my particular friend Edward,

---

* That a travel firm should have employed Patrick as a courier to New York seems improbable.

† Note that Patrick avoids claiming that he actually sailed on these!

who shared a tutor with me, had a cousin who possessed an ocean-going yacht, a converted barque-rigged merchantman, that he used to crew with undergraduates and fair-sized boys, together with some real seamen, and sail far off into the Atlantic. The young are wonderfully resilient, and although I never became much of a topman, after a while I could hand, reef and steer without disgrace, which allowed more ambitious sailoring later on.[3]

In press and television interviews he provided further details. The yacht had previously belonged to the Duke of Westminster, afterwards to Patrick's friend Edward's cousin Arthur, who sailed in it on long ocean voyages. These details identify the yacht as the *Fantôme II*, belonging to the Hon. Arthur Ernest Guinness. It is pertinent to enquire how Patrick might belatedly have become aware in old age that the vessel had once borne that name – which it had not done since the aftermath of Guinness's death in 1949 – had he in reality never enjoyed any connection with it.

Patrick's 'friend Edward' was presumably Edward Taaffe, who was best man at his wedding in 1936, and dedicatee of his short story 'The Dawn Flighting' published in 1950.* I can find no evidence of their having maintained contact thereafter, following Patrick's permanent move to France in 1949. Nor, despite enquiries with the Guinness family (some of whom I knew when at Trinity), have I been able to establish Taaffe's connexion with Arthur Guinness. However, Taaffe is a good Irish name, and cousinship can be an elastic concept in Ireland. Mr Henry McDowell, the Irish genealogist, proposed to me the interesting suggestion that: 'Ernest Guinness was said to be very kind and interested in his god-children – perhaps that is where Edward Taaffe fits in.'† This seems not unlikely, given the failure to discover a Guinness blood-relative of that name.

That Patrick 'shared a tutor' with Taaffe suggests the summer of

---

* This shows that Taaffe survived the War.
† Letter of 9 September 2002.

1933, when Patrick sat his external matriculation at Birkbeck College, London. Following his brief and erratic schooling, his father might well have accepted the necessity of professional tuition. As it was in the same year that Patrick paid his first visit to Ireland, could it be that it was Taaffe who invited him for his first visit to his homeland in 1933 – perhaps to celebrate completion of their examinations? A possible intimation that Patrick's voyage occurred no later than 1933 may also be found in his mention that Guinness 'used to crew with undergraduates and fair-sized boys, together with some real seamen'. Since Patrick was never an undergraduate or a 'real seaman', presumably he could have been one of the 'fair-sized boys'.

A curious dream recorded by Patrick in his diary on 3 March 1980 reads as follows:

> . . . so home & to an early bed where I dreamt so sadly of Taafe & Kathy. The Chelsea of 40 years ago was much the same but we were our now age: he wd not take the 1st step twds me, nor did he seem really pleased when I did so. She & I tried to make love, but I would not. They neither of them had their own faces, but their identities were the same.

That 'we were our now age' suggests that Patrick assumed Taaffe to be still living, a likely enough belief on the assumption that they were contemporaries. That he continued to bear his friend in mind is indicated by a mention in *The Commodore* (1994), where Patrick has Diana Villiers riding with 'Ned Taaffe's hounds in Ireland'. Five years later Taaffe's death in a duel is mentioned in the unfinished novel on which Patrick was working at the time of his death.

One may question whether the hypersensitive Patrick would have risked public assertion of having sailed with Edward Taaffe in his cousin's yacht, had the possibility existed of Edward's or his wife's being alive to contradict the claim if false. It might be proposed that either or both had died by the time Patrick came to mention his 'friend named Edward'. However, by that time it seems unlikely that he possessed means of learning of such an event, while I feel in any case fairly confident that had he done so he or my mother would have mentioned so poignant a loss in their diaries.

That Patrick actively sought the opportunity of sailing in his younger days is confirmed by the fact that in 1946 he made formal application to serve in a whaling expedition, which to his expressed disappointment was turned down.

Unfortunately, I have been unable to discover whether *Fantôme II* ever sailed to New York before the War, when it seems Patrick first visited the city. However, it is not unlikely, given that Arthur Guinness took her on successive oceanic cruises, including a circumnavigation of the globe in 1923–24 and a voyage to Montreal in 1937.

While I am far from suggesting that the foregoing discussion is in any way conclusive, I feel equally that Patrick's claim is by no means so demonstrably false as to be glibly dismissed as that of 'a liar'. At the least, it illustrates the extent to which much of his life in the early 1930s remains too sparsely documented to permit of facile judgements one way or another.

Postscript

The 1937 volume of *The Oxford Annual for Boys* opens with a short story by Patrick (R.P. Russ) entitled 'Two's Company'. A couple of close friends, a Scot named Ross and an Irishman called Sullivan, arrive at a desolate lighthouse, where they are to be stationed as keepers for the ensuing three months. Their adventures involve disposal of a stranded whale by means of explosives, and their capture and domestication of a sea eagle and a skua. At first contented with their lot, they volunteer for a further term of duty. This time the tedium is relieved for a while by acquisition of a violin and bagpipes, with which they entertain themselves. Eventually, however, their solitary companionship descends into accruing mutual irritation. The tension increases over several days, culminating in a ferociously mindless fight. This serves to clear the air, and for the final month their comradeship is restored.

I have often wondered whether Sullivan and Ross may not reflect Patrick and his friend Edward Taaffe. A few years later, during his wartime service with PWE, Patrick modified his originally German surname Russ to the Scotch 'Ross'. Taaffe is of course an Irish name. One of Patrick's most marked idiosyncrasies was his inability to keep company for any length of time with even the most long-standing of friends or close members of his family. Such enforced contiguity placed an intolerable strain on his nerves, which inevitably resulted either in an open quarrel or more usually ill-concealed anger.

Could something like this have occurred, had the two friends shared a cabin aboard ship on a lengthy cruise? The story was probably written in 1936, not long after the time such a voyage might have taken place. I am inclined to credit the hypothesis, although at present there exists no means of confirming it.

Notes

Preface

1   David Mamet, 'The Humble Genre Novel, Sometimes Full of Genius', *New York Times*, 17 January 2000.

I Collioure and *Three Bear Witness*

1   Nikolai Tolstoy, *Patrick O'Brian: The Making of the Novelist* (London, 2004), pp. 469–73, 483–9. Twenty years later he wrote in his diary: 'I had a great go of timor mortis conturbat me when I was 35', i.e. in 1949.

2   Patrick O'Brian, *Richard Temple* (London 1962), pp. 62–6.

3   *Daily Mail*, 3 November 2003.

4   PRO.J77/3990.

5   *Mail on Sunday*, 16 January 2000. In a court petition dated 18 June 1949, Elizabeth Russ deposed that 'the Respondent [Patrick] then arranged for him [Richard] to go to the Southey Hall Preparatory School, which was his own choice, and he proceeded there without any break whatsoever in his schooling. The Respondent paid the School fees but ceased to pay me maintenance by mutual agreement. He was then nearly eight years old [February 1945] and he remained at that school for two and a half years, when the Respondent took him away to teach him personally' (PRO J77/3990).

6   O'Brian, *Richard Temple*, p. 48.

7   *Mail on Sunday*, 16 January 2000.

8   PRO J77/3990,77.

9   Patrick O'Brian, *The Catalans* (New York, 1953), p. 26.

10   *Country Contentments: Or, The Hvsbandmans Recreations. Contayning the Wholsome Experiences in which any man ought to Recreate himselfe, after the toyle of more serious business* (London, 1649).

11   I am grateful to my friend Terry Zobeck for supplying me with this reference. My own copy of *Hussein* lacks the dustjacket.

12   A.E. Cunningham (ed.), *Patrick O'Brian: Critical Appreciations and a Bibliography* (Boston Spa, Wetherby, 1994), p. 18.

13   Patrick O'Brian, *Three Bear Witness* (London, 1952), pp. 11–12.

14 Dana Goodyear, 'Sailing Upon Ancient Seas', *Publishers Weekly* (20/12/99), p. 51.

II *The Catalans*

1 O'Brian, *Three Bear Witness*, pp. 44–6.
2 Tolstoy, *Patrick O'Brian: The Making of the Novelist*, pp. 235–8.
3 Sir James George Frazer, *The Magic Art and the Evolution of Kings* (London, 1911), i, p. 55.
4 Claude Gaignebet and Jean-Dominique Lajoux, *Art profane et religion populaire au Moyen Age* (Paris, 1985), p. 159. It is thought that the Feast of St Blaise on 3 February replaced pagan commemoration of a divine bear (ibid., pp. 254–8).
5 J.H.C. Grattan and Charles Singer, *Anglo-Saxon Magic and Medicine: Illustrated Specially from the Semi-Pagan Text 'Lacnunga'* (Oxford, 1952), pp. 54–5, 62–3.
6 Ibid., p. 114; Jacques Ruffié, *Histoire de la Louve (d'après les notes d'Émile Dateu)* (Paris, 1981), pp. 265–6.
7 Michel Brunet, *Le Roussillon: Une société contre l'État: 1780–1820* (Perpignan, 1990), pp. 177–232.
8 Isabel Savory, *The Romantic Roussillon: in the French Pyrenees* (London, 1919), p. 109.
9 Chapter IV was published earlier as a free-standing tale in William Phillips and Philip Rahv (eds), *The Avon Book of Modern Writing* (New York, 1953), pp. 98–124.
10 O'Brian, *The Catalans*, pp. 110–12.
11 Patrick O'Brian, *The Commodore* (London, 1994), p. 93.
12 O'Brian, *The Catalans*, pp. 112–20.

III New Home and New Family

1 Ben Verinder, *I Felt Like an Adventure: A Life of Mary Burkett* (Durham, 2008), pp. 14–18. While Mary's reminiscences of her visits to Collioure are authentic and useful, her general account of Patrick's career is drawn from inaccurate printed accounts. Perhaps her oddest assertion is that Patrick did not drive an ambulance during the War, but had in fact been a taxi-driver! (p. 18). I have also obtained a vivid account of their Collioure holiday from one of the schoolgirls in her party. Anne Louise Cantan (afterwards Moore), later my

contemporary at Trinity College Dublin, kindly sent me a copy of her diary of their holiday at Collioure.

2 Patrick O'Brian, *Lying in the Sun and Other Stories* (London, 1956), pp. 189–202.

3 Dean King, *Patrick O'Brian: A Life Revealed* (London, 2000), p. 177.

IV Voyages of Adventure

1 Tolstoy, *Patrick O'Brian: The Making of the Novelist*, pp. 209–10, 229.

2 Maria Callcott, *Little Arthur's History of England* (London, 1835).

3 Tolstoy, *Patrick O'Brian: The Making of the Novelist*, pp. 100–101, 205–7.

4 Ibid., pp. 202–4.

5 'An Epitome of Commodore Anson's Voyage' (Robert Beatson, *Naval and Military Memoirs of Great Britain from 1727 to 1783* (London, 1804), i, pp. 232–49).

6 Rev. Richard Walter, *A Voyage Round the World, In the Years MDCCXL, I, II, III, IV. By George Anson, Esq.; Now Lord Anson* (London, 1762).

7 O'Brian, *Lying in the Sun and Other Stories*, pp. 116–22.

8 William Burney, *A New Universal Dictionary of the Marine* (London, 1815).

9 Cunningham (ed.), *Patrick O'Brian: Critical Appreciations and a Bibliography*, p. 19.

10 Tolstoy, *Patrick O'Brian: The Making of the Novelist*, pp. 132–3.

V In the Doldrums

1 The list of Patrick's translations featured in Cunningham (ed.), *Patrick O'Brian: Critical Appreciations and a Bibliography*, pp. 127–33, omits only Francis Mazière, *The Mysteries of Easter Island*, which was published in 1969.

2 Patrick O'Brian, *Desolation Island* (London, 1978), p. 84.

VI A Family Man

1 Haroun Tazieff, *When the Earth Trembles* (Hart-Davis, 1964).

2 *Guardian*, 27 July 2003. 'He was very strict and beat me if things got very bad. But I wasn't the easiest child in the world to teach' (*Daily Telegraph*, 26 November 2003).

3 King, *Patrick O'Brian: A Life Revealed*, p. 197.

4 *Guardian*, 27 November 2003.

5 King, *Patrick O'Brian: A Life Revealed*, p. 213.

6 *Daily Telegraph*, 8 January 2000.

7 King, *Patrick O'Brian: A Life Revealed*, pp. 197–8.

8 Ross Reyburn and Michael Emery, *Jonah: the official biography of Jonah Barrington* (London, 1983), pp. 43–6. This entertaining book inadvertently telescopes Jonah's two visits to Collioure into a single one in 1963, and it was in fact during his second visit in 1964 that the fateful decision was made.

9 Françoise Mallet-Joris, *The Uncompromising Heart: a Life of Marie Mancini, Louis XIV's First Love*; Maurice Goudeket, *The Delights of Growing Old*; Simone de Beauvoir, *A Very Easy Death* – all three published in 1966.

VII *Master and Commander*

1 Bernard Fay, *Louis XVI* (1967); Francis Mazière, *The Mysteries of Easter Island* (1969).

2 Keith Wheatley, 'The Long Life of O'Brian', *Financial Times*, 11–12 January 1997. The same suggestion had been made earlier by Mark Horowitz (*New York Times Magazine*, 16 May 1993, p. 40).

3 Stephen Becker, 'Patrick O'Brian: The Art of Fiction CXLII', George Plimpton et al. (eds), *Paris Review* (New York, 1995), p. 117.

4 Patrick O'Brian, *Master and Commander* (London, 1970), p. 160.

5 David Cordingley, *Cochrane the Dauntless: The Life and Adventures of Admiral Thomas Cochrane, 1775–1860* (London, 2007), pp. 55, 216, 217–18, 259, 339–40.

6 Patrick Cumming operated as an intelligence agent, slipped ashore by Rear-Admiral Martin on the Baltic coast at the time of the French invasion of Russia in 1812 (Sir Richard Vesey Hamilton (ed.), *Letters and Papers of Admiral of the Fleet Sir Thos. Byam Martin G.C.B.* (London, 1898–1903), ii, pp. 187–8, 203, 262–4, 299–309).

7 Cf. Christopher Doorne, 'A Floating Republic? Conspiracy Theory and the Nore Mutiny of 1797', in Ann Veronica Coats and Philip MacDougall (eds), *The Naval Mutinies of 1797: Unity and Perseverance* (Woodbridge, 2011), pp. 184–7.

8 Patrick O'Brian, *Post Captain* (London, 1972), p. 358.

9 Patrick O'Brian, *The Fortune of War* (London, 1979), p. 170.

10 Reproduced in Brian Lavery and Geoff Hunt, *The Frigate Surprise: The Complete Story of the Ship Made Famous in the Novels of Patrick O'Brian* (London, 2008), p. 7.

11 *Boat U.S. Magazine*, March 2000.

VIII The Green Isle Calls

1 Richard Hill, *The Prizes of War: The Naval Prize System in the Napoleonic Wars, 1793–1815* (Stroud, 1998), p. 94.

2 Alec Guinness, *My Name Escapes Me: The Diary of a Retiring Actor* (London, 1997), p. 30.

IX *Pablo Ruiz Picasso*

1 *A Journey through the Crimea to Constantinople. In a Series of Letters from the Right Honourable Elizabeth Lady Craven, to His Serene Highness the Margrave of Brandebourg, Anspach and Bareith. Written in the Year MDCCLXXXVI* (London, 1789); *Memoirs of the Margravine of Anspach. Written by Herself* (London, 1826).

2 Cf. the admirable study by Gertje R. Utley, *Picasso: The Communist Years* (New Haven and London, 2000). Richard Ollard's initial reactions to Patrick's biography included 'Pic let off too lightly for being Communist'. In 1988 Patrick implicitly approved the artist Tom Phillips's defensive assertion that it was necessary to take into account 'the attitude of a Spaniard committed to the fight against fascism'. This defence appears weak in the extreme. In the first place, many thousands of Spaniards fought 'against fascism' without having the least desire to endorse the far more brutal ideology of Communism. In the second, Picasso remained a devoted apologist for Stalinist cruelties long after the Spanish Civil War was over.

X Shifting Currents

1 William James, *The Naval History of Great Britain, from the Declaration of War by France in 1793, to the Accession of George IV* (London, 1837), v, pp. 261–326.

2 Ibid., v, pp. 192–200, 261–313, 324–6.

3 Dean King, *Harbors and High Seas: An Atlas and Geographical Guide to the Aubrey–Maturin Novels of Patrick O'Brian* (New York, 1999), p. 84.

4   Nikolai Tolstoy, *The Half-Mad Lord: Thomas Pitt 2nd Baron Camelford (1775–1804)* (London, 1978), pp. 14–16, 205.

5   Tom Pocock, *A Thirst for Glory: The Life of Admiral Sir Sidney Smith* (London, 1996), pp. 43–63; Tolstoy, *The Half-Mad Lord*, pp. 150–7; Michael Lewis, *Napoleon and his British Captives* (London, 1962), pp. 91–6.

XI Muddied Waters

1   Simone de Beauvoir, *Quand prime le spirituel.*

2   Patrick O'Brian, *The Far Side of the World* (London, 1984), pp. 246–8.

3   Cf. Cordingley, *Cochrane the Dauntless: The Life and Adventures of Admiral Thomas Cochrane, 1775–1860*, pp. 235–54.

XII Travails of Existence

1   Patrick O'Brian, 'The Great War', in Philip Ziegler and Desmond Seward (eds), *Brooks's: A Social History* (London, 1991). Patrick describes Brooks's as 'not so much an eighteenth- or early nineteenth-century world as a wholly traditional place untied to any of the set periods and surviving them all'.

2   Richard Burn, *The Justice of the Peace, and Parish Officer* (London, 1776), ii.

3   N.A.M. Rodger, *The Wooden World: An Anatomy of the Georgian Navy* (London, 1986).

4   *Charles de Gaulle. 1, Le rebelle, 1890–1944* (Paris, 1984). Patrick's dislike of de Gaulle stemmed in large part from his wartime service with the French Department of Political Warfare Executive (PWE).

XIII Family Travails

1   A.B. Russ, *Lady Day Prodigal* (Brentwood Bay, D.C., 1989), p. 66.

2   King, *Patrick O'Brian: A Life Revealed*, pp. 301–5.

3   Ibid., pp. 303–4.

4   *Encyclopaedia Britannica; or, a Dictionary of Arts, Sciences, and Miscellaneous Literature* (Edinburgh, 1810). When transportation of the twenty bulky volumes from England was delayed, Patrick suffered frustration in the progress of his current novel: 'I want to see what they have on Kerguelen, icebergs, Amsterdam Island before going on.'

XIV The Sunlit Uplands

1 William Austen-Leigh, Richard Austen-Leigh and Deirdre Le Faye, *Jane Austen: A Family Record* (London, 1989).

2 Tolstoy, *Patrick O'Brian: The Making of the Novelist*, pp. 326–9. One serious error, however, requires correction. In my account I cited Patrick's confession that 'I was odious' as applying to a conversation between him and Horowitz on the day of his arrival. I now find that I had misread the diary passage, reference being exclusively to Patrick's mood when alone with my mother, after returning home exhausted from his troublesome journey.

3 Tolstoy, *Patrick O'Brian: The Making of the Novelist*, pp. 319–22.

4 Patrick O'Brian, *Picasso: Pablo Ruiz Picasso* (New York: G.P. Putnam's Sons, New York, 1976), p. 19. As John Raymond wrote in his review: 'Thus it is the first eighty pages of this book that the ignorant general reader is likely to find most absorbing and exciting' (*Sunday Times*, 19 September 1976).

5 *Washington Post*, 8 January 2000.

XV Epinician Acclaims

1 Brian Lavery, *Jack Aubrey Commands: An Historical Companion to the Naval World of Patrick O'Brian* (London, 2003). Another maritime scholar, David Lyon, began preparations for a prosopographical Companion, but the project was regrettably brought to a halt by his death. I am grateful to him for having sent me a manuscript copy.

2 Patrick O'Brian, *The Commodore* (London, 1994), p. 102.

3 Ibid., pp. 78–9, 142, 235–41. Patrick nicknamed their Chelsea home 'Potto Grange'.

4 Ibid., p. 238. The book's full title is Philip Junta (ed.), *POMPONIVS MELA. IVLIVS SOLINVS. ITINERARIVM ANTONINI AVG. VIBIVS SEQVESTER. P. VICTOR de regionibus urbis Romae. Dionysius Aser de Situ orbis Prisciano Interprete* (Florence, 1519).

5 'Cruising with Patrick O'Brian – The Man and the Myth', *Latitude 38* (August 2000).

6 Becker, 'Patrick O'Brian: The Art of Fiction CXLII', *Paris Review*, p. 130. Oscar Wilde was similarly gratified by American enthusiasm for his lectures, together with the good manners of his audiences (Rupert Hart-Davis (ed.), *More Letters of Oscar Wilde* (London, 1985), pp. 42–3).

7   Becker, *Paris Review*, p. 128. Becker's interview provides a perceptive account of Patrick the writer, his use of sources, and approach to writing.

8   Patrick O'Brian, *Beasts Royal* (London, 1934), p. 15.

9   William Winstanley, *The New Help to Discourse. Or Wit & Mirth, Intermix'd With more serious Matters* (London, 1716), pp. 204–7.

10 O'Brian, *Master and Commander*, p. 319; *The Reverse of the Medal* (London, 1986), p. 31.

11 Patrick O'Brian, *The Nutmeg of Consolation* (London, 1991), p. 167.

12 Patrick O'Brian, *The Yellow Admiral* (London, 1997), p. 49.

XVI Triumph and Tragedy

1   John Forester, *Novelist and Story-Teller: The Life of C.S. Forester* (Lemon Grove, CA, 2000), i, pp. 356–7.

2   T.W. Copeland et al. (eds), *The Correspondence of Edmund Burke* (Cambridge, 1958–70), i, pp. 270–1.

3   Cunningham (ed.), *Patrick O'Brian: Critical Appreciations and a Bibliography*, pp. 150–1.

XVII Melmoth the Wanderer

1   I am indebted to Sir Donnell Deeny for providing me with a copy of his reminiscences of Patrick and my mother. Patrick bestowed the name Mona Fitzpatrick on the charming little black-haired Irish girl liberated by Stephen Maturin in *The Hundred Days*, in a chapter written in January 1998.

2   Patrick O'Brian, *The Uncertain Land and Other Poems* (London, 2019), p. 44.

3   Mary H. Kingsley, *Travels in West Africa: Congo Français, Corisco and Cameroons* (London, 1897).

APPENDIX A Collioure: History and Landscape

1   E.A. Thompson, *The Goths in Spain* (Oxford, 1969), pp. 218–22.

2   Alain Ayats, *Louis XIV et les Pyrénées Catalanes de 1659 à 1681* (Canet, 2002), p. 33.

3   Virginie Raguenaud, *The Colors of Catalonia: In the Footsteps of Twentieth-Century Artists* (Boston, 2012). Another fine artist who painted in the locality was Charles Rennie Mackintosh, who stayed in Collioure in 1924 and settled in neighbouring Port-Vendres in 1925. Cf. Robin Crichton,

Monsieur Mackintosh: The Travels and paintings of Charles Rennie Mackintosh in the Pyrénées Orientales 1923–1927 (Edinburgh, 2006).

4 Ayats, *Louis XIV et les Pyrénées Catalanes*, pp. 232–4, 858. In the early 1930s, despite vigorous local protests, under direction of the infamous mayor, Léon Cristine, the philistine municipality sold land for development around the base of the glacis (Eugène Cortade, *Le château royal de Collioure* (Perpignan, 1968), pp. 54–6). After the last War, a successor administration saw fit to complete the desecration, bulldozing terraces into what remained of the splendid green rampart, in order to convert it into a car park.

5 Ayats, *Louis XIV et les Pyrénées Catalanes*, pp. 677–80.

APPENDIX B Patrick and His First Wife Elizabeth

1 *Observer*, 14 November 2004.
2 King, *Patrick O'Brian: A Life Revealed*, pp. 79–81.
3 *Daily Telegraph*, 28 February 2000. 'For my part, I do not remember anything from that time that relates to their dispute. It was all kept from me . . .' (*Guardian*, 27 November 2003).
4 *Mail on Sunday*, 16 January 2000.
5 *Guardian*, 27 November 2003.
6 PRO.J77/3990.
7 Tolstoy, *Patrick O'Brian: The Making of the Novelist*, pp. 198, 231.
8 PH/WAR/3/101.
9 PRO.J77/3990.
10 Richard Blackmore, *Prince Arthur. An Heroick Poem in Ten Books* (London, 1695).
11 18 June 1949 Elizabeth Russ Petition (PRO J77/3990).
12 Ibid.

APPENDIX C: Patrick's Sailing

1 Tolstoy, *Patrick O'Brian: The Making of the Novelist*, pp. 157–60.
2 John Scott Hughes, *Famous Yachts* (London, 1928), pp. 132–7.
3 Cunningham (ed.), *Patrick O'Brian: Critical Appreciations and a Bibliography*, p. 16. The ambiguity of his assertion that his experience aboard the ocean-going yacht 'allowed more ambitious sailoring later on' may likewise be noted, the voyage or voyages aboard the Guinness yacht being the only unequivocal claim advanced in his nautical catalogue.

Index